Engineering Design and Graphics with SolidWorks® 2023

James D. Bethune
Nathan Brown

 Pearson

Engineering Design and Graphics with SolidWorks® 2023

Images courtesy of Dassault Systèmes SolidWorks Corporation. SolidWorks® is a registered trademark of Dassault Systèmes SolidWorks Corp. All rights reserved.

Trademarks

All terms mentioned in this book that are known to be trademarks or service marks have been appropriately capitalized. Que Publishing cannot attest to the accuracy of this information. Use of a term in this book should not be regarded as affecting the validity of any trademark or service mark.

Warning and Disclaimer

Every effort has been made to make this book as complete and as accurate as possible, but no warranty or fitness is implied. The information provided is on an "as is" basis. The authors and the publisher shall have neither liability nor responsibility to any person or entity with respect to any loss or damages arising from the information contained in this book.

Special Sales

For information about buying this title in bulk quantities, or for special sales opportunities (which may include electronic versions; custom cover designs; and content particular to your business, training goals, marketing focus, or branding interests), please contact our corporate sales department at corpsales@pearsoned.com or (800) 382-3419.

For government sales inquiries, please contact governmentsales@pearsoned.com.

For questions about sales outside the U.S., please contact intlcs@pearson.com.

Acquisitions Editor: Anshul Sharma
Senior Production Editor: Tonya Simpson
Cover Designer: Chuti Prasertsith
Developmental Editor: Patrice Rutledge

Full-Service Project Management: codeMantra
Composition: codeMantra
Proofreader: Jen Hinchliffe
Indexer: Timothy Wright

1 2023

Library of Congress Control Number: 2022951068

ISBN 10: 0-13-789952-1
ISBN 13: 978-0-13789952-4

Pearson's Commitment to Diversity, Equity, and Inclusion

Pearson is dedicated to creating bias-free content that reflects the diversity of all learners. We embrace the many dimensions of diversity, including but not limited to race, ethnicity, gender, socioeconomic status, ability, age, sexual orientation, and religious or political beliefs.

Education is a powerful force for equity and change in our world. It has the potential to deliver opportunities that improve lives and enable economic mobility. As we work with authors to create content for every product and service, we acknowledge our responsibility to demonstrate inclusivity and incorporate diverse scholarship so that everyone can achieve their potential through learning. As the world's leading learning company, we have a duty to help drive change and live up to our purpose to help more people create a better life for themselves and to create a better world.

Our ambition is to purposefully contribute to a world where:

- Everyone has an equitable and lifelong opportunity to succeed through learning.
- Our educational products and services are inclusive and represent the rich diversity of learners.
- Our educational content accurately reflects the histories and experiences of the learners we serve.
- Our educational content prompts deeper discussions with learners and motivates them to expand their own learning (and worldview).

While we work hard to present unbiased content, we want to hear from you about any concerns or needs with this Pearson product so that we can investigate and address them.

Please contact us with concerns about any potential bias at https://www.pearson.com/report-bias.html.

Preface

This book shows and explains how to use SolidWorks® 2023 to create engineering designs and drawings. Emphasis is placed on creating engineering drawings including dimensions and tolerances and using standard parts and tools. Each chapter contains step-by-step sample problems that show how to apply the concepts presented in the chapter.

The book contains hundreds of projects of various degrees of difficulty specifically designed to reinforce the chapter's content. The idea is that students learn best by doing. In response to reviewers' requests, some more difficult projects have been included.

Chapters 1 and **2** show how to set up a part document and how to use the SolidWorks **Sketch** tools. **Sketch** tools are used to create 2D part entities that can then be extruded into 3D solid models. The chapters contain an explanation of how SolidWorks' colors are used and of how shapes can be fully defined. The usage of mouse gestures, S key, and origins is also included. The two chapters include 44 exercise problems (18 in Ch1 and 26 in Ch2) using both inches and millimeters so that students can practice applying the various **Sketch** tools.

Chapter 3 shows how to use the **Features** tools. **Features** tools are used to create and modify 3D solid models. In addition, reference planes are covered, and examples of how to edit existing models are given.

Chapter 4 explains how to create and interpret orthographic views. Views are created using third-angle projection in compliance with ANSI standards and conventions. The differences between first-angle and third-angle projections are demonstrated. Seven exercise problems (P4-142 to P4-149) are included to help students learn to work with the two different standards. Also included are section views, auxiliary views, and broken views. Several of the projects require that a 3D solid model be drawn from a given set of orthographic views to help students develop visualization skills.

Chapter 5 explains how to create assembly drawings using the **Assembly** tools (**Mate**, **Exploded View**) and how to document assemblies using the **Drawing Documents** tools. Topics include assembled 3D solid models, exploded isometric drawings, and bills of materials (BOMs). Assembly numbers and part numbers are discussed. Both the **Animate Collapse/Explode** and **Motion Study** tools are demonstrated. In addition, the title, release, and revision blocks are discussed. An explanation of how to use **Interference Detection** is given.

Chapter 6 shows how to create and design with threads and fasteners. Both ANSI inch and ANSI metric threads are covered. The **Design Library** is presented, and examples are used to show how to select and size screws and other fasteners for assembled parts.

Chapter 7 covers dimensioning and is in compliance with ANSI standards and conventions. There are extensive visual examples of dimensioned shapes and features that serve as references for various dimensioning applications.

Chapter 8 covers tolerances. Both linear and geometric tolerances are included. This is often a difficult topic to understand, so there are many examples of how to apply and how to interpret the various types of tolerances. Standard tolerances as presented in the title block are demonstrated.

Chapter 9 explains bearings and fit tolerances. The **Design Library** is used to create bearing drawings, and examples show how to select the correct interference tolerance between bearings and housing, and clearance tolerances between bearings and shafts.

Chapter 10 presents gears. Gear terminology, gear formulas, gear ratios, and gear creation using the SolidWorks **Toolbox** are covered. The chapter relies heavily on the **Design Library**. Keys, keyways, and set screws are discussed. Both English and metric units are covered. There is an extensive sample problem that shows how to draw a support plate for mating gears and how to create an assembly drawing for gear trains. The projects at the end of the chapter include two large gear assembly exercises.

Chapter 11 will help students prepare for the CSWA certification exam. There are many sample questions and examples. Students should time how long it takes them to do each problem. This will help them get used to working under time pressure.

The **Appendix** includes fit tables for use with projects in the text. Clearance, locational, and interference fits are included for both inch and millimeter values.

Download Instructor Resources from the Instructor Resource Center

Instructor materials are available from Pearson's Instructor Resource Center. Go to https://www.pearson.com/en-us/highered-educators.html to register, or to sign in if you already have an account.

Acknowledgments

I would like to acknowledge the reviewers of this text: Peggy Condon-Vance, Penn State Berks; Lisa Richter, Macomb Community College; Julie Korfhage, Clackamas Community College; Max P. Gassman, Iowa State University; Paul E. Lienard, Northeastern University; and Hossein Hemati, Mira Costa College.

Thanks to my family—David, Maria, Randy, Sandra, Hannah, Will, Madison, Jack, Luke, Sam, and Ben.

A special thanks to Cheryl.

James D. Bethune

I would like to acknowledge the editors of this edition: Anshul Sharma, Patrice Rutledge, and Tonya Simpson. Thanks to my family: Amanda, Jovie, and Iris. And thanks to my mentor: Gina Bertocci.

Nathan Brown

Contents

chapter one
Getting Started

CHAPTER OBJECTIVES

- Create a sketch
- Create a file/part
- Create a solid model
- Edit angular and circular shapes
- Draw holes
- Use Sketch tools
- Change units of a part

1-1 Introduction

SolidWorks is a parametric solid modeler that uses dimensions, parameters, and relationships to define and drive 3D shapes. Solid modelers make it easy to edit and modify parts as they are constructed. This capability is ideal for creating new designs.

Parametric modelers use dimensions to drive the shapes. For example, to create a line of a defined length, a line is first sketched, and then the length dimension is added. The line will assume the length of the dimension. If the dimension is changed, the length of the line will change to match the new dimension.

When using *non-parametric modelers*, a line is drawn and a dimension added. The dimension will define the length of the existing line but not drive it. If the length of the line is changed, the dimensions will not change. A new dimension is required to define the length of the line.

This chapter will show you how to start a **New** document and introduce the **Line**, **Circle**, and **Edit** tools. The **Smart Dimension** tool will be used to define and edit lines and circles. Line colors and relationships will also be introduced.

1-2 Starting a New Document

Figure 1-1 shows the initial SolidWorks screen.

Figure 1-1

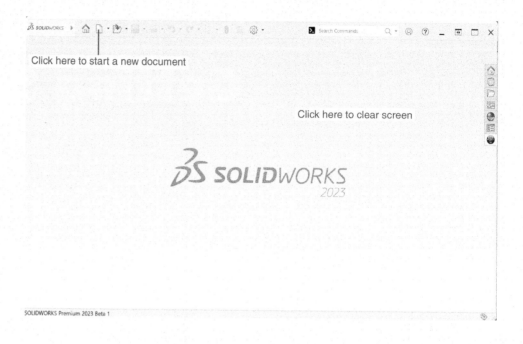

Starting a New Part Document

1 Click the **New** tool icon at the top of the SolidWorks screen.

The **New SolidWorks Document** dialog box appears, as shown on the left in Figure 1-2. This is the Novice version of the dialog box. Clicking **Advanced** opens the Advanced version, shown on the right. Either version can be used to create three types of documents: **Part**, **Assembly**, and **Drawing**.

Figure 1-2

- **Parts** are 3D solid models of individual parts.

- **Assemblies** are used to create combinations of parts and assemblies.

- **Drawings** are used to create orthographic views of a **Part** or **Assembly**. Dimensions and tolerances can be applied to **Drawings**.

2 Click the **Part** tool and then click the **OK** box.

The **Part** screen will appear. See Figure 1-3. Note the different areas of the screen. The **Sketch** tab is currently activated, so the **Features** tools are displayed. Each tool icon on the **Sketch** toolbar is accompanied by its name. These names can be removed and the toolbar condensed to expand the size of the drawing screen. For clarity these named tools will be included in the first few chapters of the book so you gain enough knowledge of the tools to work without their names.

Figure 1-3

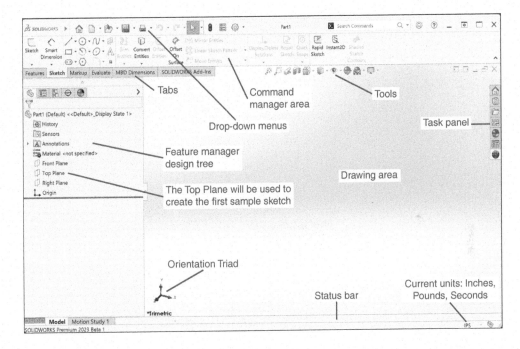

Selecting a Sketch Plane

SolidWorks uses one of three basic planes to define a part: **Front**, **Top**, and **Right**. These planes correspond to the planes used to define orthographic views that will be explained in Chapter 4. The **Top** plane will be used as a sketch plane to demonstrate the first few tools.

1 Define the plane on which the part will be created by clicking the **Top Plane** option in the **Feature manager** box on the left side of the drawing screen.

NOTE

Instruction numbering in the text and figures does not necessarily match; however, the order will be similar. Steps numbered in the figures generally pertain to clicking items in the SolidWorks user interface, whereas the text may include additional numbered steps to guide the developmental process. The numbering in the figures will generally start anew in each new figure.

See Figure 1-4. An outline of the **Top** plane will appear using a type of 3D orientation called the **Trimetric** orientation.

2 Click the **Sketch** tool as shown in Figure 1-4.

The **Top** plane's orientation will change to a 2D view. The **Top** plane is now a sketch plane and appears as a rectangle because the view is taken perpendicular to the plane. This means that all 2D shapes drawn on the plane will appear as true shapes.

Figure 1-4

3 Click the **Line** tool.

With the **Line** tool activated, locate the cursor on the origin. The origin is indicated by the two red arrows spaced 90° apart. See Figure 1-5.

Figure 1-5

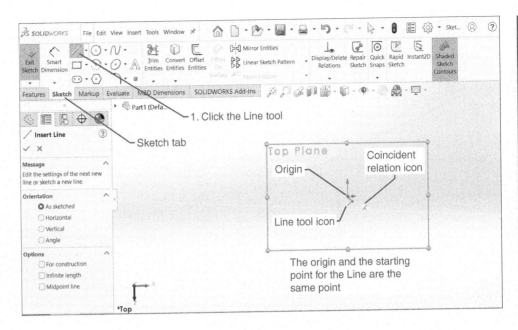

1. Click the Line tool

Sketch tab

Top Plane

Origin

Coincident relation icon

Line tool icon

The origin and the starting point for the Line are the same point

Two icons will appear on the screen: the **Line** tool icon indicating that the **Line** tool is active, and the **Coincident relation** icon indicating that the origin and the starting point for the line are on the same point.

4 Move the cursor away from the origin horizontally to the right.

As you move the cursor away from the origin, a distance and angle value will appear. See Figure 1-6. The distance is as measured from the origin or starting point for the line, and the angle is based on the SolidWorks definition of 0° as a horizontal line to the left of the starting point. We are drawing to the right, so the angular value is 180°.

Figure 1-6

1. Click the origin and move the cursor to the right

1.18, 180°

2. Left-click the mouse to define the end of the line

Line tool icon

Indicates a horizontal line is being drawn

3. Move the cursor away from the line, right-click the mouse, and click the Select option

Select

End chain (double-click)

Switch to arc (A)

Sketch Entities

Recent Commands

More Dimensions

Selected Entity

Delete

Quick Snaps

3.4in   -0.02in   0in   Under De

Figure 1-6
(Continued)

4. Click the Smart Dimension tool

A number will appear

5. Click the line and move the cursor above the line

6. Locate the dimension and click the mouse

8. Click the green check mark

7. Enter the distance value for the line

9. Click the mouse to finish the definition

3.50

Finished line distance

Two other icons will also appear: the **Line** tool icon and the horizontal relationship icon.

5 Click the mouse at the point at which you want to define the endpoint of the line.

6 Move the cursor vertically downwards. Do not click the mouse.

A new line will be drawn using the endpoint of the horizontal line as the starting point for the vertical line. Distance and angle values will appear based on the new starting point, and the **Line** and vertical relationship icons will appear.

7 Press the **<Esc>** key or right-click the mouse and click the **Select** option.

8 Click the **Smart Dimension** tool, click the line, and move the cursor away from the line.

A dimension will appear.

9 Click the mouse to define the location of the dimension.

The **Modify** dialog box will appear.

10 Enter a distance value for the line and click the green **OK** check mark.

11 Click anywhere on the empty screen to complete the line.

The dimension can be moved by locating the cursor on the dimension, pressing and holding the mouse button, and dragging the cursor.

12 Hover over the arrow next to the SolidWorks logo in the upper left and click the **File** menu located at the top of the screen, then click **Close**. See Figure 1-7.

Figure 1-7

13 Click the **Don't Save** option. See Figure 1-8.

The screen will return to the original SolidWorks screen.

Figure 1-8

1-3 SolidWorks Colors

As you work with SolidWorks you will notice that the lines change colors. These color changes let you know the status of the sketch being drawn. There are four basic colors.

Black = Fully defined
Blue = Under defined
Red = Over defined
Yellow = Redundant

1-4 Creating a Fully Defined Circle

In this section we will sketch a circle to help understand the difference between a fully defined and an under defined **Part**.

1 In the **New SolidWorks** dialog box (previously shown in Figure 1-2), click **Part** and then click OK to open a new **Part** document.

2 Click the **Top Plane** on the left (as depicted in Figure 1-4).

3 Click the **Sketch** tab. (It may already be activated.) See Figure 1-9.

Figure 1-9

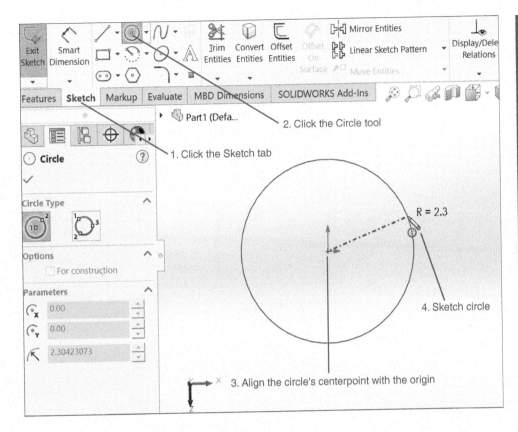

4. Sketch circle

R = 2.3

2. Click the Circle tool

1. Click the Sketch tab

3. Align the circle's centerpoint with the origin

Circle

Circle Type

Options
☐ For construction

Parameters
x 0.00
y 0.00
2.30423073

---

4 Click the **Circle** tool.

5 Locate the cursor on the origin, click the mouse, and drag the cursor away from the origin centerpoint.

Note that the Coincident relation symbol appears next to the origin, indicating that the centerpoint of the circle is located on the origin.

6 Click the mouse to define a sketch radius for the circle.

This sketched radius is a temporary radius and is not the final radius. The circle will be blue, indicating that it is not fully defined.

7 Click the **Smart Dimension** tool on the **Sketch** panel.

8 Click the circle and move the cursor away from the circle.

A dimension will appear. See Figure 1-10.

Figure 1-10

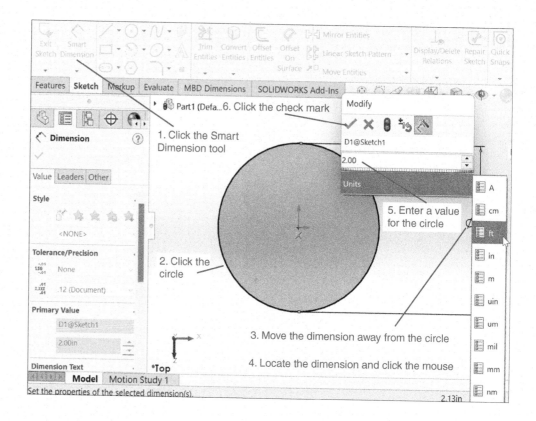

9. Select a location for the dimension and click the mouse.

The circle will initially be blue, not fully defined, until the mouse is clicked, locating the circle's dimension. When the mouse is clicked, the circle will turn black; it is now fully defined. We know the circle's diameter and location.

When the mouse is clicked, the **Modify** dialog box will appear. The sketched diameter value will be listed in the box. This sketched diameter value is now the circle's diameter until we enter a new value.

10. Enter a diameter value for the circle.

In this example a value of 2.00 was entered.

11. Click the green **OK** check mark in the **Modify** dialog box to enter the diameter value.

12. Click the green **OK** check mark in the **PropertyManager** area to finish defining the circle.

Changing an Existing Dimension

1. Double-click the **2.00** dimension.

The **Modify** dialog box will reappear.

2. Enter a new value.

In this example a value of **3.00** was entered. See Figure 1-11. The circle's diameter will change to 3.00 and the circle's color will remain black. The circle is still fully defined.

Figure 1-11

2. Click the check mark

Ø2.00

1. Double-click the 2.00 dimension and enter a value of 3.00in.

The circle is black. It is fully defined

Ø3.00

Click the drawing screen to finish the circle drawing

3 Click the green **OK** check mark in the **Modify** dialog box.

Note that the words **Fully Defined** appear at the bottom of the screen.

The circle is fully defined because both its diameter and location are known. The location was fully defined when we located the circle's centerpoint on the origin. Every circle needs a locational value and a diameter value to be fully defined. The locational value may be linear (an X and Y component value) or polar (an angular and radius value).

Fully Defined Entities

To help understand when an entity is fully defined, sketch two circles, one with its centerpoint on the origin and the other with its centerpoint not on the origin. See Figure 1-12. Both circles are under defined because the diameter values have not been defined. Both circles are sketched circles.

Figure 1-12

The centerpoint is not on the origin

Origin

The circles are not fully defined

The centerpoint is on the origin

Use the **Smart Dimension** tool and define both their diameters as **Ø2.00**. The circle located on the origin will be black. It is fully defined. Both its diameter and location are known. The circle with its centerpoint not located on the origin will remain blue. It is not fully defined. Its location is unknown. See Figure 1-13.

Figure 1-13

Dimension the circles

Blue—under defined
The centerpoint's location
has not been defined

Black—fully defined
The location and
diameter are known

Figure 1-14 shows the two Ø2.00 circles again. This time, dimensions have been added to the circle not located on the origin. The dimensions define the circle's centerpoint relative to the origin. It is now fully defined. Its color will change to black.

NOTE
Always include the origin as part of a 2D sketch.

Figure 1-14

Both circles are now black.
They are fully defined.

Figure 1-15 shows the two Ø2.00 circles with an extra dimension. The 1.20 vertical dimension is not needed to define the location of the hole not centered on the origin. A 1.20 vertical dimension already exists. The 1.20 dimension is redundant, so the dimension lines change to yellow.

Figure 1-15

Figure 1-15 also shows the **Make Dimension Driven?** dialog box. A driving dimension drives the shape and/or location of the object. If the driving dimension is changed, the shape or location will change. Driven dimensions are reference dimensions. They are sometimes added to a drawing for clarity. For example, a reference dimension could be used to show the overall value of a string of smaller dimensions. See Chapter 7. In this example it would be better to delete the extra 1.20 dimension. If you save it on the sketch, click the **Make this dimension driven** option and click **OK**. It will appear as a gray color. See Figure 1-16.

Figure 1-16

1-5 Units

This book will present examples and exercise problems using English units (inches) and Metric units (millimeters). Figure 1-17 shows the dimensioned circles created in the previous section. Note the letters **IPS** to the right of the **Fully Defined** callout. IPS stands for inch, pound, and second, the current units.

Figure 1-17

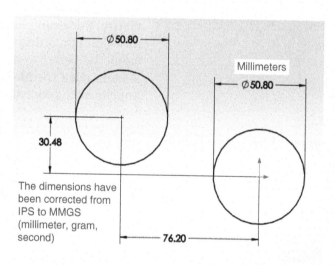

Changing Units

1 Click the **IPS** callout at the bottom of the screen.

2 Select the desired units.

In this example millimeters (**MMGS**) was selected. MMGS stands for millimeter, gram, and second. The letters **MMGS** appear at the bottom right of the screen, indicating the drawing units are now millimeters.

3 Click the **Undo** tool to return to the sketch. The new dimensions appear.

> **NOTE**
> The converted millimeter dimensions are not whole numbers as were the inch units. It is better to do a drawing in either inches or millimeters from the beginning and not to convert units as a drawing is created. This helps prevent round-off errors.

1-6 Rectangle

Rectangles are sketch tools that expedite the creation of rectangles and parallelograms. Each of these tools can be used to generate four connected lines with appropriate relations rather than drawing each line individually.

Sketching a Rectangle

The example shown in Figure 1-18 was created on the **Top** plane using the **Rectangle** tool. The units are inches.

1 Open a new **Part** document, click the **Top Plane** option, and click the **Sketch** tool.

As shown in Figure 1-18, the outline rectangle for the **Top** plane will rotate to the *Normal* orientation; that is, you are looking at the plane from a 90° orientation. This means that any shape drawn on the plane will be a true shaped line. This concept will be covered in Chapter 4 on orthographic views.

Figure 1-18

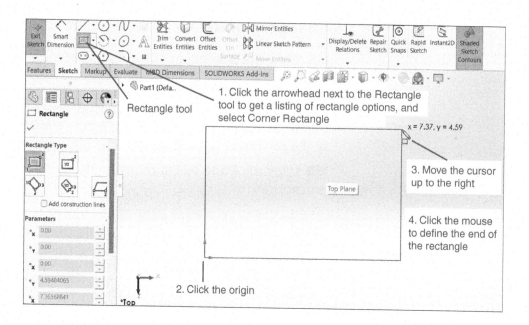

1. Click the arrowhead next to the Rectangle tool to get a listing of rectangle options, and select Corner Rectangle

Rectangle tool

x = 7.37, y = 4.59

3. Move the cursor up to the right

Top Plane

4. Click the mouse to define the end of the rectangle

2. Click the origin

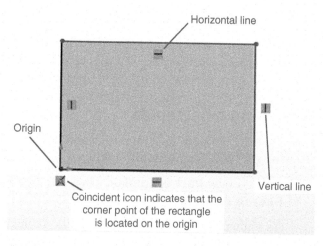

Horizontal line

Origin

Vertical line

Coincident icon indicates that the corner point of the rectangle is located on the origin

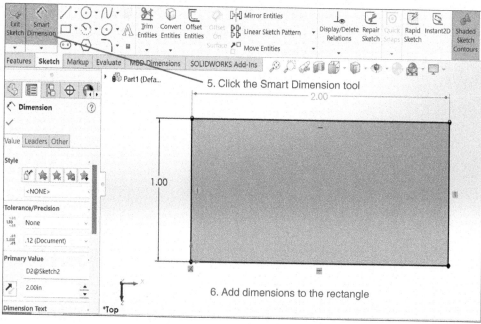

5. Click the Smart Dimension tool

6. Add dimensions to the rectangle

2 Click the arrowhead next to the **Rectangle** tool and select the **Corner Rectangle** option.

Five options for drawing a rectangle are listed. The different options are helpful when creating designs. It is recommended you take a few minutes and try each option. Only **Corner Rectangle** will be used in this chapter.

3 Click the origin and move the cursor up and to the right.

4 Click the mouse to define the rectangle's opposite corner.

5 Press the **<Esc>** key or right-click the mouse and click the **Select** option.

Note that two relationships are defined: coincident and horizontal. The starting point was located on the origin, so they are coincident and the rectangle is drawn. Note also that the rectangle is not fully defined because its size has not been defined.

Releasing the mouse button will define the length of the sketched line, but you are still in the **Sketch** mode. If you click the mouse again, a new rectangle will begin.

6 Click the **Smart Dimension** tool and use it (as previously described) to define the size of the rectangle.

Exiting the Sketch Mode

Click the **Exit Sketch** icon on the **Sketch** panel or click the **Exit Sketch** icon that appears in the upper-right corner of the drawing screen.

See Figure 1-19.

Figure 1-19

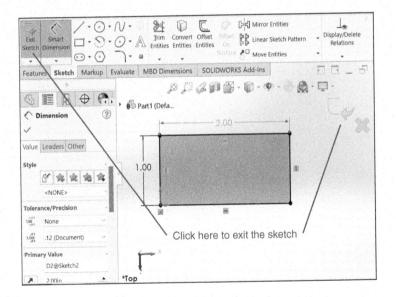

Reentering the Sketch Mode

Once you have created a sketch and left the **Sketch** mode, you can return to work on the sketch by using the **Edit Sketch** mode. See Figure 1-20.

1 Click an entity in the existing sketch.

2 Click the **Edit Sketch** tool.

Figure 1-20

2. Click Edit Sketch

Edit Sketch

1. Click one of the
lines of the rectangle

1-7 Moving Around the Drawing Screen

SolidWorks includes several methods that allow you to move entities around the screen. Entities can be moved, zoomed, or reorientated. Figure 1-21 shows the rectangle created in the previous section.

Figure 1-21

2.00

1.00

Zoom—rotate the mouse wheel

Move—hold down the <Ctrl>
key, hold down the mouse wheel, and
move the mouse

Reorientate—click the rectangle, hold
down the mouse wheel, and move the
mouse

Zooming the Rectangle

Rotate the mouse wheel. The rectangle will increase and decrease in size.

Moving the Rectangle

1 Hold down the **<Ctrl>** key; press and hold down the mouse wheel.

2 Move the mouse around.

The rectangle will follow the mouse movement.

Reorientating the Rectangle

1 Click the rectangle.

2 Hold down the mouse wheel and move the mouse.

The rectangle's orientation will follow the mouse movement.

1-8 Orientation

The rectangle in the previous sections was created in the **Top view** orientation. As you work on a sketch, the orientation may change. There are three techniques you can use to return the sketch to its original orientation.

Returning to the Top View Orientation—View Selector

1 Click the **View Orientation** tool at the top of the drawing screen.

The **View Selector** cube will appear. See Figure 1-22. If the cube does not appear, click the **View Selector** icon on the **View Orientation** tool panel.

Figure 1-22

Click the View Orientation tool

Select the Top view

Or, click the top surface of the View Selector cube

View Selector cube

Figure 1-22
(*Continued*)

A rectangle at an odd orientation

The rectangle returned to a Top view orientation

Click Y axis indicator arrow to return to a Top view orientation

Triad

2 Click the top surface of the **View Selector** cube.

The sketch will return to the **Top view** orientation.

Returning to the Top View Orientation—Top View

See Figure 1-22.

1 Click the **View Orientation** tool at the top of the drawing screen.

2 Click the **Top view** tool.

Returning to the Top View Orientation—Orientation Triad

The **Orientation Triad** is located in the lower-left corner of the drawing screen. See Figure 1-22.

SolidWorks defines the **Top** plane as the XZ plane. The Y axis is 90° to the XZ plane, so a view taken along the Y axis will generate a top view of the plane.

1 Move the cursor onto the **Orientation Triad**.

2 Click the Y axis indicator arrow.

The triad will reorientate to the **Top view** orientation.

1-9 Sample Problem SP1-1

Figure 1-23 shows a 2D shape sketched using the **Line** tool. The dimensions are in millimeters. This section will explain how to draw the shape.

1 Start a **New Part** document, select the **Front Plane**, and click the **Sketch** tool to create a sketch plane.

Figure 1-23

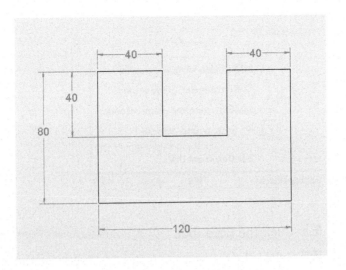

See Figure 1-24.

Figure 1-24

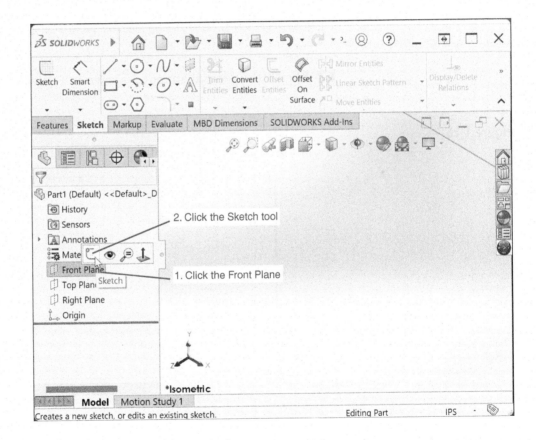

2. Click the Sketch tool

1. Click the Front Plane

2 Define the dimensional units as millimeters, **MMGS**.

See Figure 1-25.

Figure 1-25

Select the MMGS

MKS (meter, kilogram, second)

CGS (centimeter, gram, second)

MMGS (millimeter, gram, second)

✓ IPS (inch, pound, second)

Edit Document Units...

Editing Sketch1   IPS

3 Click the **Line** tool.

4 Select the origin as the starting point for the first line.

NOTE

The Line tool will generate a series of chain lines, where the endpoint of a sketched line becomes the starting point for the next line, until the line's endpoint is defined by pressing the **<Esc>** key or right-clicking the mouse and clicking the **Select** option.

5 Sketch the general shape as shown in Figure 1-26.

Figure 1-26

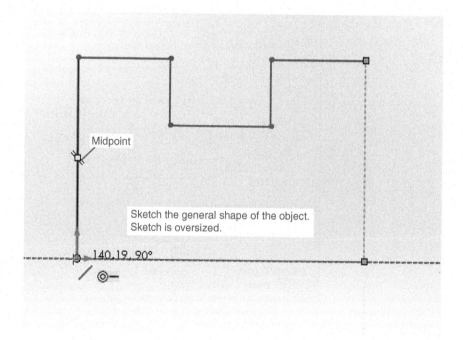

Midpoint

Sketch the general shape of the object. Sketch is oversized.

140.19, 90°

Note the double-circle relation icon that appears when the end of the last horizontal line drawn is located on the starting point of the first line. This is the **Concentric** relation icon, which indicates that the two points occupy the same location. The midpoint of the right-side vertical line is also defined.

6 Click the **Smart Dimension** tool and dimension the shape as shown in Figure 1-27 by clicking each line and entering the given dimensional value.

SolidWorks is sensitive to how the dimensions are entered. See Figure 1-27. Note that when the vertical 40 dimension was added to the right side of the shape, the adjacent horizontal 40 line moved upwards. This means that the two horizontal 40 lines are no longer aligned. The right horizontal 40 line must be fixed in place so that it remains aligned with the other horizontal 40 line when the vertical 40 dimension is added. The vertical 40 dimension will then move the bottom of the slot downwards.

Figure 1-27

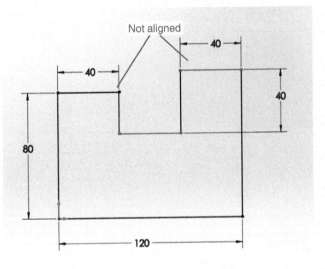

Fixing a Line in Place

1 Use the **Undo** tool to remove the vertical 40 dimension.

2 Click the right horizontal 40 line as shown in Figure 1-28.

Figure 1-28

3 Click the **Make Fixed** tool.

The **Make Fixed** tool's icon is an anchor. When the **Make Fixed** tool is activated, an anchor icon will appear below the line.

4 Use the **Smart Dimension** tool and add a vertical 40 dimension as shown.

The horizontal line at the bottom of the slot will move, accepting the 40 dimensional changes. The two horizontal lines remain aligned.

Sketch Relations

Sketch Relations are relationships shared between entities that help maintain the design intent of the sketch. The coincident relation was used previously in Figure 1-5 to align the starting point of a line with the origin. This relation ensures that the start point is always at the origin, even if the line's length changes. Figure 1-29 shows a view of the object with **Sketch Relations**.

Figure 1-29

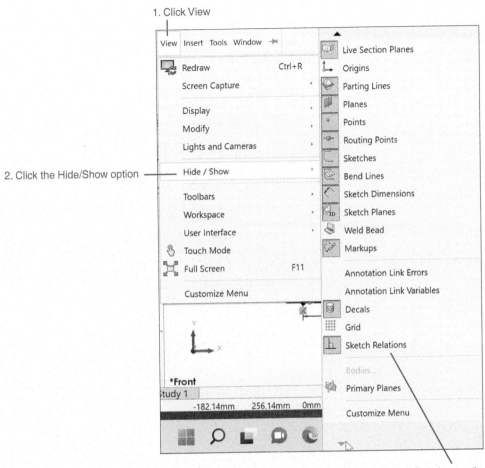

To remove the **Sketch Relations** icon:

1 Click the **View** tab at the top of the screen.

2 Click the **Hide/Show** option.

3 Click the **Sketch Relations** option.

NOTE

2D shapes should always be fully defined before creating 3D models.

1-10 Creating 3D Models

The fully defined shape shown in Figure 1-28 can now be used to create a 3D model.

Creating a 3D Model

1 Select the sketch.

2 Click the **Features** tab.

3 Click the **Extruded Boss/Base** tool.

See Figure 1-30. The shape will change orientation to the **Trimetric** orientation. The sketch was created on the **Front** plane.

Figure 1-30

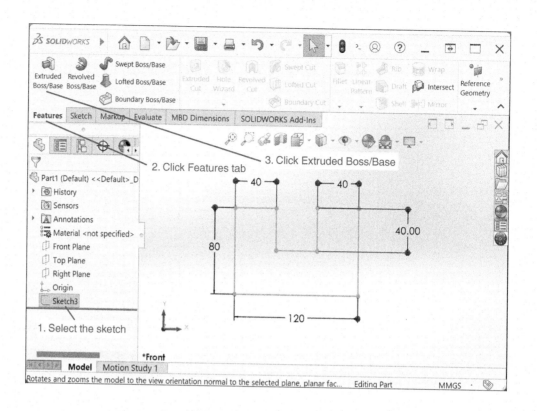

2. Click Features tab

3. Click Extruded Boss/Base

1. Select the sketch

A 3D Model

4 Define the depth as **20mm**.

5 Click the green **OK** check mark.

6 Click the drawing screen.

1-11 Saving Documents

See Figure 1-31.

Figure 1-31

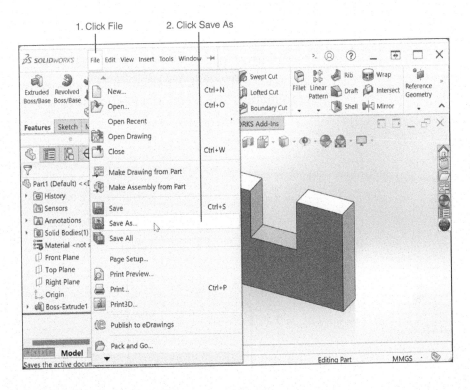

Saving a Document

1 Click the **File** menu at the top of the drawing screen. You might have to hover over the SolidWorks logo if the File menu is not visible.

A drop-down menu will appear.

2 Click the **Save As** option.

The **Save As** dialog box will appear. See Figure 1-32.

Figure 1-32

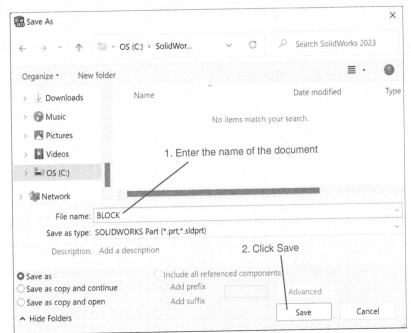

3 Enter the name of the document in the **File name** field.

In this example the name **BLOCK** was used.

4 Click the **Save** button.

1-12 Sample Problem SP1-2

Figure 1-33 shows a 2D shape that includes two angles. The dimensions are in inches. This section will show how to create the shape.

Figure 1-33

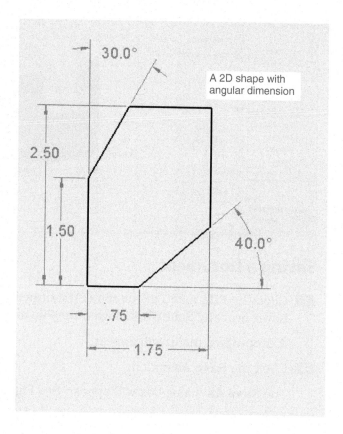

A 2D shape with angular dimension

1 Click the **Sketch** tab, click the **Front Plane** option, and then click the **Sketch** tool.

See Figure 1-34.

2 Use the **Line** tool and sketch the approximate shape.

Start the first line of the shape on the origin. Sketch the shape slightly larger than the final shape.

3 Add dimensions to the shape. See Figure 1-34.

4 Click the left vertical line and the left angled line and move the cursor away from the shape to create an angular dimension.

5 Select a location for the dimension and click the mouse.

6 In the Modify dialog box that opens, enter the angle value.

In this example the value is **30°**.

7 Click the green **OK** check mark to close the **Modify** dialog box.

8 Complete the remaining dimensions as shown in Figure 1-34.

Figure 1-34

2. Click the Sketch tool

1. Select the Front Plane

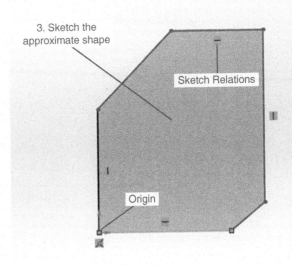

3. Sketch the approximate shape

Sketch Relations

Origin

Angular Dimension

4. Click these two lines and move the cursor away from the shape to create an angular dimension

2.24   1.50

6. Click the check mark

5. Define the angle

Figure 1-34
(*Continued*)

Angular dimension

30°

2.50

1.50

7. Click these two lines to create an angular dimension

53.79°

1.75

30°

2.50

1.50

53.79°

1.75

8. Click the existing dimension

10. Click the OK check mark

Modify

DS◊S Angle

40.00

Units

9. Enter new angular value here

11. Click the drawing screen. All lines should be black. The shape is fully defined.

30°

2.50

1.50

40°

.75

1.75

12. Finish the dimensions

9 Ensure that the shape is fully defined.

10 Click the **Features** tab, click the **Extruded Boss/Base** tool, and define the depth. See Figure 1-35.

Figure 1-35

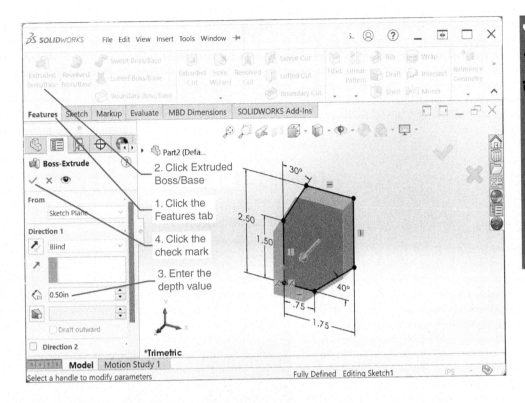

In this example, a depth of **0.50in.** was entered.

11 Click the green **OK** check mark and then click the drawing screen.

All the lines in the shape should be black, indicating the shape is fully defined. See Figure 1-36.

Figure 1-36

Finished 3D Model

1-13 Holes

There are several different ways to create holes using SolidWorks. Most holes are created using the **Hole Wizard** tool, which is explained in Chapter 3. For purposes of this introductory chapter, holes will be created using the **Circle** and **Extruded Cut** tools. A circle will be created and then cut through the 3D shape. All holes will be simple *through* holes; that is, they will go completely through the shape.

Creating a Hole

Figure 1-37 shows the 3D shape created in Sample Problem SP1-1. Two Ø20.0 holes have been added.

Figure 1-37

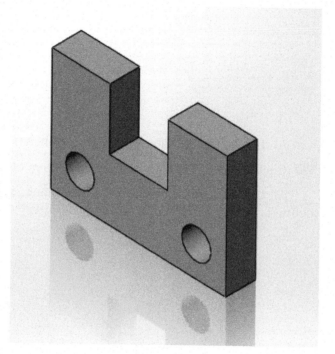

1 Click the **File** menu at the top of the screen and click the **Open** option, or click the **Open** tool.

2 Locate and click the **BLOCK** file created and saved in the last section.

See Figure 1-38. In this example the file was located on the C: drive in the folder **SolidWorks 2023**.

Figure 1-38

1. Click the BLOCK file

2. Click Open

3 Click **Open**.

The BLOCK will appear on the screen. See Figure 1-39.

Figure 1-39

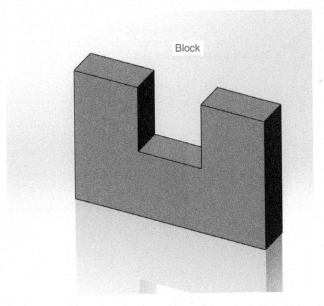

Block

4 Click the **View Orientation** tool and select the **Normal To** option.

This will create a view from an orientation point 90° to the surface. This is called a *normal* view. See Figure 1-40.

Figure 1-40

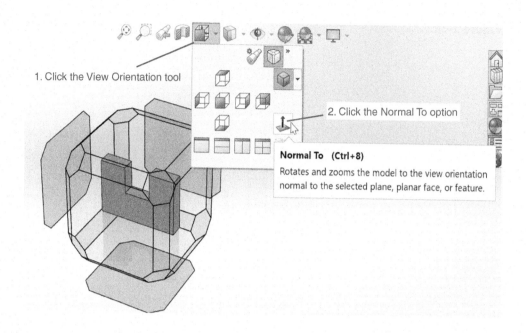

1. Click the View Orientation tool

2. Click the Normal To option

Normal To (Ctrl+8)
Rotates and zooms the model to the view orientation normal to the selected plane, planar face, or feature.

For this exercise we will work in a three-dimensional isometric plane. See Figure 1-41.

Figure 1-41

1. Click the View Orientation tool

Isometric

Click on a plane to switch views

2. Click the hexagonal corner to orient to isometric view

Figure 1-41
(*Continued*)

4. Click the Sketch tool

3. Click the front face of BLOCK

5. Sketch two holes as shown

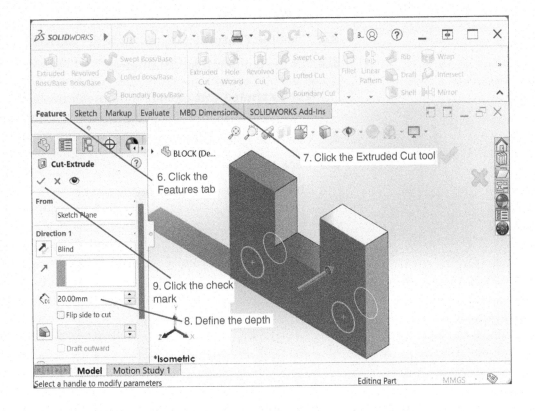

6. Click the Features tab

7. Click the Extruded Cut tool

9. Click the check mark

8. Define the depth

Figure 1-41
(*Continued*)

Holes in the
BLOCK

5 Again click the **View Orientation** tool, but this time select the small hexagonal surface to orient to **Isometric**.

6 Create a sketch plane on the front surface of the BLOCK, then use the **Circle** tool and add two circles using the given dimensions.

7 Click the **Features** tab and click the **Extruded Cut** tool.

8 Set the cut depth for **20.00mm**.

The **Extruded Cut** tool should automatically select the two circles. If it does not, click the circles. A preview should appear.

9 Click the green **OK** check mark.

10 Click the drawing screen.

The holes should appear in the shape.

Chapter Project

Project 1-1

Sketch the shapes shown in Figures P1-1 through P1-18. Create 3D models using the specified thickness values.

Figure P1-1
INCHES

Ø1.00

2.75

1.50

3.00

5.50

Thickness = 1.00

Figure P1-2
INCHES

.75 2.50

.75

Ø.50-2 HOLES

2.50

1.00

1.50

2.50

4.00

Thickness = .500

Figure P1-3
INCHES

2.00

1.00 1.25

1.00

Ø.50-2 HOLES

2.50

1.50

.50

.50 2.50

3.50

Thickness = .750

Figure P1-4
INCHES

Ø.50-2 HOLES

2.00
1.75
.50
.75
.50
.75
1.25
3.00
1.50
.75
1.00
Ø1.00
.50
2.00
3.50

Thickness = 1.125

Figure P1-5
MILLIMETERS

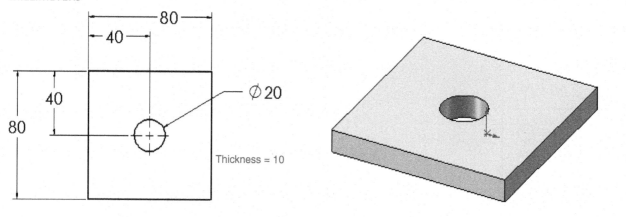

80
40
40
Ø 20
80

Thickness = 10

Figure P1-6
MILLIMETERS

120
50
40
20
Ø20-3 HOLES
110
80
60
20
50
25
45
45
140

Thickness = 15

Figure P1-7
MILLIMETERS

Ø20-3 HOLES

Thickness = 5

Figure P1-8
MILLIMETERS

Ø20-5 HOLES

Thickness = 12

Figure P1-9
MILLIMETERS

Ø20-2 HOLES

R58.31

Thickness = 20

Figure P1-10
INCHES

Figure P1-11
MILLIMETERS

Thickness = .60

Thickness = 20

Figure P1-12
MILLIMETERS

Thickness = 12

Figure P1-13
INCHES

Thickness = .875

6x Ø.50

Oject is symmetrical about the centerline.

5x.75(3.75)

Figure P1-14
MILLIMETERS

8x Ø20   Thickness = 12

Figure P1-15
MILLIMETERS

Thickness = 20

TAG	X LOC	Y LOC	SIZE
A1	1.22	57.14	Ø10
A2	10.27	84.04	Ø10
A3	15	25	Ø10
A4	32.38	75.51	Ø10
A5	38.51	25	Ø10
A6	46.50	52.61	Ø10
A7	46.50	101.88	Ø10

Figure P1-16
INCHES

Ø.50 - 4 HOLES

Thickness = .60

Figure P1-17
MILLIMETERS

Thickness = 16

Figure P1-18
MILLIMETERS

60.00°-6 PLACES

Ø15- 6 HOLES

Ø160

R65.26

Ø100

Thickness = 20

chaptertwo

Sketch Entities and Tools

CHAPTER OBJECTIVES

- Create 2D sketches
- Use most of the sketch tools
- Create more complex shapes by combining individual sketch tools

2-1 Introduction

Chapter 2 explains and demonstrates the tools on the **Sketch** panel, shown in Figure 2-1. Most of the sketch tools are initially explained and demonstrated individually. They are then combined in Sample Problems to show how they can be used together to create more complicated sketches.

Figure 2-1

The Sketch panel

Most of the sections include only one tool so that you can reference them at a later time if you need a refresher. The **Line** tool was covered in Chapter 1.

The **Circle** and **Rectangle** tools are presented in reference to an origin to create fully defined parts. However, many times sketches are added into an existing part that is already fully defined and referenced to the origin.

The added sketches are referenced to the existing part to create fully defined parts. Many of the Sketching tools will be presented without reference to an origin.

2-2 Mouse Gestures and the S Key

As you work with SolidWorks you may find yourself constantly using the same sketching tools repeatedly. The **Mouse Gestures** and **S Key** tools can be customized to help speed up the application of repetitive tools.

Mouse Gestures

Mouse Gestures is a SolidWorks feature that enables you to work faster. Selective commands, those you use most often, are linked to the movement of the mouse so that you can activate these commands by simply moving the mouse.

Figure 2-2 shows the default **Mouse Gestures** settings for the **Part** commands. Four tools are shown on the wheel: **Smart Dimension**, **Circle**, **Line**, and **Corner Rectangle**. These are the default tools settings. Up to eight tools can be added to the mouse gestures wheel.

Figure 2-2

A Mouse Gestures wheel with 8 tools

Mouse Gestures and **Mouse Gestures options** are different for each drawing mode. The tools listed in the **Drawing** and **Assembly** modes will be used when these subjects are introduced later in the book.

Using Mouse Gestures

Say you want to activate the **Line** tool and the default settings are in place.

11 Press and hold the right mouse button.

12 Move the mouse slightly to the left.

13 Still holding the right mouse button down, move the cursor onto the **Line** tool.

The selected tool will activate.

Accessing Mouse Gestures Settings

1 Click the **Tools** menu at the top of the screen.

2 Click the **Customize** option.

See Figure 2-3. The **Customize** dialog box will appear.

Figure 2-3

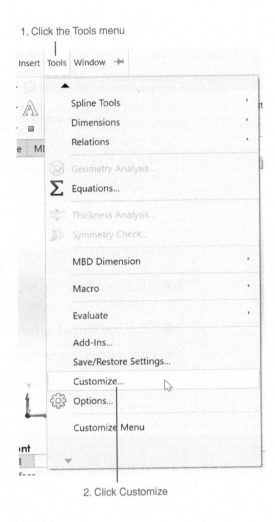

1. Click the Tools menu

2. Click Customize

3 Click the **Mouse Gestures** tab.

A listing of available tools will appear. If you select **8 Gestures** in the drop-down menu, the eight default mouse gestures settings will appear. See Figure 2-4.

Figure 2-4

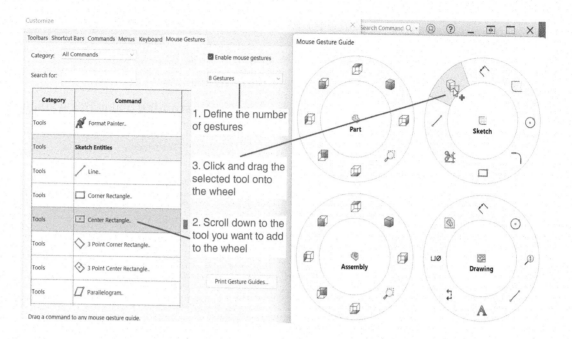

1. Define the number of gestures

3. Click and drag the selected tool onto the wheel

2. Scroll down to the tool you want to add to the wheel

Adding a Tool to a Mouse Gestures Wheel

1 Click and hold the left mouse button on the tool you want to move onto a wheel.

2 Drag the tool's icon onto the wheel.

3 Release the mouse button.

Figure 2-5 shows the new tool replacing the default tool on the wheel.

Figure 2-5

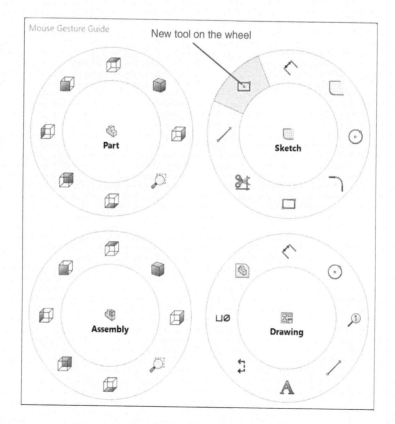

New tool on the wheel

Figure 2-6 shows the **Mouse Gestures** wheel used to create **Part** documents. Figure 2-7 shows a sample **Mouse Gestures** wheel next to a sketch.

Figure 2-6

Figure 2-7

NOTE

When you assign a new tool to a **Mouse Gestures** wheel, the existing tool will be replaced—that is, it is no longer available. If you want the removed tool on the **Mouse Gestures** wheel, you must re-enter it in a different location.

S Key

Another SolidWorks tool that helps to increase your working speed is the S *Key* option. The tools listed in the **S Key** dialog box may be customized. For this chapter we will show the **Sketching S Key**. Other **S Key** tool listings will be shown as the different modes are explained. **S Key** tools can be customized to your personal preference.

Activating the S Key

See Figure 2-8.

Figure 2-8

Press the S key on the keyboard to access the S Key toolbar

1 While in a sketch, press the **S** key on the keyboard.

The **S Key** toolbar will appear.

2 Click the desired tool.

In this example the **Line** tool was activated. See Figure 2-9.

Figure 2-9

1. Press the S key on the keyboard and click the Line tool

2. Sketch a line

Line (L)

71.14

Sketches a line. Click to place the start point, drag, and release when the line is the correct length. You can also use two clicks to place the start and end points.

Customizing the S Key Shortcut Toolbar

1 Press the **S** key on the keyboard.

2 Right-click the **S Key** toolbar.

See Figure 2-10.

Figure 2-10

1. Right-click the S Key panel

2. Click the Customize box

Customize...

3 Click the **Customize . . .** callout.

The **Customize** dialog box will appear. See Figure 2-11.

Figure 2-11

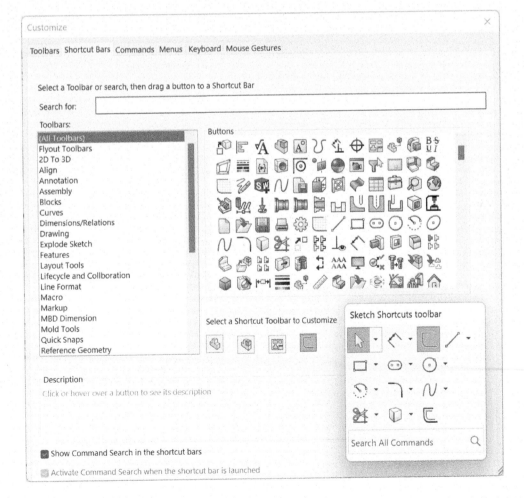

4 Click the tool to be added from the **Buttons** panel, drag the icon to the **Sketch Shortcuts toolbar** panel, and release the mouse button.

5 Click **OK**.

The tool icon will appear in the box. See Figure 2-12.

Figure 2-12

Click and drag the desired tool onto the Sketch Shortcuts panel

Figure 2-12
(*Continued*)

Chapter 2

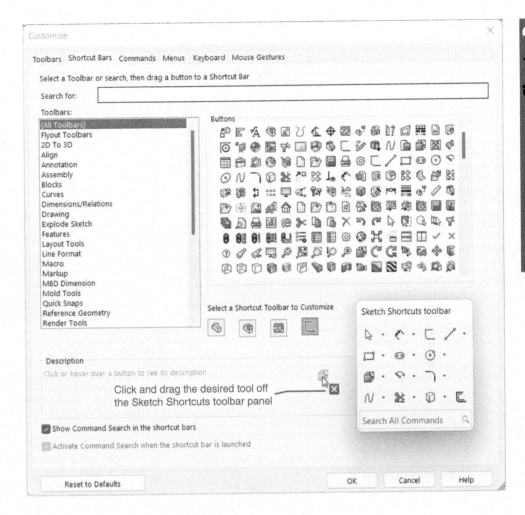

Removing a Tool from the S Key Toolbar

1 Click and drag the selected tool out and away from the toolbar. See Figure 2-12 (bottom).

2 Release the mouse button.

3 Click **OK**.

2-3 Origins

All sketches must be referenced to the drawing's origin in order to be fully defined. See Section 1-4 in Chapter 1. The easiest way to create a fully defined sketch is to start it on the origin. The drawing's origin may not always be visible.

Showing the Origin

1 Click the **View** menu at the top of the drawing screen.

2 Click the **Hide/Show** option, and click the **Origins** tool.

See Figure 2-13. The icon next to the **Origins** tool heading will become shaded when the tool is on.

Figure 2-13

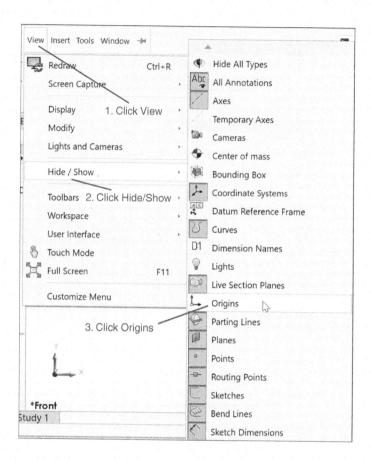

The drawing's origin icon will appear on the screen. It will remain visible on the screen until removed by clicking the shaded tool heading created when the **Origins** tool was turned on.

2-4 Circle

A circle is sketched using the **Circle** tool and then sized (that is, given a diameter value) using the **Smart Dimension** tool. There are two circle tools: **Circle** and **Perimeter Circle**.

Sketching a Circle

1 Click the **New** tool icon at the top of the screen, click the **Part** tool in the **New SolidWorks Document** dialog box, and click **OK**.

See Figure 2-14. The dimensions will be in inches.

Figure 2-14

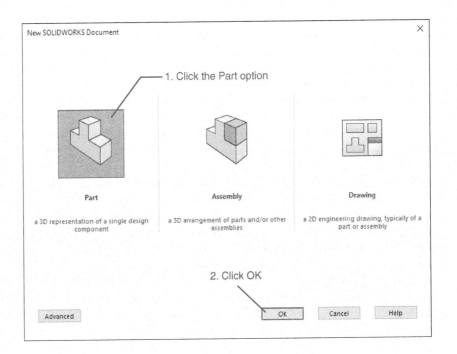

1. Click the Part option

2. Click OK

2 Click the **Front Plane** tool in the **FeatureManager Design Tree**.

A small toolbar will appear.

3 Click the **Sketch** tool.

The circle will be created on the **Front** plane in the **Sketch** mode. See Figure 2-15. Note that the origin is displayed in the center of the **Front** plane.

Figure 2-15

2. Click the Sketch tool

1. Click the Front Plane

4 Click the **Circle** tool.

5 Select the origin as the circle's centerpoint by clicking the origin and dragging the cursor away from the centerpoint.

6 Click an approximate edge point for the circle.

7 Click the **Smart Dimension** tool, click the circle, and define the circle's diameter. See Figure 2-16.

Figure 2-16

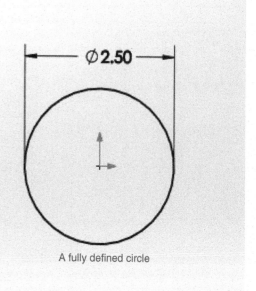

A fully defined circle

8 Right-click the mouse and click the **Select** option.

For this example a diameter of Ø2.50 was selected. The circle is black, meaning it is fully defined. The **Orientation Triad** in the lower-left corner of the screen shows the XY or **Front** plane orientation.

Sketching a Perimeter Circle Using Three Points

A perimeter circle is a circle drawn using three points. These points may be three individual points or points tangent to an existing object.

1 Create a new **Part** document.

2 Click the **Top Plane** tool in the **FeatureManager Design Tree**.

3 Click the **Sketch** tool.

4 Set the **Units** for millimeters.

5 Click the **Perimeter Circle** tool.

The **Perimeter Circle** tool is a flyout from the **Circle** tool. See Figure 2-17.

Figure 2-17

Perimeter Circle tool

6 Click three points on the screen.

Make one of the points coincidental with the origin. See Figure 2-18.

7 Click the circle to select it.

Figure 2-18

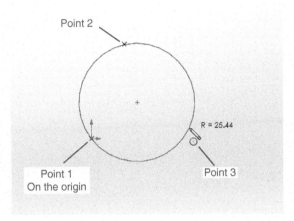

Point 2

R = 25.44

Point 1
On the origin

Point 3

Sketching a Perimeter Circle Tangent to Three Lines

Figure 2-19 shows three randomly drawn straight lines. Draw a circle tangent to each line.

1 Click the **Perimeter Circle** tool.

2 Click the approximate midpoint of each of the three lines.

Figure 2-19

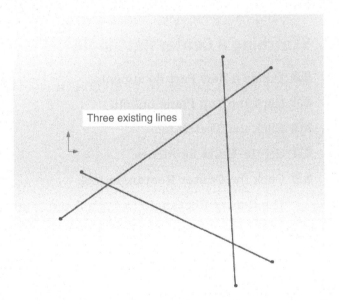

Three existing lines

A circle will appear tangent to all three lines.

When the **Sketch Relations** are shown, you can see that the circle is tangent to each of the lines. See Figure 2-20.

Figure 2-20

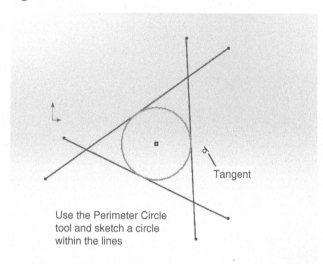

Tangent

Use the Perimeter Circle tool and sketch a circle within the lines

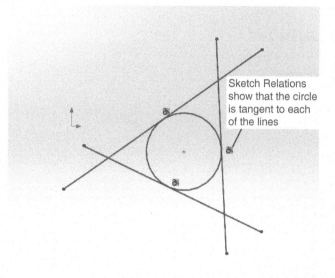

Sketch Relations show that the circle is tangent to each of the lines

2-5   Rectangle

There are five different methods that can be used to create a rectangle, including the **Corner Rectangle** tool explained in Chapter 1. This section will describe how to sketch a rectangle using the other four methods.

Sketching a Center Rectangle

1 Create a **New Part** document.

2 Click the **Top Plane** option.

3 Click the **Sketch** tool.

4 Set the **Units** for inches.

5 Click the **Center Rectangle** tool.

The **Center Rectangle** tool is a flyout from the **Rectangle** tool icon. See Figure 2-21.

Figure 2-21

Center Rectangle tool

6 Select the origin for the first corner point.

7 Move the cursor and select the second corner point, right-click the mouse, and click the **Select** option.

8 Click the **Smart Dimension** tool and add dimensions to the rectangle.

9 Right-click the mouse and click the **Select** option.

The rectangle is fully defined. See Figure 2-22.

Figure 2-22

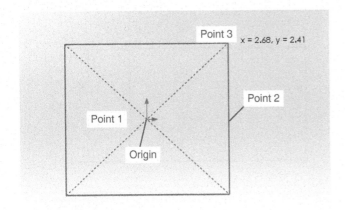

Point 3   x = 2.68, y = 2.41

Point 2

Point 1

Origin

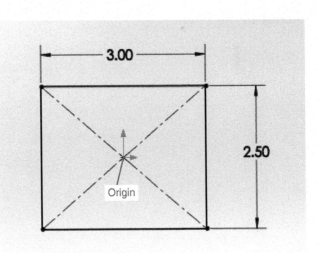

3.00

2.50

Origin

Sketching a 3 Point Corner Rectangle

1 Click the **Sketch** tab to access the **Sketching** tools, define a plane, and set the units to inches.

2 Click the **3 Point Corner Rectangle** tool.

The **3 Point Corner Rectangle** tool is a flyout from the **Rectangle** tool icon. See Figure 2-23.

Figure 2-23

3 Point Corner Rectangle

3 Locate the first point on the origin.

4 Move the cursor horizontally and define a second point.

5 Move the cursor vertically and define a third point.

6 Use the **Smart Dimension** tool and define the rectangle's size.

See Figure 2-24.

Figure 2-24

Origin

Sketching a 3 Point Center Rectangle

1 Click the **Sketch** tab to access the **Sketching** tools, define a plane, and set the units to inches.

2 Click the **3 Point Center Rectangle** tool.

The **3 Point Center Rectangle** tool is a flyout from the **Rectangle** tool icon.

3 Locate the first point on the origin.

4 Move the cursor horizontally to the right and define a second point.

5 Move the cursor vertically and define a third point.

See Figure 2-25.

Figure 2-25

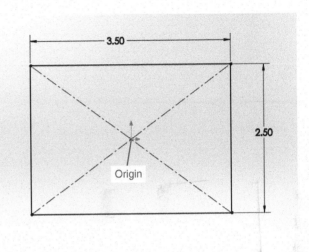

3 Point Center Rectangle

6 Use the **Smart Dimension** tool and define the rectangle's size.

Sketching a Parallelogram

1 Click the **Sketch** tab to access the **Sketching** tools, define a plane, and set the units to inches.

2 Click the **Parallelogram** tool.

The **Parallelogram** tool is a flyout from the **Rectangle** tool icon.
See Figure 2-26.

Figure 2-26

Parallelogram tool

d = 1.11, a = 72.68°

Point 3

Point 2

Point 1

Origin

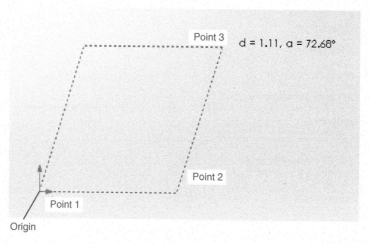

A Parallelogram

1.00

60.00°

1.25

3 Locate the first point on the origin.

4 Move the cursor horizontally and to the right and define a second point.

5 Move the cursor vertically and at an angle and define a third point.

Note that a parallelogram has four sides that are parallel and equal in length, but also includes an angle other than 90° between sides.

6 Use the **Smart Dimension** tool and define the rectangle's size.

2-6 Slots

SolidWorks has four different tools that can be used to draw slots. See Figure 2-27.

Figure 2-27

Straight Slot tool

The **Straight Slot** tool can be used to draw both internal and external slot shapes. Figure 2-28 shows examples of both internal and external slot shapes.

An internal slot shape

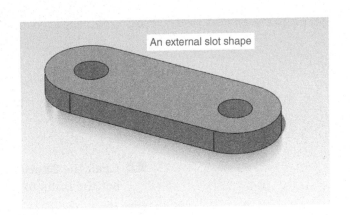

An external slot shape

Figure 2-28

Sketching a Straight Slot

See Figure 2-29.

Figure 2-29

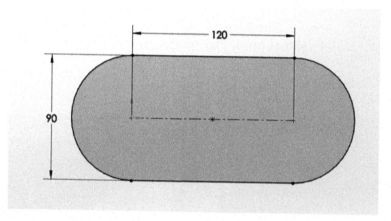

1 Click the **Sketch** tab to access the **Sketching** tools, define a plane, and set the units to millimeters.

2 Click the **Straight Slot** tool and the **Center to Center** option.

3 Click a starting point.

In this example the origin was selected.

4 Move the cursor horizontally and define a second point.

The distance between points 1 and 2 will define the slot's centerline.

5 Move the cursor and select a third point.

The distance between points 2 and 3 will define the radius of the slot's rounded ends.

6 Add dimensions as required to fully define the shape.

Sketching a Centerpoint Straight Slot

See Figure 2-30.

Figure 2-30

1. Click the **Sketch** tab to access the **Sketching** tools, define a plane, and set the units to millimeters.

2. Click the **Centerpoint Straight Slot** tool.

3. Click a starting point.

4. Move the cursor horizontally and define a second point.

5. Move the cursor and select a third point.

6. Add dimensions as required to fully define the shape.

Sketching a 3 Point Arc Slot

See Figure 2-31.

Figure 2-31

Fully defined

1 Click the **Sketch** tab to access the **Sketching** tools, define a plane, and set the units to millimeters.

2 Click the **3 Point Arc Slot** tool.

3 Click a starting point.

4 Move the cursor and define point 2.

5 Move the cursor and define point 3.

The angular distance between points 1 and 2 will define the angular length of the arc. The distance between point 3 and the arc's centerpoint will define the arc's radius.

6 Move the cursor and define point 4.

The distance between points 3 and 4 will define the radius for the slot's rounded ends.

7 Add dimensions as required.

Sketching a Centerpoint Arc Slot

See Figure 2-32.

Figure 2-32

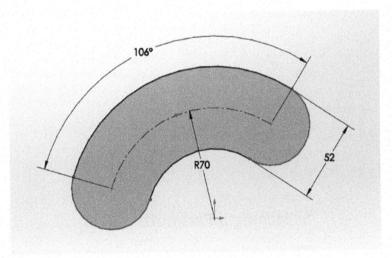

1 Click the **Sketch** tab to access the **Sketching** tools, define a plane, and set the units to inches.

2 Click the **Centerpoint Arc Slot** tool.

3 Click a starting point.

4 Move the cursor and define point 2.

The distance between the starting point, point 1, and point 2 will define the radius of a circle. The circle will be used to define the arc. The radius of the arc will be equal to the radius of the circle.

5 Move the cursor and define point 3.

The angular distance between points 2 and 3 will define the angular length of the arc.

6 Move the cursor and define point 4.

The distance between points 3 and 4 will define the radius for the slot's rounded ends.

7 Add dimensions as required.

2-7 Perimeter Circle

The **Circle** tool was presented in Section 1-4 in Chapter 1.

Perimeter circles are often drawn tangent to existing lines or arcs. Figure 2-33 shows a set of perpendicular lines and a circle. In this example a perimeter circle will be drawn tangent to the lines and circle.

Figure 2-33

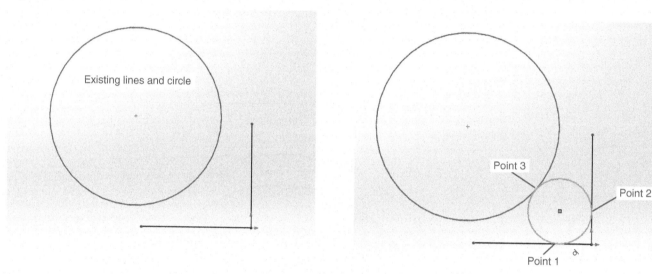

Sketching a Perimeter Circle

1 Click the **Sketch** tab to access the **Sketching** tools, define a plane, and set the units to inches.

2 Click the **Perimeter Circle** tool.

3 Click a starting point, point 1.

In this example the horizontal line was selected. Any point on the line is acceptable but it is good practice to select a point on the line near the approximate location of the tangent point.

4 Move the cursor and define point 2.

In this example the vertical line was selected.

5 Move the cursor and select point 3.

In this example the circle was selected.

6 Right-click the mouse and click the **Select** option.

2-8 Arcs

SolidWorks has three **Arc** tools: **Centerpoint Arc**, **Tangent Arc**, and **3 Point Arc**. See Figure 2-34.

Figure 2-34

Centerpoint Arc tool

Sketching a Centerpoint Arc

See Figure 2-35.

Figure 2-35

1 Click the **Sketch** tab to access the **Sketching** tools, define a plane, and set the units to millimeters.

2 Click the **Centerpoint Arc** tool.

3 Click a starting point, point 1.

4 Move the cursor and define point 2.

The distance between the starting point, point 1, and point 2 will define the radius of a circle. The circle will be used to define the arc. The radius of the arc will be equal to the radius of the circle.

5 Move the cursor and define point 3.

The angular distance between points 2 and 3 will define the angular length of the arc.

6 Add dimensions as required.

Sketching a Tangent Arc

See Figure 2-36. The **Tangent Arc** is used to draw an arc between existing entities. In this example two lines have been drawn.

Figure 2-36

1 Click the **Sketch** tab to access the **Sketching** tools, define a plane, and set the units to millimeters.

2 Click the **Tangent Arc** tool.

3 Click a starting point, point 1.

In this example the endpoint of the slanted line was selected.

4 Move the cursor and define point 2.

In this example the endpoint of the horizontal line was selected.

5 Add dimensions as required.

The radius of the arc is controlled by the radius dimensional value.

Figure 2-37 shows two parallel lines. The **Tangent Arc** tool was used to add a rounded end segment to the right end. Note that the *radius* value is **10** or half the distance between the two lines.

Figure 2-37

Figure 2-38

Sketching a 3 Point Arc

Three points can be used to define an arc. See Figure 2-38.

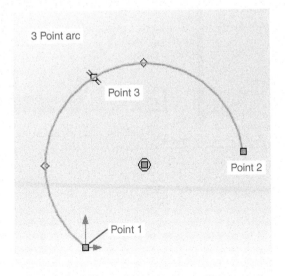

1 Click the **Sketch** tab to access the **Sketching** tools, define a plane, and set the units to millimeters.

2 Click the **3 Point Arc** tool.

3 Click a starting point, point 1.

4 Move the cursor and define point 2.

5 Move the cursor and define point 3.

6 Add dimensions as required.

2-9 Polygons

A polygon is any closed plane figure with at least three sides and three angles. SolidWorks draws regular polygons—that is, polygons with all sides and angles equal. Irregular polygons must be drawn as individual line segments.

Sketching a Hexagon

A hexagon is a polygon with six sides. For this example a regular hexagon with six equal sides and angles will be drawn. See Figure 2-39.

Figure 2-39

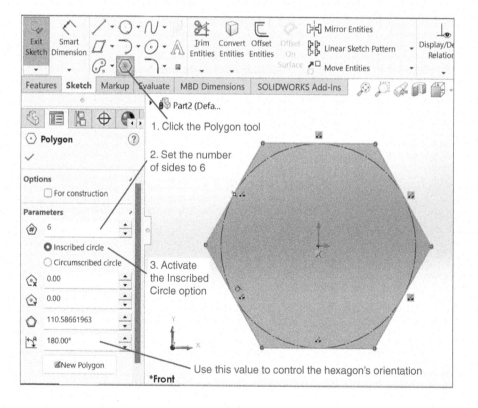

Figure 2-39
(*Continued*)

Chapter 2

1 Click the **Sketch** tab to access the **Sketching** tools, define a plane, and set the units to millimeters.

2 Click the **Polygon** tool.

3 Set the **Parameters** value to **6** and ensure that the **Inscribed circle** button is active. This will create a circumscribed hexagon.

4 Click a starting point, point 1.

5 Move the cursor and define point 2.

6 Add dimensions as required.

Figure 2-40 shows a circumscribed hexagon and an inscribed hexagon. The circumscribed hexagon is drawn around and tangent to a circle. An inscribed hexagon is drawn within a circle.

Figure 2-40

A circumscribed hexagon

An inscribed hexagon

2-10 Spline

A spline is a curved line that intersects several defined points. A spline whose starting point is coincident with its endpoint is called a closed spline. All other splines are open splines. Figure 2-41 shows examples of open and closed splines.

Figure 2-41

Sketching a Spline

See Figure 2-42.

Figure 2-42

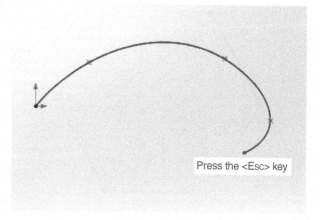

1 Click the **Sketch** tab to access the **Sketching** tools, define a plane, and set the units to millimeters.

2 Click the **Spline** tool.

3 Click a starting point, point 1.

4 Move the cursor and define point 2.

5 Move the cursor and define point 3.

6 Move the cursor and define point 4.

7 Move the cursor and define point 5.

8 Press the **<Esc>** key.

The points used to create a spline may be defined using dimensions.

Editing a Spline

See Figure 2-43.

Figure 2-43

To edit a spline, click and drag the defining points

1 Select a point on the spline.

2 Click and drag the point to a new location.

3 Click the green **OK** check mark.

A spline may also be edited by editing the dimensions used to define the spline's points.

2-11 Ellipse

There are four tools associated with the **Ellipse** tool: **Ellipse**, **Partial Ellipse**, **Parabola**, and **Conic**. See Figure 2-44. For technical drawings an ellipse is defined by its centerpoint location, its major axis, and its minor axis.

Figure 2-44

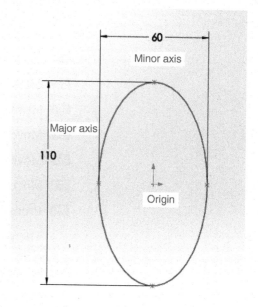

Sketching an Ellipse

See Figure 2-45.

Figure 2-45

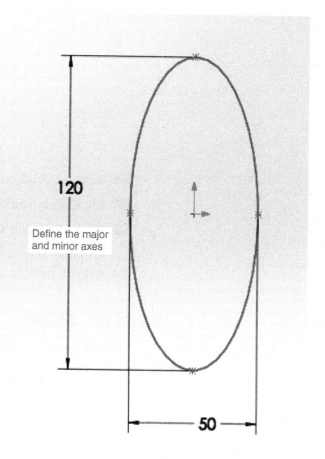

1 Click the **Sketch** tab to access the **Sketching** tools, define a plane, and set the units to millimeters.

2 Click the **Ellipse** tool.

3 Click a starting point, point 1.

4 Move the cursor and define point 2.

The distance between points 1 and 2 defines half the minor axis distance.

5 Move the cursor and define point 3.

The distance between points 1 and 3 defines half the major axis distance.

6 Add dimensions as required.

Sketching a Partial Ellipse

See Figure 2-46.

1 Click the **Sketch** tab to access the **Sketching** tools, define a plane, and set the units to millimeters.

2 Click the **Partial Ellipse** tool.

3 Click a starting point, point 1.

Figure 2-46

Figure 2-46
(*Continued*)

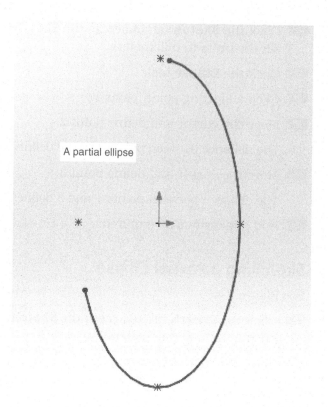

A partial ellipse

4 Move the cursor and define point 2.

The distance between points 1 and 2 defines half the minor axis distance.

5 Move the cursor and define point 3.

The distance between points 1 and 3 defines half the major axis distance.

6 Move the cursor to define the partial ellipse.

7 Add dimensions as necessary.

Sketching a Parabola

A parabola is defined as the path of a moving point that is always equidistant from a fixed point, the focus, and a fixed straight line, the directrix. See Figure 2-47.

1 Click the **Sketch** tab to access the **Sketching** tools, define a plane, and set the units to millimeters.

2 Click the **Parabola** tool.

3 Click a starting point, point 1.

Figure 2-47

2 Chapter

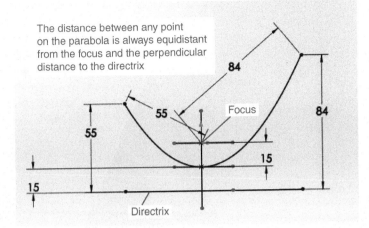

The distance between any point on the parabola is always equidistant from the focus and the perpendicular distance to the directrix

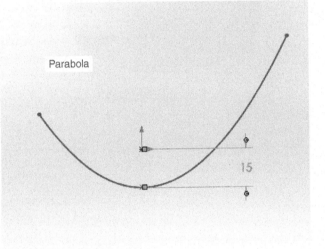

In this example the selected point 1 becomes the focus.

4 Move the cursor and define point 2.

The distance between points 1 and 2 defines half the distance to the directrix.

5 Move the cursor and define a start point for the parabola.

6 Click and drag the cursor to define the size of the parabola.

7 Add dimensions as required.

The distance between the focus and the directrix is two times the distance between the focus and the closest point of the parabola.

Conic Section

A conic section is the intersection of a plane with a cone. Ellipses, parabolas, and hyperbolas are all conic sections. See Figure 2-48.

Figure 2-48

Cone

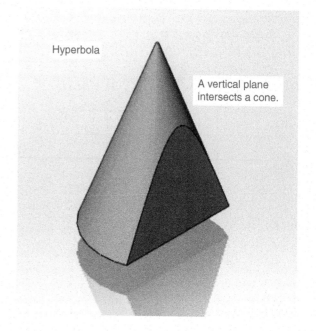

Hyperbola

A vertical plane intersects a cone.

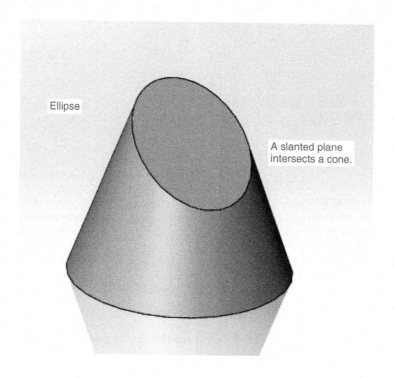

Ellipse

A slanted plane intersects a cone.

Sketching a Conic

Conic curves can be used to create smooth curves between existing endpoints. See Figure 2-49.

Figure 2-49

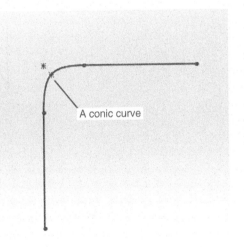

1 Click the **Sketch** tab to access the **Sketching** tools, define a plane, and set the units to millimeters.

2 Click the **Conic** tool.

3 Ensure that there is a check mark in the **Auto tangency** box.

4 Click points 1 and 2.

A conic curve will appear along with a rho value. The rho value will change as you move the cursor.

5 Select an appropriate conic shape, right-click the mouse, and click the **Select** option.

2-12 Fillets and Chamfers

A fillet is a rounded corner or edge and a chamfer is a beveled corner or edge. Both the **Sketch Fillet** and **Sketch Chamfer** tools can be applied to 2D sketches of 3D models. Figure 2-50 shows a sketch that includes a fillet and a chamfer.

Figure 2-50

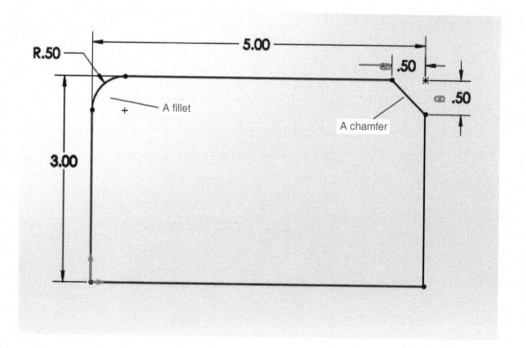

Sketching a Fillet

See Figure 2-51.

Figure 2-51

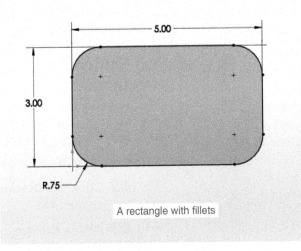

A rectangle with fillets

---

1 Click the **Fillet** tool.

2 Define the radius for the fillet.

3 Click the left vertical line.

4 Click the top horizontal line.

A preview of the fillet will appear.

5 Add fillets to the other corners of the rectangle.

Sketching a Chamfer

There are three different ways to define a chamfer: angle-distance, distance-distance—equal distance, and distance-distance—not equal distance. Figure 2-52 shows an existing 3.00 × 5.00 rectangle.

Figure 2-52

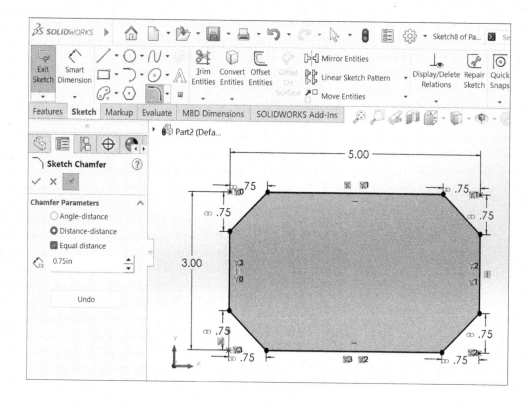

Sketching a Chamfer Using Distance-Distance—Equal Distance

See Figure 2-52.

1 Click the **Chamfer** tool.

The **Chamfer** tool is a flyout from the **Fillet** tool.

2 Click the **Distance-distance** option and check the **Equal distance** check box.

3 Define the size of the chamfer.

4 Click the left vertical line.

5 Click the top horizontal line.

A preview of the chamfer will appear.

6 Add a .75 × .75 chamfer to the other corners.

Sketching a Chamfer Using Angle-Distance

See Figure 2-53.

Figure 2-53

1 Click the **Chamfer** tool.

2 Click the **Angle-distance** option.

3 Define the chamfer's angle and distance.

4 Click the left vertical line.

5 Click the top horizontal line.

A preview of the chamfer will appear. The relative angle of the chamfer will depend on the line selection sequence. The chamfers at the top of the rectangle selected the vertical sides first and the chamfers at the bottom of the rectangle selected the bottom horizontal line first.

Note that an angle-distance chamfer created with a 45° angle will generate two equal distances.

Sketching a Chamfer Using Distance-Distance—Not Equal Distance

See Figure 2-54.

Figure 2-54

1. Click the **Chamfer** tool.

2. Click the **Distance-distance** option and uncheck the **Equal distance** check box.

3. Define the two distances.

   The direction of the chamfer depends on the line selection sequence.

4. Click the lines as shown.

2-13 Sketch Text

The **Text** tool is used to add text to a sketch. The default font for SolidWorks text is **Century Gothic**.

Adding Text

See Figure 2-55.

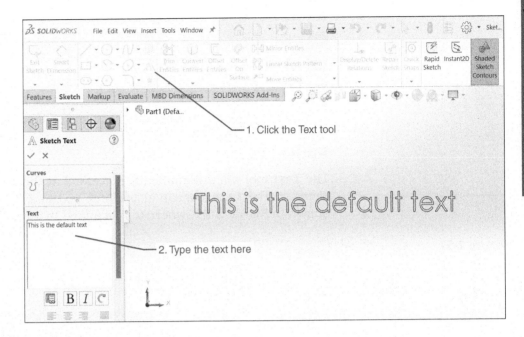

Figure 2-55

1. Click the Text tool

2. Type the text here

---

1 Click the **Text** tool.

2 Type the text in the **Text** box in the **Sketch Text** manager box.

The **Text** box text will appear on the screen. The text can be moved by clicking the cursor in a different location.

Changing the Font and Size of Text

See Figure 2-56.

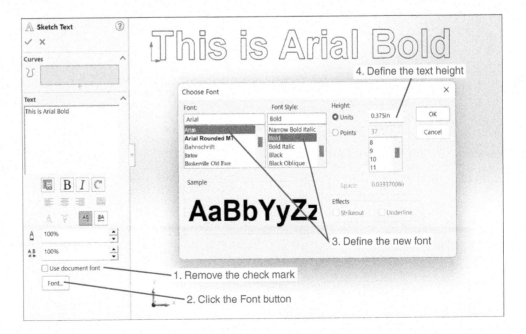

Figure 2-56

4. Define the text height

3. Define the new font

1. Remove the check mark

2. Click the Font button

1 Remove the check mark from the **Use document font** box and click the **Font** button.

The **Choose Font** dialog box will appear.

2 Define the new font and text height.

3 Click **OK**.

4 Add the text.

5 Click the green **OK** check mark.

In this example **Arial Bold** font with a height of **0.375in** was selected.

Adding Text to a Feature

The **Text** tool will automatically place text at the origin if no feature is selected. The **Text** tool can also attach text to a defined existing feature as shown in Figure 2-57, where text is added to a line on a rectangle.

Figure 2-57

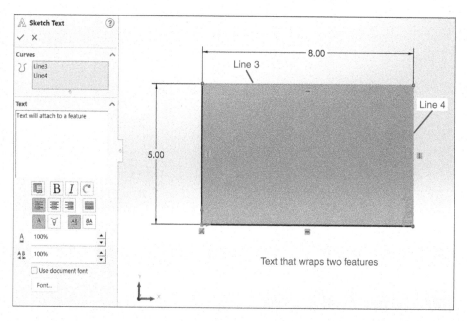

1. Draw a rectangle.

2. Click the **Text** tool.

3. Click the top line of the rectangle.

4. Type the text in the **Text** box in the **Sketch Text** manager box.

5. Click the green **OK** check mark.

Creating Text that Wraps Around Two Features

Text can also be added to two features at once.

1. Draw a rectangle.

2. Click the **Text** tool.

3. Define two of the lines in the rectangle shown as features to attach the text.

4. Type the text.

5. Click the green **OK** check mark.

2-14   Point

The **Point** tool is used to create points anywhere on the drawing screen. Points are often helpful during the construction process of a sketch. Figure 2-58 shows a point. It was created by clicking the **Point** tool and selecting a location on the drawing screen. The point can be precisely located using dimensions, by using the **Control Vertex Parameters** values listed in the **Point** manager box, or by attaching the point to an existing entity.

Figure 2-58

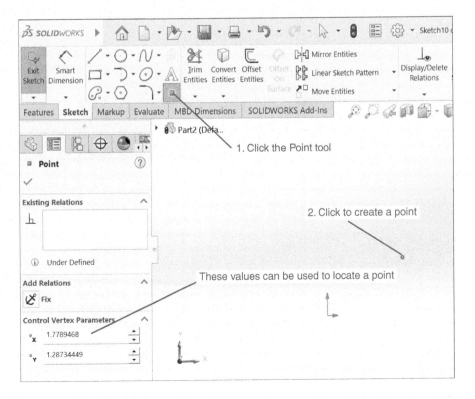

2-15   Trim Entities

The **Trim Entities** tool is used to remove unwanted entities from an existing sketch. Figure 2-59 shows a line passing through a circle and a rectangle. Say we wish to remove the portions of the line that pass through the circle and the rectangle.

Trimming Entities

1 Click the **Trim Entities** tool. If not already selected, click the **Trim to closest option**.

2 Locate the cursor on the portion of the line within the circle.

3 Click the mouse.

The line segment will be removed.

4 Locate the cursor on the portion of the line that passes through the rectangle and click the mouse.

Figure 2-59

Resulting trims

2-16   Extend Entities

The **Extend Entities** tool is on the flyout from the **Trim Entities** tool and is used to extend existing lines to new lengths.

Figure 2-60 shows an existing 1.75 × 4.00 rectangle. We wish to extend the horizontal length to 6.00.

Extending Entities in a Sketch

1 Sketch a vertical line about 6.00 from the left vertical line of the rectangle.

2 Use the **Smart Dimension** tool and define the location of the line as **6.00**.

3 Click the **Extend Entities** tool.

Figure 2-60

Figure 2-60
(*Continued*)

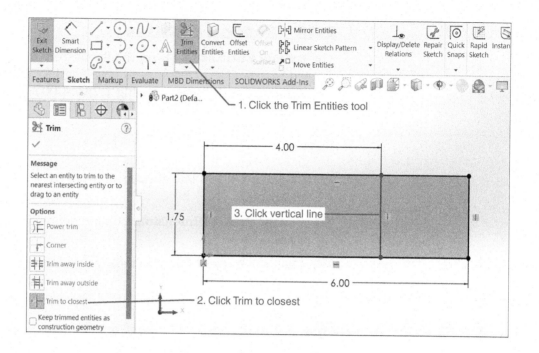

1. Click the Trim Entities tool

3. Click vertical line

2. Click Trim to closest

Extended shape

The cursor will appear with the **Extend Entities** icon attached.

4 Click the top horizontal line.

The line will extend to the vertical line located at 6.00 from the left vertical edge of the rectangle.

5 Click the lower horizontal line.

6 Click the **Trim Entities** tool, select the **Trim to closest** option, and, using the top and bottom horizontal lines as bounding lines, trim the **4.00** line.

Note that the dimension also is removed.

2-17 Offset Entities

The **Offset Entities** tool is used to sketch entities parallel to an existing entity. Figure 2-61 shows a line. Say we wish to draw a line parallel to the existing line .75 away.

Figure 2-61

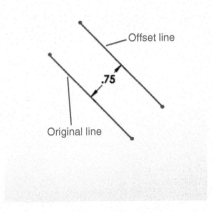

Offset line

.75

Original line

Sketching an Offset Line

1 Sketch a line.

2 Click the **Offset Entities** tool.

3 Specify the offset distance.

4 Click the existing line.

A preview will appear. In this example the offset line is initially located below the original line.

5 Click a location above the existing line.

6 Click the green **OK** check mark.

The **Offset Entities** tool can be used to offset existing enclosed shapes. See Figure 2-62.

Figure 2-62

2-18   Mirror Entities

The **Mirror Entities** tool is used to create mirror images of entities. A mirror image is different from a copy. Figure 2-63 shows both a mirror image and a copy of the same shape. Note the differences.

Figure 2-63

Creating a Mirror Entity

Figure 2-64 shows a circular shaped entity that includes a circular cutout.

1 Click the **Mirror Entities** tool.

2 Select all the curves and lines in the entity excluding the Mirror Line.

Figure 2-64

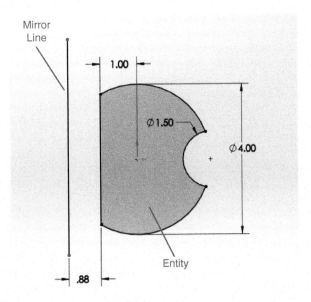

Mirror
Line

1.00

∅1.50

∅4.00

Entity

.88

The Mirror Entities tool

Define entities to mirror

Mirror line

Preview

Define mirror line

1.00

R2.00

R.75

.88

Figure 2-64
(*Continued*)

Mirror Image

A list will appear in the **Entities to mirror** box. In this example, Line1, Arc3, Arc2, and Arc1 were selected.

3 Click the **Mirror about** box.

4 Click the mirror line. In this example, Line2 was selected.

A preview of the mirrored image will appear.

5 Click the green **OK** check mark.

A line within the entity can be used as a mirror line. Figure 2-65 shows an entity mirrored about one of its edge lines.

Figure 2-65

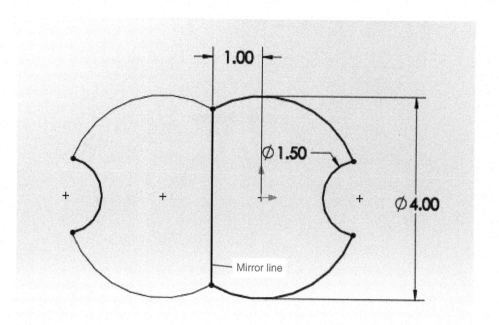

Mirror line

2-19 Linear Sketch Pattern

The **Linear Sketch Pattern** tool is used to create patterns of sketched entities in the X and Y directions. Both linear and circular patterns can also be created from 3D models.

Figure 2-66 shows an entity. Say we wish to create a 3 × 5 linear pattern of the entity.

Figure 2-66

Figure 2-66
(*Continued*)

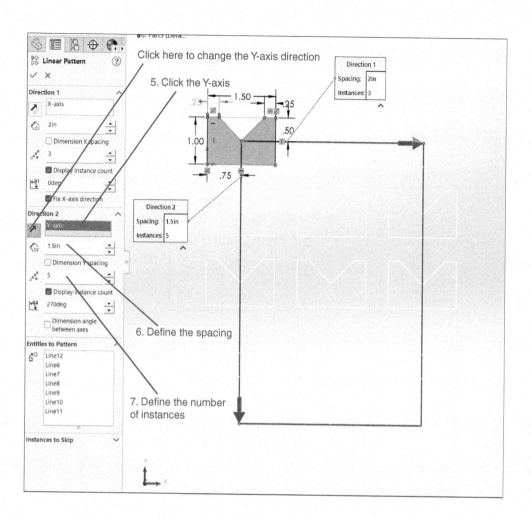

Click here to change the Y-axis direction

5. Click the Y-axis

6. Define the spacing

7. Define the number of instances

A 3 x 5 linear pattern

Creating a Linear Sketch Pattern

1 Click the **Linear Sketch Pattern** tool.

2 Click all the lines in the entity.

3 Ensure that Direction 1 is the **X-axis**.

The box will have a blue background.

4 Set the spacing distance for **2in**.

The 2.00 spacing distance is derived from the shapes' 1.50 width plus .50 clearance between each object in the X-direction.

5 Set the number of instances to **3**.

6 Click the **Y-axis** box.

7 Set the spacing distance for **1.5**.

The 1.50 spacing distance is derived from the shapes' 1.00 height plus .50 clearance between each object in the Y-direction.

8 Set the number of instances to **5**.

A preview will appear.

9 Click the green **OK** check mark.

2-20   Circular Sketch Pattern

The **Circular Sketch Pattern** tool is used to create circular patterns about a centerpoint. To demonstrate the **Circular Sketch Pattern** tool we will create a bolt circle. Figure 2-67 shows a Ø.75 circle located 2.00 from a fixed centerpoint.

Figure 2-67

Figure 2-67
(*Continued*)

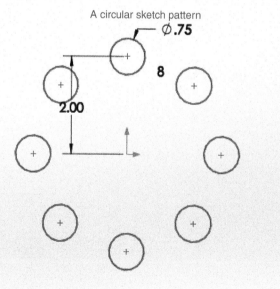

A circular sketch pattern

Creating a Circular Sketch Pattern

1 Click the **Circular Sketch Pattern** tool.

The **Circular Sketch Pattern** tool is a flyout from the **Linear Sketch Pattern** tool.

2 Define Point-1 as the origin.

3 Click the edge of the Ø.75 circle.

4 Set the number of instances in the pattern to **8**.

5 Ensure that the **Spacing** is **360deg** and that the **Entities to Pattern** contains the selected circle.

6 Click the green **OK** check mark.

2-21 Move Entities

The **Move Entities** tool is used to move an entity from one location to another. See Figure 2-68.

Figure 2-68

Moving an Entity

1 Click the **Move Entities** tool.

2 Click all the lines in the entity.

A listing of the selected lines will appear in the **Entities to Move** box.

3 Delete the check from the **Keep relations** check box.

4 Click the **Start point** box.

It should turn blue, indicating that it is active.

5 Select a **Start** point.

In this example the lower-left corner of the entity was selected.

6 Click the **Start** point and move the cursor away from the entity.

A preview of the entity will follow the cursor.

7 Select a new location for the entity.

8 Click the green **OK** check mark.

2-22 Copy Entities

The **Copy Entities** tool is used to create a duplication of an existing entity. The existing entity remains in place as the copy is created. See Figure 2-69.

Figure 2-69

Figure 2-69
(*Continued*)

Copying an Entity

1 Click the **Copy Entities** tool.

The **Copy Entities** tool is a flyout from the **Move Entities** tool.

2 Select all the lines in the entity.

3 Delete the check from the **Keep relations** check box.

4 Click the **Start point** box.

The **Start point** box will turn blue when it is active.

5 Click a selected **Start** point.

In this example the lower-left corner was selected.

6 Move the cursor and select a location for the copy.

A preview of the copy will move with the cursor.

7 Click a location for the copy.

SolidWorks will automatically generate another copy that will move with the cursor.

8 Click the green **OK** check mark.

2-23 Rotate Entities

The **Rotate Entities** tool is used to rotate an existing entity about a defined rotation point. See Figure 2-70.

Figure 2-70

A rotated entity

Rotating an Entity

1 Click the **Rotate Entities** tool.

The **Rotate Entities** tool is a flyout from the **Move Entities** tool.

2 Select all the lines in the entity.

3 Click the **Center of rotation** box.

The box will have a blue background when it is active.

4 Enter an angular value for the rotation or move the cursor to select a rotation angle.

SolidWorks defines the counterclockwise direction as the positive angular direction. A horizontal line to the right is 0.0°. In this example an angle of 30° was selected.

5 Click the green **OK** check mark.

2-24 Scale Entities

The **Scale Entities** tool is used to change the overall size of an entity while maintaining the proportions of the original entity. The **Scale Entities** tool includes a **Copy** option. If the **Copy** option is activated when the scaled entity is created, the original entity will be retained. If the **Copy** option is off (no check mark) when a scaled entity is made, the original entity will be deleted.

See Figure 2-71.

Scaling an Entity

1 Click the **Scale Entities** tool.

The **Scale Entities** tool is a flyout from the **Move Entities** tool.

2 Select all the lines in the entity.

3 Define the scale factor.

Figure 2-71

Figure 2-71
(*Continued*)

In this example a factor of **1.5** was selected.

4 Click the **Copy** box (check mark).

Checking the **Copy** box will cause the original drawing to remain when the scaled copy is created.

5 Define the **Scale** point.

In this example the lower-left corner was selected. A preview will appear.

6 Click the green **OK** check mark.

2-25 Stretch Entities

The **Stretch Entities** tool is used to extend the length of some of the lines in an entity. See Figure 2-72.

Figure 2-72

An entity

1. Click the Stretch Entities tool from the drop-down

2. Click only the lines needed to stretch

3. Define Stretch about point as the origin

4. Stretch the entity to the right

5. Click an endpoint

6. Click the dimensions and edit them as needed

Stretching an Entity

1 Click the **Stretch Entities** tool.

The **Stretch Entities** tool is a flyout from the **Move Entities** tool.

2 Click only the lines that will be involved in the stretch.

In this example five lines were selected.

3 Click the **Stretch about** box.

The box will turn blue when active.

4 Define a **Base point**.

For this example the lower-left corner (origin) was selected.

5 Click and drag the **Base point** to stretch the entity.

6 Click to specify the endpoint.

For this example, the stretch drag was along the horizontal lower line of the entity, that is, the X direction.

7 Use the **Smart Dimension** tool to size the final stretch distance.

8 Click the green **OK** check mark.

2-26   Split Entities

The **Split Entities** tool is used to trim away internal segments of an existing entity or to split an entity into two or more parts by specifying split points.

> **NOTE**
>
> Not all sketching tools are shown on the **Sketching** panel. Additional sketch tools are accessed by clicking the **Tools** heading at the top of the screen when creating a **Part** document, and clicking the **Sketch Tools** option. A listing of all sketch tools will appear. See Figure 2-73.

Splitting an Entity

See Figure 2-74.

1 Access the **Split Entities** tool by clicking **Tools**, **Sketch Tools**, and **Split Entities**.

An entity must exist for the **Split Entities** tool to activate.

2 Click two random points on the existing rectangle for the split.

In this example two points were selected on the top horizontal line of the entity.

3 Click the screen, right-click the line segment between the two points, and click the **Delete** option.

Figure 2-73

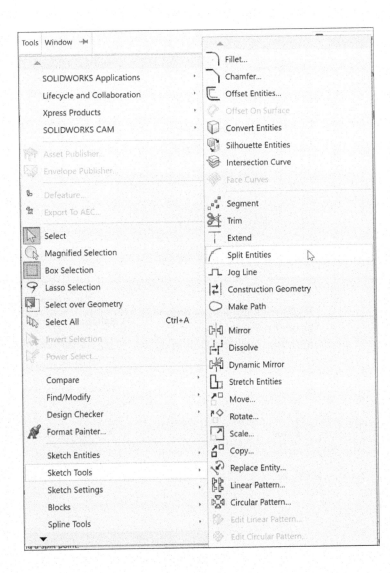

4 Use the **Smart Dimension** tool to define the split length.

5 Click the green **OK** check mark.

Figure 2-74

Figure 2-74
(*Continued*)

3.50

1.25

Select Chain

Select Midpoint

Selection Tools ▸

Zoom/Pan/Rotate ▸

Display Grid

Recent Commands ▸

Sketch Entities ▸

More Dimensions ▸

Relations

Display/Delete Relations...

Fully Define Sketch...

Selected Entity (Line13)

Delete

Detach Segment On Drag

Sketch Tools ▸

Right-click the line segment
between the two points
and then click the Delete option

'Front
dy 1

3.50

1.00   1.00

1.25

Resulting Split Entity

2-27 Jog Lines

The **Jog Line** tool is used to create a rectangular shape (jog) in a line. See Figure 2-75.

Figure 2-75

2. Click the mouse button to define the second point

5.00

1. Click and drag a selected point up and to the right to create a jog

5.00

1.00

.75

.75

1.00

1.00   1.00

3. Use the Smart Dimension tool to define the jogs

Using the Jog Line Tool

1 Access the **Jog Line** tool by clicking **Tools**, **Sketch Tools**, and **Jog Line**.

2 Click a point on the line and drag the cursor away from the line.

3 Click a point to define the approximate size of the jog.

A preview of the jog will appear.

4 Repeat the process as necessary.

5 Use the **Smart Dimension** tool to define the location and depth of the jog.

6 Right-click the mouse and click the **OK** option.

2-28 Centerline

The **Centerline** tool is used to help define and locate the center of entities.

Figure 2-76 shows an existing 2.00 × 4.00 rectangle. It is not centered on the origin, and none of its lines touch the origin. The **Centerline** tool can be used to center the rectangle on the origin.

Figure 2-76

Figure 2-76
(*Continued*)

3. Hold down the <Ctrl> key and click the Centerline and the origin

4. Click the Coincident tool

The mid point of the centerline is now located on the origin

Using the Centerline Tool

1 Click the **Centerline** tool.

The **Centerline** tool is a flyout from the **Line** tool.

2 Draw a centerline diagonally across the rectangle.

3 Right-click the mouse on the centerline near the middle of the center-line and click the **Select Midpoint** option.

4 Hold down the <Ctrl> key and click the **Origin**.

5 Click the **Coincident** option in the **Add Relations** box.

The rectangle will relocate so that the origin is on the midpoint of the centerline.

6 Click the green **OK** check mark.

2-29 Sample Problem SP2-1

Draw the shape shown in Figure 2-77.

1 Start a **New Part** document, use inch units, and create the sketch on the **Top** plane.

2 Use the **Corner Rectangle** and **Smart Dimension** tools and draw a 2.00 × 4.00 rectangle with its lower-left corner coincidental with the origin.

Figure 2-77

New Part

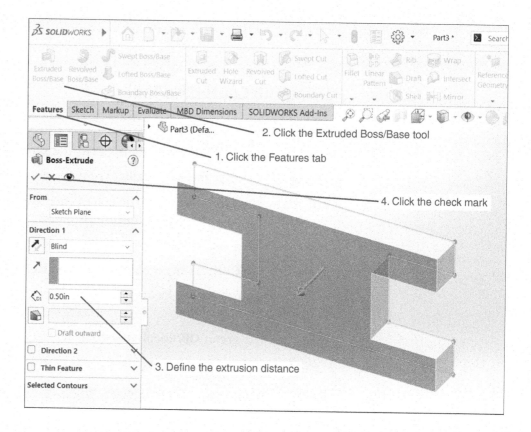

1. Click the Features tab

2. Click the Extruded Boss/Base tool

4. Click the check mark

3. Define the extrusion distance

Figure 2-77
(*Continued*)

Chapter 2

3. Use the **Jog Line** tool and add jogs at each end on the rectangle as shown. Use the **Smart Dimension** tool to size the jogs.

4. Click the **Features** tab and click the **Extruded Boss/Base** tool.

5. Set the extrude distance for **0.50in**.

6. Click the green **OK** check mark.

7. Click the **Fillet** tool on the **Features** tool panel.

This is the 3D application of the **Fillet** tool. The 2D application was discussed in Section 2-12. The fillets could have been added to the 2D sketch and then extruded.

8 Set the **Fillet radius** for **.50in**.

9 Add the fillets as shown.

10 Click the green **OK** check mark.

2-30   Sample Problem SP2-2

A circular pattern can be created using any shape. Figure 2-78 shows a slot shape located within a large circle. A circular pattern can be created from the slot shape.

1 Start a **New Part** document, use ANSI Standards, inch units, and create the sketch on the **Top** plane.

2 Sketch a Ø7.50 circle centered on the origin and add the slot shape as shown.

3 Click the **Circular Sketch Pattern** tool.

The **Circular Sketch Pattern** tool is a flyout from the **Linear Sketch Pattern** tool.

Figure 2-78

Figure 2-78
(*Continued*)

Chapter 2

A circular sketch pattern

Figure 2-78
(*Continued*)

A circular sketch pattern

4 Click all the slot components (lines and arcs) in the slot shape.

5 Set the number of instances in the pattern for **12**.

A preview will appear.

6 Click the green **OK** check mark.

7 Click the **Features** tab and click the **Extruded Boss/Base** tool.

8 Set the extrude distance for **0.3in**.

9 Click the green **OK** check mark.

The model in this sample problem could have been created by first creating a 3D disk, sketching the slot shape on the disk, and cutting out the circular pattern.

2-31 Sample Problem SP2-3

Figure 2-79 shows a shape that includes fillets and rounded shapes. Draw the shape and extrude it to a thickness of .375 inch.

Figure 2-79

ALL FILLETS AND ROUNDS = R.25
UNLESS OTHERWISE STATED.

1 Start a **New Part** document, use ANSI Standards, inch units, and create the sketch on the **Top** plane.

See Figure 2-80.

2 Sketch the approximate shape of the part.

3 Use the **Smart Dimension** tool and size the part.

4 Use the **Fillet** tool and add fillets with a 0.25 radius as shown.

Figure 2-80

Sketch the approximate shape

Use the Smart Dimension tool and size the part

Add the R = .25 fillets

Add the rectangle with R = .25 fillets

Figure 2-80
(*Continued*)

Use the Extruded Boss/Base tool
and extrude the part .375

5 Use the **Corner Rectangle** and **Smart Dimension** tools and add the 1.00 × 1.75 rectangle as shown.

6 Use the **Fillet** tool to add R0.25 fillets inside the 1.00 × 1.75 rectangle.

7 Use the **Circle**, **Line**, **Trim**, and **Smart Dimension** tools to draw and locate the slot as shown.

8 Click the **Features** tab and the **Extruded Boss/Base** tool.

9 Set the extrude distance for **0.375in**.

10 Click the green **OK** check mark.

Chapter Projects

Project 2-1:

Redraw the objects in Figures P2-1 through P2-25 using the given dimensions. Create solid models of the objects using the specified thicknesses.

Figure P2-1
INCHES

Thickness = 1.00

Figure P2-2
INCHES

Thickness = .625

Figure P2-3
MILLIMETERS

Figure P2-4
MILLIMETERS

Figure P2-5
INCHES

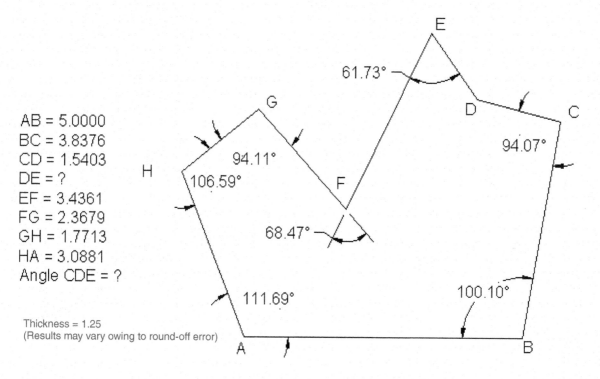

AB = 5.0000
BC = 3.8376
CD = 1.5403
DE = ?
EF = 3.4361
FG = 2.3679
GH = 1.7713
HA = 3.0881
Angle CDE = ?

Thickness = 1.25
(Results may vary owing to round-off error)

Figure P2-6
MILLIMETERS

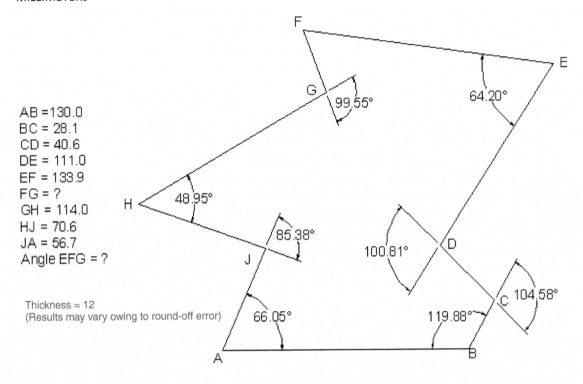

AB = 130.0
BC = 28.1
CD = 40.6
DE = 111.0
EF = 133.9
FG = ?
GH = 114.0
HJ = 70.6
JA = 56.7
Angle EFG = ?

Thickness = 12
(Results may vary owing to round-off error)

Figure P2-7
INCHES

Thickness = 1.25

Figure P2-8
MILLIMETERS

Thickness = 8

Figure P2-9
INCHES

FITTER
GUSSET

ALL FILLETS AND
ROUNDS = R.25
UNLESS OTHERWISE
STATED.

4.00
3.00
2.00
1.00
4.00
1.50
1.50
2.00
.75
Thickness = .375
1.50
2.00
5.00
R.25
2 PLACES

Figure P2-10
MILLIMETERS

DISTANCE PLATE

50
35
Ø 12-4 HOLES
SYMBOL FOR
SYMMETRY
50
35
20
10
20
Thickness = 16
10
R10-8 CORNERS

Figure P2-11
MILLIMETERS

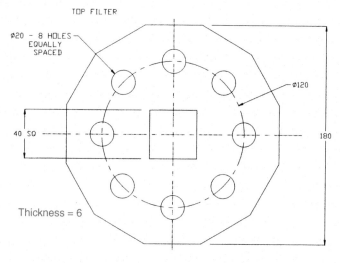

TOP FILTER

Ø20 – 8 HOLES
EQUALLY
SPACED
Ø120
40 SQ
180
Thickness = 6

Figure P2-12
MILLIMETERS

ELLIPTICAL
SPACER

65
65
20
20
20
20
30
40
70
100
55
30
20
20
Thickness = 10
40
40
5
10
15
OBJECT IS SYMMETRICAL
ABOUT THIS AXIS.

Figure P2-13
INCHES

SPACER

5.00
1.50
2.00
.75
.75
1.25
3.50
2.50
Ø 1.000 – 3 HOLES
1.00
R0.25 – 4 CORNERS
Thickness = .75

Figure P2-14
MILLIMETERS

STAR
SPACER

150
110
20
55
20
20
40
80
40
40
20
Thickness = 7.5
R10 – 4 PLACES

Figure P2-15
MILLIMETERS

STRAP
PLATE

60

30

Ø30

20

30

110

R50

30

20

30

7 X Ø12

30

15

20

6 X 20 (120)

Thickness = 5

155

Figure P2-16
MILLIMETERS

LACE
GASKET

12 × R20

12 × Ø20

12 × R30

40   40

12 × R30

Ø 160

Ø50

12 × 30°

2 × R10

Thickness = 7.5

Figure P2-17
INCHES

SLOT PLATE

2.00   3.75

1.75

R1.20
3 ARCS

STRAIGHT LINE
BOTH SIDES

R3.00
2 ARCS

1.25

.95

R.60
BOTH SLOTS

2.50 BOTH SLOTS

NOTE: Object is symmetrical
about its horizontal centerline

Thickness = .875

Figure P2-18
MILLIMETERS

STAR RATCHET

Ø24 – 4 HOLES

30° ELLIPSE

45

140

50

150

5

2.50

Ø40.0
SCALE: 4 = 1
18 REQD

Thickness = 6

Figure P2-19
MILLIMETERS

R120 - BOTH SIDES

Ø20-4 HOLES

R20-4 PLACES

40

30

15

R60 - BOTH SIDES

ALL FILLETS = R5

Thickness = 7.25

25

Figure P2-20
INCHES

Ø1.00 - 5 HOLES

1.50   1.50   1.50

R1.00 - TWO PLACES

2.00

R4.00

Thickness = .25

0.50

R1.25

Figure P2-21
MILLIMETERS

110

Ø30

70

40

30

20

35

ALL FILLETS = R5

40

R110

R20

40

70

R30

Thickness = 5

Figure P2-22
MILLIMETERS

Ø30

R30

R100

ALL FILLETS = 10R

20-4 RIBS

10-4 RIBS

Thickness = 16

Ø240

Figure P2-23
INCHES

All FILLETS AND ROUNDS = R.25

Thickness = .50

TAG	X LOC	Y LOC	SIZE
A1	.25	.25	Ø.25
A2	.25	3.10	Ø.25
A3	.88	2.64	Ø.25
A4	4.88	3.65	Ø.25
A5	6.14	.25	Ø.25
B1	.68	1.29	Ø.40
B2	1.28	.56	Ø.40
C1	1.76	2.92	Ø.29
D1	2.66	3.16	Ø.33
E1	3.38	1.13	Ø.42
F1	3.71	3.43	Ø.32
G1	4.39	.71	Ø.73

Figure P2-24
MILLIMETERS

ALL FILLETS AND ROUNDS = 5
UNLESS OTHERWISE STATED

Thickness = 20

GENEVA MECHANISM

Ø.500

R.500 - 8 ARCS

Ø.250

.250 - 8 SLOTS

Ø2.000

.250

.560

Project 2-2:

Draw a retaining ring based on the following dimensions shown in Figure P2-26 and as assigned by your instructor.

Figure P2-26

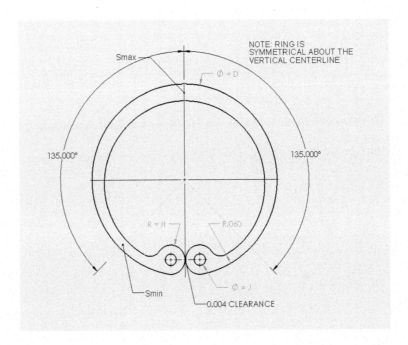

Retaining Ring - Internal - Inches

PART NO	ØD	Smax	Smin	H	A	ØJ	Thk
BU-25	.25	.025	.015	.065	.030	.031	.020
BU-50	.50	.053	.035	.114	.042	.047	.035
BU-75	.75	.070	.040	.142	.055	.060	.040
BU100	1.00	.091	.052	.155	.060	.060	.042
BU125	1.25	.120	.062	.180	.070	.075	.050
BU150	1.50	.127	.066	.180	.070	.075	.050

Retaining Ring - Internal - Millimeters

PART NO	ØD	Smax	Smin	H	A	ØJ	Thk
MBU-20	20	2.3	1.9	4.1	2.0	2.0	1.0
MBU-30	30	3.0	2.3	4.8	2.0	2.0	1.2
MBU-40	40	3.9	3.0	5.8	2.5	2.5	1.7
MBU-50	50	4.6	3.8	6.5	2.5	2.5	2.0
MBU-60	60	5.4	4.3	7.3	2.5	2.5	2.0
MBU-70	70	6.2	5.2	7.8	3.0	3.0	2.5

chapterthree

Features

CHAPTER OBJECTIVES

- Learn Features tools
- Draw 3D objects

- Use Features tools to create objects

3-1 Introduction

This chapter introduces the **Features** tools. **Features** tools are used to create 3D models. A drawing usually starts with a 2D sketch as described in Chapter 2, and **Features** tools are applied to create a 3D model. For example, the **Extruded Boss/Base** features tool can be applied to a rectangle to create a rectangular prism or box. Figure 3-1 shows the **Features** tool panel.

Figure 3-1

3-2 Extruded Boss/Base

The **Extruded Boss/Base** tool is used to add thickness or height to an existing 2D sketch. In this section we will first sketch a 2D rectangle, then extrude it into a box-like shape. All dimensions are in millimeters.

Using the Extruded Boss/Base Tool

1 Click the **New** tool, create a new **Part** document, click the **Top Plane** option, and click the **Sketch** tab.

2 Use the **Options** tool from the **Tools** menu (top of the screen), click the **Document Properties** tab, and set the **Overall** drafting standard to **ANSI**.

Figure 3-2

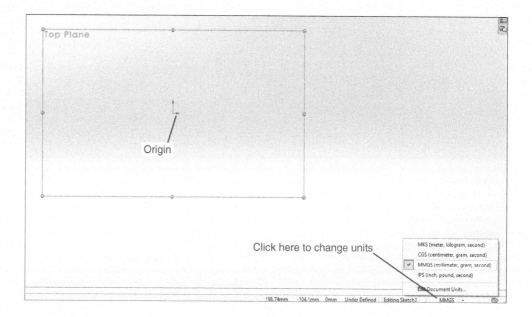

3 Define the drawing units for **MMGS** (millimeter, gram, second). Click the arrowhead next to the **IPS** heading and select the **MMGS** option.

The drawing units are referenced at the bottom of the drawing screen. See Figure 3-2.

4 Use the **Corner Rectangle** tool to sketch a **60 × 100** rectangle in the **Top** plane with one corner located on the origin. Use the **Smart Dimension** tool to size the rectangle.

See Figure 3-3.

Figure 3-3

Chapter **3**

A 60 x 100 rectangle

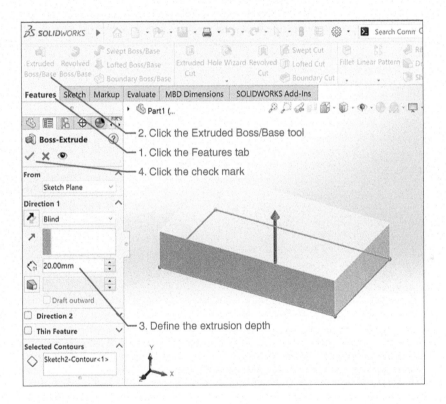

2. Click the Extruded Boss/Base tool

1. Click the Features tab

4. Click the check mark

3. Define the extrusion depth

A 20 x 60 x 100
rectangular prism (box)

Display view shaded with edges

5 Click the **Features** tab, and click the **Extruded Boss/Base** tool.

The drawing will change orientation from a 2D top view to a **Trimetric** 3D drawing. The **Boss-Extrude PropertyManager** will appear.

6 Define the extrusion depth, also known as the extrusion height or distance, as **20.00mm**. Click the screen and a real-time preview will appear.

7 Click the green **OK** check mark at the top of the **Boss-Extrude PropertyManager**. Click the drawing screen.

The finished drawing shows a 20 × 60 × 100 box.

TIP

The extrusion depth may be defined by entering a value or by using the arrows at the right of the **Depth** box. The extrusion depth may also be changed by clicking and dragging the directional arrow in the center of the box. See Figure 3-4.

Figure 3-4

Click and drag the Directional arrow to define the extrusion distance

The preceding example has perpendicular sides. The **Extruded Boss/ Base** tool may also be used to create tapered sides. Tapered sides are called *draft sides*.

Creating Inward Draft Sides

1 Sketch a **60 × 100** rectangle as described in the previous section.

2 Click the **Features** tab and click the **Extruded Boss/Base** tool.

3 Click the **Draft On/Off** tool to activate it.

4 Enter the draft angle value.

In this example a **15.00deg** value was entered. See Figure 3-5.

5 Click the green **OK** check mark at the top of the **Boss-Extrude PropertyManager** to complete the object.

The shape now has a 15° inward draft.

Figure 3-5

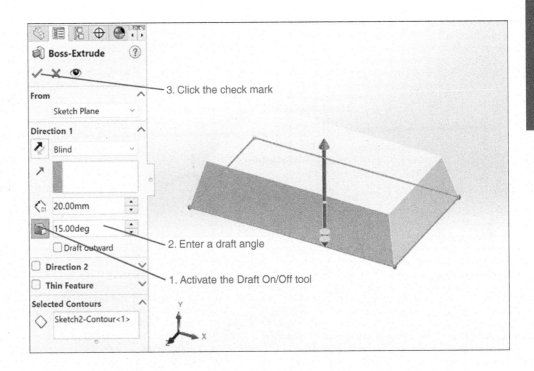

Creating an Outward Draft

Repeat the same procedure, but this time, check the **Draft outward** box.
See Figure 3-6.

Figure 3-6

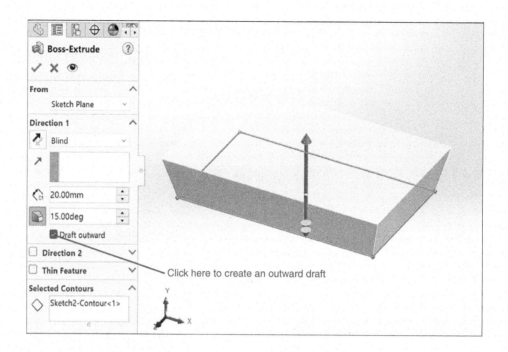

Click here to create an outward draft

Outward draft

3-3   Sample Problem SP3-1

This section shows how to draw a solid 3D model of an L-bracket using the **Extruded Boss/Base** tool.

1 Draw a **60 × 100** rectangle and extrude it to a depth of **20mm** as explained in Section 3-2.

See Figure 3-7.

Figure 3-7

A 20 x 60 x 100 Box

1. Right-click the top surface of the box

2. Click the Sketch tool

Figure 3-7
(*Continued*)

Chapter 3

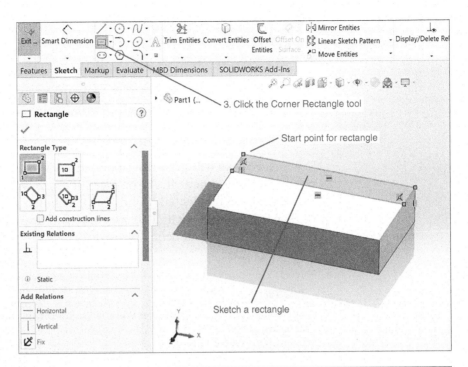

3. Click the Corner Rectangle tool

Start point for rectangle

Sketch a rectangle

5. Click the Features tab and click the Extrude Boss/Base tool

7. Click the check mark

4. Dimension the rectangle

20.00

6. Define the extrusion distance

L-bracket

2 Locate the cursor on the top surface of the box and right-click the mouse. Select the **Sketch** tool.

The 2D **Sketch** tools will be displayed across the top of the screen.

3 Click the **Corner Rectangle** tool and use it to draw a rectangle on the top surface of the box. Use the upper-left corner of the box as one corner point of the rectangle and drag the cursor to the right edge of the top surface to locate the second corner point for the rectangle.

SolidWorks will grab the upper-left corner of the rectangle when the cursor is located near it. An orange fill circle will appear indicating that the corner has been selected. SolidWorks will also grab the edge line when the cursor is located near it. The edge line will appear as an orange broken line indicating that it has been selected.

> **NOTE**
>
> The corner points and edge lines will change color when they are activated. The part is currently under defined.

4 Select the **Smart Dimension** tool and dimension the width of the rectangle as **20.0**.

5 Click the **Features** tab and select the **Extruded Boss/Base** tool.

6 Select the **20 × 100** rectangle to extrude to a depth of **40.00mm**.

7 Click the green **OK** check mark in the **Boss-Extrude PropertyManager**.

SolidWorks offers many different ways to create the same shape. Figure 3-8 shows the same L-bracket shown in Figure 3-7 created using the **Right** plane and extruded in the negative X direction.

Figure 3-8

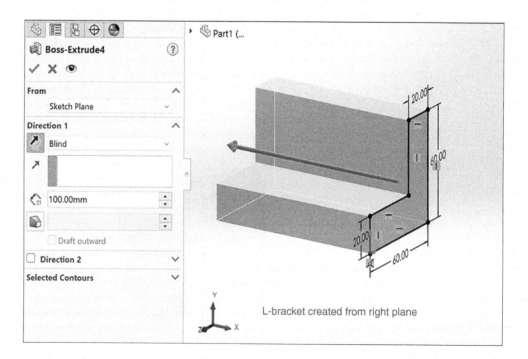

L-bracket created from right plane

Figure 3-8
(*Continued*)

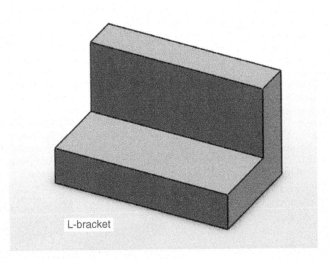

L-bracket

3-4 Extruded Cut

This section will add a cutout to the L-bracket drawn in Section 3-3 using the **Extruded Cut** tool. See Figure 3-9.

1 Locate the cursor on the lower-front horizontal surface and right-click the mouse.

2 Click the **Sketch** tool option.

3 Use the **Corner Rectangle** and **Smart Dimension** tools to draw and size a rectangle as shown.

Locate the first point of the **Corner Rectangle** on the front edge line. SolidWorks will grab the front edge line. The line will change to an orange broken line indicating that it has been selected.

Figure 3-9

1. Right-click the surface

2. Click the Sketch tool

Selection Tools
Zoom/Pan/Rotate
Recent Commands

Face
Change Transparency
Create Plane Parallel to Scree

Feature (Boss-Extrude2)
Comment
Parent/Child...
Configure Feature

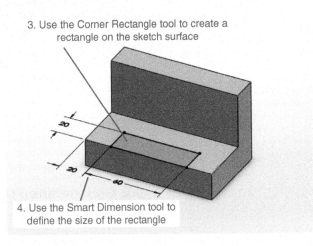

3. Use the Corner Rectangle tool to create a rectangle on the sketch surface

20

20

60

4. Use the Smart Dimension tool to define the size of the rectangle

Figure 3-9
(*Continued*)

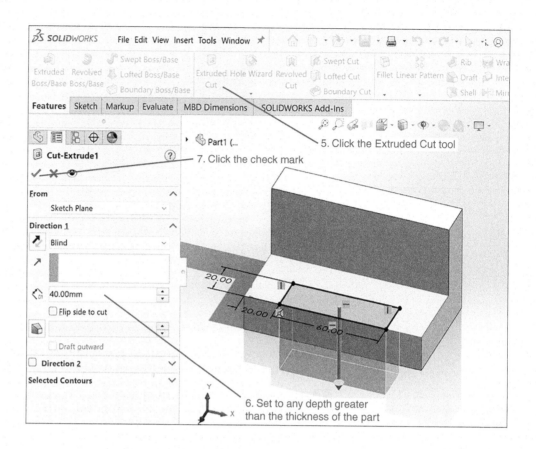

5. Click the Extruded Cut tool

7. Click the check mark

6. Set to any depth greater than the thickness of the part

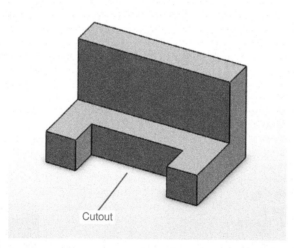

Cutout

[4] Click the **Features** tab, then click the **Extruded Cut** tool.

A preview will appear. Ensure that the **Extruded Cut** extends beyond the lower surface of the bracket.

[5] Click the green **OK** check mark in the **Cut-Extrude PropertyManager**.

3-5 Hole Wizard

This section will add a hole to the L-bracket created in Section 3-3 using the **Hole Wizard** tool. The **Hole Wizard** tool is used to add nine different types of holes and slots to an existing 3D model. The hole types include simple holes and threaded holes, among others. See Figure 3-10.

1 Click the **Features** tab, then click the **Hole Wizard** tool.

2 Select the **Hole** option.

The **Hole** option will generate a clear hole.

3 Access the **Standard** box and select **ANSI Metric**.

Figure 3-10

Figure 3-10
(*Continued*)

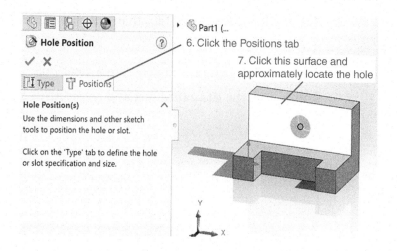

Hole Position

6. Click the Positions tab

7. Click this surface and approximately locate the hole

Type   Positions

Hole Position(s)

Use the dimensions and other sketch tools to position the hole or slot.

Click on the 'Type' tab to define the hole or slot specification and size.

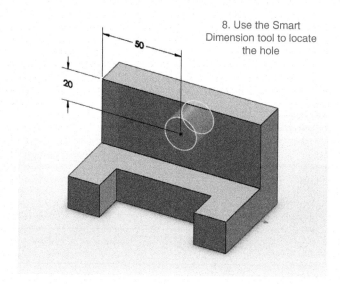

8. Use the Smart Dimension tool to locate the hole

Completed through hole

ANSI stands for American National Standards Institute. ANSI standards will be covered in detail in the chapters on orthographic views, dimensions, and tolerances.

4 Define the diameter size of the hole.

In this example a diameter of **20.0mm** was selected.

5 Define the **End Condition** as **Through All**.

6 Click the **Positions** tab on the **PropertyManager**.

7 Click an approximate location for the hole's centerpoint.

A preview of the hole will appear.

8 Use the **Smart Dimension** tool to locate the hole's centerpoint.

9 Click the green **OK** check mark and click the drawing screen.

The hole will be added to the L-bracket.

10 Save the L-bracket, as it will be used in later sections.

The hole created in Figure 3-10 is a *through hole*; that is, it goes completely through the object. Holes that do not go completely through are called *blind holes*. Note that the **Hole Wizard PropertyManager** shows a conical point at the bottom of the hole. Holes created using a circle and the **Extruded Cut** tool (see Section 1-13) will not have this conical endpoint. Blind holes created using a drill should include the conical point. For this reason, blind holes should, with a few exceptions, be created using the **Hole Wizard** tool.

3-6   Creating a Hole with the Circle and Extruded Cut Tools

Holes may also be created by using the **Circle** tool and then applying the **Extruded Cut** tool. This method should be used only for through holes. Figure 3-11 shows the L-bracket created in Section 3-3.

1 Right-click the top front plane as shown and click the **Sketch** tool.

2 Click the **Circle** tool and use it to sketch a circle.

3 Use the **Smart Dimension** tool and locate and size the circle.

4 Click the **Features** tab and select the **Extruded Cut** tool. Click the circle if necessary.

5 Click the green **OK** check mark and click the drawing screen.

Figure 3-11

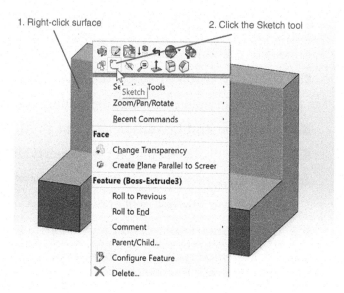

1. Right-click surface

2. Click the Sketch tool

4. Use the Smart Dimension tool to define the location of the circle

3. Sketch a circle on the surface

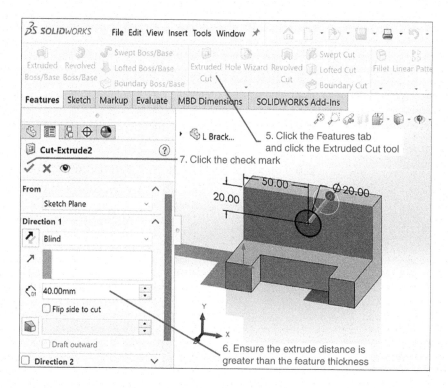

5. Click the Features tab and click the Extruded Cut tool

7. Click the check mark

6. Ensure the extrude distance is greater than the feature thickness

Figure 3-11
(*Continued*)

3-7 Blind Holes

A blind hole is a hole that does not go completely through a part. Most blind holes are created using a twist drill that includes a conical end tip. The **Hole Wizard** tool includes a conical point on blind holes.

Creating a Blind Hole—Inches

See Figure 3-12.

1 Draw a 1.00 × 1.50 × 1.25 inch box.

2 Click the **Hole Wizard** tool and click the **Hole** option.

3 Set the **Standard** for **ANSI Inch**, the **Size** for **1/2**, the **End Condition** for **Blind**, and the hole depth for **0.75in**.

Figure 3-12

A 1.00 × 1.50 × 1.25 Box

Figure 3-12
(*Continued*)

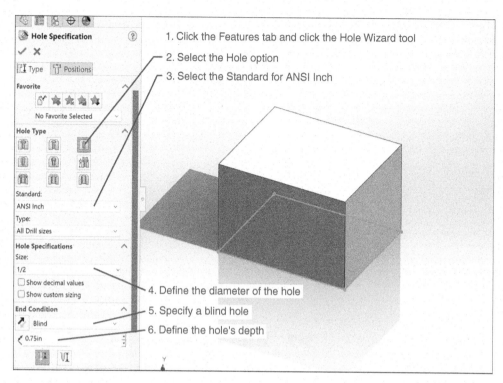

1. Click the Features tab and click the Hole Wizard tool
2. Select the Hole option
3. Select the Standard for ANSI Inch
4. Define the diameter of the hole
5. Specify a blind hole
6. Define the hole's depth

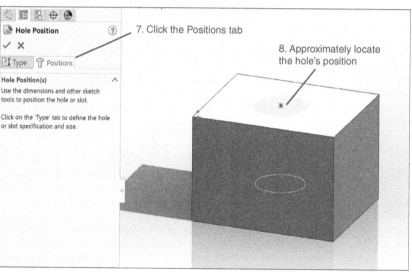

7. Click the Positions tab

8. Approximately locate the hole's position

9. Use the Smart Dimension tool to locate the hole

Conical bottom of hole

Note that the hole depth does not include the conical endpoint.

4 Click the **Positions** tab and select an approximate location for the hole.

5 Use the **Smart Dimension** tool to locate the hole.

6 Click the green **OK** check mark and click the drawing screen.

Creating a Blind Hole—Metric

See Figure 3-13.

Figure 3-13

90 x 80 x 100 Box

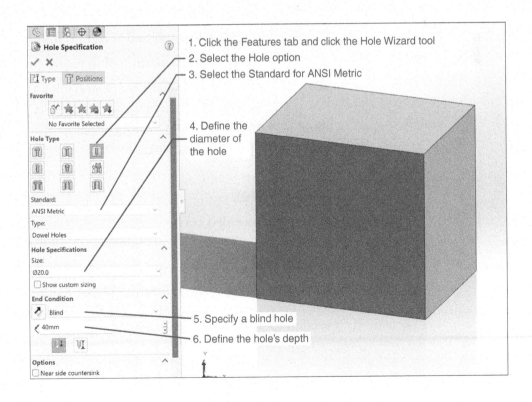

1. Click the Features tab and click the Hole Wizard tool
2. Select the Hole option
3. Select the Standard for ANSI Metric
4. Define the diameter of the hole
5. Specify a blind hole
6. Define the hole's depth

7. Click the Positions tab and approximately locate the hole

8. Use the Smart Dimension tool to locate the hole

Conical bottom of hole

1 Draw a 90 × 80 × 100 box.

2 Click the **Hole Wizard** tool and click the **Hole** option.

3 Set the **Standard** for **ANSI Metric**, the **Size** for **Ø20.0**, the **End Condition** for **Blind**, and the hole depth for **40mm**.

Note that the hole depth does not include the conical endpoint.

4 Click the **Positions** tab and select an approximate location for the hole.

5 Use the **Smart Dimension** tool to locate the hole.

6 Click the green **OK** check mark and click the drawing screen.

Figure 3-13 also shows a section view of the box. Note that the hole is blind and that it ends with a conical point. The specified hole depth does not include the conical point.

3-8 Fillet

A *fillet* is a rounded corner. Specifically, convex corners are called *rounds*, and concave corners are called *fillets*, but in general, all rounded corners are called *fillets*.

SolidWorks can draw four types of fillets: constant radius, variable radius, face fillets, and full round fillets. Figure 3-14 shows the L-bracket used previously to demonstrate the **Features** tools. It will be used in this section to demonstrate **Fillet** tools.

Figure 3-14

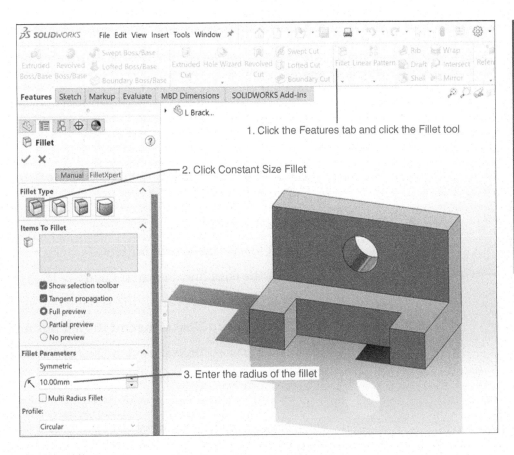

1. Click the Features tab and click the Fillet tool

2. Click Constant Size Fillet

3. Enter the radius of the fillet

Tangency line

Fillet

There is also a **2D Fillet** tool available on the **Sketch** tool panel. See Section 2-12.

1 Use the **Open** tool and open the L-bracket drawing.

If the L-bracket was not saved after the previous section, use the dimensions and procedures specified in Section 3-4 to re-create the bracket.

2 Click the **Features** tab and click the **Fillet** tool.

3 Select **Constant Size** in the **Fillet Type** box and define the fillet's radius as **10.00mm**.

Click the **Full preview** button.

4 Click the upper-right edge line of the object.

A preview of the fillet will appear.

5 Click the green **OK** check mark.

Note that there is a line across the top surface of the part. This is a tangency line. SolidWorks includes tangency lines to show the beginning and end of all fillets and rounds.

Creating a Fillet with a Variable Radius

See Figure 3-15.

1 Click the **Fillet** tool.

2 Click the **Variable Size** button.

3 Click the edge line shown in Figure 3-15.

Two boxes will appear on the screen, one at each end of the edge line.

4 Click the word **Unassigned** in the left box and enter a value of **15**.

5 Click the word **Unassigned** in the right box and enter a value of **5**.

6 Click the green **OK** check mark.

Figure 3-15

Figure 3-15
(Continued)

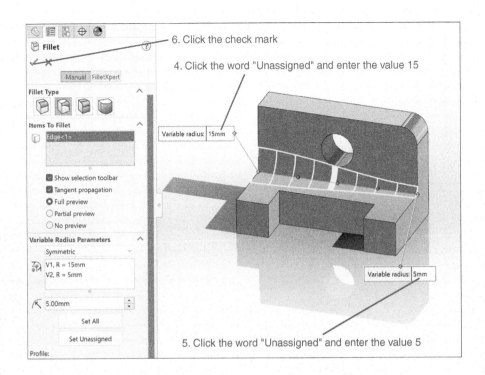

6. Click the check mark

4. Click the word "Unassigned" and enter the value 15

Variable radius: 15mm

Variable radius: 5mm

5. Click the word "Unassigned" and enter the value 5

Creating a Fillet Using the Face Fillet Option

The **Face Fillet** option draws a fillet between two faces (surfaces), whereas **Fillet** uses an edge between two surfaces to draw a fillet.

See Figure 3-16.

Figure 3-16

1 Click the **Fillet** tool.

2 Click the **Face Fillet** option.

Two boxes will appear in the **Items To Fillet** box. They will be used to define the two faces of the fillet. The blue box is the active box and is awaiting an input.

3 Define the fillet radius as **10.00mm**.

4 Define **Face 1** as shown.

The label **Face<1>** will appear in the blue box.

5 Click the lower box in the **Items To Fillet** box (it will turn blue) and define **Face 2** by clicking the surface as shown.

6 Click the green **OK** check mark and click the drawing screen.

Creating a Fillet Using the Full Round Fillet Option

See Figure 3-17.

1 Use the **Undo** tool and remove the fillets created previously.

This will return the original L-bracket shape.

2 Click the **Fillet** tool and click the **Full Round Fillet** button.

Three boxes will appear. These boxes will be used to define Side Face 1, the Center Face, and Side Face 2. The top box is blue, indicating it is awaiting an input.

In this example, the default fillet radius value of **10** will be used.

> **TIP**
>
> Objects can be rotated by holding down the mouse wheel and moving the cursor.

3 Rotate the object so that the back surface can be selected.

4 Click the back surface.

Figure 3-17

Figure 3-17
(*Continued*)

3. Select this face as Face 2

4. Define the front surface as Face 3

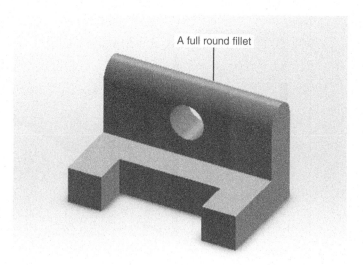

A full round fillet

The back surface is defined as **Side Face 1**.

5 Reorient the object to an isometric view.

6 Click the middle box (it will turn blue) in the **Items To Fillet** box and click the top surface of the object.

The top surface is defined as the **Center Face**.

7 Click the lower of the three boxes in the **Items To Fillet** box and click the front surface of the object as shown.

The front surface is defined as **Side Face 2**. A preview of the fillet will appear.

8 Click the green **OK** check mark.

3-9   Chamfer

A *chamfer* is a slanted surface added to a corner of an object. Chamfers are usually manufactured at 45° but may be made at any angle. Chamfers are defined using either an angle and a distance (5 × 45°) or two distances (5 × 5). A vertex chamfer may also be defined.

Defining a Chamfer Using an Angle and a Distance

See Figure 3-18. This section uses the L-bracket created in Section 3-3 and used in the previous section.

1 Use the **Undo** tool and remove the fillet created in the previous section.

2 Click the **Chamfer** tool.

The **Chamfer** tool is a flyout from the **Fillet** tool.

3 Click the **Distance-Angle** button.

4 Define the chamfer distance as **10.00mm** and accept the **45deg** default value.

5 Click the top side edge line as shown.

6 Click the green **OK** check mark.

Figure 3-18

Figure 3-18
(Continued)

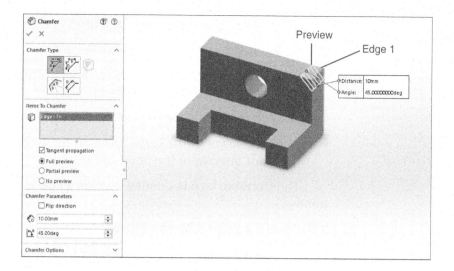

Defining a Chamfer Using Two Distances

See Figure 3-19.

1 Click the **Chamfer** tool.

2 Click the **Distance-Distance** button.

3 Select the **Asymmetric** option in the **Chamfer Parameters**.

4 Define the two distances as **15.00mm** and **5.00mm** as shown.

In this example the two distances are not equal. Distances of different lengths may be used.

Figure 3-19

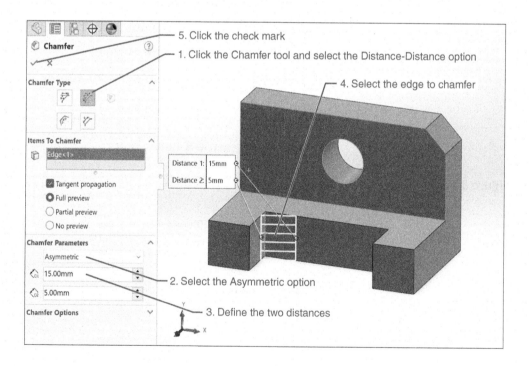

Figure 3-19
(*Continued*)

Chapter **3**

A Distance-Distance chamfer

⑤ Click the inside vertical line as shown.

⑥ Click the green **OK** check mark.

Defining a Vertex Chamfer

See Figure 3-20.

① Click the **Chamfer** tool.

② Click the **Vertex** button.

Three distance boxes will appear.

③ Define the three distances.

Figure 3-20

Figure 3-20
(*Continued*)

A vertex chamfer

In this example three equal distances of **10.00mm** were used. The three distances need not be equal.

4 Click the lower top corner point as shown.

5 Click the green **OK** check mark.

3-10 Revolved Boss/Base

The **Revolved Boss/Base** tool rotates a contour about an axis line. See Figure 3-21.

1 Start a new **Part**, click the **Sketch** tool, and click the **Top Plane** option.

2 Use the **Sketch** tools to draw a line on the screen and then draw a 2D shape next to the line. All dimensions are in inches.

3 Draw the shape shown using the given dimensions.

4 Click the **Features** tab, then click the **Revolved Boss/Base** tool.

Figure 3-21

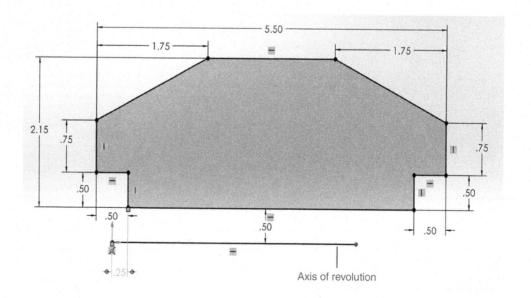

Axis of revolution

Figure 3-21
(*Continued*)

Chapter 3

1. Click the Revolved Boss/Base tool from the Features tab

Revolve options

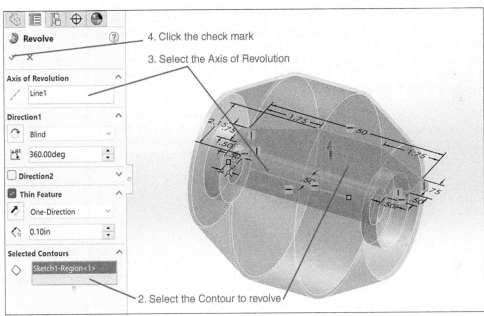

4. Click the check mark

3. Select the Axis of Revolution

2. Select the Contour to revolve

A revolved part

5 Click the **Selected Contours** box, then click the contour on the screen.

6 Click the **Axis of Revolution** box at the top of the **Revolve PropertyManager**.

> **NOTE**
> If the **Selected Contours** box is already shaded, it means that it has been activated automatically. Click the contour directly.

7 Click the **Axis of Revolution** line on the screen.

A preview of the revolved object will appear.

8 Click the green **OK** check mark.

Figure 3-22 shows an example of a sphere created using the **Revolved Boss/Base** tool. A **Centerline** was used as the axis of revolution.

Figure 3-22

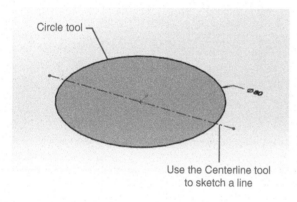

Circle tool

∅80

Use the Centerline tool to sketch a line

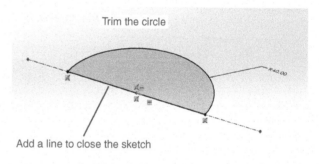

Trim the circle

R 40.00

Add a line to close the sketch

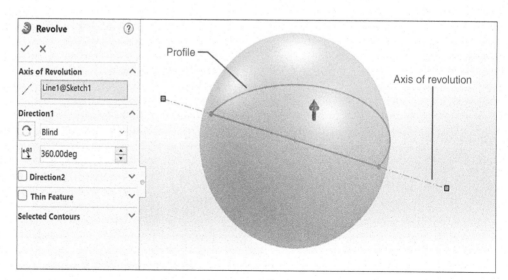

Profile

Axis of revolution

Figure 3-22
(*Continued*)

Chapter **3**

A sphere created using the Revolved Boss/Base tool

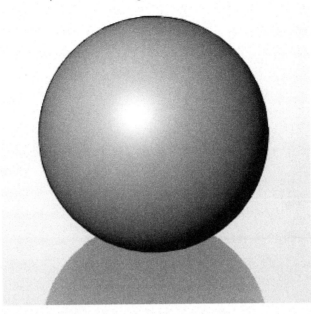

3-11 Revolved Cut

The **Revolved Cut** tool is used to cut revolved sections out of objects. Figure 3-23 shows a 40 × 60 × 100 box. All dimensions are in millimeters.

1 Create a new sketch plane (**Sketch** tool) on the top surface of the box and use the **Centerpoint Arc** tool to draw an arc of radius **40** centered about the lower corner of the top surface as shown. Use the **Smart Dimension** tool to define the radius.

2 Use the **Line** tool to draw two lines from this arc's endpoints to the corner point of the box, creating an enclosed area.

Figure 3-23

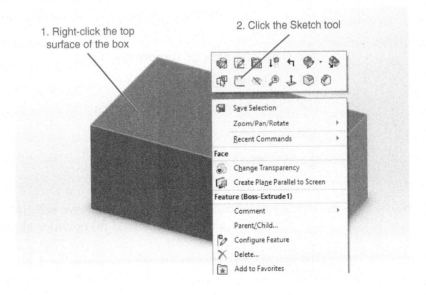

1. Right-click the top surface of the box

2. Click the Sketch tool

Save Selection
Zoom/Pan/Rotate
Recent Commands
Face
Change Transparency
Create Plane Parallel to Screen
Feature (Boss-Extrude1)
Comment
Parent/Child...
Configure Feature
Delete...
Add to Favorites

Figure 3-23
(*Continued*)

4. Use the Smart Dimension tool to define the size of the arc (R40)

3. Use the Centerpoint Arc tool to create an arc as shown

Enclosed area

Line 1

Line 2

5. Use the Line tool to add two lines creating an enclosed area

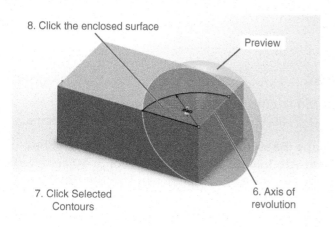

8. Click the enclosed surface

Preview

7. Click Selected Contours

6. Axis of revolution

A revolved cut

3 Click the **Features** tab and click the **Revolved Cut** tool.

4 Click the **Selected Contours** box and click the enclosed area created in Step 2.

5 Click the **Axis of Revolution** box.

6 Click the right edge line of the contour.

7 Click the green **OK** check mark and click the drawing screen.

3-12   Reference Planes

Reference planes are planes that are not part of an existing object. Until now if we needed a new sketch plane, we selected an existing surface on the object. Consider the Ø3.0 × 3.50 cylinder shown in Figure 3-24. The cylinder was drawn with its base on the **Top** plane and its centerpoint at the origin. All dimensions are in inches. How do we create a hole through the rounded sides of the cylinder? If we right-click the rounded surface, no **Sketch** tool will appear.

Creating a Reference Plane

See Figure 3-24.

1 Click the **Right Plane** option in the **FeatureManager Design Tree**.

2 Right-click the **Right Plane** feature and click **Show** to ensure that the **Right** plane is visible. (It will probably already be on.)

The **Right** plane is located at the cylinder's origin. The **Reference Geometry** tool is used to create a second plane parallel to the **Right** plane. We can offset this plane from the **Right** plane and create a sketch plane on the offset plane.

3 Click the **Reference Geometry** tool located in the **Features** panel and select the **Plane** option.

The **Plane** box will appear.

Figure 3-24

Figure 3-24
(*Continued*)

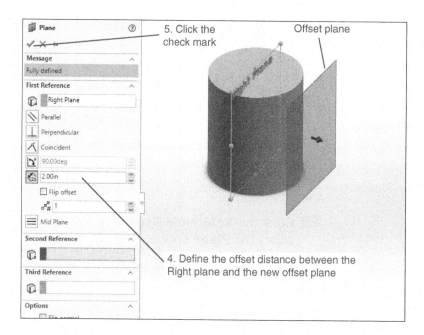

5. Click the check mark

Offset plane

4. Define the offset distance between the Right plane and the new offset plane

6. Right-click the offset plane and select the Sketch option

Figure 3-24
(*Continued*)

Chapter 3

SOLIDWORKS Add-Ins

7. If the view does not automatically change to a direct 2D view of the offset plane, click the Normal To tool

Normal To (Ctrl+8)
Rotates and zooms the model to the view orientation normal to the selected plane, planar face, or feature.

Or click this plane on the view selector cube

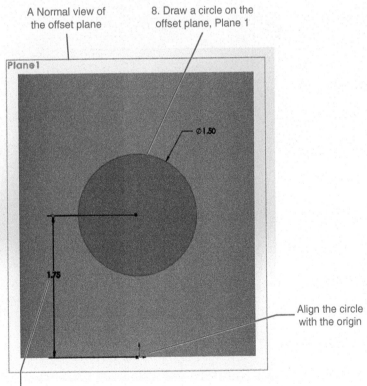

A Normal view of the offset plane

8. Draw a circle on the offset plane, Plane 1

Plane1

⌀1.50

1.75

Align the circle with the origin

9. Use the Smart Dimension tool to define the circle's diameter and location

Figure 3-24
(*Continued*)

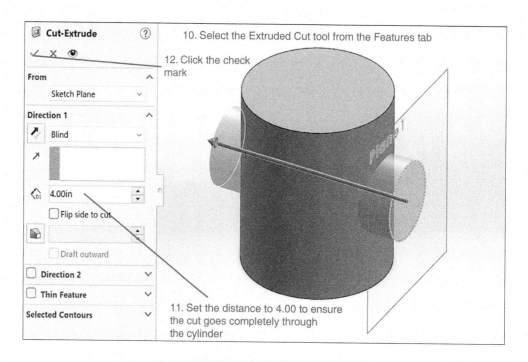

Cut-Extrude

From
Sketch Plane

Direction 1
Blind

4.00in
Flip side to cut

Draft outward

Direction 2

Thin Feature

Selected Contours

10. Select the Extruded Cut tool from the Features tab

12. Click the check mark

Plane 1

11. Set the distance to 4.00 to ensure the cut goes completely through the cylinder

A hole through a cylinder

4 Set the offset distance for **2.00in**.

This offset distance will locate a new **Front** plane offset 2.00 inches from the origin. The edge of the cylinder is 1.75 from the origin. The extra .25 distance ensures that the hole will not interfere with the edge surface.

5 Click the green **OK** check mark.

The new reference plane is defined as **Plane 1**.

6 Right-click **Plane 1** and click the **Sketch** tool.

7 Click the **View Orientation** tool, and then click the **Normal To** tool to create a right-view orientation of the cylinder.

8 Use the **Circle** tool and sketch a Ø1.50 circle located with its center-point 1.75 from the base of the cylinder as shown. Use the **Smart Dimension** tool to apply dimensions.

9 Use the **View Orientation** tool and create an isometric view of the cylinder.

10 Click the **Features** tab and click the **Extruded Cut** tool.

11 Define the length of the cutting cylinder as **4.00in** to ensure that it will pass completely through the Ø3.00 cylinder.

12 Click the green **OK** check mark.

13 Hide **Plane 1** by right-clicking on the planes and selecting the **Hide** (an icon of an eye with a slash through it) option.

3-13 Lofted Boss/Base

The **Lofted Boss/Base** tool is used to create a shape between two planes, each of which contains a defined shape. Before drawing a lofted shape we must first draw two shapes on two different planes. In this example a square is lofted to a circle.

See Figure 3-25.

Figure 3-25

Figure 3-25
(*Continued*)

1. After exiting the sketch, click the View Orientation tool

Isometric
Dimetric
Trimetric

2. Click the Trimetric view orientation

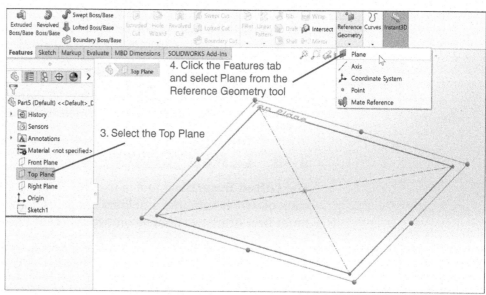

4. Click the Features tab and select Plane from the Reference Geometry tool

Plane
Axis
Coordinate System
Point
Mate Reference

3. Select the Top Plane

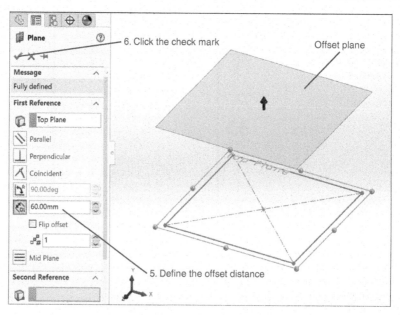

6. Click the check mark

Offset plane

5. Define the offset distance

Figure 3-25
(*Continued*)

Make Plane 1 a sketch plane. Use the origin on the offset plane that is aligned with the origin on the Top plane to draw the circle. This may be easier using a top view.

A lofted section

1 Start a new **Part**, select the **Top Plane**, click the **Sketch** tool, set the units for millimeters (**MMGS**), and set the **Drafting Standards** for **ANSI**.

2 Use the **Center Rectangle** tool and sketch a rectangle about the origin.

3 Use the **Smart Dimension** tool and create an **80** × **80** square.

The square is centered about the origin.

4 Click the **Exit Sketch** option.

5 Click the **View Orientation** tool and select a **Trimetric** orientation.

6 Click the **Features** tab.

7 Click the **Top Plane**, click the **Reference Geometry** tool, and select the **Plane** option.

A new plane, called **Plane 1**, will appear.

8 Offset **Plane 1 60.00mm** from the **Top** plane.

9 Click the green **OK** check mark.

10 Right-click **Plane 1** and click the **Sketch** option.

11 Use the **Circle** tool and sketch a circle centered about the origin in Plane 1.

12 Use the **Smart Dimension** tool and dimension the diameter of the circle to **30.0**.

13 Click the **Exit Sketch** option and click the **Lofted Boss/Base** tool on the **Features** tab.

The **Profiles** box should turn on automatically; that is, it should be blue in color.

14 Click the rectangle. The rectangle may already have been selected.

15 Click the circle.

A preview of the lofted segment should appear.

16 Click the green **OK** check mark in the **Loft PropertyManager** box.

17 Right-click **Plane 1** and select the **Hide** option.

18 Save the part as **LOFT**.

3-14 Shell

The **Shell** tool is used to hollow out existing solid parts. Figure 3-26 shows a 40 × 60 × 35 box. It was created using the **Corner Rectangle**, **Smart Dimension**, and **Extruded Boss/Base** tools.

Figure 3-26

A 40 x 60 x 35 box

35

60

40

Figure 3-26
(*Continued*)

Chapter 3

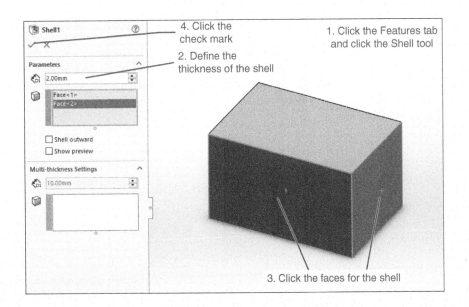

4. Click the
check mark

2. Define the
thickness of the shell

1. Click the Features tab
and click the Shell tool

3. Click the faces for the shell

Resulting shell

The **Shell** tool will be applied to the box.

1 Click the **Features** tab and click the **Shell** tool.

2 Define the shell thickness.

In this example, a thickness of **2.00mm** was selected.

3 Click the two faces of the box as indicated.

4 Click the green **OK** check mark.

Figure 3-27 shows two more examples of how the **Shell** tool can be applied to parts.

Figure 3-27

Examples of shell tool applications

3-15 Swept Boss/Base

The **Swept Boss/Base** tool is used to sweep a profile along a path line. As with the **Lofted Boss/Base** tool, existing shapes must be present before the **Swept Boss/Base** tool can be applied. In this example, a Ø.50-inch circle will be swept along an arc with a 2.50-inch radius for 120°. See Figure 3-28.

Figure 3-28

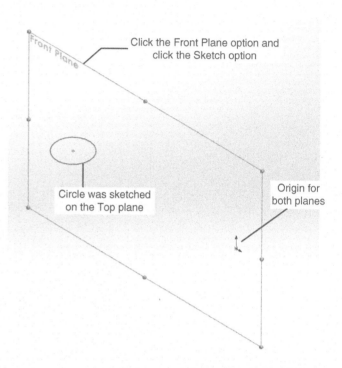

Click the Front Plane option and click the Sketch option

Circle was sketched on the Top plane

Origin for both planes

Ø.50

Origin

2.50

Sketched on the Top plane

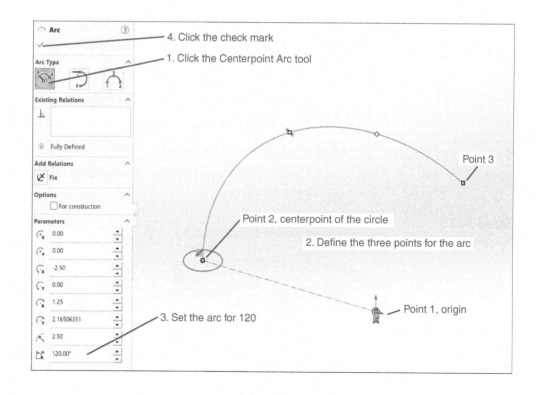

4. Click the check mark

1. Click the Centerpoint Arc tool

Point 3

Point 2, centerpoint of the circle

2. Define the three points for the arc

3. Set the arc for 120

Point 1, origin

Figure 3-28
(*Continued*)

Chapter 3

A swept part

1 Start a new **Part** and click the **Top Plane** option. Use the **Circle**, **Construction Line**, and **Smart Dimension** tools to draw a **Ø.50**-inch circle **2.50** inches from the origin.

2 Use the **View Orientation** tool and change the drawing screen to an isometric orientation.

3 Right-click the mouse and click the **Select** option.

4 Click the **Exit Sketch** option.

We are now going to create a new sketch on a different sketch plane, so we must exit the **Top** plane sketch plane.

5 Right-click the **Front Plane** tool in the **FeatureManager Design** tree and click the **Sketch** option.

6 Click the **Centerpoint Arc** tool and use it to draw an arc with a **2.50** radius with the origin as its centerpoint and an arc length of approximately 120°. Define the arc's length as **120.00°** in the **Parameters** box.

7 Click the green **OK** check mark.

8 Click the **Exit Sketch** option.

This completes the second sketch. The **Swept Boss/Base** tool can now be applied.

9 Click the **Features** tab, then click the **Swept Boss/Base** tool.

10 Select the circle as the profile and the arc as the path.

The path area will automatically be selected.

11 Click the green **OK** check mark.

> **NOTE**
> Figure 3-29 shows an object hollowed out using the **Shell** tool.

Figure 3-29

The Shell tool applied to both ends of the Part

3-16 Draft

The **Draft** tool is used to create slanted surfaces. Figure 3-30 shows a 30 × 50 × 60 box. In this example a 15° slanted surface will be added to the top surface.

Figure 3-30

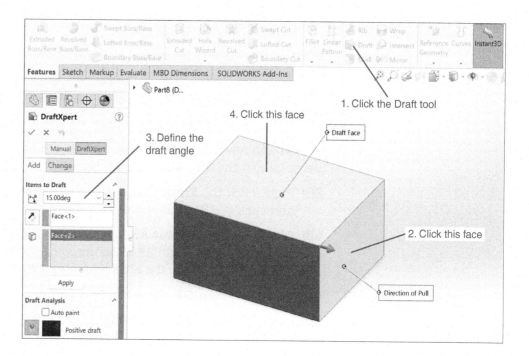

Figure 3-30
(*Continued*)

Resulting draft

1 Draw a **30 × 50 × 60** box on the **Top** plane.

2 Click the **Draft** tool.

3 Define the **Direction of Pull** by clicking the right vertical face of the box.

4 Define the **Draft angle** as **15.00deg**.

5 Select the draft face by clicking the top surface of the box.

The draft angle will be applied to the draft face relative to the 90° angle between the two faces.

6 Click the green **OK** check mark.

Figure 3-31 shows a slanted surface created by making the top surface the direction of pull and the front surface the draft face. Note how the sequence of the draft face selection affects the resulting slanted surface.

Figure 3-31

Resulting draft

3-17   Linear Sketch Pattern

The **Linear Sketch Pattern** tool is used to create rectangular patterns based on a given object.

Figure 3-32 shows a 10 × 15 × 20 box located on a 5 × 80 × 170 base. The box is located 10mm from each edge of the base as shown.

1 Draw the base and box as shown.

2 Click the **Linear Sketch Pattern** tool.

> **NOTE**
>
> The box should be selected automatically, but if it is not, use the **Features to Pattern** tool to select the box.

Figure 3-32

Figure 3-32
(*Continued*)

Chapter 3

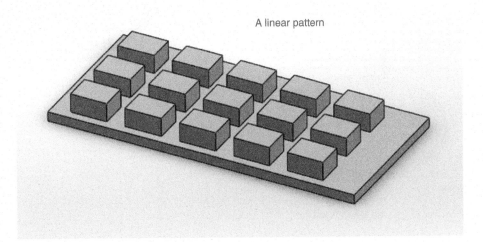

A linear pattern

3 Define **Direction 1** by clicking the back top line as shown.

4 Define the spacing as **30.00mm**.

Spacing is the distance between two of the objects in the pattern as measured from the same point on each object; for example, the distance from the lower-front corner on one object to the lower-front corner of the next object.

5 Define the number of columns in the pattern (**Instances**) as **5**.

6 Click the **Features to Pattern** box and select the 10 × 15 × 20 box.

7 Click the **Reverse Direction** option if the pattern goes in the opposite direction than desired.

8 Define **Direction 2** by clicking the left edge of the base.

9 Define the spacing for **Direction 2** as **25.00mm** and the number of rows in the pattern (**Instances**) as **3**.

A preview of the pattern will appear.

10 Click the green **OK** check mark.

3-18 Circular Sketch Pattern

The **Circular Sketch Pattern** tool is used to create circular patterns about an origin. See Figure 3-33.

Figure 3-33

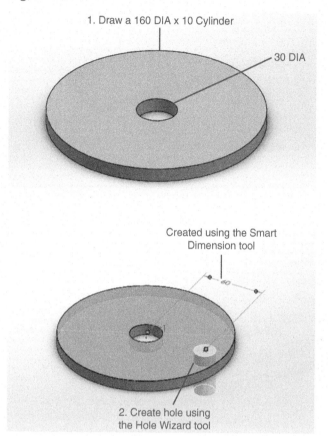

1. Draw a 160 DIA x 10 Cylinder

30 DIA

Created using the Smart Dimension tool

2. Create hole using the Hole Wizard tool

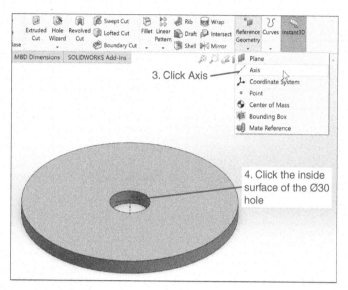

3. Click Axis

4. Click the inside surface of the Ø30 hole

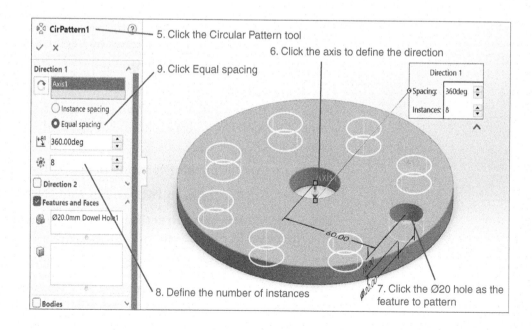

5. Click the Circular Pattern tool

6. Click the axis to define the direction

9. Click Equal spacing

4. Click the inside surface

8. Define the number of instances

7. Click the Ø20 hole as the feature to pattern

Figure 3-33
(*Continued*)

Chapter 3

Finished hole circular pattern

1 Draw a **Ø160 × 10** cylinder.

2 Draw a **Ø30** hole centered about the Ø160 cylinder's origin.

3 Create an axis for the Ø30 hole by accessing the **Reference Geometry** tool in the **Features** tab and then clicking the **Axis** option.

4 Click the **Cylindrical/Conical Face** option in the **Axis PropertyManager** and click the inside surface of the Ø30 hole.

The word **Axis** should appear on the screen and in the **Design** tree.

5 Use the **Hole Wizard** tool and create a **Ø20.0** through hole **60** from the cylinder's centerpoint by clicking the centerpoint of the Ø20 hole and the edges of the Ø30 hole.

6 Access the **Features** tab and select the **Circular Pattern** tool.

7 Define the number of features (**Instances**) in the pattern for **8**, and click the **Equal spacing** option. Define the axis of the Ø30 hole as the axis and the Ø20 hole as the **Features and Faces** to pattern.

A preview will appear.

8 Click the green **OK** check mark.

3-19 Mirror

The **Mirror** tool is used to create mirror images of features. A mirror image is not the same as a copy. In this section we will mirror the object shown in Figure 3-34.

Figure 3-34

BLOCK, MIRROR

1 Draw the object shown in Figure 3-34.

See Figure 3-35.

Figure 3-35

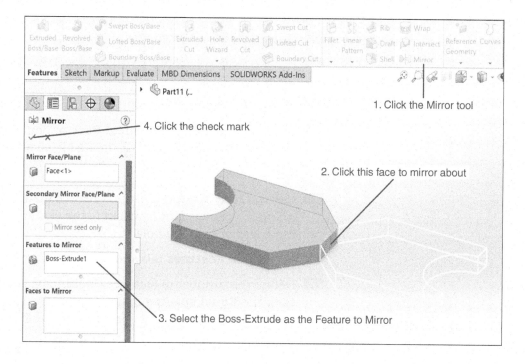

1. Click the Mirror tool

4. Click the check mark

2. Click this face to mirror about

3. Select the Boss-Extrude as the Feature to Mirror

Resulting object

2 Access the **Features** tab and click the **Mirror** tool.

3 Click the **Mirror Face/Plane** box, then click the right surface plane as shown.

The box will be blue when it is active.

4 Click the **Features to Mirror** box, then click the object.

A preview will appear.

5 Click the green **OK** check mark.

3-20 Helix Curves and Springs

SolidWorks allows you to draw springs by drawing a helix and then sweeping a circle along the helical path.

Drawing a Helix

See Figure 3-36. All dimensions are in inches.

Figure 3-36

Origin

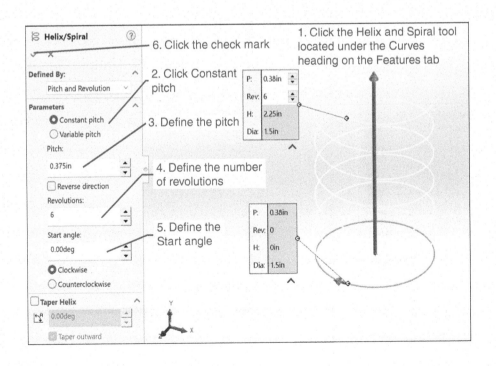

Helix/Spiral

6. Click the check mark

1. Click the Helix and Spiral tool located under the Curves heading on the Features tab

Defined By:
Pitch and Revolution

2. Click Constant pitch

P:	0.38in
Rev:	6
H:	2.25in
Dia:	1.5in

Parameters

○ Constant pitch
○ Variable pitch

3. Define the pitch

Pitch:
0.375in

☐ Reverse direction

Revolutions:
6

4. Define the number of revolutions

Start angle:
0.00deg

5. Define the Start angle

P:	0.38in
Rev:	0
H:	0in
Dia:	1.5in

○ Clockwise
○ Counterclockwise

☐ Taper Helix
0.00deg
☑ Taper outward

Helix

1 Start a new **Part**, select the **Top Plane** option, and click the **Sketch** tab.

2 Draw a **Ø1.50** circle.

In this example the circle was centered about the origin. The diameter of this circle will determine the diameter of the helix.

3 Click the **View Orientation** tool and select the **Trimetric** view orientation.

4 Click the **Features** tab, and click the **Helix** tool.

The **Helix and Spiral** tool is a flyout from the **Curves** tool on the **Features** tab.

The **Helix/Spiral PropertyManager** box will appear along with a preview of the default helix.

5 Select **Constant pitch** and enter a **Pitch** of **0.375in**, **Revolutions** of **6**, **Clockwise** direction, and **Start angle** of **0.00deg**.

Note how the Ø1.50 diameter sizes the helix.

6 Click the green **OK** check mark.

Drawing a Spring From the Given Helix

See Figure 3-37. The helix shown is the one that was created in Figure 3-36.

1 Click the endpoint of the helix and click the **Right Plane** option in the **FeatureManager**.

The endpoint of the helix had its start point at 0°; therefore, it is located on the **Front** plane. The centerpoint of the Ø1.50 circle was located on the Origin.

2 Right-click the plane and select the **Sketch** option.

Figure 3-37

Figure 3-37
(*Continued*)

Chapter 3

Spring

3 Draw a **Ø.375** circle on the front plane centered on the endpoint of the helix.

The diameter of the circle defines the wire diameter for the spring.

4 Exit the **Sketch** mode, click the **Features** tab, and click the **Swept Boss/Base** tool.

5 Click the circle as the profile and the helix as the path.

A preview will appear.

6 Click the green **OK** check mark.

7 Save the spring.

3-21 Compression Springs

Compression springs are designed to accept forces that squeeze them together. They often include ground ends that help them accept the loads while maintaining their position; that is, they don't pop out when the load is applied.

Figure 3-38 shows a spring. It has the following parameters. Dimensions are in inches.

Diameter = 1.00

Pitch = .25

Number of coils = 10

Start angle = 0.00

Wire diameter = .250

It was created using the procedure described in Section 3-20.

Figure 3-38

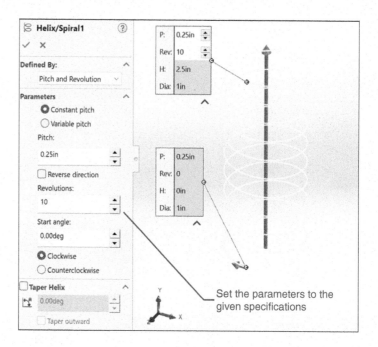

Set the parameters to the given specifications

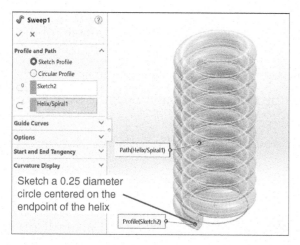

Sketch a 0.25 diameter circle centered on the endpoint of the helix

Hide the helix

Spring

Creating Ground Ends

See Figure 3-39.

1 Orient the spring in the **Trimetric** orientation.

2 Click the **Top Plane** option in the **FeatureManager Design** tree and click the **Plane** option in the **Reference Geometry** tool on the **Features** tab.

Figure 3-39

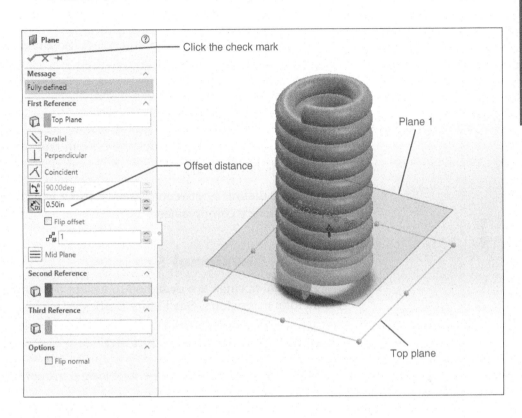

Click the check mark

Plane 1

Offset distance

Top plane

Plane 2

Plane 1

Use the Extruded Cut tool, create a rectangle, and pull to any distance greater than the length of the spring

3 Create an offset plane **.50in** from the **Top** plane and click the green **OK** check mark.

This is Plane 1.

4 Create a second offset plane **2.00in** from the **Top** plane. This is Plane 2.

5 Right-click **Plane 2** and select the **Sketch** option.

6 Sketch a large rectangle on **Plane 2**.

Any size larger than the spring is acceptable.

7 Click the **Features** tab and select the **Extruded Cut** tool.

8 Create a distance that exceeds the end of the spring.

9 Click the green **OK** check mark.

The top portion of the spring will be cut off, simulating a ground end.

10 Repeat the procedure for the bottom end of the spring.

11 Hide Planes 1 and 2.

The distance between Planes 1 and 2 will be the final height of the spring before compression.

3-22 Torsional Springs

Torsional springs are designed to accept a twisting load. They usually include extensions. See Figure 3-40.

Drawing a Torsional Spring

1 Draw a spring using the following parameters. All dimensions are in inches. See Figure 3-41.

Diameter = 1.75

Pitch = .375

Number of coils = 10

Start angle = $0°$

Wire diameter = .25

Figure 3-40

A torsional spring

Figure 3-41

Spring

Diameter = 1.75
Pitch = .375
Number of coils = 10
Wire diameter = .25

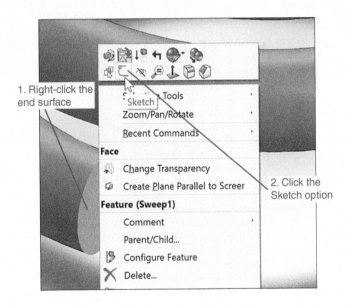

1. Right-click the end surface

2. Click the Sketch option

Figure 3-41
(*Continued*)

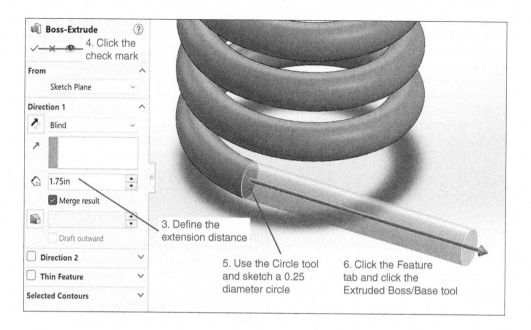

Boss-Extrude ⑦

4. Click the
check mark

From ︿

Sketch Plane ⌄

Direction 1 ︿

↗ Blind ⌄

↗

◁ 1.75in

☑ Merge result

☐ Draft outward

☐ **Direction 2** ⌄

☐ **Thin Feature** ⌄

Selected Contours ⌄

3. Define the
extension distance

5. Use the Circle tool
and sketch a 0.25
diameter circle

6. Click the Feature
tab and click the
Extruded Boss/Base tool

8. Click the Edit Feature option

7. Right-click

Material
Front Pla
Top Plan
Right Pla
Origin
Helix/Spi
Sweep1

Edit Feature

Feature (Helix/Spiral1)

Comment ▸

Parent/Child...

Configure Feature

Delete

9. Change to 9.5

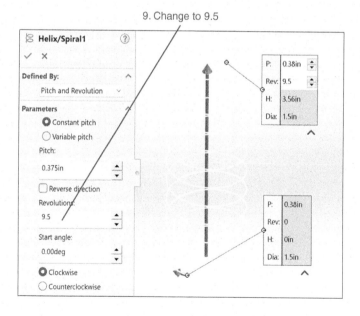

Helix/Spiral1 ⑦

✓ ✕

Defined By: ︿

Pitch and Revolution ⌄

Parameters ︿

⦿ Constant pitch
◯ Variable pitch

Pitch:

0.375in

☐ Reverse direction

Revolutions:

9.5

Start angle:

0.00deg

⦿ Clockwise
◯ Counterclockwise

P: 0.38in
Rev: 9.5
H: 3.56in
Dia: 1.5in

P: 0.38in
Rev: 0
H: 0in
Dia: 1.5in

Figure 3-41
(*Continued*)

Revised number
of coils

10. Sketch a circle

11. Extrude an
extension

2 Zoom in on the bottom endpoint of the spring, right-click the end surface, and select the **Sketch** tool.

3 Click the **Sketch** tab, click the **Circle** tool, and sketch a circle that exactly matches the existing end diameter.

In this example **Ø.25**, the wire diameter, was used.

4 Click the **Features** tab and select the **Extruded Boss/Base** tool.

5 Extrude the circle a distance of **1.75in** and click the green **OK** check mark.

6 Right-click the **Helix/Spiral** heading in the **FeatureManager Design Tree** and select the **Edit Feature** option.

7 Change the **Revolutions** value to **9.5** and click the green **OK** check mark.

This revision is necessary to make both extensions face the same direction.

8 Right-click the new top end surface of the spring, create a sketch plane, sketch a **Ø.25** circle, and draw a **1.75** extension as shown.

9 Click the green **OK** check mark and save the spring.

3-23 Extension Springs

Extension springs are designed for loads that pull them apart (that is, tension loads). Extension springs usually have hooklike ends.

Drawing an Extension Spring

See Figure 3-42.

Figure 3-42

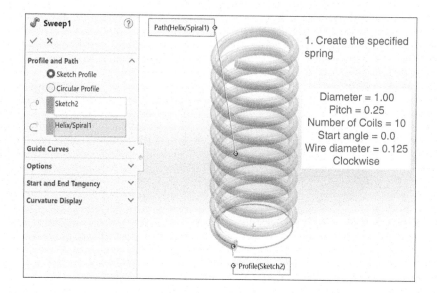

Sweep1

Profile and Path

- Sketch Profile
- Circular Profile

Sketch2

Helix/Spiral1

Guide Curves

Options

Start and End Tangency

Curvature Display

Path(Helix/Spiral1)

1. Create the specified spring

Diameter = 1.00
Pitch = 0.25
Number of Coils = 10
Start angle = 0.0
Wire diameter = 0.125
Clockwise

Profile(Sketch2)

Note that the two ends point in opposite directions

Figure 3-42
(*Continued*)

2. Sketch a .125 diameter circle

3. Create an offset Front plane centered on the circle's centerpoint

4. Make the offset plane a sketch plane

5. Use the Centerpoint Arc tool and sketch a 90 degree arc with a radius of .25

Path(Sketch4)

Profile(Sketch3)

6. Use the Swept Boss/Base tool to sweep the circle along the arc

8. Create an offset Right plane through the centerpoint of the circle

7. Sketch a circle on the end surface

9. Use the Centerpoint Arc tool and sketch a 180 degree arc with a radius of .50

Figure 3-42
(*Continued*)

10. Use the Sweep tool

1. Draw a spring as defined below. All dimensions are in inches.

   Diameter = 1.00

   Pitch = .25

   Number of coils = 10

   Start angle = 0.00

   Wire diameter = .125

   Clockwise

2. Sketch a **Ø.125** circle on the end surface of the spring as shown.

3. Use the **Plane** option under the **Reference Geometry** tool and create an offset **Front** plane offset **.50**; that is, through the centerpoint of the circle created in Step 1.

4. Right-click the mouse and select the **Sketch** tool, turning the offset plane into a sketch plane.

5. Use the **Centerpoint Arc** tool and sketch an arc from the center of the sketch circle a distance of **90°**.

Use the **Smart Dimension** tool to define the radius of the arc as **.25**.

6. Use the **Swept Boss/Base** tool and sweep the circle along the arc path; click the green **OK** check mark. Hide the planes and the sketches.

7. Sketch a circle on the arc's end surface.

8. Use the **Plane** option under the **Reference Geometry** tool and create an offset **Right** plane through the centerpoint of the circle created in Step 3.

9. Use the **Centerpoint Arc** tool and sketch a **180°** arc with a radius of .50.

10. Use the **Swept Boss/Base** tool and sweep the circle through the arc.

11. Click the **OK** check mark.

12. Hide the planes.

13. Repeat the procedure for the other end surface of the spring.

The spring shown represents one possible type of extension spring.

3-24 Wrap

The **Wrap** tool is used to wrap text or other shapes around a surface. There are three options: embossed, text that stands out from a face; debossed, text that is embedded on a face; and scribed, text that is written directly on the face.

Creating Debossed Text

See Figure 3-43.

1. Draw a **Ø3.00 × 2.50** cylinder based on the **Top** plane centered on the origin.

2. Use the **Plane** option of the **Reference Geometry** tool and create an offset **Right** plane tangent to the outside edge of the cylinder. The offset distance will be 1.50 from the origin. This is Plane 1.

3. Change the orientation of the cylinder to the **Right** plane.

4. Right-click **Plane 1** and click the **Sketch** option.

5. Click the **Text** tool and add text to the plane.

6. Use the cursor or the **Smart Dimension** tool to locate the text.

7. Change the drawing orientation to **Trimetric**.

8. Exit the **Sketch** mode.

9. Click the **Wrap** tool.

10. Click the **Deboss** option.

Figure 3-43

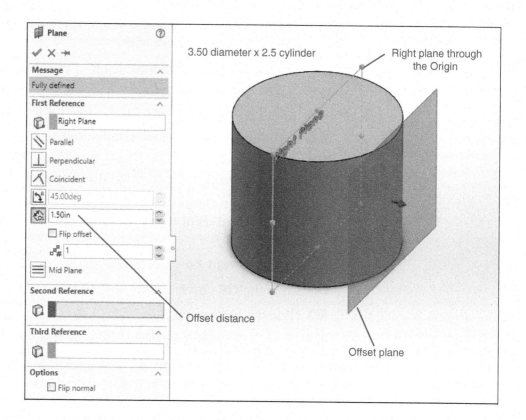

3.50 diameter x 2.5 cylinder

Right plane through the Origin

Offset distance

Offset plane

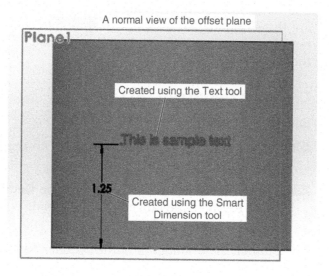

A normal view of the offset plane

Created using the Text tool

This is sample text

1.25

Created using the Smart Dimension tool

Figure 3-43
(*Continued*)

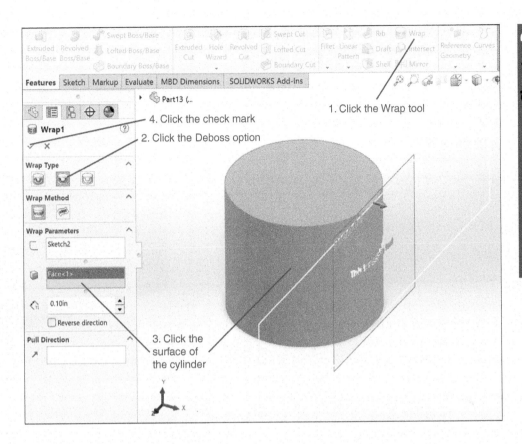

1. Click the Wrap tool

4. Click the check mark

2. Click the Deboss option

3. Click the surface of the cylinder

Font = Arial, 12 points

Debossed text

11 Click the edge surface of the cylinder to define the **Face for Wrap Sketch**.

12 Hide Plane 1.

13 Click the green **OK** check mark.

Figure 3-44 shows an example of scribed text.

Figure 3-44

Change font here

Scribe

A sample of scribed text

3-25 Editing Features

SolidWorks allows you to edit existing models. This is a very powerful feature in that you can easily make changes to a completed model without having to redraw the entire model.

TIP

The **Edit Sketch** tool is used to edit entities created using the **Sketch** tools, such as holes. The **Edit Features** tool is used to edit entities created using the **Features** tools, such as cuts or extrusions.

   Figure 3-45 shows the L-bracket originally created in Sections 3-3 through 3-6. The finished object may be edited. In this example, the hole's diameter and the size of the cutout will be changed.

Figure 3-45

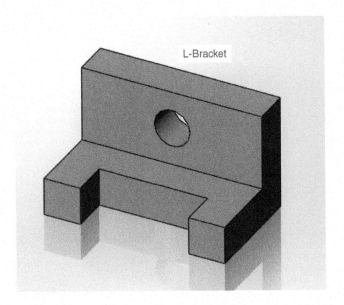

L-Bracket

TIP
The hole will be highlighted when selected.

Editing the Hole

See Figure 3-46.

 Right-click the hole on the L-bracket.

   A pop-up menu will appear.

2 Select the **Edit Sketch** option.

   The sketch used to create the hole will appear.

3 Double-click the Ø20 dimension.

Figure 3-46

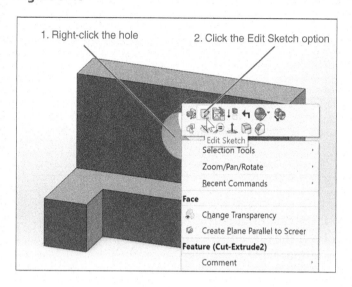

1. Right-click the hole

2. Click the Edit Sketch option

Edit Sketch
Selection Tools
Zoom/Pan/Rotate
Recent Commands

Face
Change Transparency
Create Plane Parallel to Screer

Feature (Cut-Extrude2)
Comment

4. Click the check mark

50
20

Modify
D3(
24.00mm
Units

3. Double-click the 20 dimension and change its value to 24

24 diameter

4 Change the dimension to **Ø24.00** and click the green **OK** check mark.

5 Click the **Exit Sketch** option.

Editing the Cutout

See Figure 3-47.

1 Right-click the back surface of the cutout.

The surface will be highlighted when selected. A pop-up menu will appear.

2 Click the **Edit Sketch** option.

3 Double-click the two **20** dimensions that define the length of the cutout and change their value to **30**.

Figure 3-47

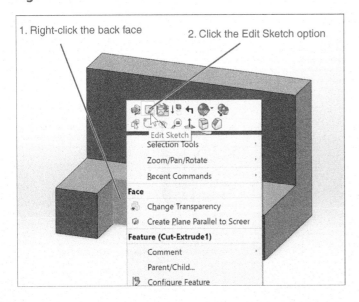

1. Right-click the back face

2. Click the Edit Sketch option

Edit Sketch
Selection Tools
Zoom/Pan/Rotate
Recent Commands

Face
Change Transparency
Create Plane Parallel to Screen

Feature (Cut-Extrude1)
Comment
Parent/Child...
Configure Feature

Double-click the 20 dimensions

Revise the two 20 dimensions to 30

Edited L-Bracket

4 Click the green **OK** check mark.

5 Click the **Exit Sketch** option.

3-26 Sample Problem SP3-2

Figure 3-48 shows a cylindrical object with a slanted surface, a cutout, and a blind hole. Figure 3-49 shows how to draw the object. The procedures presented in Figure 3-49 represent one of several possible ways to create the object.

Figure 3-48

Drawing a Cylinder

1 Start a new **Part** document.

2 Define the units as millimeters (**MMGS**), the **Overall drafting** standards should be **ANSI**, access the **Top Plane**, and make it a sketch plane.

3 Draw a **Ø58** circle centered on the origin and extrude it to **60**.

Figure 3-49

Figure 3-49
(*Continued*)

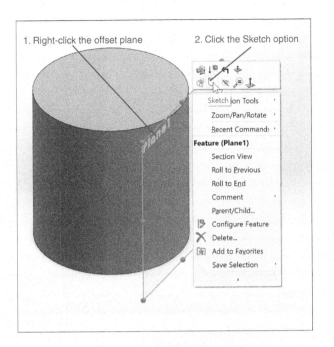

1. Right-click the offset plane

2. Click the Sketch option

Sketch ion Tools
Zoom/Pan/Rotate
Recent Commands
Feature (Plane1)
Section View
Roll to Previous
Roll to End
Comment
Parent/Child...
Configure Feature
Delete...
Add to Favorites
Save Selection

Click this face

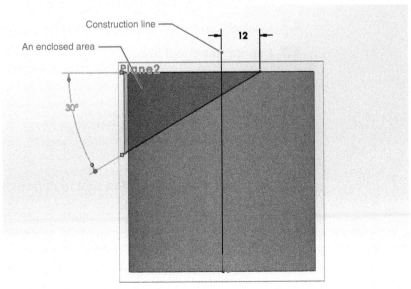

Construction line

An enclosed area

12

Plane2

30°

The dimensions are from Figure 3-48

Figure 3-49
(*Continued*)

A slanted surface

Creating a Slanted Surface on the Cylinder

1 Click the **Right Plane** option, click the **Reference Geometry** tool under the **Features** tab, and click the **Plane** option.

2 Define the offset plane distance in the **Plane PropertyManager** as **30**, and click the green **OK** check mark.

3 Right-click the offset plane and select the **Sketch** option.

4 Change the drawing orientation to the **Right** plane.

5 Use the **Line** tool and draw an enclosed triangular shape.

> **NOTE**
>
> The dimensions for the triangle came from Figure 3-48. The triangle must be an enclosed area. No gaps are permitted. A vertical construction line was added to help in the location and creation of the triangular area.

6 Use the **Smart Dimension** tool to define the size and location of the triangle.

7 Change the drawing orientation to **Dimetric** and click the **Extruded Cut** tool in the **Features** tab.

8 Set the length of the cut to **70.00mm** and click the **OK** check mark.

9 Right-click the offset plane and click the **Hide** option.

Adding the Vertical Slot

See Figure 3-50.

Figure 3-50

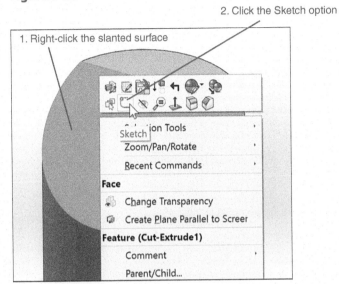

1. Right-click the slanted surface

2. Click the Sketch option

Sketch

Selection Tools
Zoom/Pan/Rotate
Recent Commands

Face
Change Transparency
Create Plane Parallel to Screen

Feature (Cut-Extrude1)
Comment
Parent/Child...

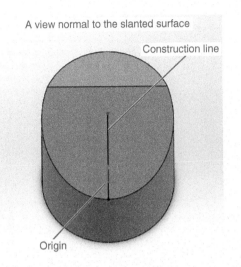

A view normal to the slanted surface

Construction line

Origin

Sketch a rectangle

8

16

Start a rectangle at
this rectangle

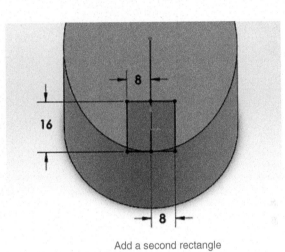

8

16

8

Add a second rectangle

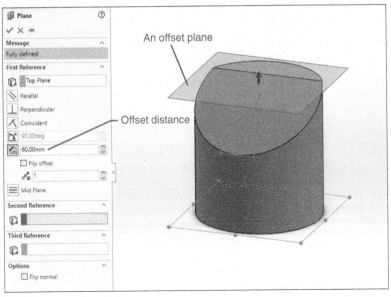

Plane

Message
Fully defined

First Reference
Top Plane
Parallel
Perpendicular
Coincident
90.00deg
60.00mm
Flip offset
1
Mid Plane

Second Reference

Third Reference

Options
Flip normal

An offset plane

Offset distance

Figure 3-50
(*Continued*)

A view normal to the top offset plane

Plane3

Origin

Use the Line tool to
create the rectangle

Use the Extruded Cut tool

Plane3

Vertical slot

1 Right-click the slanted surface and click the **Sketch** tool.

2 Click the **View Orientation** tool and click the **Normal to View** tool, or press **<Ctrl-8>**.

The original dimensions shown in Figure 3-48 define the slot along the slanted surface, so they must be applied along the slanted surface. After the dimensions are applied, they will be projected into the top surface.

3 Use the **Line** tool and sketch a vertical construction line through the origin. Start the line on the edge of the slanted surface.

4 Use the **Rectangle** tool on the **Sketch** toolbar and draw an **8 × 16** rectangle as shown. Use the **Smart Dimension** tool to size the rectangle.

The lower edge of the rectangle must align with the edge of the cylinder or extend beyond the edge to ensure the cutout removes all material.

5 Draw a second **8 × 16** rectangle as shown.

6 Change the drawing orientation to a dimetric view.

7 Exit the sketch.

8 Click the **Top Plane**, then use the **Plane** option in the **Reference Geometry** tool on the **Features** tab and create an offset **Top** plane **60.00mm** from the base of the cylinder.

> **NOTE**
>
> The **Extruded Cut** tool will extrude a shape perpendicular to the plane of the shape. In this example the plane is slanted, so the extrusion would not be vertical, as required. The rectangle is projected into the top offset plane and the extrusion tool applied there.

9 Right-click the 60 offset plane, select the **Sketch** option, and change the drawing orientation to the top view.

10 Use the **Line** tool and sketch a rectangle on the offset plane over the projected view of the 16 × 16 rectangle on the slanted plane, right-click the mouse, and click the **Select** option.

11 Change the drawing orientation to a dimetric view.

12 Use the **Extruded Cut** tool on the **Features** tab to cut out the slot.

13 Hide the 60 offset plane and hide the 16 × 16 rectangle on the slanted surface.

14 Click the green **OK** check mark.

Adding the Ø8 Hole

See Figure 3-51.

1 Right-click the flat top surface of the object, click the **Sketch** option, and create a sketch plane.

2 Change the orientation to a view normal to the flat top surface.

3 Use the **Point** tool and sketch a point on the flat portion of the top surface. Use the origin to center the point.

4 Use the **Smart Dimension** tool and locate the point according to the given dimensions, in this example 9mm.

5 Change to a **Trimetric** orientation and exit the sketch.

Figure 3-51

Figure 3-51
(*Continued*)

A trimetric view

Point

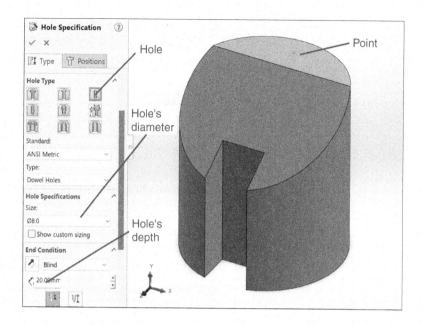

Point

Hole

Hole's diameter

Hole's depth

3. Click the Top surface

4. Click the Point

Use the Hole Wizard's position option to locate the hole

Blind hole

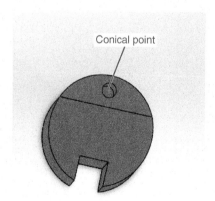

Conical point

NOTE

There are two ways to draw blind holes (holes that do not go all the way through): draw a circle and use the **Extruded Cut** tool to remove material, or use the **Hole Wizard**. In this example the **Hole Wizard** tool is used because it will generate a conical-shaped bottom to the hole. Conical-shaped hole bottoms result from using a twist drill, which has a conical-shaped cutting end.

6 Click the **Hole Wizard** tool on the **Features** tab.

7 Click the **Hole** option and define the hole's diameter and depth.

In this example the hole's diameter is **8.0mm** and the depth is **20.00mm**. Note that the hole is defined as a blind hole and that the hole's depth does not include the conical point.

8 Click the **Positions** tab in the **PropertyManager**.

9 Click the flat top surface, then click the point.

10 Click the green **OK** check mark.

11 Rotate the drawing orientation and verify that the hole has a conical-shaped bottom.

3-27 Sample Problem SP3-3

Figure 3-52 shows a dimensioned object. In this example we will start with the middle section of the object. See Figure 3-53. The solution presented represents one of many possible solutions. The solution uses metric units and ANSI Overall drafting standards.

Figure 3-52

Figure 3-53

Figure 3-53
(*Continued*)

Figure 3-53
(*Continued*)

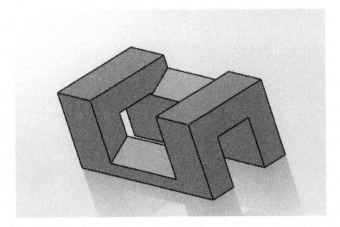

1 Sketch a profile using the **Right Plane** based on the given dimensions.

2 Use the **Extruded Boss/Base** tool to add a thickness of **40.00mm** to the profile.

3 Right-click the right surface of the object and select the **Sketch** option.

4 Use the **Rectangle** and **Smart Dimension** tools and draw a rectangle based on the given dimensions. Align the corners of the rectangle with the corners of the object.

5 Use the **Extruded Boss/Base** tool and extrude the rectangle **20** to the right.

6 Reorient the object and draw a rectangle on the left surface of the object.

7 Use the **Extruded Boss/Base** tool and extrude the rectangle **20** to the left.

8 Reorientate the object and create a sketch plane on the right side of the object. Draw a rectangle based on the given dimensions.

9 Use the **Extruded Cut** tool on the **Features** tab and cut out the rectangle over the length of the object.

3-28 Curve Driven Patterns

Figure 3-54 shows a Ø4.00 inch ring with 12 holes through its side surfaces. The holes were created using the **Curve Driven Pattern** tool.

Using the Curve Driven Pattern Tool—Example 1

See Figure 3-55.

1 Sketch the ring using the dimensions shown in Figure 3-54.

The outer diameter is Ø4.00, and the inner ring is Ø3.00. Both are centered on the origin working on the **Top** plane.

2 Use the **Extruded Boss/Base tool** and extrude the ring a distance of 1.00.

3 Click the **Front Plane** option in the **FeatureManager** box, click the **Plane** option under the **Reference Geometry** tool, and create an offset plane tangent to the front edge of the ring.

Figure 3-54

Figure 3-55

Extrude distance equals 1.00in.

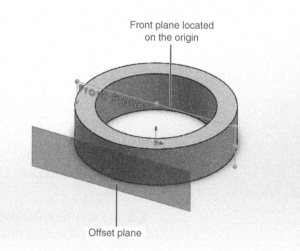

Figure 3-55
(*Continued*)

Chapter 3

A normal view of Plane 1 ⌀.38

Plane 1

.50

Use the Circle tool

Use the Extruded Cut tool to create a hole through the ring

Plane 1

⌀3

.50

Plane 2, offset .50 from the Top plane

⌀4.00

Plane 1

Use the Circle tool to sketch a diameter 4.00 circle on the Offset Plane 2

1. Click Insert menu   2. Click Pattern/Mirror

File Edit View Insert Tools Window

Boss/Base
Cut
Features
Pattern/Mirror
Fastening Feature
FeatureWorks

Surface
Face
Curve
Reference Geometry

Sheet Metal
Structure System
Weldments
Molds

Mirror Entities
Linear Sketch Pattern
Move Entities

Markup Evalu

Add-Ins

<<Default>>

s(1)
not specified>

Linear Pattern...
Circular Pattern...
Mirror...
Table Driven Pattern...
Sketch Driven Pattern...
Curve Driven Pattern...
Fill Pattern ...
Variable Pattern ...

Customize Menu

3. Click Curve Driven Pattern

Figure 3-55
(*Continued*)

A ring with 12 holes

The new plane is offset 2.00 from the origin, that is, from the center-point of the ring. The new plane is defined as Plane 1 in this example.

4 Create a sketch plane on **Plane 1**, create a normal view to the plane, and sketch a Ø0.375 circle **0.50** from the bottom edge of the ring.

5 Use the **Extruded Cut** tool and create a hole from the circle.

6 Click the **Top Plane** in the **FeatureManager** box, click the **Plane** option under the **Reference Geometry** tool, and create an offset Plane **0.50** above the initial **Top** plane used to create the ring.

In this example this plane is defined as Plane 2. Plane 2 is offset 0.50 from the initial **Top** plane or halfway up the 1.00 thickness of the ring.

7 Create a sketch plane on **Plane 2**, and create a normal view.

8 Sketch a Ø4.00 circle on the sketch plane, click the **Exit Sketch** icon, and orientate the drawing to an isometric view.

In this step we are creating a path for the new hole pattern.

9 Click the **Insert** menu at the top of the screen, click the **Pattern/Mirror** option, and click the **Curve Driven Pattern** tool.

10 Set the **Number of Instances** to **12**, click the **Equal spacing** box, click the **Tangent to curve** option for **Alignment Method**, click the **Features and Faces** box, select the hole, and click the **OK** check mark.

11 Hide Planes 1 and 2, and the circle used to define the pattern.

Using the Curve Driven Pattern Tool—Example 2

Figure 3-56 shows a part that has 12 holes offset 10 from the part's outer edge surface.

1 Use the given dimensions and draw the part as shown in Figure 3-56.

See Figure 3-57.

Figure 3-56

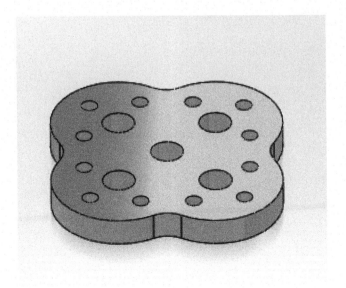

NOTE: THE CENTERPOINT FOR THE 4 - Ø12 HOLES IS ALSO THE CENTERPOINT FOR THE R25 ARCS.
THE CURVE DEFINING THE LOCATION FOR THE 12- Ø6 HOLES IS OFFSET 10 FROM THE EDGE OF THE PART ALL AROUND.

Ø50

R10 - 4 FILLETS

R25 - 4 PLACES

Ø6 - 12 HOLES EQUALLY SPACED

Ø12 - 5 HOLES

10

(100)

Figure 3-57

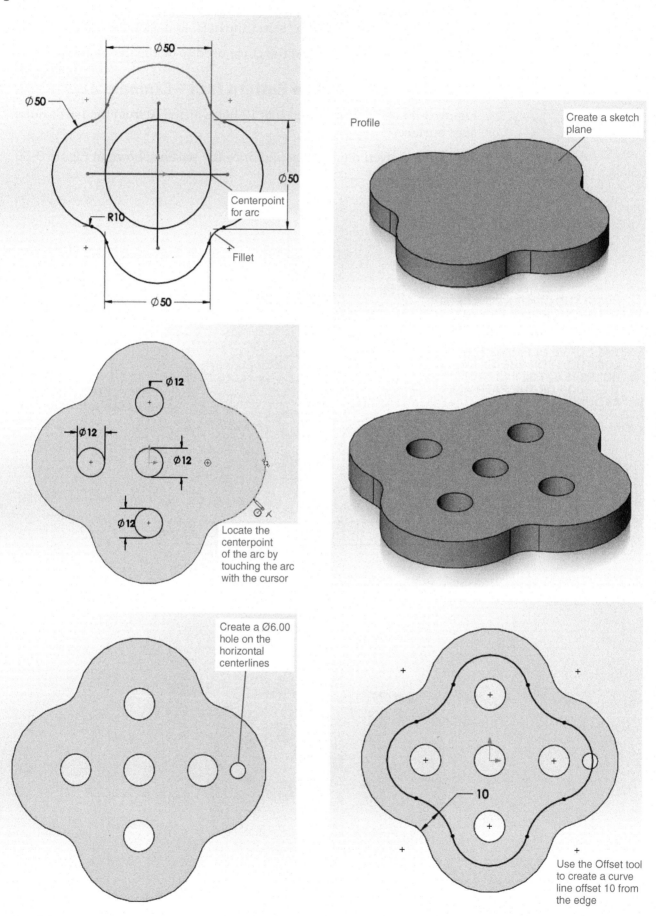

Ø50

Ø50

Ø50

Ø50

R10

Centerpoint for arc

Fillet

Profile

Create a sketch plane

Ø12

Ø12

Ø12

Ø12

Locate the centerpoint of the arc by touching the arc with the cursor

Create a Ø6.00 hole on the horizontal centerlines

10

Use the Offset tool to create a curve line offset 10 from the edge

Figure 3-57
(*Continued*)

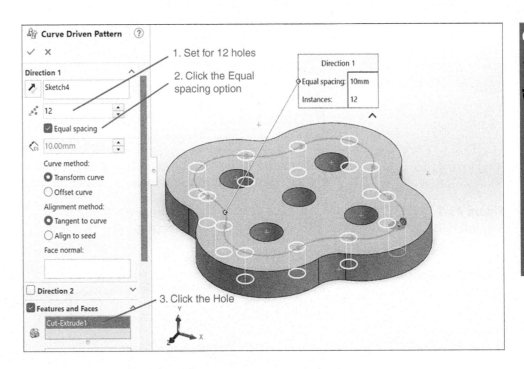

1. Set for 12 holes

2. Click the Equal spacing option

3. Click the Hole

2 Define a sketch plane on the top surface of the part and use the **Offset** tool and create a curve offset **10** from the part's outer edge.

Figure 3-57 shows a normal view of the top surface. The offset curve is created using the **Offset** tool. Both the arcs and fillets can be offset to create a continuous curve.

3 Draw a Ø6 hole centered on the intersection of the offset curve and the horizontal centerline of the part. The centerpoint is 40 from the part's origin.

4 Click the **Insert** menu at the top of the screen, click the **Pattern/ Mirror** option, and click the **Curve Driven Pattern** tool.

5 Set the **Number of Instances** to **12**, click the **Equal spacing** box, select the hole as the **Features and Faces** to pattern, the offset curve as the **Pattern Direction**, and click the **OK** check mark.

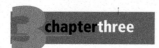

Chapter Projects

Project 3-1:

Redraw the following objects, shown in Figures P3-1 to P3-48, as solid models based on the given dimensions. Make all models from mild steel.

Figure P3-1
MILLIMETERS

Figure P3-2
INCHES

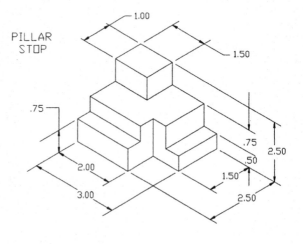

PILLAR STOP

Figure P3-3
MILLIMETERS

SPLIT BLOCK

Figure P3-4
MILLIMETERS

SQUARE CLIP

Figure P3-5
MILLIMETERS

SETTER
BRACKET
50
30
10 – ALL AROUND
40 –2 PLACES
25
15
100
30 –2 PLACES

Figure P3-6
MILLIMETERS

10 – BOTH SIDES
40
15
15
S–CLIP
40
15
10 – BOTH SIDES
50
40

MATL = 10mm SAE 1020 STEEL

Figure P3-7
INCHES

KEY CLIP
.75 BOTH SIDES
.50 BOTH SIDES
.50 ALL AROUND
.50
.25
1.50
.50
.25
1.00
1.50
2.50
2.00

Figure P3-8
MILLIMETERS

10 BOTH SIDES
15
15
10
20
25
STANDOFF – ONE
SIDE ONLY
10
20
60
80
30

Figure P3-9
MILLIMETERS

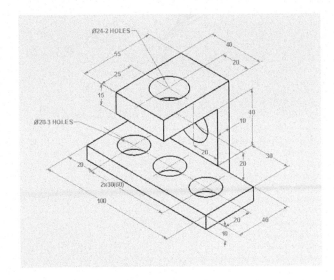

Ø24-2 HOLES
55
40
25
20
15
Ø20-3 HOLES
40
10
20
20
30
20
2x30(60)
100
20
40
40

Figure P3-10
MILLIMETERS

Ø30
50
25
Ø20
2 HOLES
13
BOTH SIDES
15
30
20
CENTERED
50
100
40
25
15
30

Figure P3-11
INCHES

Figure P3-12
MILLIMETERS

Figure P3-13
MILLIMETERS

Figure P3-14
MILLIMETERS

Figure P3-15
MILLIMETERS

20
20
105°
45
22
60°
13
45°
10
20
10
20
18
60
5
18

Figure P3-16
INCHES

1.25
1.75
1.00
.50
2.50
.63
1.63
3.50
2.38

Figure P3-17
MILLIMETERS

15
18
30
45°
50
18
A
Ø 20—THRU
PERPENDICULAR TO A
40
60
22

Figure P3-18
MILLIMETERS

15
25
Ø 14   2 HOLES
15
12
22° - BOTH
SLANTED SURFACES
27
60
38
30
100
7

Figure P3-19
MILLIMETERS

40
15
15
50
40
10
25
R13 – 4 Corners
R13 – Both Sides
R8

Figure P3-20
MILLIMETERS

∅14
18
15 BOTH SIDES
25
30
15
60
35
20
25
20
10
12
8
55
90

Figure P3-21
MILLIMETERS

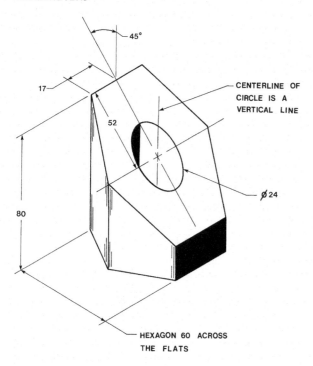

45°
17
52
80
CENTERLINE OF
CIRCLE IS A
VERTICAL LINE
∅24
HEXAGON 60 ACROSS
THE FLATS

Figure P3-22
INCHES

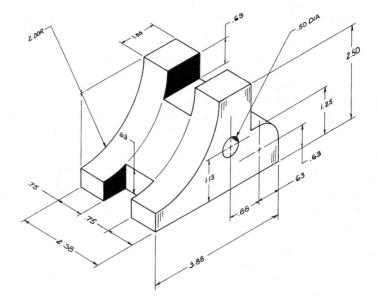

2.00R
.69
.50 DIA
2.50
1.25
.63
1.13
.63
.63
.75
.75
.88
2.38
3.88

Figure P3-23
MILLIMETERS

Figure P3-24
MILLIMETERS

Figure P3-25
INCHES (SCALE: 4 = 1)

Figure P3-26
MILLIMETERS

Note: Slot is 12 deep
from centerline

Figure P3-27
MILLIMETERS

Figure P3-28
MILLIMETERS

REGULAR HEXAGON
80 ACROSS THE CORNER

Figure P3-29
INCHES (SCALE: 4 = 1)

Figure P3-30
MILLIMETERS (SCALE: 2 = 1)

Figure P3-31
MILLIMETERS

25
BOTH ENDS

20

35 ACROSS THE FLATS
CENTERED ABOUT ℄

90

Ø 100

Figure P3-32
MILLIMETERS

6−2 PLACES

10 −2 PLACES

Ø5−2 PLACES

Ø40

90°

Ø 22

20

Ø16

60

90°

20

Figure P3-33
MILLIMETERS

R−2 PLACES

80

10

Ø 20

3

8

35

25

100

Ø32

Ø40

Figure P3-34
MILLIMETERS

Ø 40

60

Ø 12

30

19

5 x 45°

50

80

Ø 28

Figure P3-35
MILLIMETERS

70

47 REF

15

15

R47

20

Figure P3-36
MILLIMETERS

Ø 40

40

7

35

15

100

8

12

Figure P3-37
MILLIMETERS

ALL FILLETS AND ROUNDS = R3

Figure P3-38
MILLIMETERS

ALL FILLETS AND
ROUNDS = R5

Figure P3-39
MILLIMETERS (CONSIDER A SHELL)

ALL FILLETS AND ROUNDS = R3
MATL 5 THK

Figure P3-40
MILLIMETERS

MATL 5 THK
ALL INSIDE BEND RAD 5

Figure P3-41
MILLIMETERS

Figure P3-42
INCHES

Figure P3-43
MILLIMETERS

Figure P3-44
INCHES

Figure P3-45
MILLIMETERS

Figure P3-46
MILLIMETERS

Figure P3-47
INCHES

Figure P3-48
MILLIMETERS

Project 3-2:

A. Draw the following spring.

Diameter = 2.00

Wire diameter = .125

Pitch = .375

Revolutions = 16

B. Grind both ends to create a spring 2.00 long in its unloaded position.

Project 3-3:

A. Draw the following spring.

Diameter = 25

Wire diameter = 5 × 5 square

Pitch = 6

Revolutions = 8

Figure P3-49
INCHES (Project 3-2)

Figure P3-50
MILLIMETERS (Project 3-3)

Figure P3-51
INCHES (Project 3-4)

Project 3-4:

A.   Draw the following torsional spring.

Diameter = .500

Wire diameter = .06

Pitch = .125

Revolutions = 20

Extension lengths = 1.00, 90° apart

Project 3-5:

A.   Draw the following torsional spring.

Diameter = 12.00

Wire diameter = 4.0

Pitch = 6.0

Revolutions = 18

Extension lengths = 15, 180° apart

Figure P3-52
MILLIMETERS

Project 3-6:

A. Draw the following extension spring.

Diameter = 1.00

Wire diameter = .0938

Pitch = .180

Revolutions = 12

Extension radius = .125

Hook radius = .50

Project 3-7:

A. Draw the following extension spring.

Diameter = 30

Wire diameter = 6

Pitch = 30

Revolutions = 10

Extension radius = 6

Hook radius = 12

Figure P3-54
MILLIMETERS

Project 3-8:

Draw a Ø4.00 × 3.00 cylinder and deboss on one of the following. Use a font style and size of your choice, or as assigned by your instructor.

A. Your name and address

B. Your school's name and address

Project 3-9:

Redraw the following objects as solid models based on the given dimensions.

Figure P3-55
INCHES

Figure P3-56
MILLIMETERS

Figure P3-57A
MILLIMETERS

Figure P3-57B
MILLIMETERS

Orthographic Views

CHAPTER OBJECTIVES

- Implement orthographic views
- Apply ANSI standards and conventions
- Draw section and auxiliary views

4-1 Introduction

Orthographic views are two-dimensional views used to define a three-dimensional model. More than one orthographic view is needed to define a model unless the model is of uniform thickness. Standard practice calls for three orthographic views, a front, top, and side view, although more or fewer views may be used as needed.

There are two sets of standards used to define the projection and placement of orthographic views: the American National Standards Institute (ANSI) and the International Organization for Standardization (ISO). ANSI calls for orthographic views to be created using third-angle projection and is the accepted method for use in the United States. See the American Society of Mechanical Engineers publication ASME Y14.3-2012. Some countries, other than the United States, use first-angle projection. See ISO publications 128-2:2022 and 128-3:2022.

This chapter will present orthographic views using third-angle projections as defined by ANSI. However, there is so much international commerce happening today that you should be able to work in both conventions and in either inches or millimeters.

Figure 4-1 shows a three-dimensional model and three orthographic views created using third-angle projection and three orthographic views created using first-angle projection. Note the differences and similarities. The front view in both projections is the same. The top views are the same but are in different locations. The third-angle projection presents a right-side view, while the first-angle projection presents a left-side view.

Figure 4-1

3 orthographic views of the model
In compliance with ANSI
and used in the USA

Symbol for third-angle projection

In compliance with ISO
as used in some countries
other than the USA

Symbol for first-angle projection

Figure 4-2 shows the drawing symbols for first- and third-angle projections. These symbols can be added to a drawing to help the reader understand which type of projection is being used. These symbols were included in the projections presented in Figure 4-1.

Figure 4-2

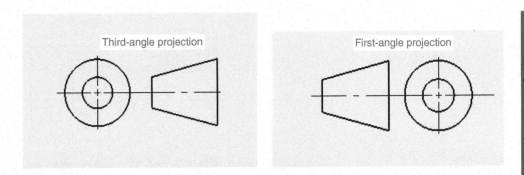

4-2 Third- and First-Angle Projections

Figure 4-3 shows an object with front and top orthographic views created using third-angle and first-angle projections. For third-angle projections the orthographic view is projected on a plane located between the viewer's position and the object. For first-angle projections the orthographic view is projected on a plane located beyond the object. The front and top views for third- and first-angle projections appear the same, but they are located in different positions relative to the front view.

Figure 4-3

The side orthographic views are different for third- and first-angle projections. Third-angle projections use a right-side view. First-angle projections use a left-side view. Figures 4-4 and 4-5 show the side views for two different objects. For third-angle projections, the viewer is located on the right side of the object and creates the side orthographic view on a plane located between the view position and the object. For first-angle projections the viewer is located on the left side of the object and creates the side orthographic view on a plane located beyond the object.

To help understand the difference between side view orientations for third- and first-angle projections, locate your right hand with the heel facing down and the thumb facing up. Rotate your hand so that the palm is facing up—this is the third-angle projection orientation. Return to the thumb-up position. Rotate your hand so that the palm is down—this is the first-angle view orientation.

Figure 4-4

Figure 4-5

4-3 Fundamentals of Orthographic Views

Figure 4-6 shows an object with its front, top, and right-side orthographic views projected from the object. The views are two-dimensional, so they show no depth. Note that in the projected right plane there are three rectangles. There is no way to determine which of the three is closest and which is farthest away if only the right-side view is considered. All views must be studied to analyze the shape of the object.

Figure 4-7 shows three orthographic views of a book. After the views are projected they are positioned as shown. The positioning of views relative to one another is critical. The views must be aligned and positioned as shown.

Figure 4-6

Figure 4-7

Normal Surfaces

Normal surfaces are surfaces that are at 90° to each other. Figures 4-8, 4-9, and 4-10 show objects that include only normal surfaces and their orthographic views.

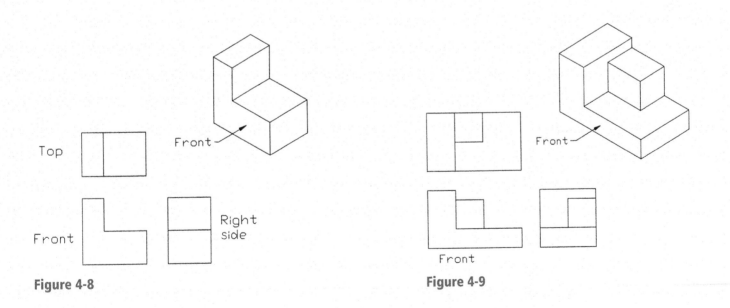

Figure 4-8

Figure 4-9

Figure 4-10

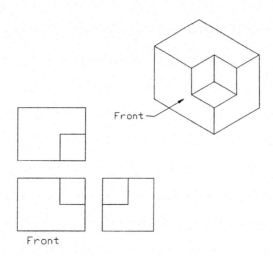

Front

Front

Hidden Lines

Hidden lines are used to show surfaces that are not directly visible. All surfaces must be shown in all views. If an edge or surface is blocked from view by another feature, it is drawn using a hidden line. Figures 4-11 and 4-12 show objects that require hidden lines in their orthographic views.

Figure 4-11

Hidden line
Used to show surfaces
that are not directly visible.

Figure 4-12

Figure 4-13 shows an object that contains an edge line, **A-B**. In the top view, line A-B is partially hidden and partially visible. The hidden portion of the line is drawn using a hidden-line pattern, and the visible portion of the line is drawn using a solid line.

Figures 4-14 and 4-15 show objects that require hidden lines in their orthographic views.

Figure 4-13

Figure 4-14

Figure 4-15

Precedence of Lines

It is not unusual for one type of line to be drawn over another type of line. Figure 4-16 shows two examples of overlap by different types of lines. Lines are shown on the views in a prescribed order of precedence. A solid line (object or continuous) takes precedence over a hidden line, and a hidden line takes precedence over a centerline.

Figure 4-16

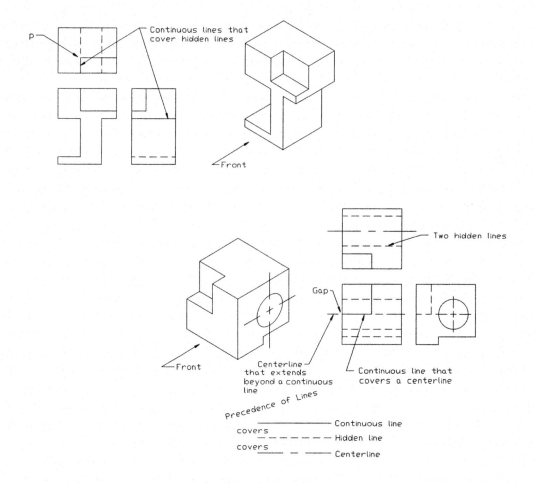

Slanted Surfaces

Slanted surfaces are surfaces drawn at an angle to each other. Figure 4-17 shows an object that contains two slanted surfaces. Surface **ABCD** appears as a rectangle in both the top and front views. Neither rectangle represents the true shape of the surface. Each is smaller than the actual surface. Also, none of the views shows enough of the object to enable the viewer to accurately define the shape of the object. The views must be used together for a correct understanding of the object's shape.

Figure 4-17

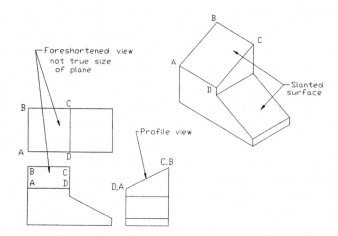

Figures 4-18 and 4-19 show objects that include slanted surfaces. Projection lines have been included to emphasize the importance of correct view location. Information is projected between the front and top views using vertical lines and between the front and side views using horizontal lines.

Figure 4-18

Figure 4-19

Compound Lines

A *compound line* is formed when two slanted surfaces intersect. Figure 4-20 shows an object that includes a compound line.

Figure 4-20

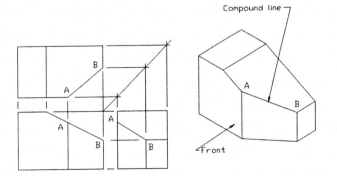

Oblique Surfaces

An *oblique surface* is a surface that is slanted in two different directions. Figures 4-21 and 4-22 show objects that include oblique surfaces.

Figure 4-21

Figure 4-22

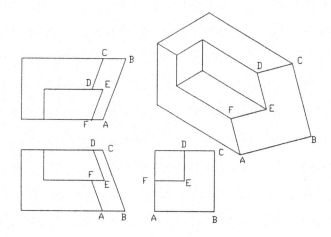

Rounded Surfaces

Figure 4-23 shows an object with two rounded surfaces. Note that as with slanted surfaces, an individual view is insufficient to define the shape of a surface. More than one view is needed to accurately define the surface's shape.

Figure 4-23

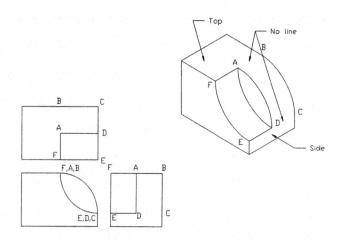

Convention calls for a smooth transition between rounded and flat surfaces; that is, no lines are drawn to indicate the tangency. SolidWorks includes a line to indicate tangencies between surfaces in the isometric drawings created using the multiview options but does not include them in the orthographic views. Tangency lines are also not included when models are rendered.

Figure 4-24 shows the drawing conventions for including lines for rounded surfaces. If a surface includes no vertical portions or no tangency, no line is included.

Figure 4-25 shows an object that includes two tangencies. Each is represented by a line. Note in Figure 4-25 that SolidWorks will add tangency lines to the 3D model. These lines will not appear in the orthographic views.

Figure 4-24

Figure 4-25

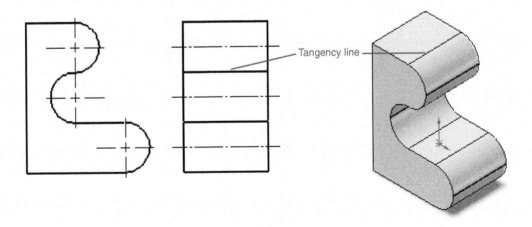

Figure 4-26 shows two objects with similar configurations; however, the boxlike portion of the lower object blends into the rounded portion exactly at its widest point, so no line is required.

Figure 4-26

4-4 Drawing Orthographic Views

SolidWorks creates orthographic views using the drawing tools found in the **New SolidWorks Document** dialog box. See Figure 4-27.

Figure 4-27

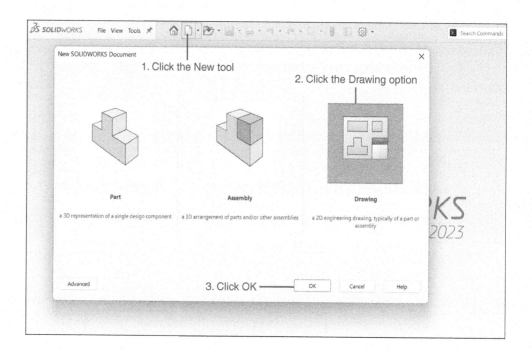

1 Start a new document by clicking the **New** tool.

2 Click the **Drawing** icon in the **New SolidWorks Document** dialog box.

3 Click **OK**.

The **Sheet Format/Size** dialog box will appear. See Figure 4-28. Keep the default format **A (ANSI) Landscape**.

Figure 4-28

TIP

Drawing sheets—that is, the paper drawings are printed on—are manufactured in standard sizes. For example, in the English unit system an A-size drawing sheet is 8.5 × 11in. In the metric unit system an A4-size drawing sheet is 210 × 297mm.

A listing of standard sheet sizes is shown in Figure 4-28.

---

4 Click **OK**.

A drawing template will appear. See Figure 4-29. The template includes a title block, a release block, a tolerance block, and two other blocks. The template format can be customized, but in this example the default template will be used. The title block will be explained in the next section.

Figure 4-29

⑤ Click the **Options** tool.

⑥ Select the **Options** option.

See Figure 4-30.

Figure 4-30

The **Document Properties** dialog box will appear. See Figure 4-31.

⑦ Click the **Document Properties** tab and ensure the **Overall drafting standard** field is set to **ANSI**.

Figure 4-31

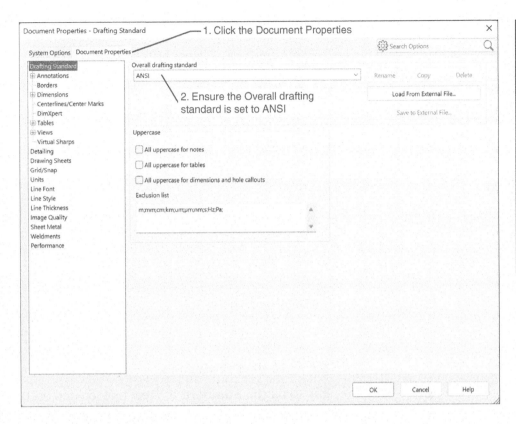

8 Click **OK.**

Third-angle projection is the format preferred by U.S. companies in compliance with ANSI (American National Standards Institute) standards. First-angle projection is used by countries that are in compliance with ISO (International Organization for Standardization). Figure 4-32 shows an L-bracket drawn in both first- and third-angle projection. Compare the differences in the projected views.

Figure 4-32 also shows a dimensioned isometric drawing of the L-bracket. The bracket was drawn in Section 3-3. If you have not previously drawn the bracket, do so now and save it as **L-bracket**.

Figure 4-32

Third-angle projection
(in compliance with
ANSI conventions)

First-angle projection
(in compliance with
ISO conventions)

Figure 4-32
(*Continued*)

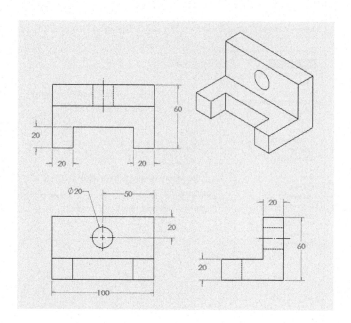

9 Click the **Drawing** tab.

10 Click the **Standard 3 View** tool located on the **Drawing** tab.

See Figure 4-33. The **Standard 3 View PropertyManager** will appear on the left side of the screen.

Figure 4-33

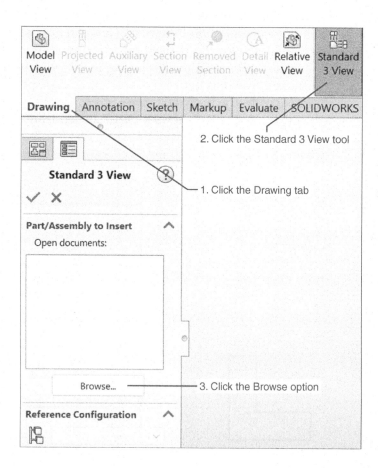

11 Click the **Browse** button.

The **Open** box will appear. See Figure 4-34.

Figure 4-34

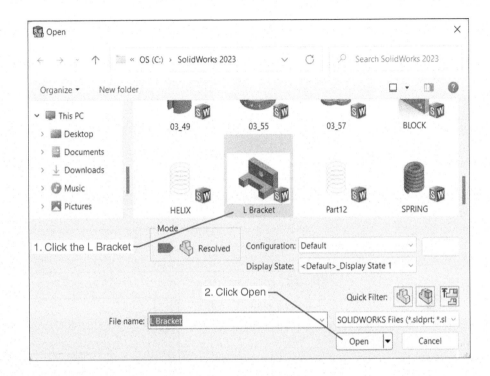

12 Click the **L Bracket** icon and click **Open**.

Three orthographic views will appear on the screen. They include no hidden lines. The hidden lines must be added. See Figure 4-35.

13 Click the top orthographic view and select the **Hidden Lines Visible** option in the **Display Style** box of the **Drawing View PropertyManager**.

The hidden lines will appear in the top view.

14 Click the right-side view, then click the **Hidden Lines Visible** option to add hidden lines to the right-side view.

Figure 4-35

Standard 3 View

No hidden lines in the top and side views

Drawing View6

Display Style
☐ Use parent style
⦿ High quality
○ Draft quality
☑ See through transparent components

Scale
⦿ Use parent scale
○ Use sheet scale
○ Use custom scale

2

B

1. Click the top view

3. Click the check mark

2. Click the Hidden Lines Visible option

Figure 4-35
(*Continued*)

Add hidden lines to both the top and side views

Notice in the top and right-side views that there are no centerlines for the hole. Centerlines are added using the **Centerline** option found on the **Annotation** tab. See Figure 4-36. The circular view of the hole will automatically generate a set of perpendicular centerlines.

Figure 4-36

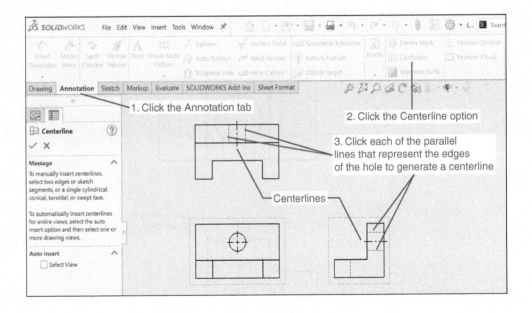

Note the difference between center marks and centerline tools.

15 Click the **Annotation** tab and select the **Centerline** option.

16 Click each of the two parallel lines in the top and side views that define the hole.

The centerlines will appear. See Figure 4-37.

Figure 4-37

Figure 4-38 shows the orthographic views of another object. The dimensions for the object are given in Figure P4-23 in the Chapter Projects section at the end of this chapter. Note the hidden lines in the side view that represent the Ø30 hole. The right vertical line is continuously straight, whereas the left vertical line has a step. Why?

Figure 4-38

Why don't the lines align?

Moving Orthographic Views

Figure 4-39 shows the orthographic views of the L-bracket generated for Figure 4-37. The views can be moved closer together or farther apart.

Figure 4-39

Click the boundary and move the view

Symbol for move

Drawing View2

Click the boundary and move the view

Views are now closer together

1 Move the cursor into the area of the top view.

An orange boundary line will appear.

2 Click and hold one of the boundary lines.

3 Drag the view to a new location.

Creating Other Views

The **Standard 3 View** tool will generate front, top, and right-side orthographic views of an object. These views are considered the standard three views. Other orthographic views and isometric views can be generated.

1 Click the **Projected View** tool.

The **Projected View** tool is one of the **Drawing** tab tools.

2 Click the front view and move the cursor to the left of the front view, creating a new orthographic view.

In this example a left-side view was created. Add hidden lines and centerlines as needed.

3 Click the left view in its new location.

4 Press the **<Esc>** key or click the green **OK** check mark.

See Figure 4-40.

5 Use the **Centerline** tool to add a centerline to the hole in the left-side view.

6 Click the **Projected View** tool and click the front view again.

7 Move the cursor to the right and upward.

An isometric view will appear.

8 Click the isometric view in its new location.

9 Press the **<Esc>** key or click the green **OK** check mark.

Left-side view

Isometric view

Click the front view and move the cursor
to the left, projecting a left-side view

Click the front view and move to the right
and upward to create an isometric view

Figure 4-40

4-5 Section Views

Some objects have internal surfaces that are not directly visible in normal orthographic views. *Section views* are used to expose these surfaces. Section views do not include hidden lines.

Any material cut when a section view is defined is hatched using section lines. There are many different styles of hatching, but the general style is evenly spaced 45° lines. This style is defined as ANSI 31 and will be applied automatically by SolidWorks.

Figure 4-41 shows a three-dimensional view of an object. The object is cut by a cutting plane. *Cutting planes* are used to define the location of the section view. Material to one side of the cutting plane is removed, exposing the section view.

Figure 4-42 shows the same object presented in Figure 4-41 using two orthographic views and a section view. The cutting plane is represented by a cutting plane line. The cutting plane line is defined as A-A, and the section view is defined as view A-A.

Figure 4-41

Figure 4-42

All surfaces directly visible must be shown in a section view. In Figure 4-43 the back portion of the object is not affected by the section view and is directly visible from the cutting plane. The section view must include these surfaces. Note how the rectangular section blocks part of the large hole. No hidden lines are used on section views.

Figure 4-43

4-6 Drawing a Section View

This section will show how to draw a section view of an existing model. In this example, the model presented as P4-22 in the Chapter Projects was used to demonstrate the concepts.

1 Start a new drawing using the **Drawing** format.

See the previous section on how to create orthographic views using SolidWorks. Select the **A (ANSI) Landscape** format and select the **ANSI standards**.

> **NOTE**
>
> See Figures 4-29 to 4-32 for an explanation of how to specify the third-angle format.

2 Click the **Model View** tool on the **Drawing** tab.

> **TIP**
>
> The **Model View** tool is similar to the **Standard 3 View** tool but creates only one orthographic view rather than three views.

3 In the **Part/Assembly to Insert** box, click **Browse**.

See Figure 4-44. The **Open** box will appear. See Figure 4-45.

Figure 4-44

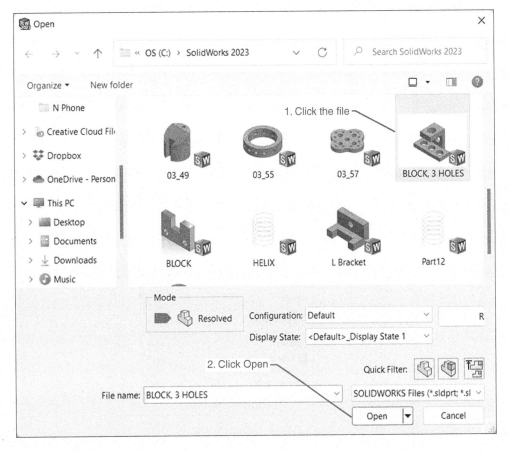

Figure 4-45

---

4. Click the model to be used to draw orthographic views, and click **Open**.

In this example the model is called **BLOCK, 3 HOLES**. The dimensions for BLOCK, 3 HOLES can be found in Figure P4-22 in the Chapter Projects section at the end of this chapter.

A rectangular outline will appear defining the boundaries of the orthographic view. By default, this will be a front view. In this example we want a top view.

5. Click the **Top view** tool.

See Figure 4-46.

6. Locate the top orthographic view on the drawing screen, click the mouse, and then click the check mark.

7. Add a centerline to the Ø24 hole.

See Figure 4-47.

8. Click the **Drawing** tab and click the **Section View** tool.

The orthographic view will be outlined by a dotted line.

Figure 4-46

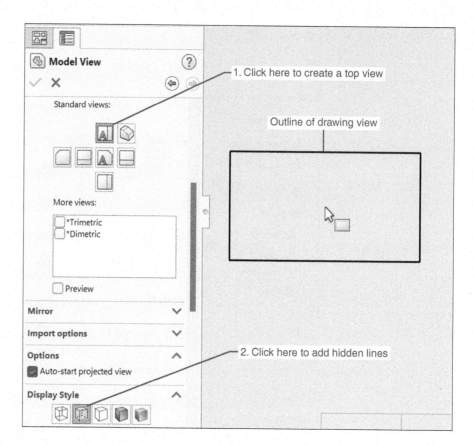

1. Click here to create a top view

Outline of drawing view

2. Click here to add hidden lines

Figure 4-47

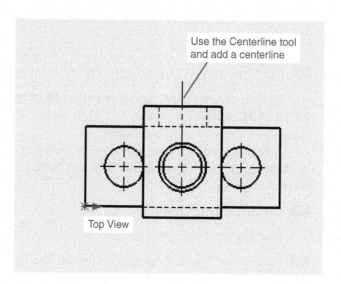

Use the Centerline tool and add a centerline

Top View

NOTE

If more than one view was present on the screen, you would first have to select which view to use to create the section view.

9 Select a horizontal cutting plane line.

10 Define the location of the cutting plane line by moving the cursor to the approximate midpoint of the left vertical line of the orthographic view.

Use the cursor to align the cutting plane line with the centerpoint of the holes.

11 Click the green **OK** check mark.

12 Move the cursor downward.

The section view will appear and move with the cursor. See Figure 4-48.

Figure 4-48

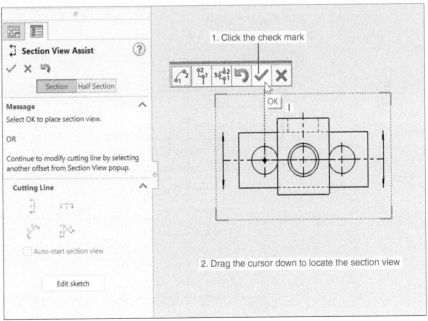

13 Select an appropriate location and click the mouse.

14 Click the **Flip direction** box if necessary.

See Figure 4-49.

15 Add centerlines.

16 Click the green **OK** check mark.

Figure 4-49

Figure 4-50

More than one section view may be taken from the same model. See Figure 4-50.

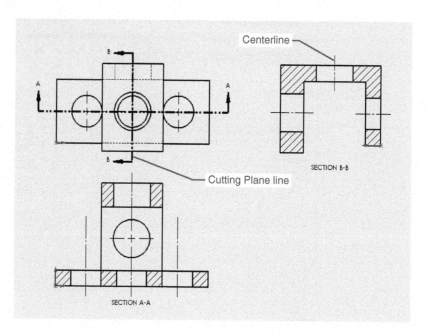

NOTE

Section views are always located behind the arrows; that is, the arrows point toward the section view. Think of the arrows as your eyes looking at the section view.

The section views shown in Figure 4-50 use a hatching pattern made from evenly spaced 45° lines. This is the most commonly used hatch pattern for section views and is designated as ANSI 31 in the ANSI hatch patterns. SolidWorks can also draw section views using one of five different styles. See Figure 4-51.

Figure 4-51

Changing the Style of a Section View

1 Move the cursor into the area of the section view and right-click the mouse.

A listing of tools will appear, and the **Display Style** box will appear.

2 Click the mouse again in the section view area to remove the list of tools.

3 Click one of the boxes in the **Display Style** box.

Figure 4-52 shows two of the styles available: **Shaded with Edges**, and **Shaded**. The hidden lines removed style is used for all other illustrations in this chapter.

Figure 4-52

4-7 Aligned Section Views

Aligned section views are most often used on circular objects and use an angled cutting plane line to include more features in the section view. Note in Figure 4-53 how section view A-A was created by rotating the cutting plane into a vertical position before projecting the section view.

Figure 4-53 shows an aligned section view created using SolidWorks. The aligned section view was created as follows.

1 Start a new **Drawing** and open the model for the aligned section view.

Figure 4-53

SECTION A-A

The model was drawn using the dimensions given in Figure 4-53.

2 Access the **Section View** tool.

3 Click the **Aligned Section View** option in the **Cutting Line** box.

See Figure 4-54.

Figure 4-54

Chapter 4

The object

4 Click the object's centerpoint.

5 Click the centerpoint of two Ø10 holes as shown.

6 Click the green **OK** check mark.

7 Move the cursor away from the object.

The aligned section will appear as the cursor is moved.

8 Add centerlines; click the green **OK** check mark.

4-8 Broken Views

It is often convenient to break long continuous shapes so that they take up less drawing space. Figure 4-55 shows a long L-bracket that has a continuous shape; that is, its shape is constant throughout its length.

Figure 4-55

Creating a Broken View

1 Draw a model of the long L-bracket using the dimensions shown in Figure 4-55. Save the model.

2 Start a new **Drawing** and insert the long L-bracket as a **Front** view.

3 Click the **Drawing** tab, and click the **Break View** tool.

See Figure 4-56.

4 Set the **Gap size** for **0.25in.** and select the **Zig Zag Cut** style.

Figure 4-56

Figure 4-56
(Continued)

4. Locate a break line   5. Locate a second break line

The finished broken-out section view

5 Move the cursor onto the long L-bracket and click a location for the first break line.

6 Click a location for the second break line.

The area between the break lines will be removed.

7 Click the green **OK** check mark.

If the break is not satisfactory, undo the break and insert a new one.

4-9 Detail Views

A *detail view* is used to clarify specific areas of a drawing. Usually, an area is enlarged so that small details are easier to see.

Drawing a Detail View

1 Create a **Part** document for the model shown in Figure P4-23 in the Chapter Projects section at the end of this chapter. Save the model.

2 Start a new **Drawing**, and create a front section view and a top orthographic view. Use third-angle projection.

3 Click the **Detail View** tool located on the **Drawing** tab.

See Figure 4-57.

4 Locate the centerpoint for a circle that will be used to define the area for the detail view by clicking a point.

In this example a point down and to the right of center was selected.

5 Move the cursor away from the point.

A detail view will appear.

6 When the circle is big enough to enclose all the area you wish to display in the detail view, click the mouse.

7 Move the cursor away from the views.

8 Select a location for the detail view and click the mouse.

9 Click the **Full outline** check box.

The scale of the detail view can be changed by changing the values in the **Scale** box in the **PropertyManager**. The callout letters are changed using the **Detail Circle** box.

Figure 4-57

4-10 Auxiliary Views

Auxiliary views are orthographic views used to present true-shaped views of a slanted surface. In Figure 4-58 neither the front nor the side view shows a true shape of the slanted surface. A top view would show a foreshortened view. Only a view taken 90° to the surface will show its true shape.

Figure 4-58

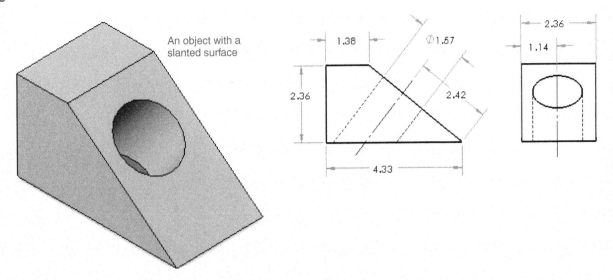

An object with a
slanted surface

Drawing an Auxiliary View

1 Draw the model with a slanted surface shown in Figure 4-58.

2 Start a new **Drawing** and create orthographic views of the model.

In this example a front and a right-side view were drawn. See
Figure 4-59.

Figure 4-59

Figure 4-59
(*Continued*)

3 Click the **Drawing** tab, then click the **Auxiliary View** tool.

4 Click the slanted edge line in the front view.

5 Move the cursor away from the slanted edge line.

6 Click the **Arrow** box in the **PropertyManager** box.

Because there is only one auxiliary view and its origin is obvious, no defining cutting plane line is needed.

7 Select a location for the auxiliary view and click the mouse.

8 If needed, adjust the font size for the view callout.

In this example the horizontal/vertical center mark for the hole in the auxiliary view was hidden and replaced with an aligned center mark.

Figures 4-60 and 4-61 show additional examples of auxiliary views.

Figure 4-60

VIEW A

Figure 4-61

VIEW A

4-11 First-Angle Projection

SolidWorks can be used to create either first-angle or third-angle projections. In this section, first-angle projection will be used to create orthographic views in compliance with ISO standards.

Creating Three Orthographic Views Using First-Angle Projection

Figure 4-62 shows an L-bracket that was used in the beginning of the chapter to demonstrate third-angle and ANSI drawing standards. The L-bracket will now be used to create orthographic views using first-angle projection.

Figure 4-62

A trimetric view

Create three orthographic views using first-angle
projections in compliance with ISO standards

1 Create a new **Drawing**, using a C sheet size.

> **NOTE**
> The icon for the drawing tools shows three orthographic views set in the first-angle
> projection.

2 Click the **Settings** heading.

3 Click the **Document Properties** tab and change the **Overall
drafting standard** field to **ISO**; then click **OK**. See Figure 4-63.

Figure 4-63

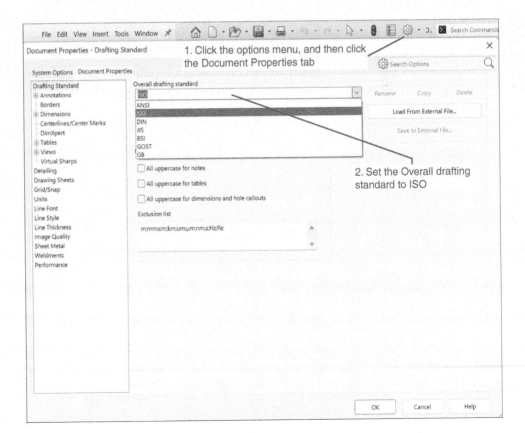

4 Click the **Model View** tool on the **Drawing** tab and create a front view of the L-bracket. Click the **Hidden Lines Visible** option. See Figure 4-64.

Figure 4-64

5 Use the **Project View** tool and create a left and top orthographic view around the front view. See Figure 4-65.

6 Drag the left view to the right side and the top view to a location directly below the front view. See Figure 4-66.

Figure 4-65

Figure 4-66

The views are now in the first-angle projections.

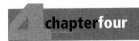

Chapter Projects

Draw a front, top, and right-side orthographic view of each of the objects in Figures P4-1 through P4-94. Do not include dimensions.

Figure P4-1
INCHES

Figure P4-2
MILLIMETERS

Figure P4-3
MILLIMETERS

Figure P4-4
INCHES

Figure P4-5
MILLIMETERS

Figure P4-6
MILLIMETERS

Figure P4-7
MILLIMETERS

Figure P4-8
MILLIMETERS

Figure P4-9
INCHES

Figure P4-10
MILLIMETERS

Figure P4-11
MILLIMETERS

Figure P4-12
INCHES

Figure P4-13
MILLIMETERS

Figure P4-14
MILLIMETERS

Figure P4-16
MILLIMETERS

Figure P4-15
MILLIMETERS

Figure P4-17
MILLIMETERS

Figure P4-18
MILLIMETERS

Figure P4-19
MILLIMETERS

Figure P4-20
MILLIMETERS

Figure P4-21
INCHES

Figure P4-22
MILLIMETERS

Figure P4-23
MILLIMETERS

Figure P4-24
INCHES

Figure P4-25
MILLIMETERS

CYLINDRICAL KEY

20
10 DEEP
Ø50
10
20
20
70
Ø80

Figure P4-26
MILLIMETERS

15
18
30
45°
50
18
A
Ø 20–THRU
PERPENDICULAR TO A
40
60
22

Figure P4-27
MILLIMETERS

30
15
Ø 16
Ø 13
R 15
12 - 2 Places
35
43
13

Figure P4-28
MILLIMETERS

15
25
Ø 14   2 HOLES
15
12
22° - BOTH
SLANTED SURFACES
27
60
30
38
100
7

Figure P4-29
MILLIMETERS

40
15
50
R13 – 4 Corners
40
10
R13 – Both Sides
25
R8

Figure P4-30
MILLIMETERS

Ø14
18
15 BOTH SIDES
60
25
30
15
35
20
25
20
10
12
8
30
55

Figure P4-31
INCHES

Figure P4-32
MILLIMETERS

Figure P4-33
INCHES

Figure P4-34
MILLIMETERS

Figure P4-35
MILLIMETERS

Figure P4-36
INCHES

Figure P4-37
MILLIMETERS

Figure P4-38
MILLIMETERS

Figure P4-39
MILLIMETERS

Figure P4-40
MILLIMETERS

Figure P4-41
INCHES

Figure P4-42
INCHES

Figure P4-43
MILLIMETERS

Figure P4-44
MILLIMETERS

Figure P4-45
MILLIMETERS

NOTE: THE SLOT
IS 15 LONG

Figure P4-46
MILLIMETERS

Figure P4-47
INCHES

Figure P4-48
INCHES

Figure P4-49
MILLIMETERS

Figure P4-50
INCHES

Figure P4-51
INCHES

Figure P4-52
MILLIMETERS

Figure P4-53
INCHES

Figure P4-54
MILLIMETERS

Figure P4-55
MILLIMETERS

Figure P4-56
MILLIMETERS

Figure P4-57
MILLIMETERS

Figure P4-58
MILLIMETERS

ALL FILLETS AND
ROUNDS = R5

Figure P4-59
MILLIMETERS

Figure P4-60
INCHES

Figure P4-61
MILLIMETERS

ALL FILLETS AND ROUNDS = R3

Figure P4-62
MILLIMETERS

Figure P4-63
MILLIMETERS

Figure P4-64
MILLIMETERS

Figure P4-65
MILLIMETERS

Figure P4-66
MILLIMETERS

Figure P4-67
MILLIMETERS

Figure P4-68
MILLIMETERS

Figure P4-69
MILLIMETERS

Figure P4-70
MILLIMETERS

Figure P4-71
MILLIMETERS

Figure P4-72
MILLIMETERS

Figure P4-73
MILLIMETERS

Figure P4-74
INCHES

Figure P4-75
INCHES

Figure P4-76
MILLIMETERS

Figure P4-77
MILLIMETERS

NOTE: ALL FILLET AND ROUNDS: R3

Figure P4-78
MILLIMETERS

MATL 5 THK

ALL INSIDE BEND RAD 5

Figure P4-79
MILLIMETERS

ALL FILLETS AND ROUNDS=R5
MATL 5 THK

Figure P4-80
MILLIMETERS

MATL 5 THK

Figure P4-81
MILLIMETERS

ALL FILLETS AND ROUNDS = R3
MATL 5 THK

Figure P4-82
MILLIMETERS

50
10
20
15
Ø10 – 2 PLACES
28
15
45
R30 – 2 PLACES
15
25
12
20
25
15
70
ALL FILLETS AND ROUNDS = R3
MATL 12 THK
R5 – 2 PLACES

Figure P4-83
MILLIMETERS

40
12
20
16
10
53
30°
40
13
10
50
20
30°
15
20
Ø10-2 HOLES
10

Figure P4-84
INCHES

Ø .375 x .500 DEEP
4 HOLES
1.75
2.25
.75
.50
1.00
.88
.63
1.63
1.13
1.25
.50
30°
.88
60°
Ø .750 x .25 DEEP
2 HOLES - BOTH
BOTTOM DRILLED
.75
.25
2.00
1.75

Figure P4-85
MILLIMETERS

45
60
15°
15
30°
30
18
85
21
15
18
12
12

Figure P4-86
MILLIMETERS

Ø – 2 HOLES
240°
R 12
8
30
30
20
20
Ø30
75
BOTH
SIDES
35
35
10
25 – 2 PLACES

Figure P4-87
INCHES

.75
2.50
1.00
2.50
1.50
.75
.75
.25 DIA
3.00
.50
2.00
.19 DIA
60°
.31

ALL FILLETS AND ROUNDS = R5

Figure P4-92
MILLIMETERS

ALL FILLETS AND ROUNDS = R5

Figure P4-93
MILLIMETERS

For Figures P4-95 through P4-100:

A. Sketch the given orthographic views, and add the top view so that the final sketch includes a front, top, and right-side view.

B. Prepare a three-dimensional sketch of the object.

Figure P4-95

Figure P4-96

Figure P4-97

Figure P4-98

Figure P4-99

For Figures P4-101 through P4-128:

A. Redraw the given views, and draw the third view.

B. Prepare a three-dimensional sketch of the object.

Figure P4-101
INCHES

Figure P4-102
INCHES

Figure P4-103
INCHES

Figure P4-104
INCHES

Figure P4-105
INCHES

Figure P4-106
INCHES

Figure P4-107
INCHES

Figure P4-108
INCHES

Figure P4-109
INCHES

All fillets and rounds = $\frac{1}{8}$ R

Figure P4-110
INCHES

Figure P4-111
INCHES

Figure P4-112
INCHES

All fillets and rounds = $\frac{1}{8}$R

Figures P4-113 through P4-128 are drawn with grid backgrounds.
The grid may be either 0.50 × 0.50 inches or 10 × 10 millimeters.

Figure P4-114

Figure P4-113

Figure P4-115

Figure P4-116

Figure P4-117

Figure P4-118

Figure P4-119

Figure P4-120

Figure P4-121

Figure P4-122

Figure P4-123

Figure P4-124

Figure P4-125

Figure P4-126

Draw the complete front, top, and side views of the two intersecting objects given in Figures P4-129 through P4-134 on the basis of the given complete and partially complete orthographic views.

Figure P4-129
MILLIMETERS

Figure P4-130
MILLIMETERS

Figure P4-131
INCHES

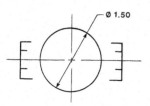

Ø 1.50

|← 1.25 →|← 2.50 →|

.75 ACROSS
THE FLATS

2.00

1.00

Figure P4-132
INCHES

50

25

60°
3 ANGLES

15   75

50   50

17   26

30   15°

40

Figure P4-133
MILLIMETERS

30°   25 SQ

20

10

32   64

50   15

22

14

Figure P4-134
MILLIMETERS

Ø 50

43   86

15°

31

EQUILATERAL TRIANGLE
30 PER SIDE

62

Draw the front, top, and side orthographic views of the objects given in Figures P4-135 through P4-138 on the basis of the partially complete isometric drawings.

Figure P4-136
MILLIMETERS

Figure P4-135
MILLIMETERS

Figure P4-138
INCHES (SCALE: 5=1)

Figure P4-137
INCHES

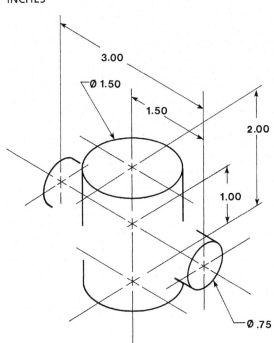

Draw Figures P4-139 through P4-141 as 3D models using the given dimensions.

Figure P4-139

Figure P4-140

Figures P4-142 through P4-149 are presented using first-angle projection per ISO standards.

Draw the objects as

A.   3D models.

B.   Orthographic views using third-angle projections per ANSI standards.

Figure P4-142

Figure P4-143

Figure P4-144

Figure P4-145

Figure P4-146

Figure P4-147A

Figure P4-147B

Figure P4-148A

NOTE: SEE BU-120 CASTING
FOR ADDITIONAL DIMENSIONS

Ø5.00

Ø9.00

Ø6

6.0

6.0

6.0

Figure P4-148B

BU-120 Casting

Ø24.0   ALL CHAMFERS R=0.5

Ø16.0

32.0

32.0

R8.0

TAPER: Ø8.0 to Ø14.0
OVER 64

Figure P4-149A   Casting

Figure P4-149B

Figure P4-149C

DETAIL A
SCALE 2 : 1

Figure P4-149D

Note: The Symbol ▼ indicates depth

5 chapterfive
Assemblies

CHAPTER OBJECTIVES

- Create assembly drawings
- Create exploded assembly drawings
- Create a parts list
- Animate an assembly
- Edit a title block

5-1 Introduction

This chapter introduces the **Assembly** tools. These tools are used to create **Assembly** documents. Assemblies can be exploded to form isometric assembly drawings that when labeled and accompanied by a parts list become working drawings. Assemblies can also be animated.

5-2 Starting an Assembly

Figure 5-1 shows a Test Block. The overall dimensions for the block are 80 × 80 × 80 mm. The cutout is 40 × 40 × 80 mm. The Test Block will be used to help introduce the **Assembly** tools. Draw the block and save it as **BLOCK, TEST**. Draw the Test Block so that one of its corners is on the origin. If the origin icon does not appear on your drawing screen, click the **View** tab, click **Hide/Show**, and click the **Origins** option. See Figure 5-2.

Figure 5-1

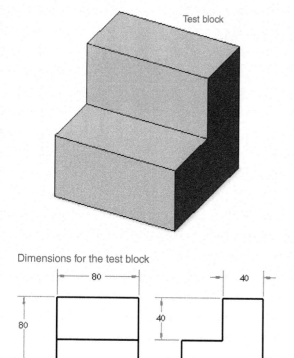

Test block

Dimensions for the test block

Figure 5-2

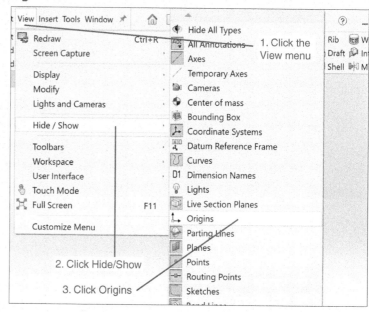

See Figure 5-3.

1 Click **New**.

2 Select the **Assembly** format.

3 Click **OK**.

The **Begin Assembly PropertyManager** will appear. See Figure 5-4.

4 Click the **Browse** button if **BLOCK, TEST** does not show automatically.

Figure 5-3

New SOLIDWORKS Document

1. Click here to start an assembly

Part

a 3D representation of a single design component

Assembly

a 3D arrangement of parts and/or other assemblies

Drawing

a 2D engineering drawing, typically of a part or assembly

2. Click OK

Advanced   OK   Cancel   Help

Figure 5-4

The **Open** dialog box will appear. See Figure 5-5.

5 Click **BLOCK, TEST,** then click **Open**.

The Test Block will appear on the screen. See Figure 5-6.

Figure 5-5

Figure 5-6

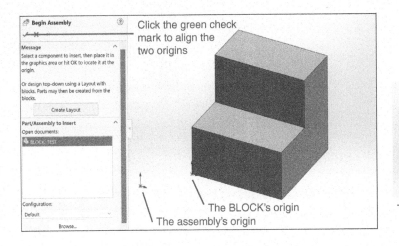

The BLOCK's origin
The assembly's origin
Click the green check mark to align the two origins

The Assembly drawing's origin and the BLOCK's origin aligned

> **NOTE**
> It is good practice to anchor the assembly to the assembly's origin.

Align the origin of the Test Block with the assembly's origin.

6 When the Test Block appears on the screen, click the green **OK** check mark in the upper-left corner of the screen.

The **Part** origin and the **Assembly** origin will align.

7 Click the **Insert Components** tool, click the **Browse** button, select the **BLOCK, TEST**, and insert a second block by clicking in the model space in a location that does not overlap the first block.

See Figure 5-7. The first block inserted is fixed in place. In any assembly drawing the first component will automatically be fixed in place. Note the **(f)** notation to the left of **BLOCK, TEST<1>** in Figure 5-7. As the assembly is created, components will move to the fixed first component.

TIP

To remove the fixed condition, locate the cursor on the **(f) BLOCK, TEST<1>** callout, right-click the mouse, and click the **Float** option. To return the block to the fixed condition or to fix another component, right-click the component name callout and select the **Fix** option.

Figure 5-7

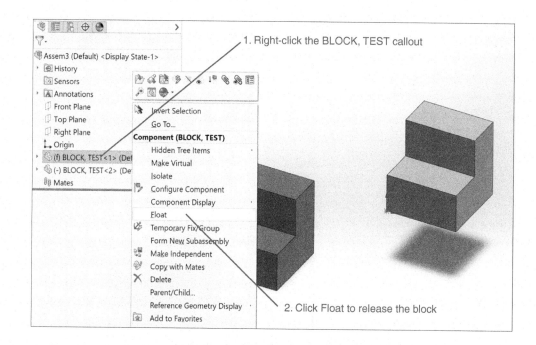

5-3 Move Component

See Figure 5-8.

1 Click the **Move Component** tool on the **Assembly** tab.

2 Click the second block inserted and hold down the left mouse button.

3 While holding down the left mouse button, move the block around the screen by moving the mouse.

4 Release the button and click the green **OK** check mark.

Figure 5-8

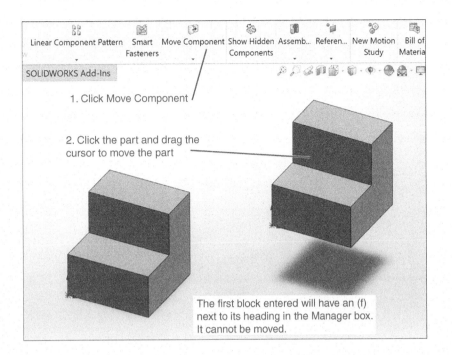

NOTE

If you try to apply the **Move** tool to the fixed block, the block will not move. **Float** must be applied before the block can be moved.

The entire assembly can be moved by pressing and holding down the **<Ctrl>** key and holding down the mouse wheel while moving the cursor. The mouse wheel can be used to zoom the assembly.

5-4 Rotate Component

See Figure 5-9.

1 Click the **Rotate Component** tool.

The **Rotate Component** tool is a flyout from the **Move Component** tool.

2 Click the second block inserted and hold down the left mouse button.

3 While holding down the left mouse button, rotate the block around the screen by moving the mouse.

4 Release the button and click the green **OK** check mark.

5 Use the **Undo** tool to return the block to its original position.

Figure 5-9

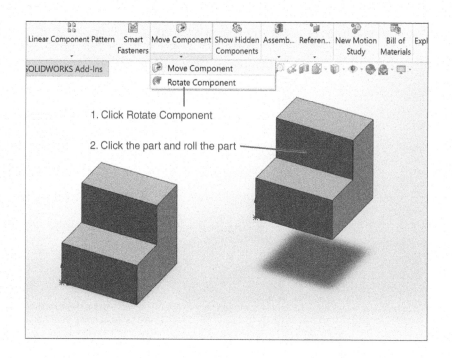

5-5 Mouse Gestures for Assemblies

The **Mouse Gestures** tools can be applied to assemblies. Mouse Gestures were introduced in Section 2-2 of Chapter 2. To access the **Mouse Gestures** tools, click the **Tools** menu and select the **Customize** option. Click the **Mouse Gestures** tab. See Figure 5-10.

Figure 5-10

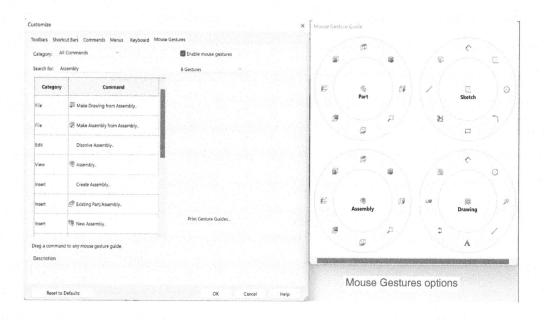

Mouse Gestures options

Scroll down the listings, watching the **Command** column for **Assembly** commands. The default settings for **Assembly** drawings are the **Front**, **Back**, **Left**, **Right**, **Top**, and **Bottom** orientation tools as well as two other tools. These may be changed as preferred. Up to 12 tools may be added to the **Mouse Gestures** tool.

To access the **Mouse Gestures**, press and hold down the right mouse button. The **Mouse Gestures** wheel will show the selected settings. While still holding down the right mouse button, move the cursor onto the selected tool and release the button. The selected tool will be applied to the assembly. See Figure 5-11.

Figure 5-11

The Mouse Gestures wheel for assemblies.
The settings can be changed.

5-6 Mate

The **Mate** tool is used to align components to create assemblies. See Figure 5-12.

Creating the First Assembly Using Mates

Mate the two Test Blocks side by side.

1 Click the **Mate** tool on the **Assembly** tab.

Figure 5-12

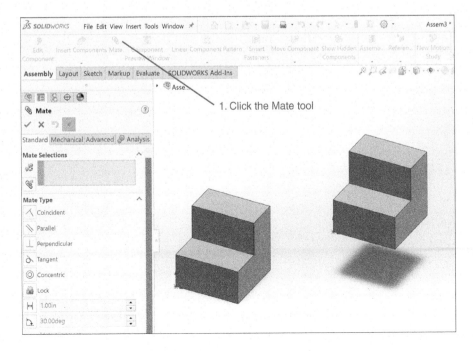

1. Click the Mate tool

See Figure 5-13. Note that the first block is listed in the **Mate Selections** box after it is selected.

2 Click the upper-right edge of the first block inserted.

3 Click the upper-left edge on the second block.

Note that the **Coincident** option became active automatically.

Figure 5-13

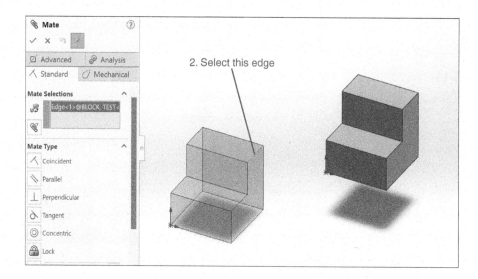

The edges will align. See Figure 5-14.

4 Click the green **OK** check mark to clear the tools.

The **Mate Selections** box should be clear.

Figure 5-14

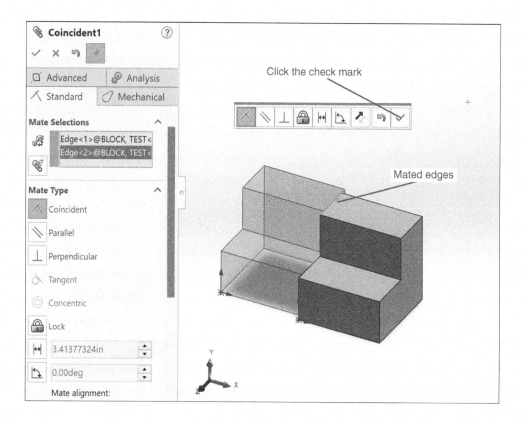

Creating a Second Assembly

Mate the two Test Blocks face to face.

1 Use the **Undo** tool and return the blocks to their original positions.

See Figure 5-15. The second Test Block must be rotated into a different position relative to the first Test Block.

Figure 5-15

Two Test Blocks

Origin

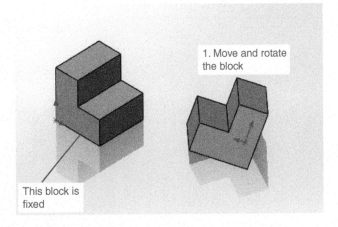

1. Move and rotate the block

This block is fixed

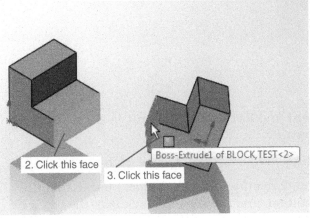

2. Click this face

3. Click this face

Boss-Extrude1 of BLOCK,TEST<2>

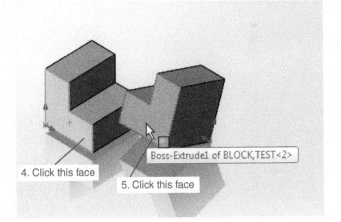

4. Click this face

5. Click this face

Boss-Extrude1 of BLOCK,TEST<2>

Figure 5-15
(*Continued*)

6. Click this edge

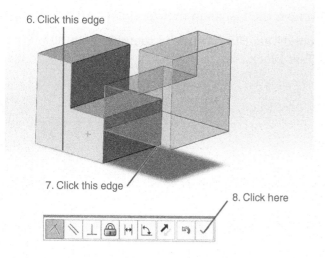

7. Click this edge

8. Click here

Edges are aligned

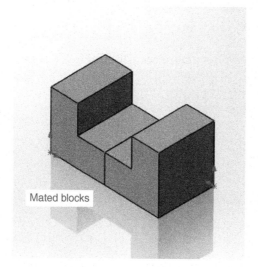

Mated blocks

2 Use the **Move Component** and **Rotate Component** tools and position the second block as shown.

3 Use the **Mate** tool and click the lower-front face of each block.

The second block will rotate relative to the first block. Recall that the first block is in the fixed condition, and the second block is in the floating condition.

4 Click the green **OK** check mark.

5 Use the **Mate** tool again and click the two faces of the Test Block as shown.

6 Click the **Add/Finish Mate** check mark on the toolbar, then click the green **OK** check mark in the **Mate PropertyManager**.

7 Use the **Mate** tool for a third time, rotate the objects as shown, and click the two edges as shown in Figure 5-16.

8 Click the green **OK** check mark.

Creating a Third Assembly

Mate the two Test Blocks to form a rectangular prism.

1 Use the **Undo** tool and return the blocks to their original positions.

2 Use the **Rotate Component** tool and position the second Test Block as shown.

3 Click the green **OK** check mark.

4 Use the **Mate** tool and click the surfaces of the blocks as shown.

Use the mouse wheel to rotate the blocks so you can click the appropriate surfaces.

5 Click the **Add/Finish Mate** check mark on the toolbar, click the green **OK** check mark in the **Mate PropertyManager**, and rotate the blocks as shown.

6 Click the front surfaces of the blocks as shown.

7 Click the **Add/Finish Mate** check mark on the toolbar, then click the green **OK** check mark in the **Mate PropertyManager**.

8 Reorient the blocks so that the bottom surfaces are visible.

9 Use the **Mate** tool and click the bottom surfaces of the blocks.

Figure 5-16 shows the finished assembly.

Figure 5-16

Figure 5-16
(*Continued*)

2. Click the surface

3. Rotate the blocks and click this surface

Boss-Extrude1 of BLOCK,TEST<2>

Surfaces are mated

4. Click this surface

5. Click this surface

7. Rotate the blocks

9. Click this surface

8. Click this surface

Isometric orientation

Surfaces are aligned

5-7 Bottom-up Assemblies

Bottom-up assemblies are assemblies that are created for existing parts; that is, the parts have already been created as models. In this example the three parts shown in Figure 5-17 have been modeled and saved.

Figure 5-17

BLOCK, BOTTOM

15   20   10   20   20   Ø15

15   60   30   40

Figure 5-17
(*Continued*)

1. Start a new document and select the **Assembly** format.

2. Click the **Browse** button, then click the **BLOCK, BOTTOM** component.

3. Click **Open**.

See Figure 5-18. The BLOCK, BOTTOM will appear on the screen.

Figure 5-18

4. Click the green **OK** check mark in the upper-left corner of the screen to align the origin of the block with the origin of the assembly.

See Figure 5-19.

Figure 5-19

3. Click the check mark to align the two origins

5. Click the **Insert Component** tool, click the **Browse** button, and select **BLOCK, TOP**.

6. Repeat the sequence and select **Ø15 POST**.

See Figure 5-20.

Figure 5-20

Add other parts

Origins for the assembly drawing and Part are coincidental

NOTE

The **BLOCK, BOTTOM** was the first part entered and is fixed in its location, as designated by the **(f)** symbol in the **PropertyManager** box.

7 Use the **Mate** tool and click the centerpoint of the edge line of the **BLOCK, BOTTOM** and the **BLOCK, TOP** as shown in Figure 5-21.

A dot will appear when the cursor is on the centerpoint of the edge. If the blocks do not align, use the **Mate** tool again to align the blocks by clicking their end surfaces.

8 Click the green **OK** check mark.

Figure 5-21

2. Click here

1. Click here

Resulting mate

9 Click the **Mate** tool and click the **Concentric** option.

See Figure 5-22.

10 Click the side of the **Ø15 POST** and the inside of the hole in the **BLOCK, TOP**.

Figure 5-22

Figure 5-22
(Continued)

NOTE

Click the surface of the components, not their edge lines. Clicking the edge lines would produce different results.

11 Click the **Add/Finish Mate** check mark on the toolbar, then click the green **OK** check mark.

12 Use the **Mate** tool and click the top surface of the **Ø15 POST** and the top surface of the **BLOCK, TOP**.

See Figure 5-23.

13 Click the **Add/Finish Mate** check mark on the toolbar, then click the green **OK** check mark.

14 Save the assembly as **Block Assembly**.

Figure 5-23

A listing of the mates can be seen by clicking the **Mates** heading in the **PropertyManager**. See Figure 5-24.

Figure 5-24

```
Block Assembly (Default) <Display State-1>
  ▶ History
    Sensors
  ▶ Annotations
    Front Plane
    Top Plane
    Right Plane
    Origin
  ▶ (f) BLOCK, BOTTOM<1> (Default) <<Default>_Display State 1>
  ▶ (-) BLOCK, TOP<1> (Default) <<Default>_Display State 1>
  ▶ (-) Ø15 POST<1> (Default) <<Default>_Display State 1>
  ▼ Mates
      Coincident1 (BLOCK, TOP<1>,BLOCK, BOTTOM<1>)
      Coincident2 (BLOCK, BOTTOM<1>,BLOCK, TOP<1>)
      Coincident3 (Ø15 POST<1>,BLOCK, TOP<1>)
      Concentric1 (BLOCK, TOP<1>,Ø15 POST<1>)
```

The origin icons can be removed from view using **View**, **Hide/Show**, **Origins**. For examples in this book the origins will be shown.

5-8 Creating an Exploded Isometric Assembly

An exploded isometric assembly shows the components of an assembly pulled apart. This makes it easier to see how the parts fit together.

1 Click the **Exploded View** tool on the **Assembly** tab.

See Figure 5-25.

2 Click the top surface of the **Ø15 POST**.

An axis system icon will appear. See Figure 5-26. The arrow in the Y-direction (the one pointing vertically) will initially be yellow.

3 Move the cursor onto the Y-direction arrow and hold down the left mouse button. The arrow will turn blue when selected.

4 Drag the **Ø15 POST** to a location above the assembly as shown.

A real-time scale will appear as you drag the **Ø15 POST**.

5 Right-click the **BLOCK, TOP** and select the **Done with step** option. Click and drag the **BLOCK, TOP** vertically to a new location between **Ø15 POST** and **BOTTOM, BLOCK**.

6 Click and move the **BOTTOM, BLOCK** vertically down if needed for more space.

Figure 5-25

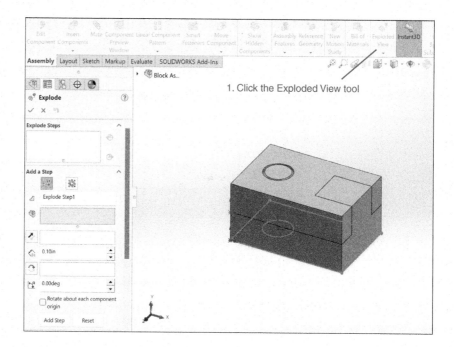

1. Click the Exploded View tool

Figure 5-26

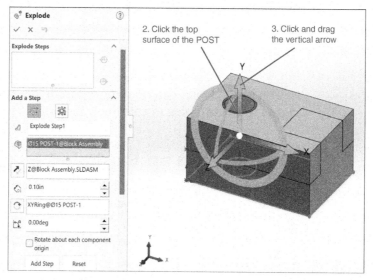

2. Click the top surface of the POST

3. Click and drag the vertical arrow

5. Place in a new location

4. Drag the POST away from the BLOCK, TOP

Figure 5-26
(*Continued*)

7. Click the Done
with step option

6. Right-click the
BLOCK, TOP

8. Click and drag the BLOCK,
TOP to a new position

An exploded isometric assembly

7 Click the green **OK** check mark.

8 Save the assembly as **Exploded Assembly**.

All three components should be listed in the **PropertyManager**.

Figure 5-26 shows the final exploded assembly.

5-9 Creating an Exploded Isometric Drawing

1 Create a new document using the **Drawing** format.

2 Select the **A-(ANSI) Landscape** sheet format.

3 Click the **Browse** button in the **Model View PropertyManager** that is open by default.

See Figure 5-27.

4 Select **Exploded Assembly**; click **Open**.

5 Set the **Orientation** for **Isometric** and the **Display Style** for **Hidden Lines Visible**.

6 Move the cursor into the drawing area.

Figure 5-27

Figure 5-27
(*Continued*)

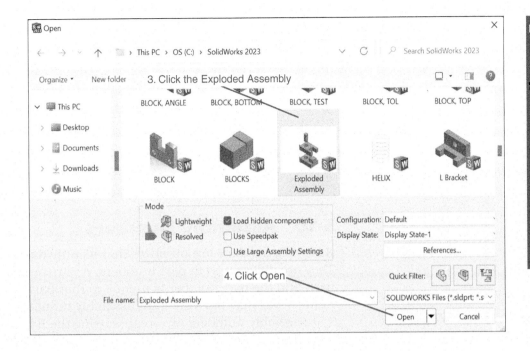

3. Click the Exploded Assembly

4. Click Open

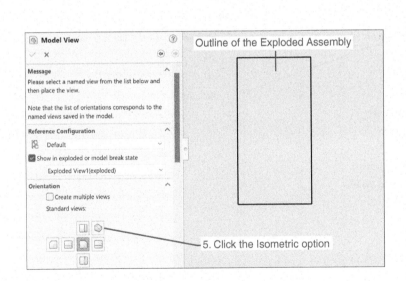

Outline of the Exploded Assembly

5. Click the Isometric option

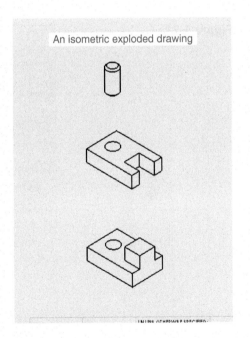

An isometric exploded drawing

A rectangular outline of the view will appear.

7 Locate the view and click the left mouse button.

Turn off the **Origins** tool if it is active.

TIP

As a general rule, hidden lines are not included on isometric drawings.

5-10 Assembly Numbers

Assembly numbers are numbers that identify a part within an assembly. They are different from part numbers. A part number identifies a specific part, and the part number is unique to that part. A part has only one part number but may have different assembly numbers in different assemblies.

Assembly numbers are created using the **Balloon** and **Auto Balloon** tools located on the **Annotation** tab. See Figure 5-28.

Figure 5-28

Figure 5-28
(*Continued*)

Auto Balloons

Click within the box

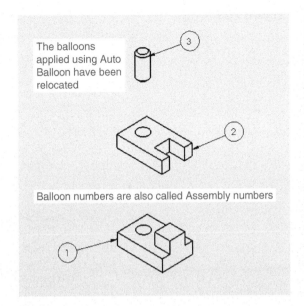

The balloons applied using Auto Balloon have been relocated

Balloon numbers are also called Assembly numbers

1 Click the **Annotation** tab.

2 Click the **Auto Balloon** tool.

3 Move the cursor into the **Block Assembly** area (a red outline will appear) and click the mouse.

The **Auto Balloon** arrangements may not always be the best presentation. The balloons may be rearranged or applied individually.

> **TIP**
>
> Balloons can be moved by first clicking them. They will change color. Click and hold either the balloon or the box that will appear on the arrow. Drag either the balloon or the arrow to a new location.

4 Use the **Undo** tool to undo the auto balloons.

5 Click the **Balloon** tool.

6 Click each part and locate the balloon.

7 Click the green **OK** check mark.

See Figure 5-29. Note that all the leader lines from the parts to the balloons are drawn at approximately the same angle. This gives the drawing a neat, organized look.

Figure 5-29

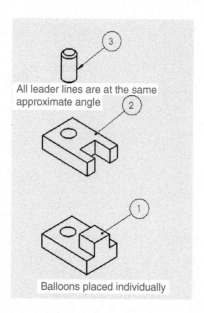

All leader lines are at the same approximate angle

Balloons placed individually

5-11 Bill of Materials (BOM or Parts List)

A *bill of materials* is a listing of all parts included in an assembly drawing. A bill of materials may also be called a *parts list*.

1 To access the **Bill of Materials** tool, click the **Annotation** tab, then the **Tables** and **Bill of Materials** tools.

See Figure 5-30.

Figure 5-30

Figure 5-30
(*Continued*)

3. Click within the box

4. Click OK and drag the BOM into the drawing screen area

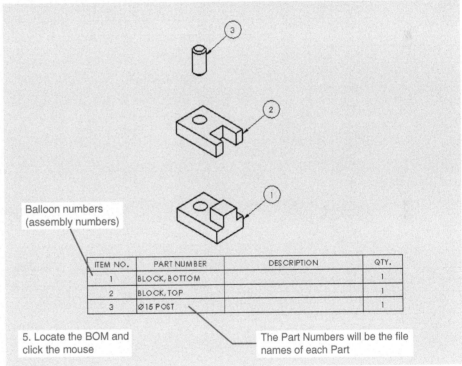

Balloon numbers
(assembly numbers)

ITEM NO.	PART NUMBER	DESCRIPTION	QTY.
1	BLOCK, BOTTOM		1
2	BLOCK, TOP		1
3	Ø15 POST		1

5. Locate the BOM and click the mouse

The Part Numbers will be the file names of each Part

2 Click the area of the **Block Assembly**.

A box will appear around the Block Assembly. Click within that box.

3 Click the green **OK** check mark.

Pull the cursor back into the drawing area. The BOM will follow. Select a location for the BOM and click the mouse.

NOTE

The information in the **PART NUMBER** column is each part's file name. These names are directly linked by SolidWorks to the original parts. They can be manually edited, but if the assembly is changed and regenerated, the original part names will appear.

Editing the BOM

1 Double-click the box directly under the heading **PART NUMBER**.

A warning dialog box will appear. See Figure 5-31.

Figure 5-31

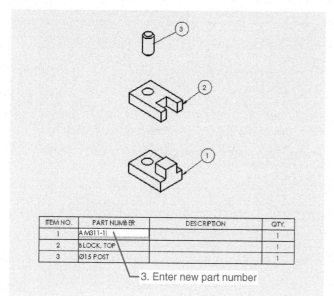

3. Enter new part number

ITEM NO.	PART NUMBER	DESCRIPTION	QTY.
1	A M311-1		1
2	A M311-2		1
3	A M311-3		1

New part numbers

2 Click the **Keep Link** box.

The **Formatting** dialog box will appear.

3 Type in a part number.

4 Click the **Left Justify** option if necessary.

5 Click the box below the one just edited and enter the part numbers.

Part numbers are different from assembly numbers (item numbers). A part number is assigned to an individual part. The part number will never change. A specific part will always have the same part number.

When a part is entered into an assembly, it receives an assembly number. The assembly number applies only to the individual assembly. The same part may also be used in a different assembly and receive a different assembly number. The original part number will remain the same.

In this example the BLOCK, BOTTOM has a part number of AM-311-1 and an assembly number of 1.

6 Click the boxes under the **DESCRIPTION** heading and enter the descriptions.

See Figure 5-32.

Figure 5-32

Adding Columns to the BOM

1 Right-click the **BLOCK, BOTTOM** box in the **DESCRIPTION** column. See Figure 5-33.

2 Click the **Insert** option, then click **Column Right**.

A new column will appear to the right of the BLOCK, BOTTOM box and a dialog box will appear above the new column.

3 Click the **Property name** box and select the **SW-Title (Title)** option.

4 Swipe and remove the **Title** entry and enter a new column heading.

In this example the heading **MATERIAL** was entered.

5 Enter the required materials for each part.

In this example a material specification of SAE 1020 Steel was added. SAE 1020 Steel is a type of mild steel.

Figure 5-33

Figure 5-33
(*Continued*)

5. Swipe and enter a new heading

New column

New Material column

Changing the Width of a Column

1 Right-click one of the cells in the new column.

See Figure 5-34.

2 Select the **Formatting** option and click **Column Width**.

The **Column Width** dialog box will appear.

3 Enter a new value.

In this example a value of **1.75in.** was entered. Figure 5-34 shows the new column width. Edit the other columns if necessary.

Figure 5-34

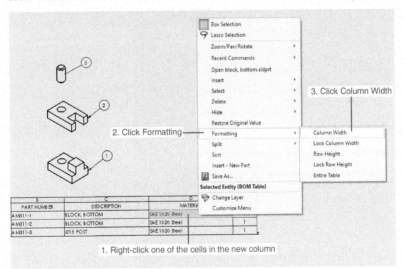

2. Click Formatting

3. Click Column Width

1. Right-click one of the cells in the new column

4. Define the width of the new column

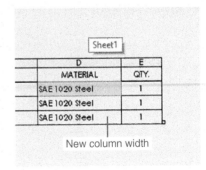

New column width

Changing the Width of Rows and Columns

The size of either rows or columns can be changed in real time by clicking and dragging the row and column lines. See Figure 5-35.

1 Click and drag the bottom horizontal line of the BOM.

2 Release the mouse button when the desired size is reached.

3 Click and drag the vertical lines to create a new format for the BOM.

Figure 5-35

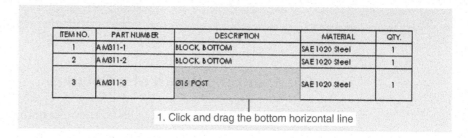

ITEM NO.	PART NUMBER	DESCRIPTION	MATERIAL	QTY.
1	A M311-1	BLOCK, BOTTOM	SAE 1020 Steel	1
2	A M311-2	BLOCK, BOTTOM	SAE 1020 Steel	1
3	A M311-3	Ø15 POST	SAE 1020 Steel	1

1. Click and drag the bottom horizontal line

D	E
MATERIAL	QTY.
SAE 1020 Steel	1
SAE 1020 Steel	1
SAE 1020 Steel	1

2. Click and drag the vertical lines

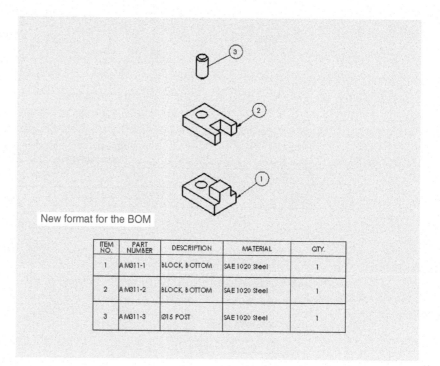

New format for the BOM

ITEM NO.	PART NUMBER	DESCRIPTION	MATERIAL	QTY.
1	A M311-1	BLOCK, BOTTOM	SAE 1020 Steel	1
2	A M311-2	BLOCK, BOTTOM	SAE 1020 Steel	1
3	A M311-3	Ø15 POST	SAE 1020 Steel	1

Changing the BOM's Font

The text font can be changed. In Figure 5-36 the font of the column heads was changed from the default SolidWorks font Century Gothic to Times New Roman and made bold.

Figure 5-36

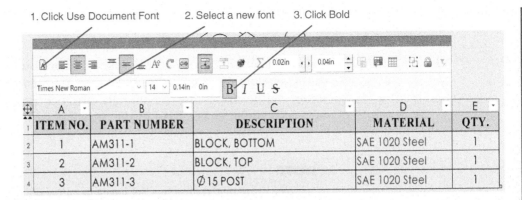

1. Click Use Document Font   2. Select a new font   3. Click Bold

ITEM NO.	PART NUMBER	DESCRIPTION	MATERIAL	QTY.
1	AM311-1	BLOCK, BOTTOM	SAE 1020 Steel	1
2	AM311-2	BLOCK, TOP	SAE 1020 Steel	1
3	AM311-3	∅15 POST	SAE 1020 Steel	1

ITEM NO.	PART NUMBER	DESCRIPTION	MATERIAL	QTY.
1	AM311-1	BLOCK, BOTTOM	SAE 1020 Steel	1
2	AM311-2	BLOCK, BOTTOM	SAE 1020 Steel	1
3	AM311-3	Ø15 POST	SAE 1020 Steel	1

New font applied to column headings

1 Swipe the text to be changed.

2 Click the **Use Document Font** tool.

3 Select a new font.

4 Click the **Bold (B)** button.

5-12 Title Blocks

A title block contains information about the drawing. See Figure 5-37. The information presented in a title block varies from company to company but usually includes the company's name, the drawing name and part number, the drawing scale, and a revision letter.

Figure 5-37

The initial title block

Revision Letters

As a drawing goes through its production cycle, changes are sometimes made. The changes may be because of errors but they may also be because of the availability of new materials, manufacturing techniques, or new customer requirements. As the changes are incorporated into the drawing, a new revision letter is added to the drawing.

NOTE

SolidWorks automatically enters the file name of the document as the part number. In the example shown in Figure 5-37 the drawing number Exploded block is not the document's part number. The title block will have to be edited and the correct part number entered.

Editing a Title Block

See Figure 5-38.

1. Right-click the mouse and select the **Edit Sheet Format** option.

2. Double-click the **Exploded block** file name.

The **Formatting** dialog box will appear.

Figure 5-38

Figure 5-38
(*Continued*)

New drawing number

3 Change the **DWG. NO.** to **BU-ME 407**.

4 Change the font size to fit the number within the DWG. NO. box.

In this example a size of **20** was selected.

5 Click the drawing screen.

The **Notes** tool is used to add text to the other boxes in the **Title Block**. See Figure 5-39.

Figure 5-39

Figure 5-39
(*Continued*)

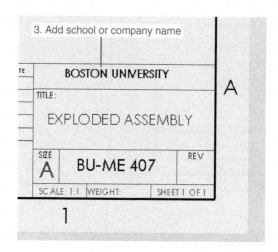

Click the **Annotation** tab, click the **Note** tool, locate the note within the title, and enter the drawing name (**EXPLODED ASSEMBLY**).

In this example the font height was changed to **16**.

Click the drawing screen.

Use the **Note** tool to add the company name.

In this example "Boston University" was added. Consider using your own school or company name.

Release Blocks

A finished engineering drawing is a legal document that goes through a release process before it becomes final. The *release block* documents the release process. For example, once you have completed a drawing, you will initial and date the **DRAWN** box located just to the left of the title block. The drawing will then go to a checker, who, after reviewing and incorporating any changes, will sign and date the **CHECKED** box. See Figure 5-40.

Figure 5-40

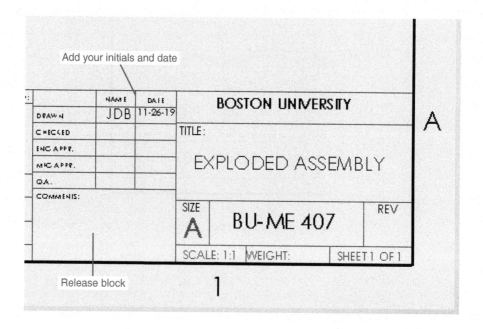

Tolerance Blocks

The tolerance block will be discussed in Chapter 8, "Tolerancing."

Application Blocks

See Figure 5-41.

Figure 5-41

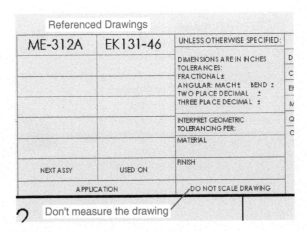

This block is used to reference closely related drawings. In this example, we know that the block assembly will be used on assembly ME-312A and that it was also used on EK131-46. This information makes it easier to access related drawings that can be checked for interfaces.

> **NOTE**
>
> The note "DO NOT SCALE DRAWING" located at the bottom of the application block is a reminder not to measure the views on the drawing. If a dimension is missing, do not measure the distance on the drawing, because the drawing may not have been reproduced at the exact 100% scale of the original.

5-13 Animate Collapse

Exploded Assemblies can be animated. In this example the **Animate Collapse** tool will be used.

1 Open the **EXPLODED ASSEMBLY**.

2 Right-click the **EXPLODED ASSEMBLY** heading in the **FeatureManager**.

See Figure 5-42.

3 Click the **Animate collapse** option.

Figure 5-42

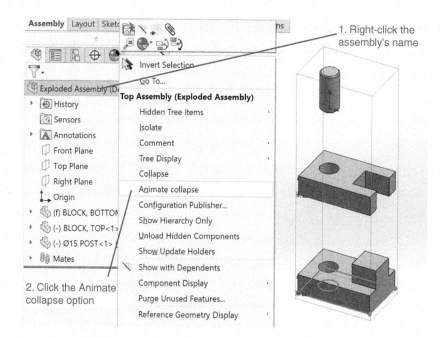

The assembly will automatically be animated and start to move. See Figure 5-43.

4 Click the **Stop** button to stop the animation and return the assembly to the exploded position.

5 Close the **Animation Controller**.

Figure 5-43

In this example the **Animate collapse** option was used because the assembly was shown in the exploded position. Had the assembly been in a closed assembled position, the **Animate explode** option would have been used.

5-14 Sample Problem SP5-1

Figure 5-44 shows the components for the Rotator Assembly. The dimensions for the components can be found in Project P5-10 at the end of the chapter. Draw and save the four Rotator Assembly components as **Part** documents.

Figure 5-44

CROSSLINK

LINK-L

LINK-L

PLATE

The origin of the PLATE is coincidental with the origin of the assembly drawing

1 Start a new **Assembly** document.

2 Insert the **PLATE**, **CROSSLINK**, and two **LINK-L**s into the assembly.

> **NOTE**
>
> Insert the **PLATE** first so it will be fixed **(f)** and align its origin with the origin of the assembly.

3 Click the **Mate** tool.

4 Click the **Concentric** tool.

5 Click the side of the bottom post of one **LINK-L** and the inside of the left hole in the **PLATE**.

See Figure 5-45. The LINK-L and PLATE will align.

TIP

Click the surfaces of the posts and holes. Do not click the edge lines.

---

6 Click the green **OK** check mark.

7 Click the **Mate** tool.

8 Click the top surface of the **PLATE** and the bottom surface of the **LINK-L**.

See Figure 5-46. Use the **Rotate View** tool to manipulate the view orientation so that the bottom surface of the LINK-L is visible. The part also can be rotated by holding down the mouse wheel and moving the cursor.

Figure 5-45

Figure 5-46

9 Click the **Distance** tool and then the **Distance** box and enter a value. In this example a value of **2.0mm** was entered.

See Figure 5-47. The initial offset values may be in inches. Enter the new value of **2.00** followed by **mm**, and the system will automatically change to metric (millimeter) distances.

Figure 5-47

Click the Distance tool

10 Click the green **OK** check mark.

The 2.00mm distance will allow for clearance between the PLATE and the LINK-L.

Figure 5-48 shows the 2mm offset between the PLATE and the LINK-L.

11 Return the assembly to the **Isometric** orientation.

12 Repeat the procedure for the other LINK-L.

See Figure 5-49.

Figure 5-49

2mm offset

Figure 5-48

2mm offset

13 Access the **Mate** tool and use the **Concentric** tool to align the top post of the first LINK-L with the left hole in the CROSSLINK.

14 Access the **Mate** tool, click the **Concentric** tool, and align the right hole in the CROSSLINK with the post on the second LINK-L.

15 Use the **Mate** tool and click the top surface of the LINK-L's post and the top surface of the CROSSLINK.

16 Use the **Mate** tool and click the top surface of the second LINK-L's post and the top surface of the CROSSLINK.

See Figure 5-50.

17 Click the green **OK** check mark.

See Figure 5-51.

Figure 5-51

Concentric

Figure 5-50

Link-L and Crosslink are concentric

Not concentric

18 Locate the cursor on the **CROSSLINK** and move it around.

The CROSSLINK and two LINK-Ls should rotate about the PLATE.

19 Save the assembly as **Rotator Assembly**.

> **TIP**
> All mates will be listed in the **FeatureManager**.

5-15 Using the Motion Study Tool

1 Access the **Rotator Assembly**.

2 Click the **Mate** tool, then click the **Parallel** tool.

3 Make the front surface line of the **CROSSLINK** parallel to the front edge of the **PLATE**; click the green **OK** check mark.

This step will ensure that the CROSSLINK rotates in an orientation parallel to the front edge of the PLATE. See Figure 5-52.

Figure 5-52

4 Click the **Motion Study** tab at the bottom of the screen.

See Figure 5-53.

Figure 5-53

5 Click the **Motor** tool.

The **Motor PropertyManager** box will appear.

See Figure 5-54.

Figure 5-54

1. Click Rotary Motor

2. Click here. The box will have a blue background when it is active.

3. Click the top surface of the LINK-L

Icon for Rotary Motor motion

6 Click the **Rotary Motor** tool.

7 Click the box under the **Component/Direction** heading, then click the top surface of the left LINK-L.

The box will have a blue background when it is active.

The left LINK-L is now the driver link. An arrow will appear indicating the direction of motion. It will drive the other components.

Viewing the Assembly Motion

1 Go to the **Motion** box on the **Motor PropertyManager** and define the assembly's motion.

In this example the default values of **Constant Speed** and **100 RPM** were accepted.

2 Click the green **OK** check mark.

See Figure 5-55.

3 Click **Play**.

Figure 5-55

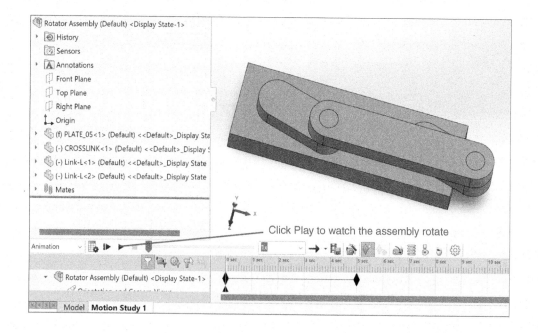

Click Play to watch the assembly rotate

5-16 Editing a Part Within an Assembly

Parts already inserted into an assembly drawing can be edited. Figure 5-56 shows the block assembly created earlier in the chapter. The general operating concept is to isolate a part, make the changes, and insert the part back into the assembly.

In this example we will change the diameter value of the hole in **BLOCK, TOP**.

Figure 5-56

An existing assembly

Edit this hole from Ø15 to Ø20

1 Click the arrowhead to the left of the **BLOCK, TOP** heading in the **FeatureManager**.

2 Click the arrowhead to the left of **Cut-Extrusion 1** under the **BLOCK, TOP** heading in the **FeatureManager**.

In this example the **Cut-Extrusion 1** is the hole in **BLOCK, TOP**. Your assembly and parts may differ. See Figure 5-57.

3 Right-click the **Sketch2** heading and click the **Edit Sketch** option.

4 Double-click the **Ø15** hole value and enter a new value.

In this example, the value was changed to **Ø20.0**. See Figure 5-58.

Figure 5-57

1. Click the arrowhead

4. Click Edit Sketch

3. Click Sketch 2

2. Click this arrowhead

Figure 5-58

Double-click the diameter 15 dimension and change it to 20

Click this icon when done modifying the hole

5 Click the green **OK** check mark.

6 Click the **Exit Sketch** option.

7 Click the **Edit Assembly** tool located in the upper-right corner of the drawing screen.

If necessary, use the **Exploded View** tool to create an exploded view of the assembly. Figure 5-59 shows **BLOCK, TOP** with the enlarged hole.

Figure 5-59

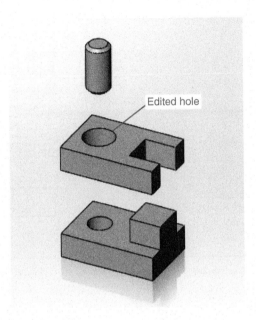

Edited hole

5-17 Interference Detection/Clearance Verification

Assemblies contain multiple parts, and these parts must fit together appropriately. SolidWorks contains **Interference Detection** and **Clearance Verification** tools that can be used to confirm that the assembly is feasibly developed with no overlapping parts.

Interference Detection

The **Interference Detection** tool is used to determine whether there are interferences within an assembly. SolidWorks will assemble parts as instructed without regard to interferences. It is possible for two parts to be put together in an assembly that would, in reality, not fit together.

Figure 5-61 shows a simple assembly made from two parts whose dimensions are shown in Figure 5-60. All the dimensions use whole numbers. There are no tolerances specified. From the given dimensions we know that there is an interference between the Base and the Top. The shaft on the Base is **Ø60** and the hole in the Top is **Ø58**. The **Interference Detection** tool can be used to highlight this interference.

Figure 5-60

BLOCK, BASE

BLOCK, TOP

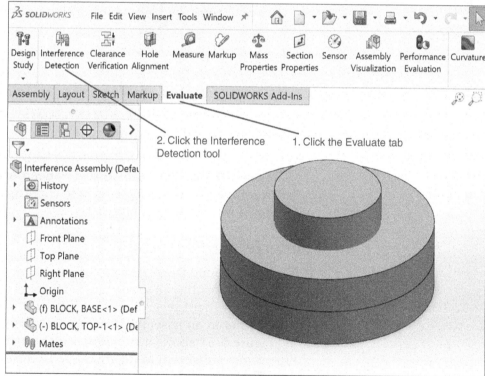

Figure 5-61

2. Click the Interference Detection tool

1. Click the Evaluate tab

Detecting an Interference

1 Click the **Evaluate** tab at the top of the screen and select the **Interference Detection** tool.

See Figure 5-62. The Assembly will appear enclosed in a wireframe box. A note will appear indicating that an interference has been detected.

Figure 5-62

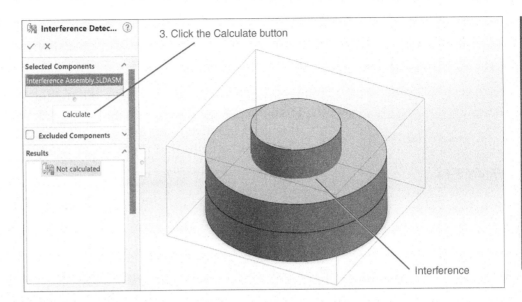

3. Click the Calculate button

Interference

2 Click the **Calculate** button.

The interference will be highlighted using a red hollow cylinder. See Figure 5-63. There will also be a sound indicating an interference has been detected.

Figure 5-63

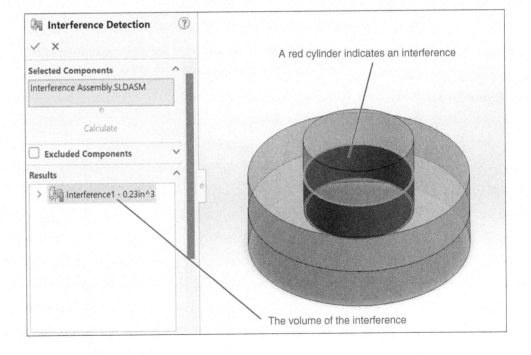

A red cylinder indicates an interference

The volume of the interference

Figure 5-64 shows an assembly. The eight fasteners in the **Base** have a diameter of Ø8.00. The eight holes in the **Cover Plate** have a diameter of Ø6.00. When the **Interference Detection** tool is applied, the interference between the fasteners and holes is detected. One fastener hole interference will be highlighted on the assembly. All the interferences will be listed in the Results box.

It is good practice to always apply the **Interference Detection** tool to an assembly to ensure that there are no interferences.

Figure 5-64

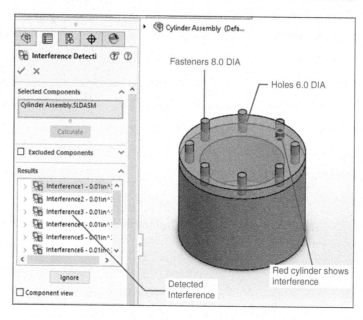

Figure 5-65 shows a similar assembly, but the eight holes in the **Cover Plate** have been enlarged to **Ø10**.

Figure 5-65

The Ø10 holes should create a clearance between the **Fasteners** and the **Cover Plate**'s holes.

Verifying the Clearance

1 Click the **Evaluate** tab and select the **Clearance Verification** tool.

See Figure 5-66. We know the clearance should be 1.0mm (10mm Hole − 8.0mm = 2.0mm; half the distance = 1.0mm).

Figure 5-66

2. Click the Clearance Verification tool

1. Click the Evaluate tab

2 Click a fastener and the **Cover Plate**.

Part file names should appear in the **Selected Components** box.

3 Click the **Calculate** button.

See Figure 5-67. SolidWorks has verified that there is a 1.0mm clearance between the fasteners and the holes in the cover plate.

Figure 5-67

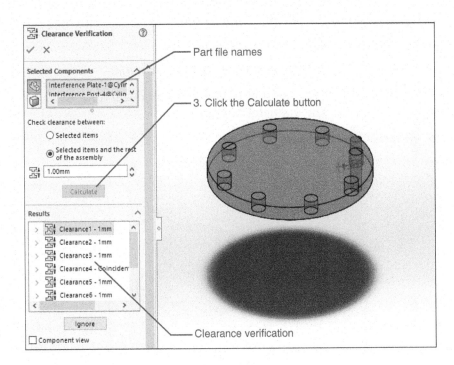

Removing the Interference

Figure 5-68 shows the assembly originally shown in Figure 5-61. There is an interference between the Post on the Base and the Hole in the Top. The interference can be removed by editing the original BLOCK, TOP part, or it can be edited in the assembly mode.

Figure 5-68

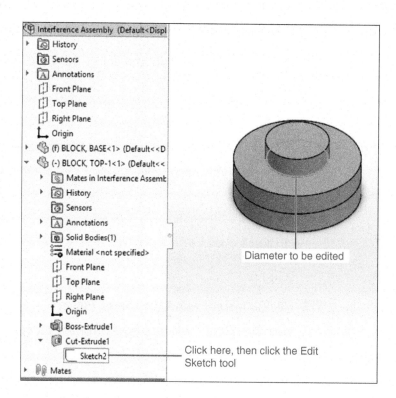

Diameter to be edited

Click here, then click the Edit Sketch tool

1 Locate the **Sketch** that created the hole in the **FeatureManager Design Tree**.

2 Right-click the **Sketch**.

3 Click the **Edit Sketch** option.

The hole's diameter value will appear. See Figure 5-69. In this example the diameter is **Ø58**.

Figure 5-69

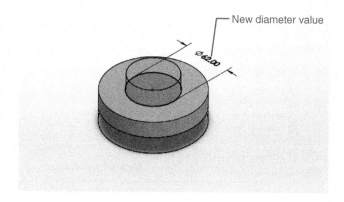

New diameter value

Ø62.00

4 Double-click the Ø58 value and change it to Ø62.

5 Click the **Exit Sketch** icon in the upper-right corner of the screen and the **Return to the FeatureManager Design Tree** icon.

There is now a clearance between the Base and Top parts.

6 Click the **Interference Detection** tool again.

7 Click the **Calculate** box.

The results box will indicate that no interferences were found. See Figure 5-70.

Figure 5-70

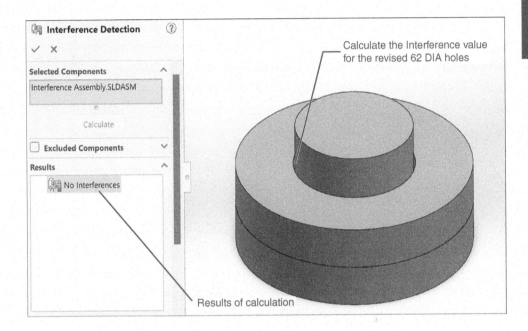

Verifying that a Clearance Exists

The **Clearance Verification** tool is used to ensure that clearances have been created.

1 Click the **Evaluate** tab at the top of the screen.

2 Click the **Clearance Verification** tool.

3 Click the two parts.

4 Click the **Calculate** box.

The **Clearance Verification** will be listed in the **Results** box and the onscreen assembly will show the clearance. See Figure 5-71.

Figure 5-71

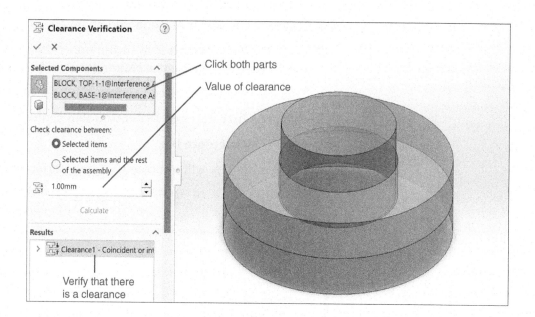

Clearance Verification

Selected Components

BLOCK, TOP-1-1@Interference
BLOCK, BASE-1@Interference As

Check clearance between:

- Selected items
- Selected items and the rest of the assembly

1.00mm

Calculate

Results

> Clearance1 - Coincident or int

Verify that there is a clearance

Click both parts

Value of clearance

Chapter Projects

Project 5-1:

Create a **Part** document of the SQBLOCK using the given dimensions.
Create assemblies using two SQBLOCKS, positioning the blocks as shown
in Figures P5-1A through P5-1G.

Pages 305–316 show a group of parts. These parts are used to create the assemblies presented as problems in this section. Use the given
descriptions, part numbers, and materials when creating BOMs for the
assemblies.

Figure P5-1
MILLIMETERS

E

F

G

Project 5-2:

Redraw the models in Figure P5-2 and save them as **Standard (mm).ipn** files. All dimensions are in millimeters.

Figure P5-2
MILLIMETERS

SPACER
P/N ME311-1
MATL: SAE 1020 Steel

SPACER DOUBLE
P/N ME311-2
MATL: SAE 1020 Steel

SPACER TRIPLE
P/N ME311-3
MATL: SAE 1020 Steel

Figure P5-2
(*Continued*)

DESCRIPTION	PART NO.	D-VALUE
PEG, SHORT	PG20-1	20
PEG	PG30-1	30
PEG, LONG	PG40-1	40

PEGS
MATL: Steel

DESCRIPTION	PART NO.	D-VALUE
PEG, SHORT	PG20-1	20
PEG	PG30-1	30
PEG, LONG	PG40-1	40

DESCRIPTION	PART NO.	D
PEG, SHORT	PG20-1	20
PEG	PG30-1	30
PEG, LONG	PG40-1	40

ALL DISTANCES IN MILLIMETERS

L-BRACKET
P/N BK20-1
MATL: SAE 1040 Steel

Z-BRACKET
P/N BK20-2
MATL: SAE 1040 Steel

C-BRACKET
P/N BK20-3
MATL: SAE 1040 Steel

PLATE, QUAD
P/N ME311-4
MATL: SAE 1020 Steel

PART NO.	TOTAL NO. OF HOLES	L	W	HOLE PATTERN
PL110-9	9	90	90	3×3
PL110-16	16	120	120	4×4
PL110-6	6	60	90	2×3
PL110-8	8	60	120	2×4
PL110-4	4	60	60	2×2

PLATE, BASE
P/N ME311-5
MATL: SAE 1020 Steel

Ø10 - AS NEEDED

PART NO.	TOTAL NO. OF HOLES	L	W	HOLE PATTERN
PL110-9	9	90	90	3 × 3
PL110-16	16	120	120	4 × 4
PL110-6	6	60	60	2 × 3
PL110-8	8	60	120	2 × 4
PL110-4	4	60	60	2 × 2

Project 5-3:

Create an exploded isometric assembly drawing of the shown in Figure P5-3. Create a BOM.

Figure P5-3
MILLIMETERS

ITEM NO.	PART NUMBER	DESCRIPTION	QTY.
1	ME311-4	PLATE, QUAD	2
2	BK20-3	C-BRACKET	2
3	PG20-1	Ø12×20 PEG	4

Project 5-4:

Create an exploded isometric assembly drawing of the shown in Figure P5-4. Create a BOM.

Figure P5-4
MILLIMETERS

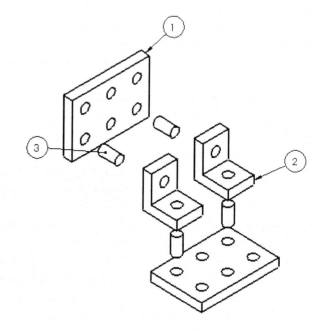

Project 5-5:

Create an exploded isometric assembly drawing of the shown in Figure P5-5. Create a BOM.

Figure P5-5
MILLIMETERS

PEG20
STEEL
4 REQD

SPACER, QUAD
STEEL
3 REQD

PEG30
STEEL
2 REQD

Z-BRACKET
STEEL
2 REQD

PL80-4
STEEL
2 REQD

Project 5-6:

Create an exploded isometric assembly drawing of the shown in Figure P5-6. Create a BOM.

Figure P5-6
MILLIMETERS

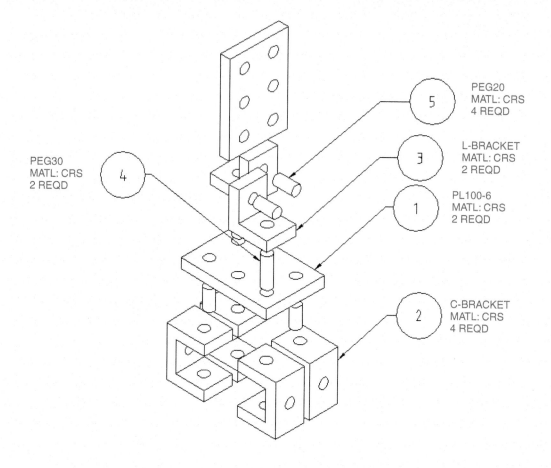

PEG30
MATL: CRS
2 REQD

PEG20
MATL: CRS
4 REQD

L-BRACKET
MATL: CRS
2 REQD

PL100-6
MATL: CRS
2 REQD

C-BRACKET
MATL: CRS
4 REQD

Project 5-7:

Create an exploded isometric assembly drawing of the shown in
Figure P5-7. Create a BOM.

Figure P5-7
MILLIMETERS

Figure P5-7
(*Continued*)

L-BRACKET
MATL: ANSI-SAE 4024 STEEL
1 REQD

PEG20
MATL: STEEL
4 REQD

Z-BRACKET
MATL: ANSI-SAE 4024 STEEL
2 REQD

SPACER, QUAD
MATL: ANSI-SAE 4024 STEEL
2 REQD

Project 5-8:

Create an exploded isometric assembly drawing of the shown in
Figure P5-8. Create a BOM.

Figure P5-8
MILLIMETERS

Z-BRACKET
MATL: PTFE
2 REQD

PEG20
MATL: NYLON
8 REQD

SPACER, QUAD
MATL: PTFE

L-BRACKET
MATL: PTFE
2 REQD

PL110-16
MATL: PTFE
2 REQD

Project 5-9:

Create an original assembly and drawing based on the parts shown on pages 347–349. Include an isometric view, an exploded isometric view with assembly numbers, and a BOM. Use at least 12 parts.

Project 5-10:

Draw the ROTATOR ASSEMBLY shown in Figure P5-10. Include the following:

A.   An assembly drawing

B.   An exploded isometric drawing with assembly numbers

C.   A parts list

D.   LINKs should carry the CROSSLINK. The CROSSLINK should remain parallel during the rotation.

NOTE

This assembly was used in the section on animating assemblies. See page 341.

LINK-L
P/N AM311-1
MATL: SAE1020 STEEL

30 — R10

Ø10 - 2 HOLES

10

10

15

CROSSLINK
P/N 311-2
MATL: SAE1020 STEEL

80 — R10

Ø10 - 2 HOLES

10

PLATE
P/N AM311-3
MATL: SAE1020 STEEL

20 — 80

40

20

Ø10 - 2 HOLES

15

120

ROTATOR ASSEMBLY

Project 5-11:

Draw the FLY ASSEMBLY shown in Figure P5-11. Include the following:

A. An assembly drawing

B. An exploded isometric drawing with assembly numbers

C. A parts list

D. An animated assembly; the FLYLINK should rotate around the SUPPORT base.

FLY ASSEMBLY

FLYLINK
BU200A
SAE 1040

3

60

Ø5-2 HOLES

R2.5

40

10

R5 BOTH ENDS

PEGØ5
BU200C
SAE1040

20

Ø5

PLATE, SUPPORT
BU200B
SAE 1040

54

23

10

12

28

Ø5-2 HOLES

R2.0 FOR ALL FILLETS AND ROUNDS

Ø10

Ø5

27

27

3

2

4

10

3.6

16

43

8

Project 5-12:

Draw the ROCKER ASSEMBLY shown in Figure P5-12. Include the following:

A. An assembly drawing

B. An exploded isometric drawing with assembly numbers

C. A parts list

D. An animated assembly

Figure P5-12
MILLIMETERS

ROCKER ASSEMBLY

DRIVELINK

Ø10 × 10 PEG

PLATE, WEB

CENTERLINK

Ø10 × 15 PEG

Ø10 × 15 PEG

ROCKERLINK

DRIVELINK
AM312-2
SAE 1040
5 mm THK

30

R10 BOTH ENDS

Ø10-2 HOLES

Ø10

R15

PLATE,WEB
AM312-1
SAE 1040
10 mm THK

ALL FILLETS AND ROUNDS = R3

40

30

Ø5-7 HOLES

26

6 TYP

12 TYP

80

R15

40

4

R15

R15

Ø10

R10

20

26

30

80

ROCKERLINK
AM312-4
SAE 1040
5 mm THK

Ø10 BOTH HOLES

R10 BOTH ENDS

10

100

70

15

CENTERLINK
AM312-3
SAE 1040
5 mm THK

Ø10 × 10 PEG
AM312-5
SAE 1020

Ø10 × 15 PEG
AM312-6
SAE 1020

Project 5-13:

Draw the LINK ASSEMBLY shown in Figure P5-13. Include the following:

A. An assembly drawing

B. An exploded isometric drawing with assembly numbers

C. A parts list

D. An animated assembly; the HOLDER ARM should rotate between –30° and +30°.

Figure P5-13
MILLIMETERS

LINK ASSEMBLY

HOLDER ARM
AM-311-A3
7075-T6 AL
5 mm THK

Offset all mating
surfaces 1.00 mm.

CROSSLINK
AM-311-A4
7075-T6 AL
5 mm THK

BUSHING-A
AM-311-A5
TEFLON

BASE, HOLDER
AM-311-A1
6061-T6 AL

ALL FILLETS AND
ROUNDS = R3

SIDELINK
AM-311-A2
7075-T6 AL
5 mm THK
2 REQD

Project 5-14:

Draw the PIVOT ASSEMBLY shown in Figure P5-14 using the dimensioned components given. Include the following:

A.   A 3D exploded isometric drawing

B.   A parts list

PIVOT ASSEMBLY

BOX, PIVOT
P/N: ENG-A43
MATL: SAE 1020 STEEL

POST, HANDLE
P/N: ENG-A44
MATL: SAE 1020 STEEL

LINK
P/N: ENG-A45
MATL: SAE 1020 STEEL

Figure P5-14
(*Continued*)

HANDLE
P/N: AM300-1
MATL: STEEL

R30.00

26.00

Ø12.00 ⊤ 12.00

Presentation drawing

Parts List				
ITEM	PART NUMBER	DESCRIPTION	MATERIAL	QTY
1	ENG-A43	BOX,PIVOT	SAE1020	1
2	ENG-A44	POST,HANDLE	SAE1020	1
3	ENG-A45	LINK	SAE1020	1
4	AM300-1	HANDLE	STEEL	1
5	EK-132	POST-Ø6x14	STEEL	1
6	EK-131	POST-Ø6x26	STEEL	1

Project 5-15:

Soma Cube Puzzle

The Soma Cube puzzle was invented by Piet Hein in 1933. It makes an interesting assembly problem. Each of the 27 cubes used is the same size. They are combined to form seven solid shapes, each of which has an internal edge. When correctly combined they will form a $3 \times 3 \times 3$ cube.

A.   Specify a cube size.

B.   Create the seven different shapes shown in Figure P5-15.

C.   Assemble the seven shapes to create a $3 \times 3 \times 3$ cube.

D.   Physically build the seven shapes out of poster board and assemble them.

Figure P5-15
MILLIMETERS

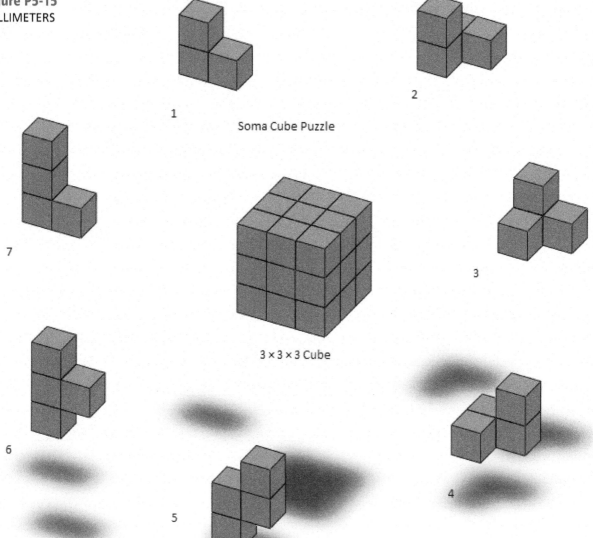

Soma Cube Puzzle

$3 \times 3 \times 3$ Cube

Project 5-16:

Draw the assembly shown in Figure P5-16.

A. An assembly drawing

B. An exploded isometric drawing with assembly numbers

C. A parts list

D. An animated assembly. Make the **Crank** the driver.

Figure P5-16

CRANK
P/N OA4-33
MATL: 2024-T4 AL

FOLLOWER
P/N OA4-34
MATL: 2024-T4 AL

COUPLER
P/N OA4-35
MATL: 2024-T4 AL

CRANK = 50
FOLLOWER = 80
COUPLER = 160

Ø10 BOTH ENDS

R9 BOTH ENDS

R5 - 4 PLACES

5

4-PIN SHORT 1
P/N PS1-100
MATL: 2024-T4 AL

Ø10
Ø14

5
12
5

PIN-1
P/N P16-H17
MATL: 2024-T4 AL

Ø10
Ø14

5
17
10

Project 5-17:

Slider Assembly—Millimeters

Draw the Slider Assembly shown in Figure P5-17.

A. An assembly drawing

B. An exploded isometric drawing with assembly numbers

C. A parts list

D. An animated assembly. Make the **Driver Wheel** the driver.

Figure P5-17

BASE, SLIDER
P/N S4001
MATL: 1020 STEEL

Ø 5 ▽ 10 - 4 HOLES

20

10

Ø10

115

160

44

280

20

20

5

24

5

R4 BOTH SIDES

60

DRIVER WHEEL
P/N S4002
MATL: 1020 STEEL

32

Ø22

Ø8

Ø80

Ø 10

5

5

SLIDER
P/N S4003
MATL: 1020 STEEL

30

15

Ø 5 ▽ 5

12

6

Ø 8

16

Figure P5-17
(*Continued*)

Ø5 ⍐ 10 - 2 HOLES

R10 - 2 PLACES

Ø8

4 × 45° CHAMFER
2 PLACES

R5

Ø5 - 2 HOLES

Ø8

PIN, DRIVER
P/N S4007
MATL: 1020 STEEL

Ø10

Ø8

Ø5

PIN, SHORT
P/N S4008
MATL: 1020 STEEL

Ø5

chaptersix

Threads and Fasteners

CHAPTER OBJECTIVES

- Learn thread terminology and conventions
- Draw threads
- Size both internal and external threads
- Use standard-sized threads
- Use and size washers, nuts, and set screws

6-1 Introduction

This chapter explains how to draw threads, washers, and nuts. It also explains how to select fasteners, washers, nuts, and set screws.

Internal threads are created using the **Hole Wizard** tool, which is located on the **Features** toolbar. Predrawn fasteners and other standard components may be accessed using the **Design Library**.

All threads in this book are in compliance with ANSI (American National Standards Institute) standards—ANSI Inch and ANSI Metric threads.

6-2 Thread Terminology

Figure 6-1 shows a thread. The peak of a thread is called the *crest*, and the valley portion is called the *root*. The *major diameter* of a thread is the distance across the thread from crest to crest. The *minor diameter* is the distance across the thread from root to root.

Figure 6-1

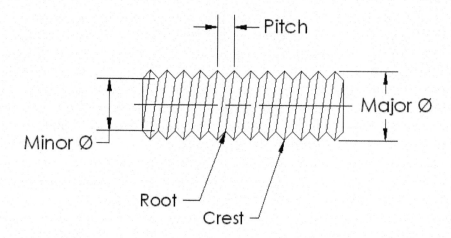

Pitch

The pitch of a thread is the distance from the center of one thread to the center of the next thread. By definition the pitch of a thread is equal to one over the number of threads per distance unit. The formula for pitch is

Pitch = 1/Number of threads per inch (millimeter)

Number of threads per inch (millimeter) = 1/Pitch

6-3   Thread Callouts—ANSI Metric Units

Threads are specified on a drawing using drawing callouts. See Figure 6-2. The M at the beginning of a drawing callout specifies that the callout is for a metric thread. Holes that are not threaded use the Ø symbol.

Figure 6-2

The number following the M is the major diameter of the thread. An M10 thread has a major diameter of 10mm. The pitch of a metric thread is assumed to be a coarse thread unless otherwise stated. The callout M10 × 30 assumes a coarse thread, or a thread length of 1.5mm per thread. The number 30 is the thread length in millimeters. The "×" is read as "by," so the thread is called a "ten by thirty."

> **NOTE**
>
> For metric threads the pitch is specified, not the number of threads per millimeter.

Figure 6-3

Standard listing of ANSI metric sizes

The callout M10 × 1.25 × 30 specifies a pitch of 1.25mm per thread. This is not a standard coarse thread size, so the pitch must be specified.

Figure 6-3 shows a listing of standard metric thread sizes available in the SolidWorks **Design Library** for one type of hex head bolt. The sizes are in compliance with ANSI Metric specifications.

Whenever possible, design using preferred thread sizes. Preferred thread sizes are readily available and are usually cheaper than nonstandard sizes. In addition, tooling such as wrenches is also readily available for preferred sizes.

6-4 Thread Callouts—ANSI Unified Screw Threads

ANSI Unified Screw Threads (English units) always include a thread form specification. Thread form specifications are designated by capital letters, as shown in Figure 6-4, and are defined as follows:

UNC—Unified National Coarse

UNF—Unified National Fine

UNEF—Unified National Extra Fine

UN—Unified National, or constant-pitch threads

An ANSI (English units) thread callout starts by defining the major diameter of the thread followed by the pitch specification. The callout .500-13 UNC means a thread whose major diameter is .500in. with 13 threads per inch. The thread is manufactured to the UNC standards. The pitch for a .500-13 UNC thread is 1/13 = .08 or 1/Number of threads per inch.

There are three possible classes of fit for a thread: 1, 2, and 3. The different class specifications specify a set of manufacturing tolerances. A class 1 thread is the loosest and a class 3 the most exact. A class 2 fit is the most common.

The letter A designates an external thread and the letter B designates an internal thread. The symbol × means "by" as in 2 × 4, "two by four." The thread length (3.00) may be followed by the word LONG to prevent confusion about which value represents the length.

Drawing callouts for ANSI (English unit) threads are sometimes shortened, such as in Figure 6-4. The callout .500-13 UNC-2A × 3.00 LONG is shortened to .500-13 × 3.00. Only a coarse thread has 13 threads per inch,

Figure 6-4

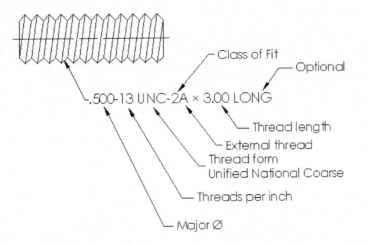

Class of Fit

Optional

.500-13 UNC-2A × 3.00 LONG

Thread length

External thread

Thread form

Unified National Coarse

Threads per inch

Major Ø

Shortened Version
.500-13×3.00

Figure 6-5

A listing of standard
ANSI inch sizes

and it should be obvious whether a thread is internal or external, so these specifications may be dropped. Most threads are class 2, so it is tacitly accepted that all threads are class 2 unless otherwise specified. The shortened callout form is not universally accepted. When in doubt, use a complete thread callout.

A listing of standard ANSI (English unit) threads, as presented in Solid-Works, is shown in Figure 6-5.

6-5 Thread Representations

There are three ways to graphically represent threads on a technical drawing: detailed, schematic, and simplified. Figure 6-6 shows an external detailed representation, and both the external and internal simplified and schematic representations.

Figure 6-7 shows an internal and an external thread created using SolidWorks. Note that no thread representations appear. This is called the **Simplified** representation. SolidWorks uses the **Simplified** thread representation as a way to minimize file size. Cosmetic thread representations can be created and will be discussed later in the chapter. Actual threads may be drawn using the **Helix** tool. SolidWorks can also draw a **Schematic** thread representation.

Figure 6-6

Drawing thread representations

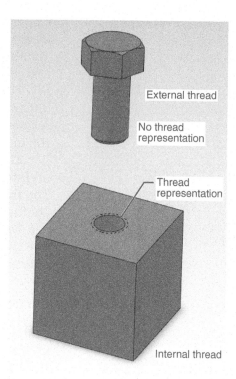

Figure 6-7

6-6 Internal Threads—Inches

Internal threads are drawn using the **Hole Wizard**. Figure 6-8 shows a 1.5 × 2.0 × 1.0 block. In this section a 3/8-16 UNC hole will be located in the center of the block.

Figure 6-8

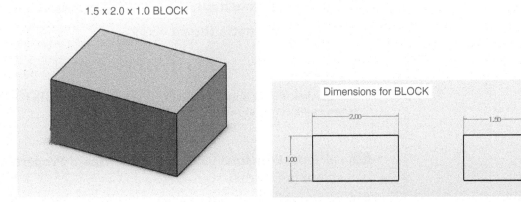

1.5 × 2.0 × 1.0 BLOCK

Dimensions for BLOCK

1 Draw a **1.5 × 2.0 × 1.0** block.

2 Orient the block in the **Isometric** view.

3 Click the **Hole Wizard** tool on the **Features** tab.

4 Click the **Straight Tap** option, set the **Standard** for **ANSI Inch**, set the **Type** for **Tapped hole**, define the thread's size, and set the **End Condition** to **Through All**.

In this example an internal 3/8-16 UNC thread will be created. The thread will go completely through the block. See Figure 6-9.

Figure 6-9

1. Click Straight Tap option

2. Specify ANSI Inch standards

3. Select Tapped hole

4. Select 3/8-16

5. Select Through All

6. Select Cosmetic thread option

5 Select a **3/8-16** thread size in the **Hole Specifications** box.

The thread will have a major diameter of 3/8 with 16 threads per inch and a pitch of 1/16 = .06.

6 Select the **Through All** option in the **End Condition** box.

7 Click the **Cosmetic thread** option.

NOTE

The **Cosmetic thread** option will create a hidden line around the finished hole that serves to indicate that the hole is threaded.

---

8 Click the **Positions** tab in the **Hole Wizard PropertyManager**, as shown in Figure 6-10.

9 Click a location near the center of the top surface of the block to identify the surface for the thread.

Figure 6-10

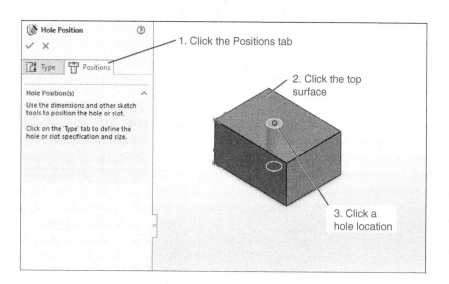

Use the Smart Dimension tool to locate the hole's centerpoint

A threaded hole - Cosmetic representation

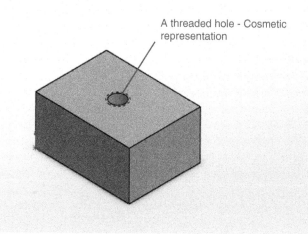

10 Click the mouse again to approximately locate the threaded hole.

11 Use the **Smart Dimension** tool and locate the centerpoint of the hole.

12 Click the green **OK** check mark.

The hidden line surrounding the hole is a cosmetic thread and indicates that the hole is threaded. Note that there are threads on the inside of the hole.

6-7 Threaded Blind Holes—Inches

A *blind hole* is one that does not go completely though an object. See Figure 6-11.

Figure 6-11

1.5 x 2.00 x 2.00 BLOCK

Blind hole

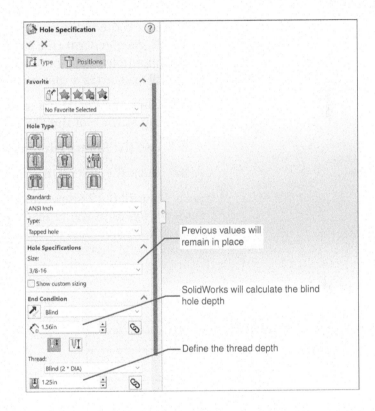

Previous values will remain in place

SolidWorks will calculate the blind hole depth

Define the thread depth

1 Use the **Undo** tool and remove the hole added to the 1.5 × 2.0 × 1.0 block.

2 Edit the block so that it is **2.00** thick.

3 Click the **Hole Wizard** tool.

SolidWorks will remember the last hole setting used, so the hole specifications will be the same as those used to create the 3/8-16 through hole: ANSI standard, tapped hole, with a cosmetic thread.

4 Size the hole to **3/8-16**, set the **End Condition** for **Blind**, and set the **Tap Thread Depth** in the **End Condition** box to **1.25in**.

In this example the tap Blind Hole Depth was automatically calculated as 1.56in. When a threaded hole is created, a hole (pilot hole) is first drilled and then the threads are cut (tapped hole) into the sides of the hole. The pilot hole must always be longer than the threaded portion of the hole. A tapping bit only cuts threads; it has no cutting surfaces on its bottom surface. If the bit bottoms out—that is, hits the bottom of the hole—it may break. As a general rule a distance greater than two pitches is added to the pilot hole depth beyond the threaded hole depth. In this example SolidWorks adds a distance of approximately four pitches.

5 Click the **Positions** tab and locate a centerpoint near the center of the top surface of the block.

6 Use the **Smart Dimension** tool to locate the centerpoint.

7 Click the green **OK** check mark.

Figure 6-12 shows an orthographic view of the block and a section view. Note that the tapped hole extends beyond the end of the threads and ends with a conical point. The depth of the tapped hole does not include the conical end point.

Figure 6-12

6-8 Internal Threads—Metric

Metric threads are designated by the letter M. For example, M10 × 30 is the callout for a metric thread of diameter 10 and a length of 30. The thread is assumed to be a coarse thread.

TIP

For metric thread drawings, the symbol Ø indicates a hole or cylinder without threads; the symbol **M** indicates metric threads.

1 Draw a **20** × **30** × **15** block.

See Figure 6-13.

Figure 6-13

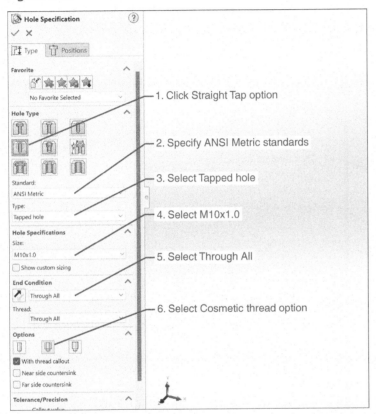

1. Click Straight Tap option

2. Specify ANSI Metric standards

3. Select Tapped hole

4. Select M10x1.0

5. Select Through All

6. Select Cosmetic thread option

Use the Smart Dimension tool to locate the hole's centerpoint

M10 x 1.0 Through hole

2 Click the **Hole Wizard**.

3 Click the **Straight Tap** option, select the **Tapped hole** option, set the **Standard** for **ANSI Metric**, set the hole size for **M10** × **1.0**, and set the depth for **Through All**.

The number 1.0 is the pitch of the thread. An M10 thread can be cut with several different pitch sizes.

4 Click the **Cosmetic thread** option.

5 Click the **Positions** tab and click the top surface of the block, and click the mouse again to select the approximate location for the hole.

6 Use the **Smart Dimension** tool to locate the hole's centerpoint.

7 Click the green **OK** check mark.

Figure 6-14 shows the specifications for an M10 × 1.0 × 20 deep blind hole. The pilot hole depth is approximately 5 pitches deeper than the threaded portion of the hole.

Figure 6-14

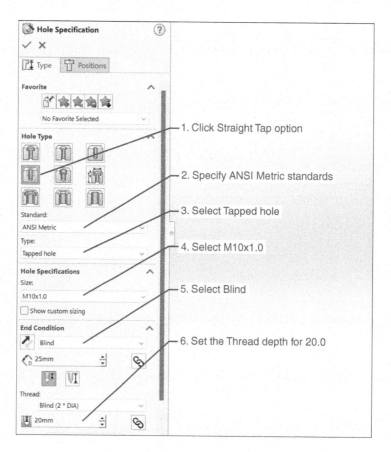

6-9 Accessing the Design Library

SolidWorks includes a **Design Library**. The **Design Library** contains a listing of predrawn standard components such as bolts, nuts, and washers. These components may be accessed and inserted into assemblies. Figure 6-15 shows how to access hex bolts in the **Design Library**.

Figure 6-15

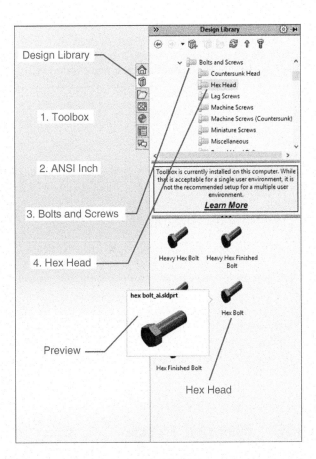

The **Design Library** is accessed by clicking the **Design Library** icon located on the right side of the screen. The **Design Library** can only be used in an **Assembly** document.

1 Create an **Assembly** document and click the **Design Library** tab.

2 Click **Toolbox**.

If the **Add in Now** tool appears, click **Add in Now**.

3 Click **ANSI Inch**.

4 Click **Bolts and Screws**.

5 Click **Hex Head**.

A listing of various types of hex head bolts will appear.

6 Click the **Hex Bolt**, drag it into the drawing screen area, and click **Create Part**.

7 Define the needed size and length.

In this example a 1/4-20 UNC × 2.00 HEX HEAD BOLT was created.

8 Define the **Thread Display** style.

9 Click the green **OK** check mark.

Figure 6-16

6-10 Thread Pitch

Thread pitch for an ANSI Inch fastener is defined as

$$P = \frac{1}{N}$$

where

P = pitch

N = number of threads per inch

In ANSI Inch standards a sample bolt callout is 1/4-20 UNC × length. The 20 value is the number of threads per inch, so the pitch is 1/20 or 0.05. The pitch for a 1/4-28 UNF thread would be 1/28, or 0.036.

A sample thread callout for ANSI Metric is written M10 × 1.0 × 30, where 1.0 is the pitch. No calculation is required to determine the pitch for metric threads. It is included directly in the thread callout.

6-11 Determining an External Thread Length—Inches

Figure 6-17 shows three blocks stacked together. Their dimensions are given. They are to be held together using a hex bolt, two washers, and a nut. The bolt will be a 3/8-16 UNC. What length should be used?

Figure 6-17

3–1.5 × 1.5 × 0.5
BLOCKS, BOLT

Block and Assembly origins
are coincidental.

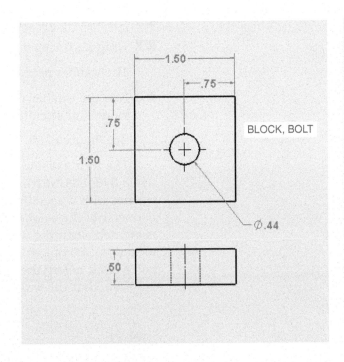

BLOCK, BOLT

Ø.44

1. Draw a **1.5 × 1.5 × 0.50** block. Draw a **Ø.44** (7/16) hole through the center of the block. Save the block as **BLOCK, BOLT**.

The Ø.44 was selected because it allows for clearance between the bolt and the block.

2. Create an **Assembly**, enter three **BLOCK, BOLT**s, and assemble them as shown.

3. Save the assembly as **3-BLOCK ASSEMBLY**.

4. Access the **Design Library**, then click **Toolbox**, **ANSI Inch**, **Washers**, and **Plain Washers (Type A)**.

See Figure 6-18.

Figure 6-18

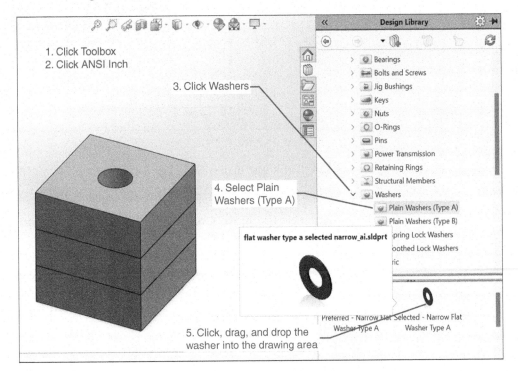

5 Click and hold the **Preferred – Narrow Flat Washer Type A**.

6 Drag-and-drop it into the drawing screen.

The washer preview will appear in the drawing area.

7 Size the washer by clicking the arrow to the right of the initial **Size** value and selecting a nominal value.

See Figure 6-19.

The term *nominal* refers to a starting value. In this case we are going to use a 3/8-16 UNC thread. The 3/8 value is a nominal value. We select a washer with a specified 3/8 nominal inside diameter. The actual inside diameter of the washer is .406. Clearance between the washer and the bolt is created when the washer is manufactured. The fastener will also not measure .375 but will be slightly smaller. The .375 size is the size of the bolt's shaft before the threads were cut.

Note that the washer thickness is .065 (about 1/16).

> **NOTE**
>
> Washers are identified using Inside Diameter × Outside Diameter × Thickness; for example: .406 × .812 × .065 PLAIN WASHER.

Figure 6-19

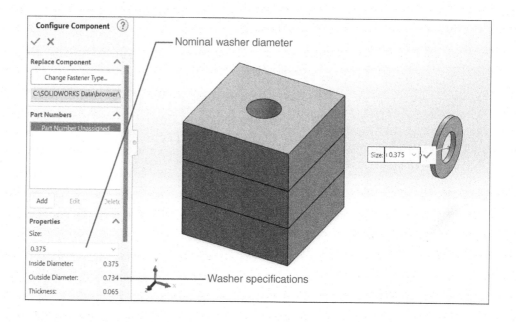

8 Click the green **OK** check mark.

9 Add a second washer into the assembly.

10 Use the **Mate Concentric** and **Mate Coincident** tools to position the washers around the block's holes as shown.

See Figure 6-20.

11 Access the **Design Library**, then click **Toolbox**, **ANSI Inch**, **Nuts**, **Hex Nuts**, **Hex Jam Nut**, and drag-and-drop the nut into the drawing area.

See Figure 6-21.

Figure 6-20

Use the Mate tool to position the washers

The Origin icons have been hidden

Figure 6-21

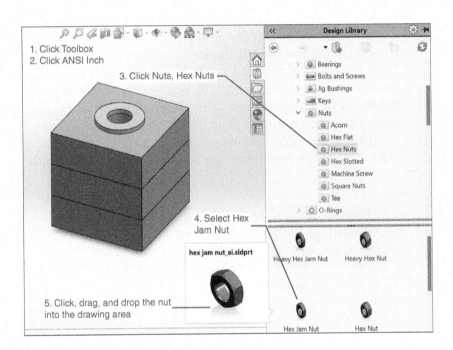

1. Click Toolbox
2. Click ANSI Inch

3. Click Nuts, Hex Nuts

4. Select Hex Jam Nut

hex jam nut_ai.sldprt

5. Click, drag, and drop the nut into the drawing area

Heavy Hex Jam Nut   Heavy Hex Nut

Hex Jam Nut   Hex Nut

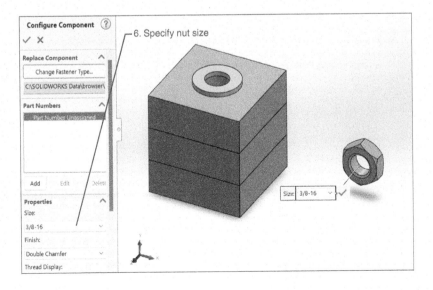

6. Specify nut size

Size: 3/8-16

Configure Component ?
✓ ✕

Replace Component ∧
Change Fastener Type...
C:\SOLIDWORKS Data\browser\

Part Numbers ∧
Part Number Unassigned

Add   Edit   Delete

Properties ∧
Size:
3/8-16
Finish:
Double Chamfer
Thread Display:

Figure 6-22

Position the nut

12 Size the nut to 3/8-16 UNC to match the 3/8-16 UNC thread on the bolt.

13 Use the **Mate** tool and position the nut as shown in Figure 6-22.

The nut thickness is .227. This value was obtained by using the **Edit Feature** tool and determining the extrusion value used to create the nut. The nut is defined as 3/8-16 UNC Hex Jam Nut.

> **NOTE**
>
> Bolt threads must extend beyond the nut to ensure 100% contact with the nut. The extension must be a minimum of two pitches (2P).

Figure 6-23

Standard bolt lengths

Thread Length:

So far, the bolt must pass through three blocks (.50 × 3 = 1.50), two washers (.065 × 2 = .13), and one nut (.227). Therefore, the initial bolt length is 1.50 + .13 + .227 = 1.857.

Calculations used to determine the strength of a bolt/nut combination assume that there is 100% contact between the bolt and the nut; that is, all threads of the nut are in contact with the threads of the bolt. However, there is no assurance that the last thread on a bolt is 360°, so at least two threads must extend beyond the nut to ensure 100% contact. The 2P requirement is a minimum value. More than 2P is acceptable. SolidWorks will automatically add at least 4P unless defined otherwise.

In this example the thread pitch is .0625 (1/16). Two pitches (2P) is .125. This value must be added to the initial thread length:

$$1.857 + .125 = 1.982$$

Therefore, the minimum bolt length is 1.982. This value must in turn be rounded up to the nearest standard size. Figure 6-23 shows a listing of standard sizes for a 1 3/8-16 UNC Hex Head bolt.

The final thread length for the given blocks, washers, nut, and 2P is 2.00. The bolt callout is

3/8-16 UNC × 2.00 Hex Head Bolt

14 Click the **Design Library, Toolbox, ANSI Inch, Bolts and Screws, Hex Head, Hex Bolt,** and click and drag-and-drop the bolt into the drawing.

15 Define the **Size** as **3/8-16** and the **Length** as **2**.

See Figures 6-24 and 6-25. Note how the bolt extends beyond the nut.

Figure 6-24

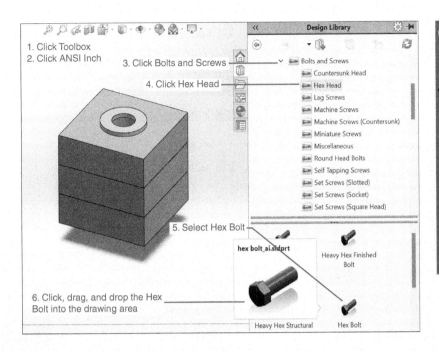

1. Click Toolbox
2. Click ANSI Inch
3. Click Bolts and Screws
4. Click Hex Head
5. Select Hex Bolt
6. Click, drag, and drop the Hex Bolt into the drawing area

Design Library

Bolts and Screws
- Countersunk Head
- Hex Head
- Lag Screws
- Machine Screws
- Machine Screws (Countersunk)
- Miniature Screws
- Miscellaneous
- Round Head Bolts
- Self Tapping Screws
- Set Screws (Slotted)
- Set Screws (Socket)
- Set Screws (Square Head)

hex bolt_ai.sldprt

Heavy Hex Finished Bolt

Heavy Hex Structural

Hex Bolt

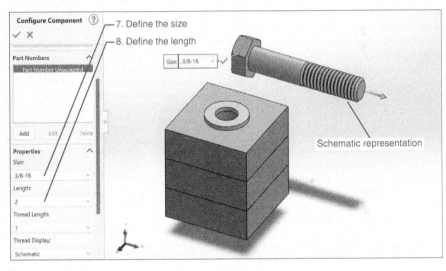

Configure Component

7. Define the size
8. Define the length

Part Numbers
Part Number Unassigned

Add   Edit   Delete

Properties
Size:
3/8-16
Length:
2
Thread Length:
1
Thread Display:
Schematic

Size: 3/8-16

Schematic representation

Figure 6-25

3/8-16 UNC x 2.00 HEX HEAD BOLT

Threads should extend beyond the nut

6-12 Smart Fasteners

The **Smart Fasteners** tool will automatically create the correct bolt. Given the three blocks, two washers, and nut shown in Figure 6-26, use the **Smart Fasteners** tool to add the appropriate bolt.

1 Click the **Smart Fasteners** tool located on the **Assembly** tab.

A dialog box will appear.

2 Click **OK**.

Figure 6-26

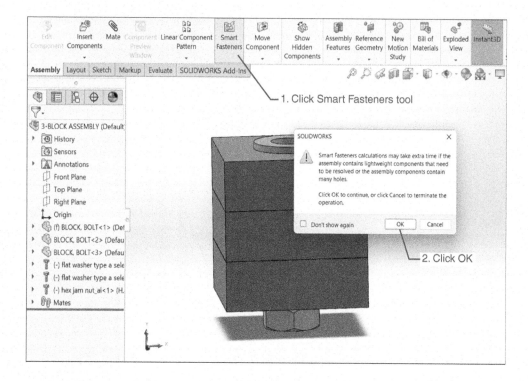

The **Smart Fasteners PropertyManager** will appear. See Figure 6-27.

3 Click the hole in the top block of the three blocks.

Figure 6-27

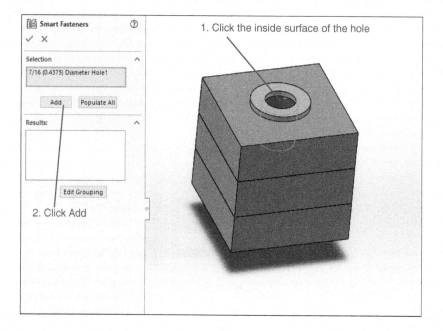

The selected hole will appear in the **Selection** box.

4 Click **Add**.

A fastener will appear in the hole. This may take a few seconds. In this example a **Socket Head Cap Screw** appeared in the hole. Once the screw is added to the assembly it can be edited as needed.

5 Right-click the **Socket Head Cap Screw** heading in the **Fastener** box.

6 Click the **Change fastener type** option.

See Figure 6-28. The **Smart Fastener** dialog box will appear.

Figure 6-28

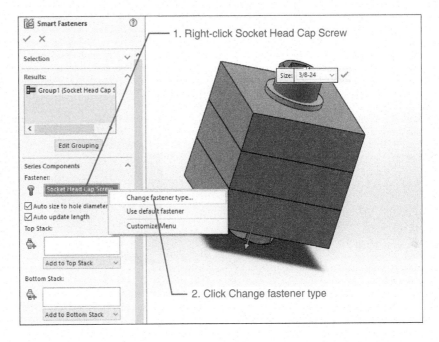

7 Scroll down the list of fasteners and select a **Hex Head** type, as shown in Figure 6-29.

8 Click **OK**.

The **Series Components** manager will appear. See Figure 6-30.

9 Scroll down and access the **Properties** box.

10 Define the thread size, number of threads per inch, and the thread length.

11 Click the green **OK** check mark.

Note that the fastener extends beyond the nut. See Figure 6-31.

Figure 6-29

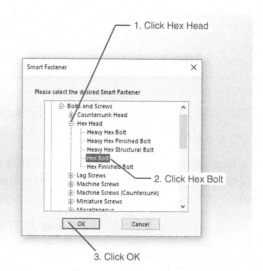

1. Click Hex Head

2. Click Hex Bolt

3. Click OK

Figure 6-30

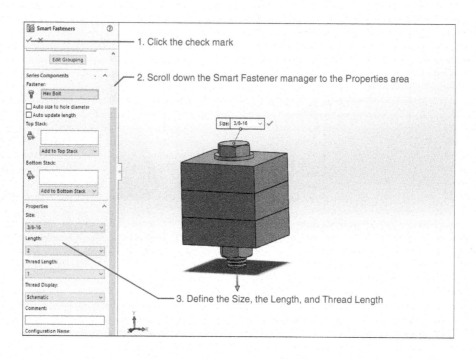

1. Click the check mark

2. Scroll down the Smart Fastener manager to the Properties area

3. Define the Size, the Length, and Thread Length

Figure 6-31

Threads should extend beyond the nut

6-13 Determining an Internal Thread Length

Figure 6-32 shows two blocks: **Block, Cover** and **Block, Base**. Their dimensions are also shown. The two blocks are to be assembled and held together using an M10 × 1.25 × 25 hex head screw. What should be the threaded hole in the **Block, Base**?

Note in Figure 6-32 that the tapped hole extends beyond the threaded portion of the hole. This is to prevent damage to the tapping bit. SolidWorks will automatically calculate the excess length needed, but as a general rule it is at least two pitches (2P) beyond the threaded portion of the hole.

The threaded hole should always be longer than the fastener so that the fastener doesn't "bottom out"—that is, hit the bottom of the threads before the fastener is completely in the hole. Again, the general rule is to allow at least two pitches (2P) beyond the length of the fastener, but more are acceptable depending on the situation.

> **TIP**
> Metric thread callouts give the pitch directly.

Figure 6-32

In this example the thread pitch is **1.25**. Two pitches = 2.50. The bolt length is 25, but it must initially pass through the 10-thick **Block, Cover**, so the length of the bolt in the **Block, Base** is 15. Adding 2.50 to this value yields a minimum thread length of 17.50. Rounding the value up determines that the threaded hole in the **Block, Base** should be M10 × 1.25 × 18 deep. See Figure 6-33. The 18 depth is a minimum value and can be greater.

Figure 6-33

1 Draw the parts as dimensioned in Figure 6-32 and use the **Hole Wizard** to add an M10 × 1.25 × 18 deep hole to the **Block, Base**.

The **Ø12** hole in the **Cover** block is a clearance hole; that is, it is larger than the fastener. It has no threads. See Figure 6-34.

Figure 6-34

2 Assemble the parts as shown.

3 Access the **Design Library**. Click **Toolbox**, **ANSI Metric**, **Bolts and Screws**, **Hex Head**, and access **Formed Hex Screw ANSI B18.2.3.2M**.

4 Click and drag the bolt onto the screen.

See Figure 6-35.

Figure 6-35

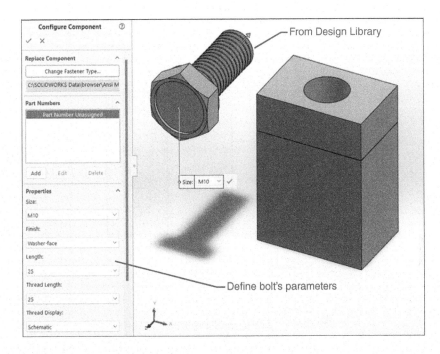

From Design Library

Define bolt's parameters

5 Define the **Size** of the screw as **M10** and the **Length** as **25** with **Thread Length** of **25**.

The **Ø12mm** hole in the **Cover Block** is **10mm** thick. The threaded hole has threads **18mm** deep. The screw is **25mm** long. There are three unused threads in the hole.

6 Use the **Mate Concentric** and **Mate Coincident** tools to place the screw into the assembly.

7 Save the assembly. See Figure 6-36.

Figure 6-37 shows an isometric view, an orthographic view, and a section view of the internal thread assembly.

Figure 6-36

Screw inserted

Figure 6-37

SECTION B-B

6-14   Set Screws

Set screws are fasteners used to hold parts like gears and pulleys to rotating shafts or other moving objects to prevent slippage between the two objects. See Figure 6-38.

Most set screws have recessed heads to help prevent interference with other parts.

Figure 6-38

Many different head styles and point styles are available. See Figure 6-39. The dimensions shown in Figure 6-39 are general sizes for use in this book. For actual sizes, see manufacturers' specifications.

Figure 6-39

SLOTTED HEAD

HEX SOCKET HEAD

SQUARE HEAD

øD

.13D × .19D DEEP

RD

LENGTH

FLAT POINT

.2D

øD

.5D

.75D

R.75D

OVAL POINT

D

SEE HEAD SHAPES

Ø.25D

.75D

LENGTH

45°

CONE POINT

Note: The dimensions listed are for reference only. See manufacturers' specifications for the actual sizes.

45°

.5D

.75D

FULL DOG POINT

45°

.25D

.75D

HALF DOG POINT

45°

120°

.25D

CUP POINT

6-15 Drawing a Threaded Hole in the Side of a Cylinder

Figure 6-40 shows a Ø.75 × Ø1.00 × 1.00 collar with a #10-24 threaded hole. This section will explain how to add a threaded hole through the sides of a cylinder.

1 Draw the collar as a **Ø1.00 × 1.00** cylinder with a **Ø.75** hole through the length of the cylinder.

Figure 6-40

Ø.75

Ø1.00

#10-24 Tapped Hole

1.00

.75

Collar

.25

#10-24 Tapped Hole

See Figure 6-41. In this example the Ø1.00 × 1.00 cylinder was centered about the origin.

Figure 6-41

2 Select the **Plane** tool flyout from the **Reference Geometry** tool.

3 Choose the **Right Plane** as the **First Reference** and set the **Offset distance** to **0.50in**, which is tangent to the outside edge of the cylinder.

See Figure 6-42. The plane will be offset .50 from the origin.

Figure 6-42

4 Click the **Hole Wizard** tool and define the **Size** of the hole as **#10-24** with a thread depth of **.38**.

The .38 distance is enough to have the threads go through the wall of the collar, but not go completely through the cylinder. The collar wall is .125 (1.00 − .75 = .25/2 = .125). Use the **Straight Tap** option. See Figure 6-43.

Figure 6-43

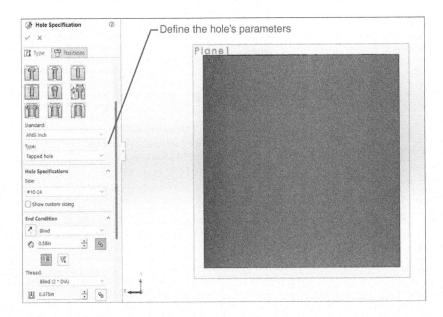

TIP

Do not use the **Through All** option, as this will create holes in both sides of the collar.

---

5 Use the **View Orientation** tool and create a **Right** view of the collar, that is, Normal to the offset plane.

This view orientation will give a direct 90° view of Plane 1. The holes must be located at exactly 90° to the cylinder.

6 Click the **Positions** tab and click the offset right plane within the boundaries of the rectangular face of the cylinder.

This will define the face for the hole location.

7 Locate the centerpoint of the threaded hole as near as possible to the defined location and click the mouse.

See Figure 6-44. This will locate the hole. The location will not be perfect, but it can easily be corrected.

8 Click the **Smart Dimension** tool, and click the hole's centerpoint again.

A listing of parameters will appear. See Figure 6-45.

Figure 6-44

1. Click the Positions tab

Normal view of Right offset plane

2. Approximately locate the hole's centerpoint

Figure 6-45

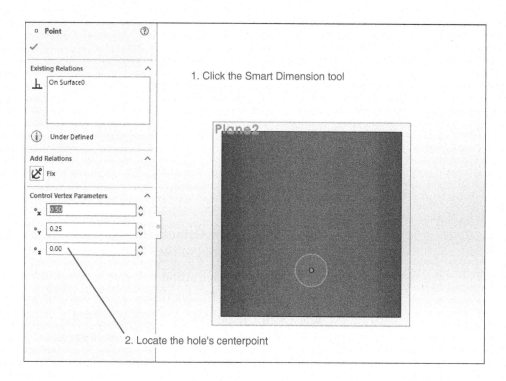

9 Change the **Z** value to **0.00** and the **Y** value to **0.25**.

The Z value of 0.00 will locate the hole's centerpoint directly on the Z-axis. Remember that the original cylinder's centerpoint is on the origin, so this Z value will locate the hole's centerpoint on the Z-axis. The X location will be 0.50, or a point tangent to the outside edge of the cylinder.

The 0.25 value comes from the given .25 dimension. See Figure 6-40.

10 Use the **Hole Wizard** tool again and repeat the procedure and locate a second threaded hole **0.75** from the base as shown in Figure 6-46.

Figure 6-46

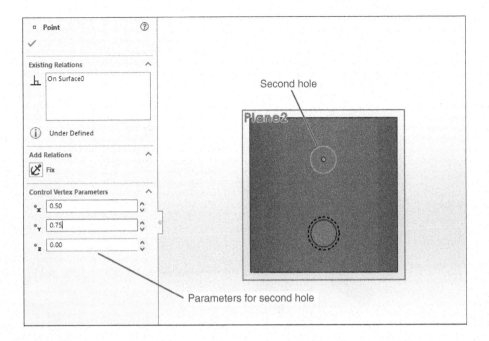

Figure 6-47

Two threaded holes

11 Hide the **Offset Plane** by right-clicking the plane and selecting the **Hide** option.

12 Save the collar as **Ø1.00 COLLAR**.

The Ø symbol is created using **<Alt> 0216**.

Figure 6-47 shows the resulting holes.

6-16 Adding Set Screws to the Collar

Figure 6-49 shows the collar with two set screws. This section will explain how to add and insert the set screws.

1 Start a new **Assembly**.

2 Use the **Browse** tool and locate the **Ø1.00 COLLAR** on the screen.

Locate the origin of the **COLLAR** on the origin of the assembly.

3 Access the **Design Library**, then click **Toolbox**, **ANSI Inch**, **Bolts and Screws**, and **Set Screws (Slotted)**.

See Figure 6-48.

4 Select the **Slotted Set Screw Cup Point** option and click and drag the set screw into the assembly.

See Figure 6-49.

Figure 6-48

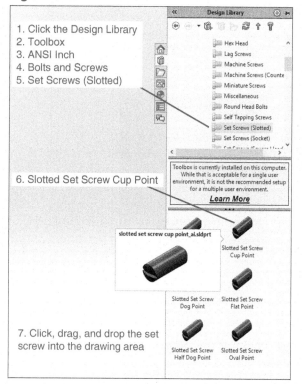

1. Click the Design Library
2. Toolbox
3. ANSI Inch
4. Bolts and Screws
5. Set Screws (Slotted)

6. Slotted Set Screw Cup Point

7. Click, drag, and drop the set screw into the drawing area

Figure 6-49

Two Set Screws

5 Define the **Size** of the set screw as **#10-24** and the **Length** as **0.315**.

0.315 is a standard length. It is good design practice to use standard lengths whenever possible.

6 Click the green **OK** check mark.

A second screw will automatically be attached to the cursor.

7 Add a second set screw and press the **<Esc>** key.

See Figure 6-50.

Figure 6-50

Inserted set screws

Slotted set screws

8 Use the **Mate** tool and insert the set screws into the collar.

9 Save the assembly.

Chapter Projects

Project 6-1: Millimeters

Figure P6-1 shows three blocks. Assume that the blocks are each 30 × 30 × 10 and that the hole is Ø9. Assemble the three blocks so that their holes are aligned and they are held together by a hex head bolt secured by an appropriate hex nut. Locate a washer between the bolt head and the top block and between the nut and the bottom block. Create all drawings using either an A4 or A3 drawing sheet, as needed. Include a title block on all drawing sheets.

A. Define the bolt.

B. Define the nut.

C. Define the washers.

D. Create an assembly drawing including all components.

E. Create a BOM for the assembly.

F. Create an isometric exploded drawing of the assembly.

G. Create an animation of the assembly.

Figure P6-1

Three blocks, each 30 x 30 x 10
with a centered Ø9 hole
P/N AM311-10M

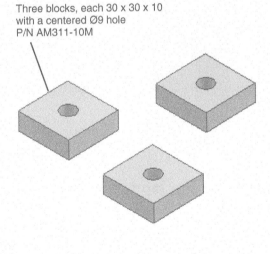

Assemble the three blocks
using a hex head bolt, a hex
nut, and two plain narrow
washers

Project 6-2: Millimeters

Figure P6-2 shows three blocks, one 30 × 30 × 50 block with a centered M8 threaded hole, and two 30 × 30 × 10 blocks with centered Ø9 holes. Join the two 30 × 30 × 10 blocks to the 30 × 30 × 50 block using an M8 hex head bolt. Locate a regular plain washer under the bolt head.

A. Define the bolt.

B. Define the thread depth.

C. Define the hole depth.

D. Define the washers.

E. Create an assembly drawing including all components.

F. Create a BOM for the assembly.

G. Create an isometric exploded drawing of the assembly.

H. Create an animation of the assembly.

Figure P6-2

Ø9

30 × 30 × 10 Block
2 REQD
P/N AM-311-10M

M8

30 × 30 × 50 Block
2 REQD
P/N AM-311-10M

Project 6-3: Inches

Figure P6-3 shows three blocks. Assume that each block is 1.00 × 1.00 × .375 and that the hole is Ø.375. Assemble the three blocks so that their holes are aligned and that they are held together by a 5/16-18 UNC indented regular hex head bolt secured by an appropriate hex nut. Locate a washer between the bolt head and the top block and between the nut and the bottom block. Create all drawings using either an A4 or A3 drawing sheet, as needed. Include a title block on all drawing sheets.

A. Define the bolt.

B. Define the nut.

C. Define the washers.

D. Create an assembly drawing including all components.

E. Create a BOM for the assembly.

F. Create an isometric exploded drawing of the assembly.

G. Create an animation of the assembly.

5/16-18 UNC indented regular hex head bolt

Ø.375

1.00 × 1.00 × .375 Block
3 REQD
P/N AM311-10

Project 6-4: Inches

Figure P6-4 shows three blocks, one 1.00 × 1.00 × 2.00 with a centered threaded hole, and two 1.00 × 1.00 × .375 blocks with centered Ø.375 holes. Join the two 1.00 × 1.00 × .375 blocks to the 1.00 × 1.00 × 2.00 block using a 5/16-18 UNC hex head bolt. Locate a regular plain washer under the bolt head.

Figure P6-4

1.00 × 1.00 × .375 Block
2 REQD
P/N AM311-10

Ø.375 Centered hole

5/16-18 UNC

1.00 × 1.00 × 2.00 Block
P/N AM312-2

A. Define the bolt.

B. Define the thread depth.

C. Define the hole depth.

D. Define the washer.

E. Create an assembly drawing including all components.

F. Create a BOM for the assembly.

G. Create an isometric exploded drawing of the assembly.

H. Create an animation of the assembly.

Project 6-5: Inches or Millimeters

Figure P6-5 shows a centering block. Create an assembly drawing of the block and insert three set screws into the three threaded holes so that they extend at least .25in. or 6mm into the center hole.

Figure P6-5

Centering Block
P/N BU2004-5
SAE 1020 Steel

DIMENSION	INCHES	mm
A	1.00	26
B	.50	13
C	1.00	26
D	.50	13
E	.38	10
F	.190 – 32 UNF	M8X1
G	2.38	60
H	1.38	34
J	.164 – 36 UNF	M6
K	Ø1.25	Ø30
L	1.00	26
M	2.00	52

A. Use the inch dimensions.

B. Use the millimeter dimensions.

C. Define the set screws.

D. Create an assembly drawing including all components.

E. Create a BOM for the assembly.

F. Create an isometric exploded drawing of the assembly.

G. Create an animation of the assembly.

Project 6-6: Millimeters

Figure P6-6 shows two parts: a head cylinder and a base cylinder. The head cylinder has outside dimensions of Ø40 × 20, and the base cylinder has outside dimensions of Ø40 × 50. The holes in both parts are located on a Ø24 bolt circle. Assemble the two parts using hex head bolts.

Figure P6-6

Cylinder Head
P/N EK130-1
SAE 1040 Steel

Counterbored holes
on a Ø24 bolt circle

Cylinder Base
P/N EK130-2
SAE 1040 Steel

A. Define the bolt.

B. Define the holes in the head cylinder, the counterbore diameter and depth, and the clearance hole diameter.

C. Define the thread depth in the base cylinder.

D. Define the hole depth in the base cylinder.

E. Create an assembly drawing including all components.

F. Create a BOM for the assembly.

G. Create an isometric exploded drawing of the assembly.

H. Create an animation of the assembly.

Project 6-7: Millimeters

Figure P6-7 shows a pressure cylinder assembly.

Figure P6-7

A. Create an assembly drawing including all components.

B. Create a BOM for the assembly.

C. Create an isometric exploded drawing of the assembly.

D. Create an animation of the assembly.

Project 6-8: Millimeters

Revise the pressure cylinder assembly shown in Figure P6-7.

A. Use M10 × 35 hex head bolts.

B. Create an assembly drawing including all components.

C. Create a BOM for the assembly.

D. Create an isometric exploded drawing of the assembly.

E. Create an animation of the assembly.

Project 6-9: Inches and Millimeters

Figure P6-9 shows a C-block assembly.

A. Use one of the following fasteners assigned by your instructor:

- M12 hex head

- M10 square head

- 1/4-20 UNC hex head

- 3/8-16 UNC square head

- M10 socket head

- M8 slotted head

- 1/4-20 UNC slotted head

- 3/8-16 UNC socket head

B. Define the bolt.

C. Define the nut.

D. Define the washers.

E. Create an assembly drawing including all components.

F. Create a BOM for the assembly.

G. Create an isometric exploded drawing of the assembly.

H. Create an animation of the assembly.

DIMENSION	INCHES	mm
A	1.25	32
B	.63	16
C	.50	13
D	3.25	82
E	2.00	50
F	.63	16
G	.38	10
H	1.25	32
J	4.13	106
K	.63	16
L	.50	13
M	.75	10
N	3.38	86

Project 6-10: Millimeters

Figure P6-10 shows an exploded assembly drawing. There are no standard parts, so each part must be drawn individually.

A. Create an assembly drawing including all components.

B. Create a BOM for the assembly.

C. Create an isometric exploded drawing of the assembly.

D. Create an animation of the assembly.

Project 6-11: Millimeters

Figure P6-11 shows an exploded assembly.

A. Create an assembly drawing including all components.

B. Create a BOM for the assembly.

C. Create an isometric exploded drawing of the assembly.

D. Create an animation of the assembly.

Figure P6-10

REAR VIEW OF
PART 1

M 10

60
30
15
30

Ø 10

4

M 10

15

42

2 X 45°
CHAMFER

9 SQ

3

15

Ø 14

M 12

20

75

3 X 45° CHAMFER

Ø 14

15

1

15

20

13
2 HOLES

13

20

M 12

40

Ø 16

R 12 BOTH ENDS

55

10

Ø 12

2

Figure P6-11

2

25 ACROSS THE
FLATS

5

25

5
2 GROOVES

73

23

Ø 20

Ø 15 – 2 GROOVES

M 20

3 X 45° CHAMFER

Ø 36

Ø 22

1

3

41.5

M 6
2 HOLES

M 6 X 10 HEX
HEAD SCREW

3

3

21.5

24

28

100

4

M 20

Project 6-12: Inches or Millimeters

Figure P6-12 shows an exploded assembly. No dimensions are given. If parts 3 and 5 have either M10 or 3/8-16 UNC threads, size parts 1 and 2. Based on these values, estimate and create the remaining sizes and dimensions.

A.   Create an assembly drawing including all components.

B.   Create a BOM for the assembly.

C.   Create an isometric exploded drawing of the assembly.

D.   Create an animation of the assembly.

Figure P6-12

Project 6-13: Inches

Figure P6-13 shows an assembly and detail drawings of a surface gauge.

A.   Create an assembly drawing including all components.

B.   Create a BOM for the assembly.

C.   Create an isometric exploded drawing of the assembly.

D.   Create an animation of the assembly.

Figure P6-13   SIMPLIFIED SURFACE GAUGE

NOTE: ALL PARTS MADE
FROM SAE 1020 STEEL

Project 6-14: Millimeters

Figure P6-14 shows an assembly made from parts defined in Project 5-2 on pages [358-360].

Assemble the parts using M10 threaded fasteners.

A.   Define the bolt.

B.   Define the nut.

C.   Create an assembly drawing including all components.

D.   Create a BOM for the assembly.

E.   Create an isometric exploded drawing of the assembly.

F.   Create an animation of the assembly.

G.   Consider possible interference between the nuts and ends of the fasteners both during and after assembly. Recommend an assembly sequence.

Figure P6-14

PLATE, QUAD
P/N AM311-4
2 REQD

C-BRACKET
P/N BK20-3
2 REQD

Project 6-15: Millimeters

Figure P6-15 shows an assembly made from parts defined on pages [358–360]. Assemble the parts using M10 threaded fasteners.

A.   Define the bolt.

B.   Define the nut.

C.   Create an assembly drawing including all components.

D.   Create a BOM for the assembly.

E. Create an isometric exploded drawing of the assembly.

F. Create an animation of the assembly.

G. Consider possible interference between the nuts and ends of the fasteners both during and after assembly. Recommend an assembly sequence.

Figure P6-15

L-BRACKET
P/N BK20-1
2 REQD

PLATE
PL100-6
2 REQD

Project 6-16: Millimeters

Figure P6-16 shows an assembly made from parts defined in Project 5-2 on pages [358-360].

Assemble the parts using M10 threaded fasteners.

A. Define the bolt.

B. Define the nut.

C. Create an assembly drawing including all components.

D. Create a BOM for the assembly.

E. Create an isometric exploded drawing of the assembly.

F. Create an animation of the assembly.

G. Consider possible interference between the nuts and ends of the fasteners both during and after assembly. Recommend an assembly sequence.

Project 6-17: Access Controller

Design an access controller based on the information given in Figure P6-17. The controller works by moving an internal cylinder up and down within the base so the cylinder aligns with output holes A and B. Liquids will enter the internal cylinder from the top, then exit the base through holes A and B. Include as many holes in the internal cylinder as necessary to create the following liquid–exit combinations.

Figure P6-17

INTERNAL CYLINDER

ALIGNMENT SLOT

M20 - 16 DEEP

Ø40

AS NEEDED

AS MANY HOLES AS NEEDED - Ø8

SLOTS FOR SPRING-LOADED STOP BUTTON AS NEEDED

Ø40 NOMINAL

ALIGNMENT GUIDE

60 SQUARE

STOP BUTTON ASSEMBLY

40 NOMINAL May be increased as needed

AS NEEDED

BRACKET
Redesign as necessary for attachment to the base. Add holes to the base and specify fasteners.

STOP BUTTON

M10

SPRING located here

KNURLED HANDLE

MATCH TO STOP BUTTON

SPACER

BASE

1. A open, B closed
2. A open, B open
3. A closed, B open

The internal cylinder is to be held in place by an alignment key and a stop button. The stop button is to be spring-loaded so that it will always be held in place. The internal cylinder will be moved by pulling out the stop button, repositioning the cylinder, then reinserting the stop button.

Prepare the following drawings:

A. An assembly drawing.

B. Detail drawings of each nonstandard part. Include positional tolerances for all holes.

C. A BOM.

Project 6-18: Grinding Wheel

Design a hand-operated grinding wheel as shown in Figure P6-18 specifically for sharpening a chisel. The chisel is to be located on an adjustable rest while it is being sharpened. The mechanism should be able to be clamped to a table during operation using two thumbscrews. A standard grinding wheel is 6.00in. and 1/2in. thick, and has an internal mounting hole with a 50.00±.03 bore.

Prepare the following drawings:

A. An assembly drawing.

B. Detail drawings of each nonstandard part. Include positional tolerances for all holes.

C. A BOM.

Project 6-19: Millimeters

Given the assembly shown in Figure P6-19, add the indicated fasteners and prepare the following drawings:

1. Create an assembly drawing.

2. Create a parts list including assembly numbers.

3. Create a dimensioned drawing of the support block and specify a dimension for each hole including the thread size and the depth required.

30 degrees to the bottom surface

CHISEL

GRINDING WHEEL

ADJUSTABLE REST
The pictured triangular shape is only a suggestion; any shape rest can be specified.

HOLDING SCREW
More than one may be used.

SUPPORT

GRINDING WHEEL
1/2" Thick, Ø6",
50.00±.03 Bore

This support may be designed as a casting.

SHAFT

At least 1" opening

Insert HANDLE here.

LINK

Locate BEARING here, if specified.

THUMBSCREWS

Metal threaded end

HANDLE ASSEMBLY
wooden, metal threaded end

SUPPORT

GRINDING WHEEL

BEARING

SPACER

SPACER

NUT

SHAFT

This is a nominal setup. It may be improved. Consider how the SPACERs rub against the stationary SUPPORT, and consider double NUTs at each end of the shaft.

NUT

SPACER

LINK

SPACER

Figure P6-19

BLOCK, TOP

ASSEMBLY
Material: Mild Steel
All Parts

GASKET

HOLE PATTERN TO MATCH BLOCK,TOP

BASE

HOLE PATTERN TO MATCH BLOCK,TOP

0.75 OR AS REQUIRED

Fasteners:

A.

1. M10 × 35 HEX HEAD BOLT
2. M10 × 35 HEX HEAD BOLT
3. M10 × 30 HEX HEAD BOLT
4. M10 × 25 HEX HEAD BOLT

B.

1. M10 × 1.5 × 35 HEX HEAD BOLT
2. M8 × 35 ROUND HEAD BOLT
3. M10 × 30 HEXAGON SOCKET HEAD CAP SCREW
4. M6 × 30 SQUARE BOLT

Project 6-20: Inches

Given the assembly shown in Figure P6-19, add the indicated fasteners and prepare the following drawings:

1. Create an assembly drawing.
2. Create a BOM including assembly numbers.
3. Create a dimensioned drawing of the base and specify a dimension for each hole including the thread size and the depth required.

Fasteners:

A.

1. 3/8-16 UNC × 2.50 HEX HEAD BOLT
2. 1/4-20 UNC × 2.00 HEX HEAD BOLT
3. 7/16-14 UNC × 1.75 HEX HEAD BOLT
4. 5/16-18 UNC × 2.25 HEX HEAD BOLT

B.

1. 1/4-28 UNF × 2.00 HEX HEAD BOLT
2. #8 (.164)-32 UNC × 2.00 HEX HEAD BOLT
3. 3/8-16 UNC × 1.75 PAN HEAD MACHINE BOLT
4. 5/16-18 UNC × 1.75 HEXAGON SOCKET HEAD CAP BOLT

Project 6-21: Millimeters

Given the collar shown in Figure P6-21, add the indicated set screws and prepare the following drawings:

1. Create an assembly drawing.
2. Create a BOM.
3. Create a dimensioned drawing of the collar. Specify a thread specification for each hole as required by the designated set screw.

Figure P6-21

COLLAR
Mild steel

40.00
35.00
25.00
15.00
5.00

Ø30.00
Ø24.00 THRU
Ø AS REQUIRED

A.
1. M4 × 6 ANSI B18.3.5M SOCKET SET SCREW-HALF-DOG POINT
2. M3 × 3 SOCKET SET SCREW-OVAL POINT
3. M2.5 × 4 B18.3.6M SOCKET SET SCREW-FLAT POINT
4. M4 × 5 B18.3.1M SOCKET HEAD CAP SCREW

B.
1. M2 × 4 B18.3.4M SOCKET BUTTON HEAD CAP SCREW
2. M3 × 6 B18.3.6M SOCKET SET SCREW-CONE POINT
3. M4 × 5 B18.3.6M SOCKET SET SCREW-FLAT POINT
4. M1.6 × 4 B18.3.6M SOCKET SET SCREW-CUP POINT

Project 6-22: Inches

Given the collar shown in Figure P6-22, add the indicated set screws and prepare the following drawings:

1. Create an assembly drawing.
2. Create a BOM.
3. Create a dimensioned drawing of the collar. Specify a thread specification for each hole as required by the designated set screw.

Figure P6-22

Holes:

A.

1. #10 (0.190) × .375 SQUARE HEAD SET SCREW-HALF-DOG POINT-INCH
2. #6 (0.138) × .125 SLOTTED HEADLESS SET SCREW-FLAT POINT-INCH
3. #8 (0.164) × 3.75 SOCKET SET SCREW-CUP POINT-INCH
4. #5 (0.126) × .45 HEXAGON SOCKET SET SCREW-CONE POINT-INCH

B.

1. #6 (0.138) × .25 TYPE D-SOCKET SET SCREW-CUP POINT-INCH
2. #8 (0.164) × .1875 SLOTTED HEADLESS SET SCREW-DOG POINT-INCH
3. #10 (0.190) × .58 HEXAGON SOCKET SET SCREW-FLAT POINT-INCH
4. #6 (0.138) × .3125 SOCKET SET SCREW-HALF-DOG POINT-INCH

Project 6-23: Millimeters

Given the components shown in Figure P6-23:

1. Create an assembly drawing.
2. Animate the assembly.
3. Create an exploded isometric drawing.
4. Create a BOM.

Figure P6-23

60.00

10.00   10.00

Ø6.00

M6x1 - 6g
BOTH ENDS

1×1 CHAMFER
BOTH ENDS

139.00

25.00

12.50

M12x1.75 - 6g   9.00

Ø20.00

Ø6.00

5.00   Ø8.00

Ø7.00 THRU

NOTE: ALL CHAMFERS 1×1

18.00

9.00

3.50

2.00

10.00

R2 - 4 CORNERS

R1 - BOTH SIDES

R3.00

100.00

10.00   10.00

R5-4 CORNERS

OBJECT IS SYMMETRICAL
ABOUT THIS CENTERLINE

25.00

8.00

6.00   8.00

12.00

9.00

55.00

19.50

8.00

M5x0.8 - 6H ⊽8
6 HOLES

NOTE: ALL FILLETS = R2

Project 6-24: Inches

Given the assembly shown in Figure P6-24:

Figure P6-24

ADJUSTABLE ASSEMBLY

NOTE: ALL FILLETS AND ROUNDS = R0.125 UNLESS OTHERWISE STATED.

Figure P6-24
(*Continued*)

R0.38 - BOTH ENDS

5.25

0.63

4.00

Ø0.25 +0.00 +0.02 - 2 HOLES

0.12 BOTH ENDS

0.25 BOTH ENDS

Ø1.00

NOTE: ALL FILLETS = R 0.125

NOTE: ALL FILLETS = R0.125

R5.50

R5.00

R5.25

5°
5°
5°
5°
5°
30°

0.50

1.63

5 × Ø0.25

3/8-16 UNC - 1A

Ø0.25
2 HOLES

R0.38
BOTH
SIDES

1.00

0.50

1.50

1.63

0.53

3/8-16 UNC - 1A

1.00

0.25 ALL AROUND

R0.38

R0.13

ITEM NO.	PART NUMBER	DESCRIPTION	MATL	QTY.
1	SP6-24a	BASE, CAST #4	CAST IRON	1
2	SP6-24c	SUPPORT, ROUND	SAE 1020	1
3	SP6-24d	POST, ADJUSTABLE	SAE 1020	1
4	SP6-24b	YOKE	SAE 1040	1
5	AI 18.15_type2 0.25x2.22-N-0.75	EYEBOLT, TYPE 2 FORGED	STEEL	1
6	SPS 0.25x1.125	PIN, SPRING, SLOTTED	STEEL	1
7	HHJNUT 0.2500-20-D-N	HEX NUT	STEEL	1
8	HHJNUT 0.3750-16-D-N	HEX NUT	STEEL	2

1. Create an assembly drawing.
2. Animate the assembly.
3. Create an exploded isometric drawing.
4. Create a BOM.

Project 6-25: Inches

Given the assembly shown in Figure P6-25:

1. Create an assembly drawing.
2. Animate the assembly.
3. Create an exploded isometric drawing.
4. Create a BOM.

Figure P6-25

ITEM NO.	PART NUMBER	DESCRIPTION	QTY.
1	ME 311-1	WHEEL BRACKET	1
2	ME 311-2	WHEEL SUPPORT	1
3		1.00 × 1.75 × .06 PLAIN WASHER	2
4		1 × 8 UNC HEX NUT	1
5	ME 311-3	SUPPORT ARM	2
6		1/4 - 28 UNF ×1.25 HEX HEAD	4
7		1/4 - 28 UNF × 1.75 HEX HEAD	2
8		1/4 - 28 UNF HEX NUT	6
9	ME 311-4	PIVOT SHAFT	1
10		.500 × .875 .750 BEARING	2
11	ME 311-5	STATIONARY ARM	2
12		#6-32 × .560 UNC SET SCREW CONE POINT	2

NOTE: ALL FILLETS AND ROUNDS R= .25
UNLESS OTHERWISE STATED.

Project 6-26: Inches

Given the assembly shown in Figure P6-26:

1. Create an assembly drawing.
2. Animate the assembly.
3. Create an exploded isometric drawing.
4. Create a BOM.

Figure P6-26

0.09

0.06 - 2 PLACES

5/16-18 UNC - 1B

0.29

0.19

0.50

A   B

A   B

1.44

Ø.313 x .125 DEEP

0.79

0.40

0.10

0.25

R0.10

SECTION A-A
SCALE 2 : 1

R0.19 - 2 PLACES

0.50

0.25

SECTION B-B
SCALE 2 : 1

CHAIN,HANNDLE
P/N: CHN-3
MATL: MILD STEEL

2.00

Ø0.19

0.03 CHAMFER - BOTH ENDS

1.75

Ø0.31

0.13 ROUND

5/16 18 UNC

Ø0.19 THRU

0.03 CHAMFER

.01 CHAMFER

Ø0.33

0.25

0.50

1.13

1.95

Ø0.13

Project 6-27: Inches

Given the assembly shown in Figure P6-27:

1. Create an assembly drawing.
2. Animate the assembly.
3. Create an exploded isometric drawing.
4. Create a BOM.

Figure P6-27

Parts List				
ITEM	PART NUMBER	DESCRIPTION	MATERIAL	QTY
1	AM311-1	BASE	Steel, Mild	1
2	AM311-2	PLATE,END	Steel, Mild	2
3	AM311-3	POST, GUIDE	Steel, Mild	3
4	EK-152	WEIGHT	Steel, Mild	3
5	AS 2465 - 1/2 UNC	HEX NUT	Steel, Mild	6
6		COMPRESSION SPRING	Steel, Mild	6
7	AS 2465 - 1/4 x 2 1/2 UNC	HEX BOLT	Steel, Mild	8

Figure P6-27
(Continued)

BASE
P/N AM311-1
MILD STEEL
1 REQD

1/4-20 UNC - 1B

END PLATE
P/N AM311-2
MILD STEEL
2 REQD

Ø0.53 THRU - 3 HOLES

Ø1.25 ▼ 0.75
3 HOLES

Ø0.28 - 4 HOLES

GUIDE POST
P/N AM311-3
MILD STEEL
3 REQD

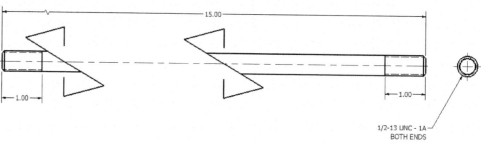

15.00

1.00

1.00

1/2-13 UNC - 1A
BOTH ENDS

WEIGHT
P/N EK-152
MILD STEEL
3 REQD

8.00

Ø1.75

Ø0.56

SPRING
Grind both ends
Inside Ø = .563
Wire Ø = .063
Natural finished
Length = .500
Number of coils
= at least 7

Project 6-28: Inches

Figure P6-28 shows five pipe segments. Use the segments to create the following assemblies:

A. Pipe assembly-1

B. Pipe assembly-2

C. Pipe assembly-3

D. Pipe assembly-4

E. An assembly as defined by your instructor.

For each assembly join the segments using a 1/4-20 UNC × 1.375 Hex Head Screw and a 1/4-20 UNC Hex Nut and create the following:

1. Assembly drawing
2. An isometric exploded drawing
3. A BOM

Figure P6-28

TRAN 6" – 9"

6" ELBOW

Figure P6-28
(*Continued*)

9" ELBOW

∅11.00
BOTH ENDS

∅.250
12 HOLES
EVENLY SPACED

R5.00
BOTH ENDS

∅9.00

∅8.50

90.0°

.50 BOTH
FLANGES

R9.00

STRAIGHT - 9"

TRAN 6" – 9"

6" ELBOW

1/4 – 20 UNC × 1.375
HEX HEAD SCREW

1/4 – 20 UNC × 1.375
HEX HEAD NUT

STRAIGHT - 6"

PIPE ASSEMBLY - 1

9" ELBOW - 60° downward

STRAIGHT - 9"

STRAIGHT - 9"

9" ELBOW

STRAIGHT - 9"

PIPE ASSEMBLY - 2

STRAIGHT - 9"

TRAN 6" – 9"

STRAIGHT - 6"

STRAIGHT - 6"

TRAN 6" – 9"

PIPE ASSEMBLY - 3

PIPE ASSEMBLY - 4

6" ELBOW

6" ELBOW

STRAIGHT - 6"

STRAIGHT - 6"

6" ELBOW

6" ELBOW

Dimensioning

CHAPTER OBJECTIVES

- Dimension objects
- Learn ANSI standards and conventions

- Dimension different shapes and features
- Learn fundamentals of 3D dimensioning

7-1 Introduction

Dimensions are added to SolidWorks on **Drawing** documents. Dimensions will appear in **Part** documents, but these are construction dimensions. These sketch dimensions are used to create a part and are used when a sketch is edited. They may be modified as the part is being created using the **Smart Dimension** tool. They will not appear on the finished model or in **Assembly** documents.

Figure 7-1 shows a dimensioned shape. The drawing on the left in Figure 7-1 shows the sketch dimensions that were used as the part was being created. The drawing on the right in Figure 7-1 shows dimensions that were created using the **Smart Dimension** tool in a **Drawing** document. These are defining dimensions and will appear on the working drawings. This chapter will show how to apply these types of dimensions.

SolidWorks has ANSI Inch and ANSI Metric dimensions available. Other dimensioning systems such as ISO also are available. This text is in compliance with ANSI standards.

Figure 7-1

7-2 Terminology and Conventions—ANSI

Dimensions are added to drawings to define the part and guide manufacturing. General rules and conventions are used to dimension a drawing in a complete, orderly, and succinct manner.

Common Terms

Figure 7-2 shows both ANSI- and ISO-style dimensions. The terms apply to both styles.

Figure 7-2

Dimension lines: In mechanical drawings, lines between extension lines that end with an arrowhead and include a numerical dimensional value located within the line.

Extension lines: Lines that extend away from an object and allow dimensions to be located off the surface of an object.

Leader lines: Lines drawn at an angle, not horizontal or vertical, that are used to dimension specific shapes such as holes. The start point of a leader line includes an arrowhead. Numerical values are drawn at the end opposite the arrowhead.

Linear dimensions: Dimensions that define the straight-line distance between two points.

Angular dimensions: Dimensions that define the angular value, measured in degrees, between two straight lines.

Dimensioning Conventions

There are general guidelines you should follow when dimensioning drawings. Figure 7-3 shows some of the following guidelines applied to a dimensioned part.

Figure 7-3

- Dimension lines should be drawn evenly spaced; that is, the distance between dimension lines should be uniform. A general rule of thumb is to locate dimension lines about 1/2in. or 15mm apart.

- There should be a noticeable gap between the edge of a part and the beginning of an extension line. This serves as a visual break between the object and the extension line. The visual difference between the line types can be enhanced by using different colors for the two types of lines.

- Leader lines are used to define the size of holes and should be positioned so that the arrowhead points toward the center of the hole.

- Centerlines may be used as extension lines. No gap is used when a centerline is extended beyond the edge lines of an object.

- Align dimension lines whenever possible to give the drawing a neat, organized appearance.

Common Errors to Avoid

See Figure 7-4.

Figure 7-4

- Avoid crossing extension lines. Place longer dimensions farther away from the object than shorter dimensions.

- Do not locate dimensions within cutouts; always use extension lines.

- Do not locate any dimension close to the object. Dimension lines should be at least 1/2in. or 15mm from the edge of the object.

- Avoid long extension lines. Locate dimensions in the same general area as the feature being defined.

7-3 Adding Dimensions to a Drawing

Figure 7-5 shows a part that includes two holes. This section will explain how to add dimensions to the part. The part was drawn as a **Part** document and saved as **BLOCK, 2 HOLES**. See Figure 7-10 for the part's dimensions. The part is 0.50 thick. Save the part and start a new **Drawing** document.

Figure 7-5

Block, 2 Holes

1 Click **New**, **Drawing**, and **OK** to start a new drawing. Use a **B (ANSI) Landscape** sheet size.

2 Click the **View Layout** tab, **Model View**, and create a top view of the **BLOCK, 2 HOLES** part.

In this example we will work with only one view. See Figure 7-6.

Figure 7-6

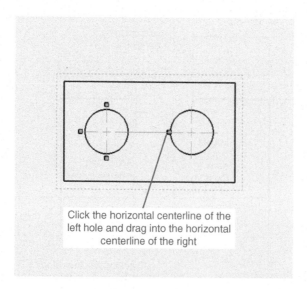

Click the horizontal centerline of the left hole and drag into the horizontal centerline of the right

Extend the horizontal center mark from the left hole to the horizontal centerline of the right hole.

3 Click the horizontal centerline of the left hole. Small blue boxes will appear on the center mark.

4 Click and drag the horizontal centerline from the left hole to the right hole.

The holes now have the same horizontal centerline so only one vertical dimension can be used to define the hole's location. See Figure 7-7.

Figure 7-7

Use the Smart dimension tool and add dimensions to the drawing

2.00

In general, add dimensions from the inside out

TIP
Centerlines can be extended by first clicking them and then dragging an endpoint to a new location.

---

5 Use the **Smart Dimension** tool and add the horizontal and vertical dimensions as shown.

See Figure 7-8.

Figure 7-8

Aligned

Equal distance spacing

4.00

1.00   2.00

1.13

2.25

Shorter dimensions closest to the part

Note that the dimension values for the vertical dimensions are written horizontally. This is in compliance with ANSI standards. For this example, the Century Gothic font was made bold with 14-point height.

> **RULE**
>
> Keep dimension lines aligned and evenly spaced.

6 Click the **Hole Callout** tool located on the **Annotation** panel, click the edge of the left hole, and move the cursor away from the hole.

Note that the leader arrow always points to the center of the hole.

7 Select a location off the surface of the part and click the mouse.

> **RULE**
>
> Never locate dimensions on the surface of the part.

See Figure 7-9. The word THRU is optional. Some companies require it and some do not.

Figure 7-9

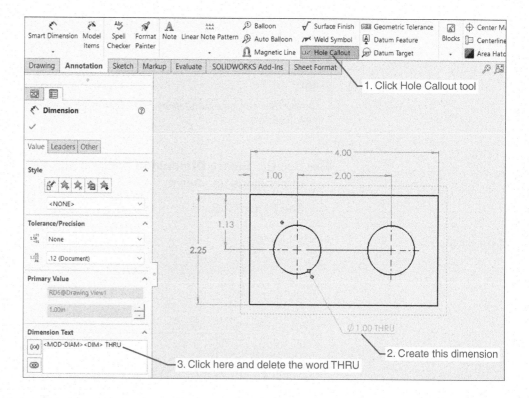

Figure 7-9
(*Continued*)

Chapter 7

8. Go to the **Dimension PropertyManager** at the left of the screen, locate the cursor in the **Dimension Text** box, and delete the word THRU.

   The text already in the box defines the hole's diameter.

9. Move the cursor to the end of the existing text line, and type **- 2 HOLES**.

10. Click the green **OK** check mark.

    Move the dimensions if needed to create neat, uniform dimensions.

    See Figure 7-10.

11. Save the drawing.

Figure 7-10

Controlling Dimensions

Various aspects of dimensions can be edited, such as text height, arrow location, and text values.

1 Click the **Options** tool at the top of the screen.

The **Documents Properties - Drafting Standard** dialog box will appear. See Figure 7-11.

2 Click the **Document Properties** tab.

3 Click the **Dimensions** option.

The **Document Properties - Dimensions** dialog box can be used to edit the style and form of dimensions. It can also be used to change the way arrows are applied.

4 Click the **Font** option.

The **Choose Font** dialog box will appear. See Figure 7-11. This dialog box can be used to change the font, font style, and height of dimension text. The height of text can be measured in inches, millimeters, or points. A *point* refers to a space that equals about 1/72 of an inch. (There are 12 points to a *pica*.)

Figure 7-11

Figure 7-11
(Continued)

An example of Times New Roman font

4.00
1.00 2.00
1.13
2.25
Ø1.00 - 2 HOLES

5 Click the **Height: Units** radio button and change the height to **0.250in**.

Note that the SolidWorks default font is Century Gothic.

6 Click **OK**, then **OK**.

Figure 7-11 shows dimensions created using the Times New Roman font. Fonts for drawings should always be easy to read and not too stylistic.

Dimensioning Short Distances

Figure 7-12 shows an object that includes several short distances. We will start by using the standard dimensions settings and show how to edit them for a particular situation.

1 Use the **Smart Dimension** tool and add dimensions to the drawing.

Note that the arrows for the .50 dimension are aligned with the arrows for the 1.00 dimensions. Dimensions that are aligned in a single row are called *chain dimensions*. Note that the .25 dimension is crowded between the two extension lines.

RULE
Never squeeze dimension values. Dimension values should always be presented clearly and legible.

There are several possible solutions to the crowded .25 value.

2 Click and drag the .25 dimension to the right outside the extension lines.

3 Add the **4.00** overall dimension.

Dimensions that define the total length and width of an object are called *overall dimensions*. In this example the dimension 4.00 defines the total length of the part, so it is an overall dimension. Overall dimensions are located farthest away from the edge of the part.

The right edge of the part, the section below the .25, does not need a dimension. The reason for this will be discussed in the next chapter on tolerancing.

Figure 7-12 shows two other options for dimensioning. The first is the baseline method, in which all dimensions are taken from the same datum line. The second method is a combination of chain and baseline dimensions.

Figure 7-12

Dimension this shape

Figure 7-13 shows an example of double dimensioning. The top edge distance is dimensioned twice: once using the 1.00 + .50 + 1.00 + .25 + 1.25 dimensions, and a second time using the 4.00 dimension. One of the dimensions must be omitted. Double dimensioning will be explained in more detail in Chapter 8.

Figure 7-13

ERROR—double dimensions

The top edge is dimensioned twice

Autodimension Tool

The **Autodimension** tool will automatically add dimensions to a drawing.

Figure 7-14 shows a shape to be dimensioned using the **Autodimension** tool.

1 Click the **Annotation** tab, click the **Smart Dimension** tool, and click the **Autodimension** tab.

2 Select the **Chain Scheme**, define **Edge 1** and **Edge 2**, click the **Apply** box, and click the **OK** check mark.

SolidWorks will automatically pick edges 1 and 2. If it does not, or the edges selected are not the ones you want, click the **Edge** box, then click the edge. The word **Edge<1>** should appear in the box.

Figure 7-14 shows the dimensions applied using the **Autodimension** tool. They are not in acceptable positions.

3 Rearrange the dimensions to comply with standard conventions.

Figure 7-14

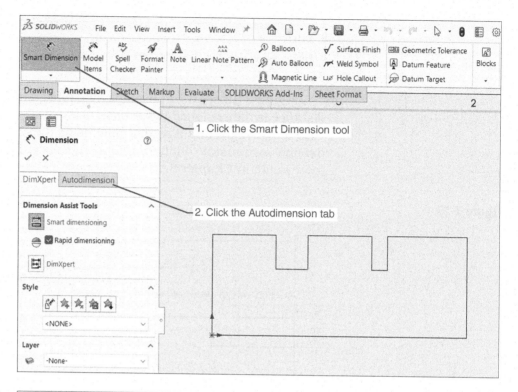

1. Click the Smart Dimension tool

2. Click the Autodimension tab

3. Select Chain Scheme

Edge 2 (Pink)

Edge 1 (Purple)

4. Click Apply

Chain dimensions created using the Autodimension tool

Dimensions must be repositioned

Chain dimensions in compliance with ANSI

Figure 7-15 shows the shape shown in Figure 7-14 dimensioned using the baseline scheme, which is created as follows.

Figure 7-15

Creating Baseline Dimensions

1 Access the **Autodimension** tool and select the **Baseline Scheme**.

2 Select **Edge 1** and **Edge 2**.

3 Click **Apply**.

4 Click the green **OK** check mark.

Figure 7-15 shows the dimensions created by the **Autodimension** tool and how the dimensions can be rearranged.

Creating Ordinate Dimensions

Figure 7-16 shows the object dimensioned using the **Ordinate Scheme** of the **Autodimension** tool. The **Autodimension** tool did better placing the ordinate dimensions in this instance, but if some of the created dimensions are located on the surface of the part, this would be a violation of the convention that dimensions should never be located on the surface of the part. Figure 7-16 shows how the ordinate dimensions were rearranged.

Figure 7-16

7-4 Drawing Scale

Drawings are often drawn "to scale" because the actual part is either too big to fit on a sheet of drawing paper or too small to be seen. For example, a microchip circuit must be drawn at several thousand times its actual size to be seen.

Drawing scales are written using the following formats:

SCALE: 1 = 1

SCALE: FULL

SCALE: 1000 = 1

SCALE: .25 = 1

In each example the value on the left indicates the scale factor. A value greater than 1 indicates that the drawing is larger than actual size. A value smaller than 1 indicates that the drawing is smaller than actual size.

Regardless of the drawing scale selected, the dimension values must be true size. Figure 7-17 shows the same rectangle drawn at two different scales. The top rectangle is drawn at a scale of 1 = 1, or its true size. The bottom rectangle is drawn at a scale of 2 = 1, or twice its true size. In both examples the 3.00 dimension remains the same.

Figure 7-17

SCALE: FULL

Figure 7-18

TOLERANCES UNLESS OTHERWISE STATED	
X	± 1
.X	± .1
.xx	± .01
.XXX	± .005
X°	± 1°
.X°	± .1°

7-5   Units

It is important to understand that dimension values are not the same as mathematical units. Dimension values are manufacturing instructions and always include a tolerance, even if the tolerance value is not stated. Manufacturers use a predefined set of standard dimensions that are applied to any dimensional value that does not include a written tolerance. Standard tolerance values differ from organization to organization. Figure 7-18 shows a chart of standard tolerances.

In Figure 7-19 a distance is dimensioned twice: once as 5.50 and a second time as 5.5000. Mathematically these two values are equal, but they are not the same manufacturing instruction. The 5.50 value could, for example, have a standard tolerance of ±.01, whereas the 5.5000 value could have a standard tolerance of ±.0005. A tolerance of ±.0005 is more difficult and therefore more expensive to manufacture than a tolerance of ±.01.

Figure 7-20 shows examples of units expressed in millimeters and in decimal inches. A zero is not required to the left of the decimal point for decimal inch values less than one. Millimeter values do not require zeros to the right of the decimal point. Millimeter and decimal inch values never include symbols; the units will be defined in the title block of the drawing.

Figure 7-19

These dimensions are not the same. They have different tolerance requirements.

Figure 7-20

Millimeters

0.25	0.5	0.033
32	14.5	3

Zero required

No zero required

Inches

.25	.05	.033
32.00	14.50	3.000

Aligned Dimensions

Aligned dimensions are dimensions that are parallel to a slanted edge or surface. They are not horizontal or vertical. The units for aligned dimensions should be written horizontally. This is called *unidirectional dimensioning*.

Figure 7-21 shows the front, right-side, and isometric views of a part with a slanted surface. The dimensions were applied using the **Smart Dimension** tool. Note that the slanted dimension, aligned with the slanted surface, has unidirectional (horizontal) text. The hole dimension was created using the **Note** tool from the **Annotation** tab.

Hole Dimensions

Figure 7-22 shows an object that has two holes, one blind and one completely through. The object has filleted corners. In this section we will add dimensions to the views.

Figure 7-21

Figure 7-22

The holes were drawn using the **Hole Wizard** tool. The **Hole Wizard** tool will automatically create a conical point to a blind hole.

1 Use the **Smart Dimension** tool and locate the two holes.

See Figure 7-23. In general, dimensions are applied from the inside out; that is, starting with the features in the middle of the part and working out to the overall dimensions. Leader lines are generally applied last, as they have more freedom of location.

2 Use the **Linear Center Mark** tool to draw a centerline between the two holes and use the **Centerline** tool to add the vertical centerline in the front and side views.

The centerline between the two holes indicates that the vertical 30 dimension applies to both holes.

> **NOTE**
>
> Centerlines should extend beyond the edges of the part. Centerlines can be extended by first clicking the centerline. Blue end boxes will appear. Click and drag the blue end boxes to a point beyond the edges of the part.

Figure 7-23

3 Use the **Smart Dimension** tool and add a dimension to one of the filleted corners.

See Figure 7-24.

Figure 7-24

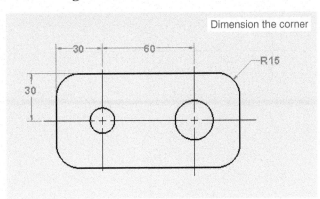

4 Click the fillet dimension again, go to the **Dimension Text** block on the **Dimension PropertyManager**, and type **- 4 CORNERS** as shown in Figure 7-25.

Figure 7-25

5 Click **OK**, **Apply**, and **OK**.

6 Use the **Hole Callout** tool on the **Annotation** panel and dimension the Ø16 hole.

The Ø16 hole goes completely through the part, so no depth specification is required. See Figure 7-26. The word THRU is optional and may be removed.

7 Use the **Hole Callout** tool and **Dimension** the Ø25 hole.

Figure 7-26

The hole callout will include the depth symbol (see Figure 7-27) and a depth value of **30** (see Figure 7-28).

Complete the dimensions.

See Figure 7-29.

Figure 7-28

Figure 7-27

Figure 7-29

NOTE

If the **Smart Dimension** tool had been used, the dimension would have to be edited in the **Dimension Text** area and the depth symbol and a numerical value added.

7-6 Dimensioning Holes and Fillets

A *blind hole* is a hole that does not go completely through an object. It has a depth requirement. Figure 7-30 shows a 2.00 × 2.00 × 2.00 cube with a blind Ø.50 × 1.18 DEEP hole. It was created as follows.

Dimensioning a Blind Hole

1 Draw the block.

2 Click the **Hole Wizard** tool.

See Figure 7-30.

Figure 7-30

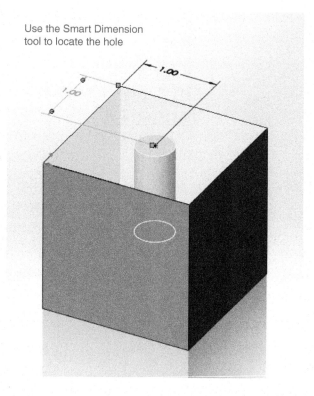

Use the Smart Dimension tool to locate the hole

1. Click the Hole Type option

2. Define Standard

3. Define Hole Size

4. Define hole's depth

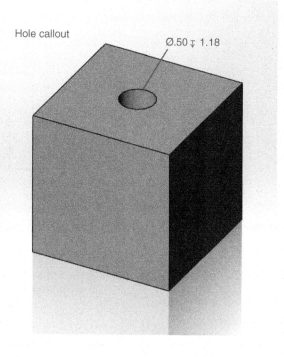

Hole callout

Ø.50 ⬇ 1.18

Figure 7-30
(*Continued*)

Chapter 7

Symbol for depth

Hole depth

⌀ .50 ⍌ 1.18

Hole callout

1.00

1.00

2.00

2.00

(1.18)

2.00

2.00

Not included in depth

This dimension is not needed. It is included here to verify that the stated hole depth does not include the conical point.

3 Click the **Hole** tool in the **Hole Type** box. Define the hole using the **ANSI Inch** standard with a **Size** of **1/2** and a **Blind Hole Depth** of **1.18in**.

4 Click the **Positions** tab.

5 Locate the hole as shown.

The initial location is an approximation. Use the **Smart Dimension** tool to specify the exact location of the hole's centerpoint.

6 Click the green **OK** check mark.

7 Save the drawing as **Block, Blind**.

8 Start a new **Drawing** document and create a front and a top orthographic view of the **Block, Blind**.

9 Add dimensions to the views.

10 Click the **Annotation** tab and click the **Hole Callout** option.

11 Click the edge of the hole, move the cursor away from the hole, define a location for the hole callout, and click the mouse. The hole callout dimension will initially appear as a rectangular box.

Change the height of the text font if necessary.

12 Save the drawing.

Note that the hole includes a conical point. Holes manufactured using twist drills will have conical points. The conical point is not included in the hole's depth dimension. A special drill bit can be used to create a flat-bottomed hole.

Figure 7-31 shows three different methods that can be used to dimension a blind hole.

Figure 7-31

Dimensions for holes with depth

Figure 7-32

Section views of holes with depth

Figure 7-32 shows three methods of dimensioning holes in section views. The single line note version is the preferred method.

Dimensioning Hole Patterns

Figure 7-33 shows two different hole patterns dimensioned. The circular pattern includes the note **Ø10 – 4 HOLES**. This note serves to define all four holes within the object.

Figure 7-33 also shows a rectangular object that contains five holes of equal diameter, equally spaced from one another. The notation **5 × Ø10** specifies five holes of 10 diameter. The notation **4 × 20 (=80)** means four equal spaces of 20. The notation **(=80)** is a reference dimension and is included for convenience. Reference dimensions are explained in Chapter 9.

Figure 7-33

Figure 7-34 shows two additional methods for dimensioning repeating hole patterns. Figure 7-35 shows a circular hole pattern that includes two different hole diameters. The hole diameters are not noticeably different and could be confused. One group is defined by indicating letter **A**; the other is dimensioned in a normal manner.

Figure 7-34

Figure 7-35

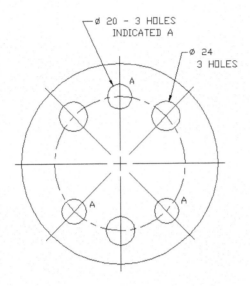

7-7 Dimensioning Counterbored and Countersunk Holes

Counterbored holes are dimensioned in the sequence of their manufacture. First the hole's diameter is given, then the counterbore diameter, then the depth of the counterbore.

Figure 7-36 shows a part that contains two counterbored holes; one goes completely through and the other is blind. Dimensions will be applied to both.

1 Create a **3.00 × 4.00 × 1.75** block.

2 Click the **Hole Wizard** tool, click the **Counterbore** option, and insert the counterbored hole that goes completely through.

3 Specify the **Standard** as **ANSI Inch**, the **Type** as **Hex Screw**, the **Size** as a **3/8** diameter, and the **End Condition** as **Through All**.

See Figure 7-37. SolidWorks will automatically select the diameter for the counterbored hole that will accommodate a Ø3/8 Hex Head Screw.

Depending on your default settings, the counterbored hole may have a small chamfer added. The countersink can be removed by removing the check mark in the **Options** box on the **Hole Specification** manager.

Figure 7-36

Figure 7-37

Locate the counterbore hole

Figure 7-37
(*Continued*)

Chapter 7

Position the second hole

Finished block

4 Position the hole using the given dimensions.

5 Add the second hole, setting the **End Condition** to **Blind** and **1.00** deep.

6 Position the hole using the given dimensions.

7 Save the block as **Block, Cbore**.

8 Start a new **Drawing** document and create a front and a top orthographic view of the **Block, Cbore**.

9 Click the **Annotation** tab and add all dimensions and centerlines other than the hole dimensions.

10 Click the **Hole Callout** tool.

See Figure 7-38.

11 Click the edge of each hole, move the cursor away from the hole, and click the mouse when a suitable location is found.

The counterbored hole's dimension note is interpreted as shown in Figure 7-38.

Figure 7-38

Figure 7-39 shows the **Block, Cbore** assembled with hex head screws inserted into the counterbored holes. SolidWorks will automatically generate the correct size counterbored hole for a specified screw. The counterbore depth will align the top of the screw head with the top surface of the part and will define a hole diameter that includes clearance between the fastener and the hole. In this example a clearance hole with a diameter of **Ø.40** was generated. The hole is .02 larger than the specified .38 fastener diameter.

If clearance is required between the top of the screw and the top surface of the part, check the **Head clearance** box under **Options** in the **Hole Specification** section of the **Hole Wizard PropertyManager**. See Figure 7-40.

Figure 7-40

Click Hole Wizard and
Hole Specification

Specify the clearance

Figure 7-39

3/8 Hex Head screw

Tool clearance

The diameter of the counterbored hole can be made larger than the clearance generated by SolidWorks to allow for tool clearance. Tool clearance allowance increases the diameter of the counterbore so that it is large enough to allow a socket wrench to fit over the head of the fastener and still fit within the hole.

Counterbored Hole with Threads

Figure 7-41 shows a 3.00 × 4.00 × 2.00 block with two counterbored holes. Both holes are threaded.

1 Create the block.

2 Click the **Hole Wizard** tool, select the **Straight Tap** option, and specify a **3/8-16 UNC** thread that goes completely through.

3 Click the **Positions** tab and locate the hole.

4 Click the green **OK** check mark.

This will locate a 3/8-16 UNC thread hole in the block. Now, we add the counterbore.

5 Click the top surface of the block and click the **Sketch** option.

6 Click the **Circle** tool and draw a **Ø.88** circle on the top surface centered on the same centerpoint as the Ø3/8-16 hole.

The dimensions for this example came from Figure 7-38.

Figure 7-41
(*Continued*)

1. Click Straight Tap

2. Select ANSI Inch

3. Select Tapped hole

4. Specify 3/8-16

5. Specify Through All

Figure 7-41
(*Continued*)

7 Click the **Features** tab, click the **Extruded Cut** tool, and specify a cut depth of **0.27**.

8 Click the green **OK** check mark.

9 Repeat the procedure, adding a second hole with a thread to a depth of **0.85**.

See Figure 7-42.

Figure 7-42

10 Save the block as **Block, Threads**.

11 Create a new **Drawing** document and create front and top orthographic views of the **Block, Threads**.

12 Add centerlines to the front view and add dimensions as shown.

See Figure 7-43.

13 Use the **Hole Callout** tool and click the left threaded hole.

Do not click the outside of the counterbored hole. This will generate a note that includes only the counterbore. In Figure 7-42 the callouts 3/8-16 Tapped Hole appear on the front view. Remove the callouts from view by right-clicking the callouts and selecting the **Hide** option. The thread information will be included in the counterbore hole callout.

14 Locate the text and click the mouse.

The initial note may show the counterbore callout above the thread callout. Convention calls for the note to read in the sequence of manufacture. The threaded hole is cut first and then the counterbore is added; therefore, the thread callout should come before the counterbore callout.

15 Modify the callout to list the thread callout above the counterbore callout.

Access the **Dimension Text** box on the **Dimension Manager** by clicking the **.31 THRU ALL** dimension, delete the first line of text, and replace the dimension with a new dimension, **3/8-16 UNC THRU**.

Figure 7-43

1. Click this dimension to access the Dimension Text

2. Change the text here

3. Hide the Tapped dimensions

16 Click the green **OK** check mark.

17 Click the threaded portion of the right hole.

18 Locate the text and click the mouse.

19 Modify the callout as shown.

Figure 7-44 shows dimensioned counterbored holes using metric units. The **Hole Callout** tool was used to dimension the counterbored holes. Note that the hole's diameter is listed as Ø11. The fastener size was specified as M10, and the Ø11 hole is a clearance hole.

Figure 7-44

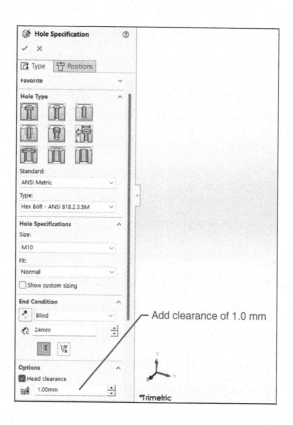

Add clearance of 1.0 mm

Dimensioning Countersink Holes

Countersink holes are used with flat head screws to create assemblies in which the fasteners do not protrude above the surfaces.

Figure 7-45 shows a part with two countersunk holes; one goes completely through, the other has a depth specification.

Figure 7-45

Two countersunk holes

1 Draw a 40 × 80 × 60 block.

2 Use the **Hole Wizard** tool, click the **Countersink** type, specify the **ANSI Metric** standard, select an **M10** size for a flat head screw, and specify a hole that goes all the way through. Define a head clearance of **2.00mm**.

3 Click the **Positions** tab and position the countersunk hole's centerpoint as shown using the **Smart Dimension** tool.

4 Click the green **OK** check mark.

5 Click the **Hole Wizard** tool, click the **Countersink** type, specify the **ANSI Metric** standard, select an **M10** size for a flat head screw, and specify a depth requirement of **25.00mm** for a **Blind** hole. Define a head clearance of **2.00mm**.

6 Click the **Positions** tab and locate the hole as shown.

7 Click the green **OK** check mark.

8 Save the drawing as **Block, CSink**.

Dimensioning the Block

1 Create a new **Drawing** document with a front and a top orthographic view of the **Block, CSink**.

2 Use the **Smart Dimension** tool and add the appropriate dimensions.

3 Use the **Center Mark** tool to add a centerline between the two holes indicating they are aligned.

4 Click the **Annotation** tab, click the **Hole Callout** tool, and dimension the two countersunk holes.

See Figure 7-46.

Figure 7-46

Completed dimensions

7-8 Angular Dimensions

Figure 7-47 shows a model that includes a slanted surface and dimensioned orthographic views of the model. The dimension values are located beyond the model between two extension lines. Locating dimensions between extension lines is preferred to locating the value between an extension line and the edge of the model.

Figure 7-47

A model with slanted surfaces

Angular dimension

Extension line

Extension line

Figure 7-48 shows a shape that includes a slanted surface dimensioned in two different ways. The shape on the left uses an angular dimension; the one on the right does not. Both are acceptable.

Figure 7-48

20.00

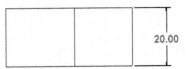

20.00

No dimension here

There are different ways to dimension the same model. Do not include more dimensions than are needed.

38.3°

30.00

3.91

45.00

24.41

No dimension here

30.00

3.91

45.00

Figure 7-49 shows two objects dimensioned using angular dimensions. One has an evenly spaced hole pattern; the other has an uneven hole pattern.

Figure 7-49

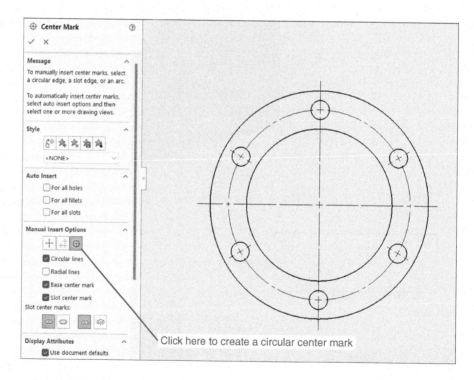

Figure 7-49
(*Continued*)

Chapter **7**

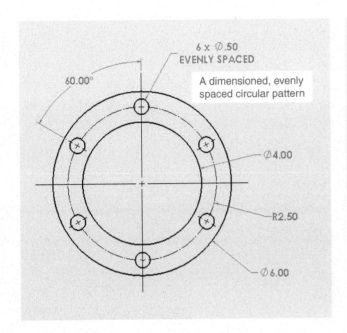

6 x ⌀.50
EVENLY SPACED

60.00°

A dimensioned, evenly
spaced circular pattern

⌀4.00

R2.50

⌀6.00

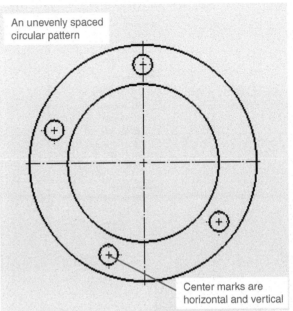

An unevenly spaced
circular pattern

Center marks are
horizontal and vertical

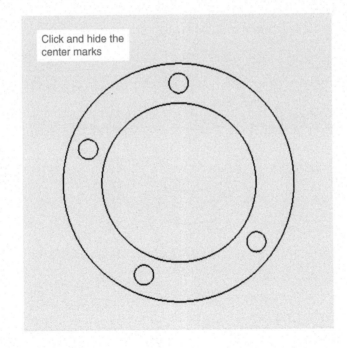

Click and hide the
center marks

Figure 7-49
(*Continued*)

Dimensioning an Evenly Spaced Hole Pattern

1 Start a new drawing of the object and create a view as shown in Figure 7-49.

The object will automatically include circular centerlines. The circular centerline is called a *bolt circle*. Note that the center marks are not horizontal and vertical but point at the centerpoint of the pattern.

Circular centerlines and center marks can be created using the **Manual Insert Options** located on the **Center Mark PropertyManager**.

2 Add dimensions to the pattern and the object.

The six holes are evenly spaced and are all the same size, so only one angular dimension and a note are needed, as shown. All the holes are the same distance from the centerpoint, so the circular centerline needs only one dimension that will include the six holes.

The size and text position of the angular dimension can be edited using the **System** tool, **Document Properties**, **Dimensions**, **Angle**, and entering edits.

Figure 7-49 shows a similar object but with an uneven hole pattern. Each hole must be dimensioned separately.

When the drawing view first appears on the screen, all the center marks are horizontal and vertical. A circular centerline pattern is preferred. Click each center mark and **Hide** the mark. Click the **Center Mark** tool and the **Circular Center Mark** tool located under the **Manual Insert Options**, and click each hole. A circular centerline pattern will appear. The shape can then be dimensioned using the circular pattern.

7-9 Ordinate Dimensions

Ordinate dimensions are dimensions based on an XY coordinate system. Ordinate dimensions do not include extension lines, dimension lines, or arrowheads but simply horizontal and vertical leader lines drawn directly from the features of the object. Ordinate dimensions are particularly useful when dimensioning an object that includes many small holes.

Figure 7-50 shows a part that is to be dimensioned using ordinate dimensions. Ordinate dimensions' values are calculated from the XY origin, which, in this example, is the lower-left corner of the front view of the model.

Figure 7-50

Creating Ordinate Dimensions

See Figure 7-51.

1 Start a new **Drawing** document and create a top orthographic view of the part.

Use the dimensions shown in Figure 7-52 to create the drawing.

2 Click and extend the center marks and draw centerlines between the four corner holes.

Figure 7-51

Figure 7-51
(Continued)

Vertical Ordinate
Dimensions

3 Click the arrowhead located under the **Smart Dimension** tool and click the **Horizontal Ordinate Dimension** option.

4 Click the lower-left corner of the part to establish the origin for the dimensions.

5 Move the cursor away from the origin and define a location for the "0" dimension.

All other horizontal dimensions will align with this location.

6 Click the lower portion of each hole's vertical centerline and the lower-right corner of the part.

7 Click the arrowhead located under the **Smart Dimension** tool and click the **Vertical Ordinate Dimension** option.

8 Click the lower-left corner of the part to establish the origin for the dimensions.

9 Click the left portion of each hole's horizontal centerline and the upper-left corner of the part.

10 Add dimensions for the holes.

Figure 7-52 shows the dimensioned part.

Figure 7-52

7-10 Baseline Dimensions

Baseline dimensions are a series of dimensions that originate from a common baseline or datum line. Baseline dimensions are very useful because they help eliminate the tolerance buildup that is associated with chain-type dimensions.

Creating Baseline Dimensions

See Figure 7-53.

1 Start a new **Drawing** document and create a top orthographic view of the part.

2 Use the **Linear Center Mark** tool and add connection centerlines between the four corner holes.

3 Click the arrowhead under the **Smart Dimension** tool and click the **Baseline Dimension** option.

4 Click the left vertical edge of the part and the lower portion of the first vertical centerline.

This will establish the baseline.

5 Click the lower portion of each vertical centerline and the right vertical edge line and locate the dimensions.

Figure 7-53

Baseline dimensions

Add hole dimensions

6 Click the arrowhead under the **Smart Dimension** tool and click the **Baseline Dimension** option.

7 Click the lower horizontal edge of the part and the left end of the first horizontal centerline.

8 Click the left end of each horizontal centerline and the right top horizontal edge line.

The alignment of the vertical dimension lines can be changed by right-clicking the individual dimension and selecting the **Break Alignment** option.

9 Add the hole dimensions.

Hole Tables

Hole tables are a method for dimensioning parts that have large numbers of holes where standard dimensioning may be cluttered and difficult to read. See Figure 7-54.

Figure 7-54

Figure 7-54
(*Continued*)

Chapter 7

1. Click the corner

2. Click each hole

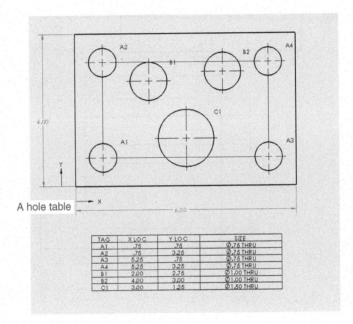

A hole table

TAG	X LOC	Y LOC	SIZE
A1	.75	.75	Ø.75 THRU
A2	.75	3.25	Ø.75 THRU
A3	5.25	.75	Ø.75 THRU
A4	5.25	3.25	Ø.75 THRU
B1	2.00	2.75	Ø1.00 THRU
B2	4.00	3.00	Ø1.00 THRU
C1	3.00	1.25	Ø1.50 THRU

1 Start a new **Drawing** document and create a top orthographic view of the part.

2 Use the **Linear Center Mark** tool and add connection centerlines between the four corner holes.

3 Click the **Annotation** tab, click **Tables**, and click **Hole Table**.

4 Click the lower-left corner of the part to establish an origin.

5 Click each hole.

As the holes are clicked they should be listed in the **Holes** box located in the **Hole Table PropertyManager**.

6 Click the green **OK** check mark and locate the hole table.

7 Add the overall dimensions.

8 Move the hole tags as needed to present a clear, easy-to-read drawing.

In this example all tags were located to the upper-right of the holes they define. Tables can be edited using the instructions presented in Section 5-11 for BOMs.

7-11 Locating Dimensions

There are eight general rules concerning the location of dimensions. See Figure 7-55.

Figure 7-55

1. Locate dimensions near the features they are defining.

2. Do not locate dimensions on the surface of the object.

3. Align and group dimensions so that they are neat and easy to understand.

4. Avoid crossing extension lines.

Sometimes it is impossible not to cross extension lines because of the complex shape of the object, but whenever possible, avoid crossing extension lines.

5. Do not cross dimension lines.

6. Locate shorter dimensions closer to the object than longer dimensions.

7. Always locate overall dimensions the farthest away from the object.

8. Do not dimension the same distance twice. This is called *double dimensioning* and will be discussed in Chapter 8 in association with tolerancing.

7-12   Fillets and Rounds

Fillets and rounds may be dimensioned individually or by a note. In many design situations all the fillets and rounds are the same size, so a note as shown in Figure 7-56 is used. Any fillets or rounds that have a different radius from that specified by the note are dimensioned individually.

Figure 7-56

NOTE: ALL FILLETS AND
ROUNDS = R0.25 UNLESS
OTHERWISE STATED.

7-13   Rounded Shapes—Internal

Internal rounded shapes are called *slots*. Figure 7-57 shows three different methods for dimensioning slots. The end radii are indicated by the note **R-2 PLACES**, but no numerical value is given. The width of the slot is dimensioned, and it is assumed that the radius of the rounded ends is exactly half of the stated width.

Figure 7-57

7-14 Rounded Shapes—External

Figure 7-58 shows two shapes with external rounded ends. As with internal rounded shapes, the end radii are indicated, but no value is given. The width of the object is given, and the radius of the rounded end is assumed to be exactly half of the stated width.

Figure 7-58

The second example shown in Figure 7-58 shows an object dimensioned using the object's centerline. This type of dimensioning is done when the distance between the holes is more important than the overall length of the object; that is, the tolerance for the distance between the holes is more exact than the tolerance for the overall length of the object.

The overall length of the object is given as a reference dimension (100). This means the object will be manufactured based on the other dimensions, and the 100 value will be used only for reference.

Objects with partially rounded edges should be dimensioned as shown in Figure 7-58. The radii of the end features are dimensioned. The center-point of the radii is implied to be on the object centerline. The overall dimension is given; it is not referenced unless specific radii values are included.

7-15   Irregular Surfaces

There are three different methods for dimensioning irregular surfaces: tabular, baseline, and baseline with oblique extension lines. Figure 7-59 shows an irregular surface dimensioned using the tabular method. An XY axis is defined using the edges of the object. Points are then defined relative to the XY axis. The points are assigned reference numbers, and the reference numbers and XY coordinate values are listed in chart form as shown.

Figure 7-59

STATION	1	2	3	4	5	6
X	0	20	40	55	62	70
Y	40	38	30	16	10	0

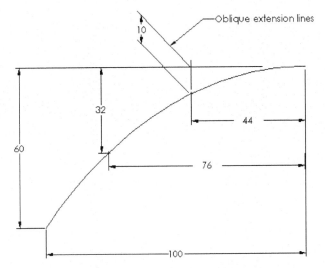

Figure 7-60 shows an irregular curve dimensioned using baseline dimensions. The baseline method references all dimensions to specified baselines. Usually there are two baselines, one horizontal and one vertical.

Figure 7-60

It is considered poor practice to use a centerline as a baseline. Centerlines are imaginary lines that do not exist on the object and would make it more difficult to manufacture and inspect the finished objects.

Baseline dimensioning is very common because it helps eliminate tolerance buildup and is easily adaptable to many manufacturing processes.

7-16 Polar Dimensions

Polar dimensions are similar to polar coordinates. A location is defined by a radius (distance) and an angle. Figure 7-61 shows an object that includes polar dimensions. The holes are located on a circular centerline, and their positions from the vertical centerline are specified using angles.

Figure 7-61

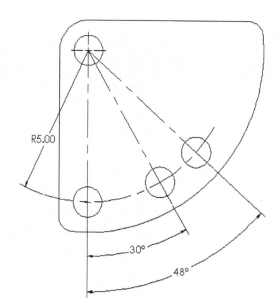

Figure 7-62 shows an example of a hole pattern dimensioned using polar dimensions.

Figure 7-62

7-17 Chamfers

Chamfers are angular cuts made on the edges of objects. They are usually used to make it easier to fit two parts together. They are most often made at 45° angles but may be made at any angle. Figure 7-63 shows two objects with chamfers between surfaces 90° apart and two examples between surfaces that are not 90° apart. Either of the two types of dimensions shown for the 45° dimension may be used. If an angle other than 45° is used, the angle and setback distance must be specified.

Figure 7-63

Figure 7-64 shows two examples of internal chamfers. Both define the chamfer using an angle and diameter. Internal chamfers are very similar to countersunk holes.

Figure 7-64

7-18 Symbols and Abbreviations

Symbols are used in dimensioning to help accurately display the meaning of the dimension. Symbols also help eliminate language barriers when reading drawings.

Abbreviations should be used very carefully on drawings. Whenever possible, write out the full word, including correct punctuation. The **Dimension PropertyManager Value** tab includes a group of symbols and words commonly used on technical drawings. Figure 7-65 lists several standard abbreviations used on technical drawings.

Figure 7-65

AL	= Aluminum
CBORE	= Counterbore
CRS	= Cold Rolled Steel
CSK	= Countersink
DIA	= Diameter
EQ	= Equal
HEX	= Hexagon
MAT'L	= Material
R	= Radius
SAE	= Society of Automotive Engineers
SFACE	= Spotface
ST	= Steel
SQ	= Square
REQD	= Required

Figure 7-66 shows a list of symbols available in the **Dimension PropertyManager Value** tab.

Figure 7-66

Diameter

Click here

TIP
To access the **Dimension PropertyManager Value** tab, click an existing dimension.

More symbols are available by clicking the **More** box. A list of available symbols will appear. Click a new symbol. A preview of the selected symbol will appear. Click **OK** and the symbol will appear on the drawing next to the existing symbol.

7-19 Symmetrical and Centerline Symbols

An object is symmetrical about an axis when one side is the exact mirror image of the other. Figure 7-67 shows a symmetrical object. The symbol of two short parallel lines or the note OBJECT IS SYMMETRICAL ABOUT THIS AXIS (centerline) may be used to designate symmetry.

If an object is symmetrical, only half the object needs to be dimensioned. The other dimensions are implied by the symmetry note or symbol.

Figure 7-67

The centerline is slightly different from the axis of symmetry. An object may or may not be symmetrical about its centerline. See Figure 7-67. Centerlines are used to define the center of both individual features and entire objects. Use the centerline symbol when a line is a centerline, but do not use it in place of the symmetry symbol.

7-20 Dimensioning to a Point

Curved surfaces can be dimensioned using theoretical points. See Figure 7-68. There should be a small gap between the surface of the object and the lines used to define the theoretical point. The point should be defined by the intersection of at least two lines.

There should also be a small gap between the extension lines and the theoretical point used to locate the point.

Figure 7-68

7-21 Dimensioning Section Views

Section views are dimensioned. See Figure 7-69. The section lines should be drawn at an angle that allows the viewer to clearly distinguish between the section lines and the extension lines.

Figure 7-69

SECTION C-C

7-22 Dimensioning Orthographic Views

Dimensions should be added to orthographic views where the features appear in contour. Holes should be dimensioned in their circular views. Figure 7-70 shows three views of an object that has been dimensioned.

Figure 7-70

The hole dimensions are added to the top view, where the hole appears circular. The slot is also dimensioned in the top view because it appears in contour. The slanted surface is dimensioned in the front view.

The height of surface A is given in the side view rather than run along extension lines across the front view. The length of surface A is given in the front view. This is a contour view of the surface.

It is considered good practice to keep dimensions in groups. This makes it easier for the viewer to find dimensions.

Be careful not to double dimension a distance. A distance should be dimensioned only once. If a 30 dimension were added above the 25 dimension on the right-side view, it would be an error. The distance would be double dimensioned: once with the 25 + 30 dimension, and again with the 55 overall dimension. The 25 + 30 dimensions are mathematically equal to the 55 overall dimension, but there is a distinct difference in how they affect the manufacturing tolerances. Double dimensions are explained more fully in Chapter 8.

Dimensions Using Centerlines

Figure 7-71 shows an object dimensioned from its centerline. This type of dimensioning is used when the distance between the holes relative to each other is critical.

Figure 7-71

Chapter Projects

Project 7-1:

Measure and redraw the shapes in Figures P7-1 through P7-24. The dotted grid background has either .50in. or 10mm spacing. All holes are through holes. Specify the units and scale of the drawing. Use the **Part** template to create a model. Use the grid background pattern to determine the dimensions. Use the **Drawing** template to create the orthographic view shown. Use the **Smart Dimension** tool to dimension the view.

    A.   Measure using millimeters.

    B.   Measure using inches.

    All dimensions are within either .25in. or 5mm. All fillets and rounds are R.50in., R.25in. or R10mm, R5mm.

Figure P7-1

THICKNESS:
40mm
1.50in.

Figure P7-2

THICKNESS:
20mm
.75in.

Figure P7-3

THICKNESS:
35mm
1.25in.

Figure P7-4

THICKNESS:
15mm
.50in.

Figure P7-5

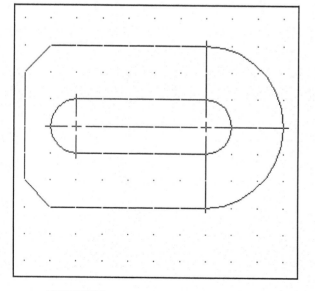

THICKNESS:
10mm
.50in.

Figure P7-6

THICKNESS:
5mm
.25in.

Figure P7-7

THICKNESS:
12mm
.50in.

Figure P7-8

THICKNESS:
25mm
1.00in.

Figure P7-9

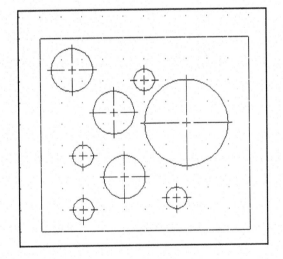

THICKNESS:
5mm
.25in.

Figure P7-10

THICKNESS:
20mm
.75in.

Figure P7-11

THICKNESS:
18mm
.625in.

Figure P7-12

THICKNESS:
24mm
1.00in.

Figure P7-13

THICKNESS:
10mm
.25in.

Figure P7-14

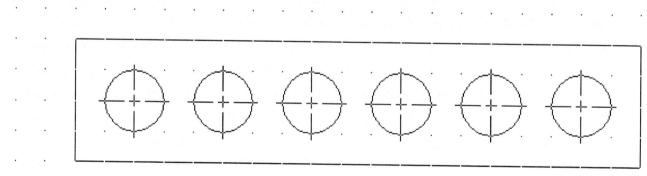

THICKNESS:
8mm
.25in.

Figure P7-15

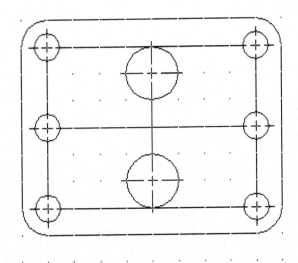

THICKNESS:
20mm
.75in.

Figure P7-16

THICKNESS:
20mm
.75in.

THICKNESS:
20mm
.75in.

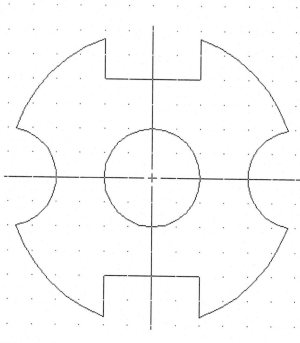

THICKNESS:
30mm
1.375in.

Figure P7-19

THICKNESS:
12mm
.30in.

THICKNESS:
5mm
.125in.

Figure P7-21

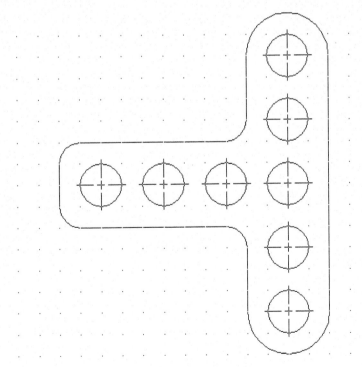

THICKNESS:
10mm
.25in.

Dimension using baseline dimensions

Figure P7-22

THICKNESS:
15mm
.50in.

Dimension using
A. Baseline dimensions C. Chain dimensions
B. Ordinate dimensions D. Hole table

Figure P7-23

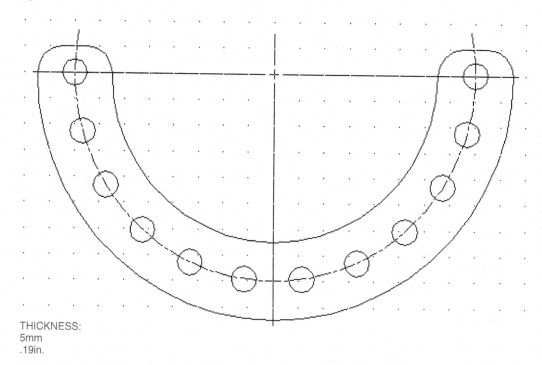

THICKNESS:
5mm
.19in.

Figure P7-24

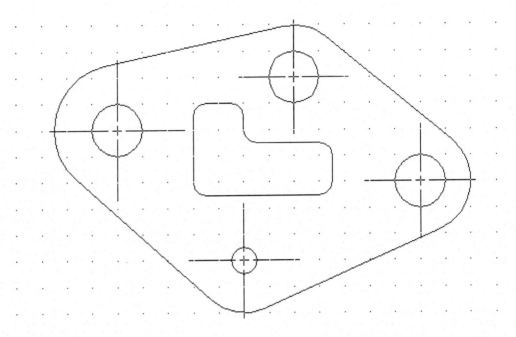

THICKNESS:
15mm
.625in.

Project 7-2:

Use the **Part** template to draw models of the objects shown in Figures P7-25 through P7-42.

1. Create orthographic views of the objects. Dimension the orthographic views.

2. Create 3D models of the objects. Dimension the 3D models.

Figure P7-25
MILLIMETERS

Figure P7-26
MILLIMETERS

Figure P7-27
INCHES

KEY CLIP

.75 BOTH SIDES
.50 BOTH SIDES
.50 ALL AROUND
.50
.25
1.50
1.00
1.50
2.50
2.00

Figure P7-28
MILLIMETERS

ALIGNMENT
BRACKET

20-2 HOLES
40
10
Ø30
55
15
25
40
20
10
20
2×30
100
40
20
Ø20

Figure P7-29
MILLIMETERS

Ø30
50
25
Ø20
2 HOLES
13
BOTH SIDES
15
30
20
CENTERED
50
15
100
40
25
30

Figure P7-30
INCHES

POSITIONER
BLOCK

.50
Ø1.500 THRU
1.00
.50
3.50
1.50
1.50
1.00
4.00
2.00
2.50

Figure P7-31
MILLIMETERS

CYLINDRICAL
KEY

20
10 DEEP
Ø50
10
20
20
70
Ø80

Figure P7-32
INCHES

.50
.50
.25
30°
.75
.25
.75
.25
2.38
1.25
1.50

Figure P7-33
MILLIMETERS

Ø 14   2 HOLES

22° - BOTH
SLANTED SURFACES

15
25
15
12
27
30
60
38
100
7

Figure P7-34
INCHES

2.00R
.69
.50 DIA
1.00
.63
2.50
1.25
.75
.75
1.13
.63
.63
.88
2.38
3.88

Figure P7-35
MILLIMETERS

100
10
75
10
30
35
65
30
35
60
25
20
R15

Figure P7-36
MILLIMETERS

R 6—4 PLACES
50
5
40
5
10
25
15
60
R 5—4 PLACES
25
12.5
Ø 8
45°
20
30°
14
12
18
60
12
25

Figure P7-37
INCHES

Figure P7-38
MILLIMETERS

NOTE: ALL FILLETS AND ROUNDS=R3

Figure P7-39
MILLIMETERS

Figure P7-40
MILLIMETERS

ALL FILLETS AND ROUNDS=R5
MATL 5 THK

Figure P7-41
MILLIMETERS

Figure P7-42
MILLIMETERS

Project 7-3:

1. Draw a 3D model from the given top orthographic and section views in Figure P7-43.

2. Draw a top orthographic view and a section view of the object and add dimensions.

Figure P7-43
MILLIMETERS

SECTION A-A
SCALE 1 : 1

Figure P7-44
MILLIMETERS

SECTION A-A
SCALE 1 : 1

Project 7-4:

1. Draw a 3D model from the given top orthographic and section views in Figure P7-44.

2. Draw a top orthographic view and a section view of the object and add dimensions.

Project 7-5:

1. Draw a 3D model from the given top orthographic and section views in Figure P7-45.

2. Draw a top orthographic view and a section view of the object and add dimensions.

Project 7-6:

1. Draw a 3D model from the given top orthographic and section views in Figure P7-46.

2. Draw a top orthographic view and a section view of the object and add dimensions.

Figure P7-45
INCHES

Figure P7-46
INCHES

Project 7-7:

Redraw the given shapes in Figures P7-47 through P7-49 and dimension them using the following dimension styles.

1. Baseline

2. Ordinate

3. Hole Table

Figure P7-47
MILLIMETERS

Figure P7-48
MILLIMETERS

Figure P7-49
INCHES

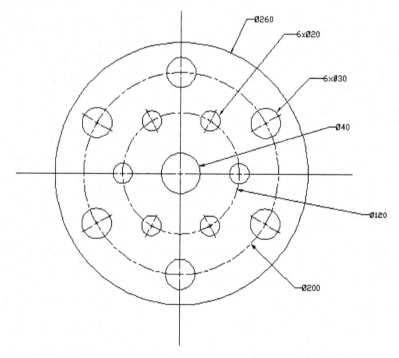

8 chaptereight
Tolerancing

CHAPTER OBJECTIVES

- Understand tolerance conventions
- Understand the meaning of tolerances
- Apply tolerances
- Understand geometric tolerances
- Understand positional tolerances

8-1 Introduction

Tolerances define the manufacturing limits for dimensions. All dimensions have tolerances either written directly on the drawing as part of the dimension or implied by a predefined set of standard tolerances that apply to any dimension that does not have a stated tolerance.

This chapter explains general tolerance conventions and how they are applied using SolidWorks. It includes a sample tolerance study and an explanation of standard fits and surface finishes.

8-2 Direct Tolerance Methods

There are two methods used to include tolerances as part of a dimension: *plus and minus*, and *limits*. Plus and minus tolerances can be expressed in either bilateral (symmetric) or unilateral (deviation) form.

A *bilateral tolerance* has both a plus and a minus value, whereas a *unilateral tolerance* has either the plus or the minus value equal to 0. Figure 8-1 shows a horizontal dimension of 60mm that includes a bilateral tolerance of plus or minus 1 and another dimension of 60.00mm that includes a bilateral tolerance of plus 0.20 or minus 0.10. Figure 8-1 also shows a dimension of 65mm that includes a unilateral tolerance of plus 1 or minus 0.

Figure 8-1

Plus or minus tolerances define a range for manufacturing. If inspection shows that all dimensioned distances on an object fall within their specified tolerance range, the object is considered acceptable; that is, it has been manufactured correctly.

A dimension and tolerance of 60±0.1 means that the part must be manufactured within a range no greater than 60.1 nor less than 59.9. A dimension and tolerance of 65 +1/–0 defines the tolerance range as 65 to 66.

Figure 8-2 shows some bilateral and unilateral tolerances applied using decimal inch values. Inch dimensions and tolerances are written using a slightly different format than millimeter dimensions and tolerances, but they also define manufacturing ranges for dimension values. The horizontal bilateral dimension and tolerance 2.50±.02 defines the longest acceptable distance as 2.52 inches and the shortest as 2.48. The unilateral dimension 2.50 +.02/–.00 defines the longest acceptable distance as 2.52 and the shortest as 2.50.

Figure 8-2

8-3 Tolerance Expressions

Dimension and tolerance values are written differently for inch and millimeter values. See Figure 8-3. Unilateral dimensions for millimeter values specify a zero limit with a single 0. A zero limit for inch values must include the same number of decimal places given for the dimension value. In the example shown in Figure 8-3, the dimension value .500 has a unilateral tolerance with minus zero tolerance. The zero limit is written as .000, three decimal places for both the dimension and the tolerance.

Figure 8-3

Both values in a bilateral tolerance for inch values must contain the same number of decimal places; for millimeter values the tolerance values need not include the same number of decimal places as the dimension value. In Figure 8-3 the dimension value 32 is accompanied by tolerances of +0.25 and –0.10. This form is not acceptable for inch dimensions and tolerances. An equivalent inch dimension and tolerance would be written 32.00 + .25/–.00.

Degree values must include the same number of decimal places in both the dimension and the tolerance values for bilateral tolerances. A single 0 may be used for unilateral tolerances.

8-4 Understanding Plus and Minus Tolerances

A millimeter dimension and tolerance of 12.0 +0.2/−0.1 means that the longest acceptable distance is 12.2000... 0, and the shortest is 11.9000... 0. The total range is 0.3000... 0.

After an object is manufactured, it is inspected to ensure that the object has been manufactured correctly. Each dimensioned distance is measured and, if it is within the specified tolerance, is accepted. If the measured distance is not within the specified tolerance, the part is rejected. Some rejected objects may be reworked to bring them into the specified tolerance range, whereas others are simply scrapped.

Figure 8-4 shows a dimension with a tolerance. Assume that five objects were manufactured using the same 12.0 +0.2/−0.1 dimension and tolerance. The objects were then inspected and the results were as listed. Inspected measurements are usually expressed to at least one more decimal place than that specified in the tolerance. Which objects are acceptable and which are not? Object 3 is too long, and object 5 is too short because their measured distances are not within the specified tolerances.

Figure 8-5 shows a dimension and tolerance of 3.50 ±.02in. Object 3 is not acceptable because it is too short, and object 4 is too long.

Figure 8-4

GIVEN (mm):

$12\,{}^{+0.2}_{-0.1}$

MEANS:
TOL MAX = 12.2
TOL MIN = 11.9
TOTAL TOL = 0.3

OBJECT	AS MEASURED	ACCEPTABLE ?
1	12.160	OK
2	12.020	OK
3	12.203	Too Long
4	11.920	OK
5	11.895	Too Short

Figure 8-5

GIVEN (inches):

3.50±.02

MEANS:
TOL MAX = 3.52
TOL MIN = 3.48
TOTAL TOL = .04

OBJECT	AS MEASURED	ACCEPTABLE ?
1	3.520	OK
2	3.486	OK
3	3.470	Too Short
4	3.521	Too Long
5	3.515	OK

8-5 Creating Plus and Minus Tolerances

Figure 8-6 shows a dimensioned view. This section will show how to add plus and minus to the existing dimensions.

Figure 8-6

MAT'L = .50   ⌀1.00-2 HOLES

Create a part using the dimensions shown. The part thickness is 0.50.

2. Save the part as **BLOCK, TOL**.

3. Create a **Drawing** document of the **BLOCK, TOL** and create an orthographic view as shown.

4. Add dimensions as shown.

See Figure 8-7.

Figure 8-7

5. Click the horizontal **2.00** dimension.

6. Click the arrow in the **Tolerance/Precision** box as shown.

7. Select the **Bilateral** option.

8. Enter a plus tolerance of **0.02in** and a minus tolerance of **0.01in**.

See Figure 8-8.

9. Click the green **OK** check mark.

Figure 8-8

Adding Plus and Minus Symmetric Tolerances Using the Dimension Text Box

See Figure 8-9.

Figure 8-9

1 Click the vertical **1.13** dimension.

Note the entry in the **Dimension Text** box: **<DIM>**. This represents the existing text value taken from the part's construction dimensions.

2 Move the cursor into the **Dimension Text** box to the right of the <DIM> notation and click the ± symbol.

Note that the entry in the **Dimension Text** box now reads **<DIM MOD-PM>**. This indicates that the ± symbol has been added to the dimension text.

3 Type **.01** after <MOD-PM>.

4 Click the green **OK** check mark.

5 Save the **BLOCK, TOL** drawing.

Note how the dimensions and tolerances have been aligned and moved to create a neat, uncluttered appearance.

TIP
A symmetric tolerance can also be created using the **Symmetric** option in the **Tolerance/Precision** box.

8-6 Creating Limit Tolerances

Figure 8-10 shows examples of limit tolerances. Limit tolerances replace dimension values. Two values are given: the upper and lower limits for the dimension value. The limit tolerance 62.1 and 61.9 is mathematically equal to 62±0.1, but the stated limit tolerance is considered easier to read and understand.

Figure 8-10

Limit tolerances define a range for manufacture. Final distances on an object must fall within the specified range to be acceptable.

This section uses the **BLOCK, TOL** drawing created in the previous section. See Figure 8-11.

1 Click the vertical **2.25** dimension.

2 Select the **Limit** option as shown.

3 Set the upper limit for **0.02in** and the lower limit for **0.01in**.

4 Click the green **OK** check mark.

Figure 8-11

8-7 Creating Angular Tolerances

Figure 8-12 shows an example of an angular dimension with a symmetric tolerance. The procedures explained for applying different types of tolerances to linear dimensions also apply to angular dimensions.

See Figure 8-12.

1 Draw the part shown in Figure 8-12. Extrude the part to a thickness of **.50**.

2 Save the part as **BLOCK, ANGLE**.

3 Create a **Drawing** document of the **BLOCK, ANGLE** and create an orthographic view as shown.

Figure 8-12

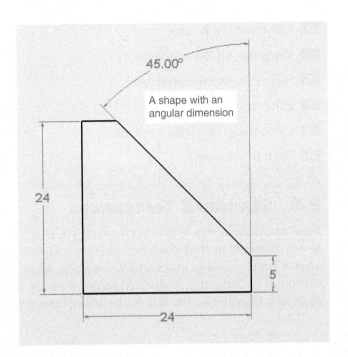

A shape with an
angular dimension

1. Click here

2. Click here

3. Click here

Symmetrical tolerance

4. Enter tolerance value

4 Dimension the view.

5 Click the **45.00°** dimension.

6 Select the **Symmetric** option.

7 Enter a value of **.02**.

8 Click the green **OK** check mark.

9 Save the drawing.

8-8 Standard Tolerances

Most manufacturers establish a set of standard tolerances that are applied to any dimension that does not include a specific tolerance. Figure 8-13 shows some possible standard tolerances. Standard tolerances vary from company to company. Standard tolerances are usually listed on the first page of a drawing to the left of the title block, but this location may vary.

Figure 8-13

The X value used when specifying standard tolerances means any X stated in that format. A dimension value of 52.00 would have an implied tolerance of ±.01 because the stated standard tolerance is .XX ±.01. Thus, any dimension value with two decimal places has a standard implied tolerance of ±.01. A dimension value of 52.000 would have an implied tolerance of ±.001.

8-9 Double-Dimensioning Errors

It is an error to dimension the same distance twice. This mistake is called *double dimensioning*. Double dimensioning is an error because it does not allow for tolerance buildup across a distance.

Figure 8-14 shows an object that has been dimensioned twice across its horizontal length, once using three 30mm dimensions and a second time using the 90mm overall dimension. The two dimensions are mathematically equal but are not equal when tolerances are considered. Assume that each dimension has a standard tolerance of ±1mm. The three 30mm dimensions could create an acceptable distance of 90±3mm, or a maximum distance of 93 and a minimum distance of 87. The overall dimension of 90mm allows a maximum distance of 91 and a minimum distance of 89. The two dimensions yield different results when tolerances are considered.

Figure 8-14

The size and location of a tolerance depend on the design objectives of the object, how it will be manufactured, and how it will be inspected. Even objects that have similar shapes may be dimensioned and toleranced very differently.

One possible solution to the double dimensioning shown in Figure 8-14 is to remove one of the 30mm dimensions and allow that distance to "float," that is, absorb the cumulated tolerances. The choice of which 30mm dimension to eliminate depends on the design objectives of the part. For this example the far-right dimension was eliminated to remove the double-dimensioning error.

Another possible solution to the double-dimensioning error is to retain the three 30mm dimensions and to change the 90mm overall dimension to a reference dimension. A reference dimension is used only for mathematical convenience. It is not used during the manufacturing or inspection process. A reference dimension is designated on a drawing using parentheses: (90).

If the 90mm dimension was referenced, then only the three 30mm dimensions would be used to manufacture and inspect the object. This would eliminate the double-dimensioning error.

8-10 Chain Dimensions and Baseline Dimensions

There are two systems for applying dimensions and tolerances to a drawing: chain and baseline. Figure 8-15 shows examples of both systems. *Chain dimensions* dimension each feature to the feature next to it. *Baseline dimensions* dimension all features from a single baseline or datum.

Chain and baseline dimensions may be used together. Figure 8-15 also shows two objects with repetitive features; one object includes two slots, and the other includes three sets of three holes. In each example, the center of the repetitive feature is dimensioned to the left side of the object, which serves as a baseline. The sizes of the individual features are dimensioned using chain dimensions referenced to centerlines.

Figure 8-15

CHAIN DIMENSIONS

BASELINE DIMENSIONS

⊈ = Symbol for centerline

Baseline dimensions eliminate tolerance buildup and can be related directly to the reference axis of many machines. They tend to take up much more area on a drawing than do chain dimensions.

Chain dimensions are useful in relating one feature to another, such as the repetitive hole pattern shown in Figure 8-15. In this example the distance between the holes is more important than the individual hole's distance from the baseline.

Figure 8-16 shows the same object dimensioned twice, once using chain dimensions and once using baseline dimensions. All distances are assigned a tolerance range of 2mm using limit tolerances. The maximum distance for surface A is 28mm using the chain system and 27mm using the baseline system. The 1mm difference comes from the elimination of the first 26–24 limit dimension found on the chain example but not on the baseline.

Figure 8-16

The total tolerance difference is 6mm for the chain dimensions and 4mm for the baseline dimensions. The baseline method reduces the tolerance variations for the object simply because it applies the tolerances and dimensions differently. So why not always use baseline dimensions? For most applications, the baseline system is probably better, but if the distance between the individual features is more critical than the distance from the feature to the baseline, use the chain system.

Baseline Dimensions

See Figure 8-17. See also Chapter 7, "Dimensioning."

Note in the example of baseline dimensioning shown in Figure 8-17 that each dimension is independent of the other. This means that if one of the dimensions is manufactured incorrectly, it will not affect the other dimensions.

Figure 8-17

8-11 Tolerance Studies

The term *tolerance study* is used when analyzing the effects of a group of tolerances on one another and on an object. Figure 8-18 shows an object with two horizontal dimensions. The horizontal distance A is not dimensioned. Its length depends on the tolerances of the two horizontal dimensions.

Figure 8-18

Calculating the Maximum Length of A

Distance A will be longest when the overall distance is at its longest and the other distance is at its shortest.

$$
\begin{array}{r}
65.2 \\
-29.8 \\
\hline
35.4
\end{array}
$$

Calculating the Minimum Length of A

Distance A will be shortest when the overall length is at its shortest and the other length is at its longest.

$$\begin{array}{r} 64.9 \\ -30.1 \\ \hline 34.8 \end{array}$$

8-12 Rectangular Dimensions

Figure 8-19 shows an example of rectangular dimensions referenced to baselines. Figure 8-20 shows a circular object on which dimensions are referenced to a circle's centerlines. Dimensioning to a circle's centerline is critical to accurate hole location.

Figure 8-19

Rectangular Dimensions

Figure 8-20

8-13 Hole Locations

When rectangular dimensions are used, the location of a hole's centerpoint is defined by two linear dimensions. The result is a rectangular tolerance zone whose size is based on the linear dimension's tolerances. The shape of the centerpoint's tolerance zone may be changed to circular using positioning tolerancing, as described later in the chapter.

Figure 8-21 shows the location and size dimensions for a hole. Also shown are the resulting tolerance zone and the overall possible hole shape. The centerpoint's tolerance is .2 by .3 based on the given linear locating tolerances.

NOTE

Linear tolerances generate a square or rectangular tolerance zone.

The hole diameter has a tolerance of ±.05. This value must be added to the centerpoint location tolerances to define the maximum overall possible shape of the hole. The maximum possible hole shape is determined by drawing the maximum radius from the four corner points of the tolerance zone.

This means that the left edge of the hole could be as close to the vertical baseline as 12.75 or as far as 13.25. The 12.75 value was derived by subtracting the maximum hole diameter value 12.05 from the minimum linear distance 24.80 (24.80 – 12.05 = 12.75). The 13.25 value was derived by subtracting the minimum hole diameter 11.95 from the maximum linear distance 25.20 (25.20 – 11.95 = 13.25).

Figure 8-21

Figure 8-22 shows a hole's tolerance zone based on polar dimensions. The zone has a sector shape, and the possible hole shape is determined by locating the maximum radius at the four corner points of the tolerance zone.

Figure 8-22

Ø45 ± 0.2

30° ± 0.2°

0.4

0.4

Shape of tolerance zone for hole's centerpoint

8-14   Choosing a Shaft for a Toleranced Hole

Given the hole location and size shown in Figure 8-21, what is the largest diameter shaft that will always fit into the hole?

Figure 8-23 shows the hole's centerpoint tolerance zone based on the given linear locating tolerances. Four circles have been drawn centered at the four corners on the linear tolerance zone that represents the smallest possible hole diameter. The circles define an area that represents the maximum shaft size that will always fit into the hole, regardless of how the given dimensions are applied.

Figure 8-23

NOT TO SCALE

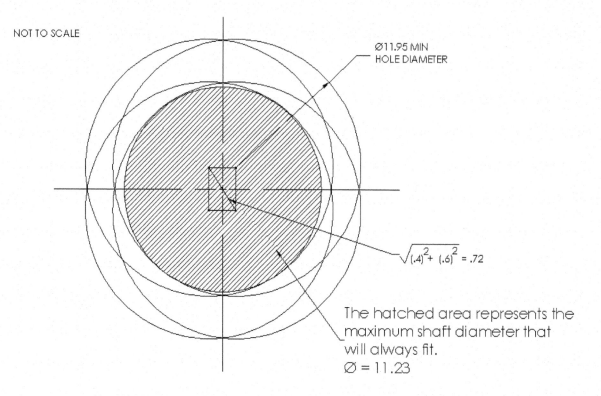

Ø11.95 MIN
HOLE DIAMETER

$$\sqrt{(.4)^2 + (.6)^2} = .72$$

The hatched area represents the maximum shaft diameter that will always fit.
Ø = 11.23

The diameter size of this circular area can be calculated by subtracting the maximum diagonal distance across the linear tolerance zone (corner to corner) from the minimum hole diameter.

The results can be expressed as a formula.

For Linear Dimensions and Tolerances

$$S_{max} = H_{min} - DTZ$$

where

S_{max} = maximum shaft diameter

H_{min} = minimum hole diameter

DTZ = diagonal distance across the tolerance zone

In the example shown the diagonal distance is determined using the Pythagorean theorem:

$$DTZ = \sqrt{(.4)^2 + (.6)^2}$$
$$= \sqrt{.16 + .36}$$
$$DTZ = .72$$

This means that the maximum shaft diameter that will always fit into the given hole is 11.43:

$$S_{max} = H_{min} - DTZ$$
$$= 11.95 - .72$$
$$S_{max} = 11.23$$

This procedure represents a restricted application of the general formula presented later in the chapter for positioning tolerances.

Once the maximum shaft size has been established, a tolerance can be applied to the shaft. If the shaft had a total tolerance of .25, the minimum shaft diameter would be 11.43 − .25, or 11.18. Figure 8-23 shows a shaft dimensioned and toleranced using these values.

The formula presented is based on the assumption that the shaft is perfectly placed on the hole's centerpoint. This assumption is reasonable if two objects are joined by a fastener and both objects are free to move. When both objects are free to move about a common fastener, they are called *floating objects*.

8-15 Sample Problem SP8-1

Parts A and B in Figure 8-24 are to be joined by a common shaft. The total tolerance for the shaft is to be .05. What are the maximum and minimum shaft diameters?

Figure 8-24

NOTE: Dimensions are the same for both objects.

Both objects have the same dimensions and tolerances and are floating relative to each other.

$$S_{max} = H_{min} - DTZ$$
$$= 15.93 - .85$$
$$S_{max} = 15.08$$

The shaft's minimum diameter is found by subtracting the total tolerance requirement from the calculated maximum diameter:

$$15.08 - .05 = 15.03$$

Therefore,

Shaft max = 15.08

Shaft min = 15.03

8-16 Sample Problem SP8-2

The procedure presented in Sample Problem SP8-1 can be worked in reverse to determine the maximum and minimum hole size based on a given shaft size.

Objects AA and BB as shown in Figure 8-25 are to be joined using a bolt whose maximum diameter is .248. What is the minimum hole size for objects that will always accept the bolt? What is the maximum hole size if the total hole tolerance is .005?

$$S_{max} = H_{min} - DTZ$$

In this example H_{min} is the unknown factor, so the equation is rewritten as

$$H_{min} = S_{max} + DTZ$$
$$H_{min} = .248 + .001$$
$$H_{min} = .249$$

This is the minimum hole diameter, so the total tolerance requirement is added to this value:

$$.249 + .005 = .254$$

Figure 8-25

Therefore,

Hole max = .254

Hole min = .249

8-17 Nominal Sizes

The term *nominal* refers to the approximate size of an object that matches a common fraction or whole number. A shaft with a dimension of 1.500 + .003 is said to have a nominal size of "one and a half inches." A dimension of 1.500 +.000/−.005 is still said to have a nominal size of one and a half inches. In both examples 1.5 is the closest common fraction.

8-18   Standard Fits (Metric Values)

Calculating tolerances between holes and shafts that fit together is so common in engineering design that a group of standard values and notations has been established. These values may be calculated using the **Limits and Fits** option of the **Design Library**.

There are three possible types of fits between a shaft and a hole: clearance, transitional, and interference. There are several subclassifications within each of these categories.

A *clearance fit* always defines the maximum shaft diameter as smaller than the minimum hole diameter. The difference between the two diameters is the amount of clearance. It is possible for a clearance fit to be defined with zero clearance; that is, the maximum shaft diameter is equal to the minimum hole diameter.

An *interference fit* always defines the minimum shaft diameter as larger than the maximum hole diameter; that is, the shaft is always bigger than the hole. This definition means that an interference fit is the converse of a clearance fit. The difference between the diameter of the shaft and the hole is the amount of interference.

An interference fit is primarily used to assemble objects together. Interference fits eliminate the need for threads, welds, or other joining methods. Using an interference for joining two objects is generally limited to light load applications.

It is sometimes difficult to visualize how a shaft can be assembled into a hole with a diameter smaller than that of the shaft. It is sometimes done using a hydraulic press that slowly forces the two parts together. The joining process can be augmented by the use of lubricants or heat. The hole is heated, causing it to expand, the shaft is inserted, and the hole is allowed to cool and shrink around the shaft.

A *transition fit* may be either a clearance or an interference fit. It may have a clearance between the shaft and the hole or an interference.

The notations are based on Standard International Tolerance values. A specific description for each category of fit follows.

Clearance Fits

H11/c11 or C11/h11 = loose running fit

H8/d8 or D8/h8 = free running fit

H8/f7 or F8/h7 = close running fit

H7/g6 or G7/h6 = sliding fit

H7/h6 = locational clearance fit

Transitional Fits

H7/k6 or K7/h6 = locational transition fit

H7/n6 or N7/h6 = locational transition fit

Interference Fits

H7/p6 or P7/h6 = locational transition fit

H7/s6 or S7/h6 = medium drive fit

H7/u6 or U7/h6 = force fit

8-19 Standard Fits (Inch Values)

Inch values are accessed in the **Design Library** by selecting the **ANSI-Inch** standards.

Fits defined using inch values are classified as follows:

RC = running and sliding fits

LC = locational clearance fits

LT = locational transition fits

LN = interference fits

FN = force fits

Each of these general categories has several subclassifications within it defined by a number, for example, Class RC1, Class RC2, through Class RC8. The letter designations are based on International Tolerance Standards, as are metric designations.

> **TIP**
> Charts of tolerance values can be found in the appendix.

Adding a Fit Callout to a Drawing

Figure 8-26 shows a block and post. Figure 8-27 shows a drawing containing a front and a top orthographic view of the block and post assembly.

1 Draw the block and post and create an assembly drawing as shown in Figure 8-26.

Figure 8-26

Figure 8-27

Block/Post
assembly

Add the dimension

Ø.50

Top
view

Front
view

2 Draw a front and a top orthographic view of the assembly as shown.

3 Add a **Ø.50** dimension to the top view.

4 Click the **Ø.50** dimension.

The **Dimension Value PropertyManager** will appear. See Figure 8-28.

5 Select the **Fit** option from the **Tolerance/Precision** box as shown.

6 Select an **H5** tolerance for the hole.

7 Select the **g4** tolerance for the shaft.

8 Change the number of decimal places in the Ø.50 dimension to four places, **Ø.5000.**

9 Click the green **OK** check mark.

Figure 8-28

Reading Fit Tables

There are several fit tables in the appendix for both English units and metric units. The metric tables can be read directly, as they state hole and shaft dimension. For example, the tolerance for a Preferred Clearance Fit for a 10mm nominal hole using a loose running fit is 10.090/10.000 for the hole and 9.920/9.830 for the shaft. The tolerance callout would be H11/c11. English unit tables require interpretation.

Figure 8-29 shows the table values for a .5000 nominal hole using an H5/g4 tolerance. The tolerance values are in thousandths of an inch; that is, a listed value of 0.25 equals 0.0025in. The Ø.5000 nominal value is in the 0.40–0.71 size range, so the tolerance values are as shown. These values can be applied to the detail drawings of the block and shaft. See Figure 8-30.

Figure 8-29

Figure 8-30

8-20 Preferred and Standard Sizes

It is important that designers always consider preferred and standard sizes when selecting sizes for designs. Most tooling is set up to match these sizes, so manufacturing is greatly simplified when preferred and standard sizes are specified. Figure 8-31 shows a listing of preferred sizes for metric values.

Figure 8-31

PREFERRED SIZES			
1	1.1	12	14
1.2	1.4	16	18
1.6	1.8	20	22
2	2.2	25	28
2.5	2.8	30	35
3	3.5	40	45
4	4.5	50	55
5	5.5	60	70
6	7	80	90
8	9	100	110
10	11	120	140

Consider the case of design calculations that call for a 42mm diameter hole. A 42mm diameter hole is not a preferred size. A diameter of 40mm is the closest preferred size, and a 45mm diameter is a second choice. A 42mm hole could be manufactured but would require an unusual drill size that might not be available. It would be wise to reconsider the design to see if a 40mm diameter hole could be used, and if not, possibly a 45mm diameter hole.

A production run of a very large quantity could possibly justify the cost of special tooling, but for smaller runs it is probably better to use preferred sizes. Machinists will have the required drills, and maintenance people will have the appropriate tools for these sizes.

Figure 8-32 shows a listing of standard fractional drill sizes. Most companies now specify metric units or decimal inches; however, many standard items are still available in fractional sizes, and many older objects may still require fractional-sized tools and replacement parts. A more complete listing is available in the appendix.

Figure 8-32

STANDARD TWIST DRILL SIZES					
Fraction	Decimal Equivalent	Fraction	Decimal Equivalent	Fraction	Decimal Equivalent
7/16	0.1094	21/64	0.3281	11/16	0.6875
1/8	0.1250	11/64	0.3438	3/4	0.7500
9/64	0.1406	23/64	0.3594	13/16	0.8125
5/32	0.1562	3/8	0.3750	7/8	0.8750
11/64	0.1719	25/64	0.3906	15/16	0.9375
3/16	0.1875	13/32	0.4062	1	1.0000
13/64	0.2031	27/64	0.4219		
7/32	0.2188	7/16	0.4375		
1/4	0.2500	29/64	0.4531		
17/64	0.2656	15/32	0.4688		
9/32	0.2812	1/2	0.5000		
19/64	0.2969	9/16	0.5625		
5/16	0.3125	5/8	0.6250		

8-21 Surface Finishes

The term *surface finish* refers to the accuracy (flatness) of a surface. Metric values are measured using micrometers (μm), and inch values are measured in microinches (μin).

The accuracy of a surface depends on the manufacturing process used to produce the surface. Figure 8-33 shows a listing of manufacturing processes and the quality of the surface finish they can be expected to produce.

Figure 8-33

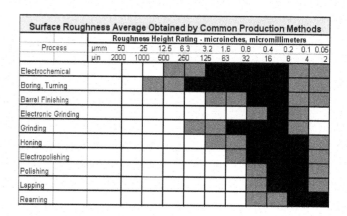

Surface finishes have several design applications. *Datum surfaces*, or surfaces used for baseline dimensioning, should have fairly accurate surface finishes to help assure accurate measurements. Bearing surfaces should have good-quality surface finishes for better load distribution, and parts that operate at high speeds should have smooth finishes to help reduce friction. Figure 8-34 shows a screw head sitting on a very wavy surface. Note that the head of the screw is actually in contact with only two wave peaks, which means that the entire bearing load is concentrated on the two peaks. This situation could cause stress cracks and greatly weaken the surface. A better-quality surface finish would increase the bearing contact area.

Figure 8-34

Bearing Load

Sliding Surfaces

Figure 8-34 also shows two very rough surfaces moving in contact with each other. The result will be excess wear to both surfaces because the surfaces touch only on the peaks, and these peaks will tend to wear faster than flatter areas. Excess vibration can also result when interfacing surfaces are too rough.

Surface finishes are classified into three categories: surface texture, roughness, and lay. *Surface texture* is a general term that refers to the overall quality and accuracy of a surface.

Roughness is a measure of the average deviation of a surface's peaks and valleys. See Figure 8-35.

Figure 8-35

Lay refers to the direction of machine marks on a surface. See Figure 8-35. The lay of a surface is particularly important when two moving objects are in contact with each other, especially at high speeds.

8-22 Surface Control Symbols

Surface finishes are indicated on a drawing using surface control symbols. See Figure 8-36. The general surface control symbol looks like a check mark. Roughness values may be included with the symbol to specify the required accuracy. Surface control symbols can also be used to specify the manufacturing process that may or may not be used to produce a surface.

Figure 8-36

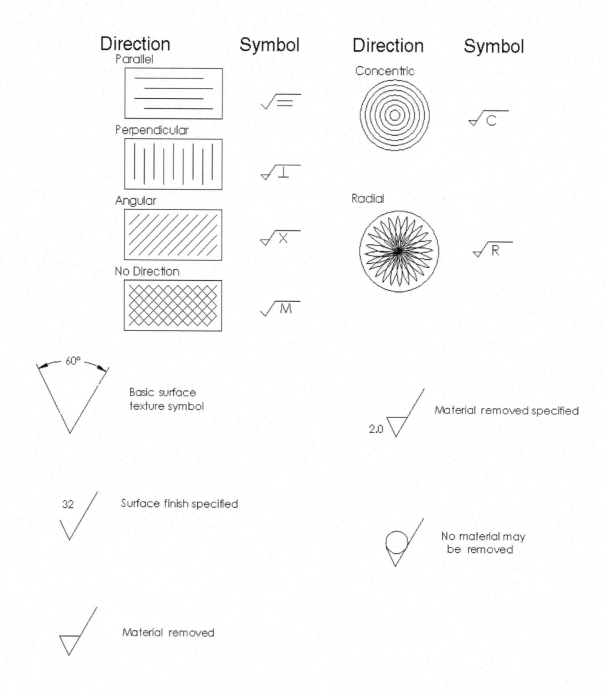

Figure 8-37 shows two applications of surface control symbols. In the first example, a 0.8-μm (32μin) surface finish is specified on the surface that serves as a datum for several horizontal dimensions. A 0.8-μm surface finish is generally considered the minimum acceptable finish for datums.

A second finish mark with a value of 0.4μm is located on an extension line that refers to a surface that will be in contact with a moving object. The extra flatness will help prevent wear between the two surfaces.

Figure 8-37

8-23 Applying Surface Control Symbols

Figure 8-38 shows a dimensioned orthographic view. Surface symbols will be added to this view.

1 Click the **Annotation** tab and select the **Surface Finish** tool.

Figure 8-38

See Figure 8-39.

2 Select the **Basic** symbol and enter a value of **32**.

3 Move the cursor into the drawing area and locate the surface control symbol on an extension line as shown.

4 Press the **<Esc>** key.

5 Click the green **OK** check mark.

6 Save the drawing.

Figure 8-39

Adding a Lay Symbol to a Drawing

Use the same drawing as in Figure 8-39.

1 Click the **Annotation** tab and select the **Surface Finish** tool.

See Figure 8-40.

2 Click the **Machining Required** symbol box.

3 Click the **Lay Direction** box and select the **Multi-Directional** option.

Figure 8-40

4 Move the cursor into the drawing area and locate the surface control symbol on an extension line as shown.

5 Press the **<Esc>** key.

6 Click the green **OK** check mark.

8-24 Design Problems

Figure 8-41 shows two objects that are to be fitted together using a fastener such as a screw-and-nut combination. For this example a cylinder will be used to represent a fastener. Only two nominal dimensions are given. The dimensions and tolerances were derived as follows.

Figure 8-41

The distance between the centers of the holes is given as 50 nominal. The term *nominal* means that the stated value is only a starting point. The final dimensions will be close to the given value but do not have to equal it.

Assigning tolerances is an iteration process; that is, a tolerance is selected and other tolerance values are calculated from the selected initial values. If the results are not satisfactory, go back and modify the initial value and calculate the other values again. As your experience grows you will become better at selecting realistic initial values.

In the example shown in Figure 8-41, start by assigning a tolerance of ±.01 to both the top and bottom parts for both the horizontal and vertical dimensions used to locate the holes. This means that there is a possible centerpoint variation of .02 for both parts. The parts must always fit together, so tolerances must be assigned based on the worst-case condition, or when the parts are made at the extreme ends of the assigned tolerances.

Figure 8-42 shows a greatly enlarged picture of the worst-case condition created by a tolerance of ±.01. The centerpoints of the holes could be as much as .028 apart if the two centerpoints were located at opposite corners of the tolerance zones. This means that the minimum hole diameter must always be at least .028 larger than the maximum stud diameter. In addition, there should be a clearance tolerance assigned so that the hole and stud are never exactly the same size. Figure 8-43 shows the resulting tolerances.

> **TIP**
>
> The tolerance zones in this section are created by line dimensions that generated square tolerance zones.

Figure 8-42

NOT TO SCALE

Tolerance zones for the centerpoints of the holes using the linear tolerance 50±.01

Figure 8-43

Fastener

Tolerance for fastener

Tolerance for both holes

Holes

The 19.96 value includes a .01 clearance allowance, and the 19.94 value is the result of an assigned feature tolerance of .02.

Floating Condition

The top and bottom parts shown in Figure 8-41 are to be joined by two independent fasteners; that is, the location of one fastener does not depend on the location of the other. This situation is called a *floating condition*.

This means that the tolerance zones for both the top and bottom parts can be assigned the same values and that a fastener diameter selected to fit one part will also fit the other part.

The final tolerances were developed by first defining a minimum hole size of 20.00. An arbitrary tolerance of .02 was assigned to the hole and was expressed as 20.00 1.02/20, so the hole can never be any smaller than 20.00.

The 20.00 minimum hole diameter dictates that the maximum fastener diameter can be no greater than 19.97, or .03 (the rounded-off diagonal distance across the tolerance zone—.028) less than the minimum hole diameter. A .01 clearance was assigned. The clearance ensures that the hole and fastener are never exactly the same diameter. The resulting maximum allowable diameter for the fastener is 19.96. Again, an arbitrary tolerance of .02 was assigned to the fastener. The final fastener dimensions are therefore 19.96 to 19.94.

The assigned tolerances ensure that there will always be at least .01 clearance between the fastener and the hole. The other extreme condition occurs when the hole is at its largest possible size (20.02) and the fastener is at its smallest (19.94). This means that there could be as much as .08 clearance between the parts. If this much clearance is not acceptable, then the assigned tolerances will have to be reevaluated.

Figure 8-44 shows the top and bottom parts dimensioned and toleranced. Any dimensions that do not have assigned tolerances are assumed to have standard tolerances.

Figure 8-44

Note, in Figure 8-44, that the top edge of each part has been assigned a surface finish. This was done to help ensure the accuracy of the 20±.01 dimension. If this edge surface were rough, it could affect the tolerance measurements.

This example will be done later in the chapter using geometric tolerances. Geometric tolerance zones are circular rather than rectangular.

Fixed Condition

Figure 8-45 shows the same nominal conditions presented in Figure 8-41, but the fasteners are now fixed to the top part. This situation is called the *fixed condition*. In analyzing the tolerance zones for the fixed condition, two positional tolerances must be considered: the positional tolerances for the holes in the bottom part, and the positional tolerances for the fixed fasteners in the top part. This relationship may be expressed in an equation, as follows:

Figure 8-45

$$S_{max} + DTSZ = H_{min} - DTZ$$

where

S_{max} = maximum shaft (fastener) diameter

H_{min} = minimum hole diameter

DTSZ = diagonal distance across the shaft's centerpoint tolerance zone

DTZ = diagonal distance across the hole's centerpoint tolerance zone

If a dimension and tolerance of 50±.01 is assigned to both the center distance between the holes and the center distance between the fixed fasteners, the values for DTSZ and DTZ will be equal. The formula can then be simplified as follows.

$$S_{max} = H_{min} - 2(DTZ)$$

where DTZ equals the diagonal distance across the tolerance zone. If a hole tolerance of 20.00 +.02/–0 also is defined, the resulting maximum shaft size can be determined, assuming that the calculated distance of .028 is rounded off to .03. See Figure 8-46.

$$S_{max} = 20.00 - 2(0.03)$$

$$= 19.94$$

This means that 19.94 is the largest possible shaft diameter that will fit without interference. If a clearance tolerance of .01 is assumed to ensure that the shaft and hole are never exactly the same size, the maximum shaft diameter becomes 19.93. See Figure 8-47.

A feature tolerance of .02 on the shaft will result in a minimum shaft diameter of 19.91. Note that the .01 clearance tolerance and the .02 feature tolerance were arbitrarily chosen. Other values could have been used.

Figure 8-47

Figure 8-46

Designing a Hole Given a Fastener Size

The previous two examples started by selecting a minimum hole diameter and then calculating the resulting fastener size. Figure 8-48 shows a situation in which the fastener size is defined, and the problem is to determine the appropriate hole sizes. Figure 8-49 shows the dimensions and tolerances for both top and bottom parts.

Requirements:

Clearance, minimum = .003

Hole tolerances = .005

Positional tolerance = .002

Figure 8-48

Figure 8-49

All dimensions not assigned a tolerance will be assumed to have a standard tolerance.

8-25   Geometric Tolerances

Geometric tolerancing is a dimensioning and tolerancing system based on the geometric shape of an object. Surfaces may be defined in terms of their flatness or roundness, or in terms of how perpendicular or parallel they are to other surfaces.

Geometric tolerances allow a more exact definition of the shape of an object than do conventional coordinate-type tolerances. Objects can be toleranced in a manner more closely related to their design function or so that their features and surfaces are more directly related to each other.

8-26   Tolerances of Form

Tolerances of form are used to define the shape of a surface relative to itself. There are four classifications: flatness, straightness, roundness, and cylindricity. Tolerances of form are not related to other surfaces but apply only to an individual surface.

8-27   Flatness

Flatness tolerances are used to define the amount of variation permitted in an individual surface. The surface is thought of as a plane not related to the rest of the object.

Figure 8-50 shows a rectangular object. How flat is the top surface? The given plus or minus tolerances allow a variation of (±0.5) across the surface. Without additional tolerances the surface could look like a series of waves varying between 30.5 and 29.5.

Figure 8-50

If the example in Figure 8-50 was assigned a flatness tolerance of 0.3, the height of the object—the feature tolerance—could continue to vary based on the 30±0.5 tolerance, but the surface itself could not vary by more than 0.3. In the most extreme condition, one end of the surface could be 30.5 above the bottom surface and the other end 29.5, but the surface would still be limited to within two parallel planes 0.3 apart as shown.

To better understand the meaning of flatness, consider how the surface would be inspected. The surface would be acceptable if a gauge could be moved all around the surface and never vary by more than 0.3. See Figure 8-51. Every point in the plane must be within the specified tolerance.

Figure 8-51

0   0.3 —— Total amount of
flatness variation

A reading may be
taken at any point
on the surface.

Inspection
for flatness

Figure 8-52

8-28 Straightness

Straightness tolerances are used to measure the variation of an individual feature along a straight line in a specified direction. Figure 8-52 shows an object with a straightness tolerance applied to its top surface. Straightness differs from flatness because straightness measurements are checked by moving a gauge directly across the surface in a single direction. The gauge is not moved randomly about the surface, as is required by flatness.

Straightness tolerances are most often applied to circular or matching objects to help ensure that the parts are not barreled or warped within the given feature tolerance range and, therefore, do not fit together well. Figure 8-53 shows a cylindrical object dimensioned and toleranced using a standard feature tolerance. The surface of the cylinder may vary within the specified tolerance range as shown.

Figure 8-53

Figure 8-54 shows the same object shown in Figure 8-53 dimensioned and toleranced using the same feature tolerance but also including a 0.05 straightness tolerance. The straightness tolerance limits the surface variation to 0.05 as shown.

Figure 8-54

Given:

Ø20 ± 1

Interpretation

No Ø symbol

Straightness tolerance zone

0.05

0.05

Within feature tolerance zone

8-29 Straightness (RFS and MMC)

Figure 8-55 again shows the same cylinder shown in Figures 8-53 and 8-54. This time the straightness tolerance is applied about the cylinder's centerline. This type of tolerance permits the feature tolerance and geometric tolerance to be used together to define a *virtual condition*. A virtual condition is used to determine the maximum possible size variation of the cylinder or the smallest diameter hole that will always accept the cylinder.

Figure 8-55

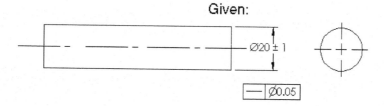

Given:

Ø20 ± 1

Ø0.05

Interpretation

Virtual condition
21 + 0.05 = 21.05

Tolerance zone of centerline
Ø0.05 RFS

The geometric tolerance specified in Figure 8-55 is applied to any circular segment along the cylinder, regardless of the cylinder's diameter. This means that the 0.05 tolerance is applied equally when the cylinder's diameter measures 19 or when it measures 21. This application is called RFS, *regardless of feature size.* RFS condition applies if no material condition is specified. In Figure 8-55 no symbol is listed after the 0.05 value, so it is assumed to be applied RFS.

Figure 8-56 shows the cylinder dimensioned with an MMC condition applied to the straightness tolerance. MMC stands for *maximum material condition* and means that the specified straightness tolerance (0.05) is applied only at the MMC condition or when the cylinder is at its maximum diameter size (21).

Figure 8-56

Measured Size	Allowable Tolerance Zone	Virtual Condition
21.0	0.05	21.05
20.9	0.15	21.15
20.8	0.25	21.25
.	.	.
.	.	.
.	.	.
20.0	1.05	22.05
.	.	.
.	.	.
19.0	2.05	23.05

A shaft is an external feature, so its largest possible size or MMC occurs when it is at its maximum diameter. A hole is an internal feature. A hole's MMC condition occurs when it is at its smallest diameter. The MMC condition for holes will be discussed later in the chapter along with positional tolerances.

Applying a straightness tolerance at MMC allows for a variation in the resulting tolerance zone. Because the 0.05 flatness tolerance is applied at MMC, the virtual condition is still 21.05, the same as with the RFS condition; however, the tolerance is applied only at MMC. As the cylinder's diameter varies within the specified feature tolerance range the acceptable tolerance zone may vary to maintain the same virtual condition.

The table in Figure 8-56 shows how the tolerance zone varies as the cylinder's diameter varies. When the cylinder is at its largest size or MMC, the tolerance zone equals 0.05, or the specified flatness variation. When the cylinder is at its smallest diameter, the tolerance zone equals 2.05, or the total feature size plus the total flatness size. In all variations the virtual size remains the same, so at any given cylinder diameter value, the size of the tolerance zone can be determined by subtracting the cylinder's diameter value from the virtual condition.

NOTE

Geometric tolerance applied at MMC allows the tolerance zone to grow.

Figure 8-57 shows a comparison between different methods used to dimension and tolerance a .750 shaft. The first example uses only a feature tolerance. This tolerance sets an upper limit of .755 and a lower limit of .745. Any variations within that range are acceptable.

Figure 8-57

The second example in Figure 8-57 sets a straightness tolerance of .003 about the cylinder's centerline. No conditions are defined, so the tolerance is applied RFS. This limits the variations in straightness to .003 at all feature sizes. For example, when the shaft is at its smallest possible feature size of .745, the .003 still applies. This means that a shaft measuring .745 that had a straightness variation greater than .003 would be rejected. If the tolerance had been applied at MMC, the part would be accepted. This does not mean that straightness tolerances should always be applied at MMC. If straightness is critical to the design integrity or function of the part, then straightness should be applied in the RFS condition.

The third example in Figure 8-57 applies the straightness tolerance about the centerline at MMC. This tolerance creates a virtual condition of .758. The MMC condition allows the tolerance to vary as the feature tolerance varies, so when the shaft is at its smallest feature size, .745, a straightness tolerance of .003 is acceptable (.005 feature tolerance + .003 straightness tolerance).

If the tolerance specification for the cylinder shown in Figure 8-57 was 0.000 applied at MMC, it would mean that the shaft would have to be perfectly straight at MMC or when the shaft was at its maximum value (.755); however, the straightness tolerance can vary as the feature size varies, as discussed for the other tolerance conditions. A 0.000 tolerance means that the MMC and the virtual conditions are equal.

Figure 8-58 shows a very long .750 diameter shaft. Its straightness tolerance includes a length qualifier that serves to limit the straightness variations over each inch of the shaft length and to prevent excess waviness over the full length. The tolerance .002/1.000 means that the total straightness may vary over the entire length of the shaft by .003 but that the variation is limited to .002 per 1.000 of shaft length.

Figure 8-58

A maximum of .002 straightness allowed within every 1.000 unit of length

8-30 Circularity

A *circularity tolerance* is used to limit the amount of variation in the roundness of a surface of revolution. It is measured at individual cross sections along the length of the object. The measurements are limited to the individual cross sections and are not related to other cross sections. This means that in extreme conditions the shaft shown in Figure 8-59 could actually taper from a diameter of 21 to a diameter of 19 and never violate the circularity requirement. It also means that qualifications such as MMC cannot be applied.

Figure 8-59

Figure 8-59 shows a shaft that includes a feature tolerance and a circularity tolerance of 0.07. To understand circularity tolerances, consider an individual cross section or slice of the cylinder. The actual shape of the outside edge of the slice varies around the slice. The difference between the maximum diameter and the minimum diameter of the slice can never exceed the stated circularity tolerance.

Circularity tolerances can be applied to tapered sections and spheres, as shown in Figure 8-60. In both applications, circularity is measured around individual cross sections, as it was for the shaft shown in Figure 8-59.

Figure 8-60

8-31   Cylindricity

Cylindricity tolerances are used to define a tolerance zone both around individual circular cross sections of an object and also along its length. The resulting tolerance zone looks like two concentric cylinders.

Figure 8-61 shows a shaft that includes a cylindricity tolerance that establishes a tolerance zone of .007. This means that if the maximum measured diameter is determined to be .755, the minimum diameter cannot be less than .748 anywhere on the cylindrical surface. Cylindricity and circularity are somewhat analogous to flatness and straightness. Flatness and cylindricity are concerned with variations across an entire surface or plane. In the case of cylindricity, the plane is shaped like a cylinder. Straightness and circularity are concerned with variations of a single element of a surface: a straight line across the plane in a specified direction for straightness, and a path around a single cross section for circularity.

Figure 8-61

8-32 Geometric Tolerances Using SolidWorks

Geometric tolerances are tolerances that limit dimensional variations based on the geometric properties. Figure 8-62 shows three different ways geometric tolerance boxes can be added to a drawing.

Figure 8-63 shows lists of geometric tolerance symbols.

Figure 8-62

Figure 8-63

	TYPE OF TOLERANCE	CHARACTERISTIC	SYMBOL
FOR INDIVIDUAL FEATURES	FORM	STRAIGHTNESS	—
		FLATNESS	▱
		CIRCULARITY	○
		CYLINDRICITY	⌭
INDIVIDUAL OR RELATED FEATURES	PROFILE	PROFILE OF A LINE	⌒
		PROFILE OF A SURFACE	⌓
RELATED FEATURES	ORIENTATION	ANGULARITY	∠
		PERPENDICULARITY	⊥
		PARALLELISM	//
	LOCATION	POSITION	⊕
		CONCENTRICITY	◎
	RUNOUT	CIRCULAR RUNOUT	↗
		TOTAL RUNOUT	↗↗

TERM	SYMBOL
AT MAXIMUM MATERIAL CONDITION	Ⓜ
REGARDLESS OF FEATURE SIZE	Ⓢ
AT LEAST MATERIAL CONDITION	Ⓛ
PROJECTED TOLERANCE ZONE	Ⓟ
DIAMETER	⌀
SPHERICAL DIAMETER	s⌀
RADIUS	R
SPHERICAL RADIUS	SR
REFERENCE	( )
ARC LENGTH	⌒

8-33 Datums

A *datum* is a point, axis, or surface used as a starting reference point for dimensions and tolerances. Figure 8-64 and Figure 8-65 show a rectangular object with three datum planes labeled A, B, and C. The three datum planes are called the primary, secondary, and tertiary datums, respectively. The three datum planes are, by definition, exactly 90° to one another.

Figure 8-66 shows a cylindrical datum frame that includes three datum planes. The X and Y planes are perpendicular to each other, and the base A plane is perpendicular to the datum axis between the X and Y planes.

Figure 8-64

Figure 8-65

Figure 8-66

Datum planes are assumed to be perfectly flat. When assigning a datum status to a surface, be sure that the surface is reasonably flat. This means that datum surfaces should be toleranced using surface finishes or created using machine techniques that produce flat surfaces.

Adding a Datum Indicator

Figure 8-67 shows a dimensioned orthographic view. This section shows how to define the lower surface as a datum feature, datum A. Note that a surface finish of 16 has been added to the lower surface. Datum surfaces are assumed to be flat and smooth.

1 Click the **Annotation** tab and select the **Datum Feature** tool.

The **Datum Feature PropertyManager** will appear.

2 Enter the letter **A** in the **Label Settings** field and select the **Filled Triangle With Shoulder** option under **Leader**.

Figure 8-67

Chapter 8 | Tolerancing **563**

3 Locate the datum symbol on the drawing as shown.

4 Press the **<Esc>** key.

5 Click the green **OK** check mark.

> **TIP**
>
> Once in place, a datum symbol can be repositioned by clicking and dragging the symbol.

Defining a Perpendicular Tolerance

Define the right vertical edge of the part as datum B and perpendicular to datum A within a tolerance of .001.

1 Click the **Annotation** tab and click the **Datum Feature** tool and define the right vertical surface as datum **B** using the same procedure as used to define datum A.

2 Click the **Annotation** tab and click the **Geometric Tolerance** tool.

See Figure 8-68. The **Properties/Geometric Tolerance** dialog box will appear.

3 Locate the Geometric Tolerance.

4 Click the **No Leader** option.

5 Select the **Perpendicular** symbol from the popup box.

6 Enter the **Tolerance** and click **Add Datum** in the next popup box.

7 Enter datum **A** and click **Done** in the next popup box.

8 Locate the geometric symbol on the extension line as shown.

9 Click the green **OK** check mark.

Figure 8-68

1. Click Annotation   2. Click Geometric Tolerance

Figure 8-68
(*Continued*)

Defining a Straightness Value for Datum Surface A

The surface finish value of 16 defines the smoothness of the surface but not the straightness. Think of surface finish as waves, and straightness as an angle. A straightness value of .002 indicates that there is a band of width .002 located .001 on either side of a theoretically perfectly straight line. The surface may vary but must always be within the .002 boundary. See Figure 8-69.

1 Click the **Annotation** tab and select the **Geometric Tolerance** tool.

2 Locate the Geometric Tolerance.

3 Click the **No Leader** option.

4 Select the **Straightness** symbol from the popup box, and define the tolerance as **.002** in the next popup box.

5 Click **Done**.

6 Locate the symbol under the datum A symbol as shown.

7 Click the green **OK** check mark.

Figure 8-69

8-34 Tolerances of Orientation

Tolerances of orientation are used to relate a feature or surface to another feature or surface. Tolerances of orientation include perpendicularity, parallelism, and angularity. They may be applied using RFS or MMC conditions, but they cannot be applied to individual features by themselves. To define a surface as parallel to another surface is very much like assigning a flatness value to the surface. The difference is that flatness applies only within the surface; every point on the surface is related to a defined set of limiting parallel planes. Parallelism defines every point in the surface relative to another surface. The two surfaces are therefore directly related to each other, and the condition of one affects the other.

Orientation tolerances are used with locational tolerances. A feature is first located, then it is oriented within the locational tolerances. This means that the orientation tolerance must always be less than the locational tolerances. The next four sections will further explain this requirement.

8-35 Perpendicularity

Perpendicularity tolerances are used to limit the amount of variation for a surface or feature within two planes perpendicular to a specified datum. Figure 8-70 shows a rectangular object. The bottom surface is assigned as datum A, and the right vertical edge is toleranced so that it must be perpendicular within a limit of 0.05 to datum A. The perpendicularity tolerance defines a tolerance zone 0.05 wide between two parallel planes that are perpendicular to datum A.

The object also includes a horizontal dimension and tolerance of 40±1. This tolerance is called a *locational tolerance* because it serves to locate the right edge of the object. As with rectangular coordinate tolerances, discussed earlier in the chapter, the 40±1 controls the location of the edge—how far away or how close it can be to the left edge—but does not directly control the shape of the edge. Any shape that falls within the specified tolerance range is acceptable. This may in fact be sufficient for a given design, but if a more controlled shape is required, a perpendicularity tolerance must be added. The perpendicularity tolerance works within the locational tolerance to ensure that the edge is not only within the locational tolerance but also perpendicular to datum A.

Figure 8-70 shows the two extreme conditions for the 40±1 locational tolerance. The perpendicularity tolerance is applied by first measuring the surface and determining its maximum and minimum lengths. The difference between these two measurements must be less than 0.05. Thus, if the measured maximum distance is 41, then no other part of the surface may be less than 41 − 0.05 = 40.95.

Figure 8-70

Tolerances of perpendicularity serve to complement locational tolerances, to make the shape more exact, so tolerances of perpendicularity must always be smaller than tolerances of location. It would be of little use, for example, to assign a perpendicularity tolerance of 1.5 for the object shown in Figure 8-71. The locational tolerance would prevent the variation from ever reaching the limits specified by such a large perpendicularity tolerance.

Figure 8-72 shows a perpendicularity tolerance applied to cylindrical features: a shaft and a hole. The figure includes examples of both RFS and MMC applications. As with straightness tolerances applied at MMC, perpendicularity tolerances applied about a hole or shaft's centerline allow the tolerance zone to vary as the feature size varies.

The inclusion of the Ø symbol in a geometric tolerance is critical to its interpretation. See Figure 8-73. If the Ø symbol is not included, the tolerance applies only to the view in which it is written. This means that the tolerance zone is shaped like a rectangular slice, not a cylinder, as would be the case if the Ø symbol were included. In general it is better to always include the Ø symbol for cylindrical features because it generates a tolerance zone more like that used in positional tolerancing.

Figure 8-71

RFS tolerance applies regardless of feature sign

Tolerance zone is perpendicular to datum A

MMC tolerance applies only at the maximum material condition

Figure 8-72

If tolerance is

Ø20±0.03

| 0.02 | A |

Feature Tolerance	Allowable Tolerance
20.03	.02
20.02	.02
20.01	.02
20.00	.02
19.99	.02
19.98	.02
19.97	.02

Tolerance zone shape

0.02 SQUARE

If tolerance is

Ø20±0.03

| Ø0.02 Ⓜ | A |

Feature Tolerance	Allowable Tolerance
20.03	.02
20.02	.03
20.01	.04
20.00	.05
19.99	.06
19.98	.07
19.97	.08

Tolerance zone shape

Ø0.02

Figure 8-73

Tolerance zone applies to the edges of the slot as well.

0.04 Ⓜ | A

0.04 Perpendicular to datum A

Figure 8-73 shows a perpendicularity tolerance applied to a slot, a non-cylindrical feature. Again, the MMC specification is always for variations in the tolerance zone.

8-36 Parallelism

Parallelism tolerances are used to ensure that all points within a plane are within two parallel planes that are parallel to a referenced datum plane. Figure 8-74 shows a rectangular object that is toleranced so that its top surface is parallel to the bottom surface within 0.02. This means that every point on the top surface must be within a set of parallel planes 0.02 apart. These parallel tolerancing planes are located by determining the maximum and minimum distances from the datum surface. The difference between the maximum and minimum values may not exceed the stated 0.02 tolerance.

In the extreme condition of maximum feature size, the top surface is located 40.5 above the datum plane. The parallelism tolerance is then applied, meaning that no point on the surface may be closer than 40.3 to the datum. This is an RFS condition. The MMC condition may also be applied, thereby allowing the tolerance zone to vary as the feature size varies.

Figure 8-74

8-37 Angularity

Angularity tolerances are used to limit the variance of surfaces and axes that are at an angle relative to a datum. Angularity tolerances are applied like perpendicularity and parallelism tolerances as a way to better control the shape of locational tolerances.

Figure 8-75 shows an angularity tolerance and several ways it is interpreted at extreme conditions.

Figure 8-75

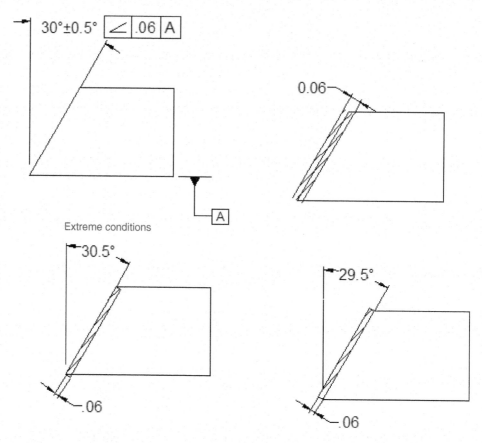

Extreme conditions

8-38 Profiles

Profile tolerances are used to limit the variations of irregular surfaces. They may be assigned as either bilateral or unilateral tolerances. There are two types of profile tolerances: surface and line. *Surface* profile tolerances limit the variation of an entire surface, whereas a *line* profile tolerance limits the variations along a single line across a surface.

Figure 8-76 shows an object that includes a surface profile tolerance referenced to an irregular surface. The tolerance is considered a bilateral tolerance because no other specification is given. This means that all points on the surface must be located between two parallel planes 0.08 apart that are centered about the irregular surface. The measurements are taken perpendicular to the surface.

Figure 8-76

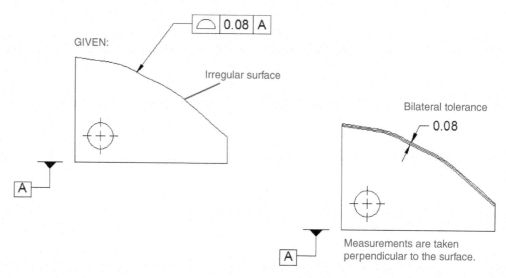

Unilateral applications of surface profile tolerances must be indicated on the drawing using phantom lines. The phantom line indicates the side of the true profile line of the irregular surface on which the tolerance is to be applied. A phantom line above the irregular surface indicates that the tolerance is to be applied using the true profile line as 0, and then the specified tolerance range is to be added above that line. See Figures 8-77 and 8-78.

Figure 8-77

Figure 8-78

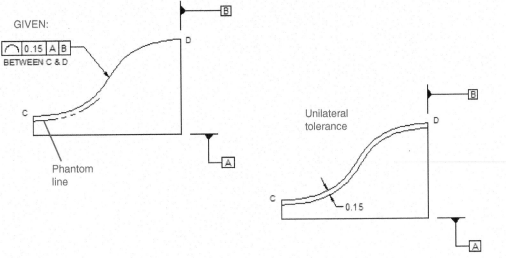

Chapter 8 | Tolerancing **571**

Profiles of line tolerances are applied to irregular surfaces, as shown in Figure 8-78. Profiles of line tolerances are particularly helpful when tolerancing an irregular surface that is constantly changing, such as the surface of an airplane wing.

Surface and line profile tolerances are somewhat analogous to flatness and straightness tolerances. Flatness and surface profile tolerances are applied across an entire surface, whereas straightness and line profile tolerances are applied only along a single line across the surface.

8-39 Runouts

A *runout tolerance* is used to limit the variations between features of an object and a datum. More specifically, they are applied to surfaces around a datum axis such as a cylinder or to a surface constructed perpendicular to a datum axis. There are two types of runout tolerances: circular and total.

Figure 8-79 shows a cylinder that includes a circular runout tolerance. The runout requirements are checked by rotating the object about its longitudinal axis or datum axis while holding an indicator gauge in a fixed position on the object's surface.

Runout tolerances may be either bilateral or unilateral. A runout tolerance is assumed to be bilateral unless otherwise indicated. If a runout tolerance is to be unilateral, a phantom line is used to indicate the side of the object's true surface to which the tolerance is to be applied. See Figure 8-80.

Figure 8-79

Figure 8-80

Runout tolerances may be applied to tapered areas of cylindrical objects, as shown in Figure 8-81. The tolerance is checked by rotating the object about a datum axis while holding an indicator gauge in place.

A total runout tolerance limits the variation across an entire surface. See Figure 8-82. An indicator gauge is not held in place while the object is rotated, as it is for circular runout tolerances, but is moved about the rotating surface.

Figure 8-83 shows a circular runout tolerance that references two datums. The two datums serve as one datum. The object can then be rotated about both datums simultaneously as the runout tolerances are checked.

Figure 8-81

Figure 8-82

Runout tolerance

Figure 8-83

8-40 Positional Tolerances

As defined earlier, *positional tolerances* are used to locate and tolerance holes. Positional tolerances create a circular tolerance zone for hole center-point locations, in contrast with the rectangular tolerance zone created by linear coordinate dimensions. See Figure 8-84. The circular tolerance zone allows for an increase in acceptable tolerance variation without compromising the design integrity of the object.

Note how some of the possible hole centerpoints fall in an area outside the rectangular tolerance zone but are still within the circular tolerance zone. If the hole had been located using linear coordinate dimensions, centerpoints located beyond the rectangular tolerance zone would have been rejected as beyond tolerance, and yet holes produced using these locations would function correctly from a design standpoint. The centerpoint locations would be acceptable if positional tolerances had been specified. The finished hole is round, so a round tolerance zone is appropriate. The rectangular tolerance zone rejects some holes unnecessarily.

Figure 8-84

Linear bilateral tolerances

Feature tolerance

1.00±.01

1.00±.01

Ø1.000±.003

These tolerances will generate a square tolerance zone for the hole's centerpoint.

Basic dimension

Ø1.000±.003

⊕ | Ø.027 Ⓜ

Feature tolerance

Positional tolerance

1.00

1.00

These tolerances will generate a circular tolerance zone for the hole's centerpoint.

Holes are dimensioned and toleranced using geometric tolerances by a combination of locating dimensions, feature dimensions and tolerances, and positional tolerances. See Figure 8-85. The locating dimensions are enclosed in rectangular boxes and are called *basic dimensions*. Basic dimensions are assumed to be exact.

The feature tolerances for the hole are as presented earlier in the chapter. They can be presented using plus or minus or limit-type tolerances. In the example shown in Figure 8-85 the diameter of the hole is toleranced using a plus and minus 0.05 tolerance.

The basic locating dimensions of 45 and 50 are assumed to be exact. The tolerances that would normally accompany linear locational dimensions are replaced by the positional tolerance. The positional tolerance also specifies that the tolerance be applied at the centerline at maximum material condition. The resulting tolerance zones are as shown in Figure 8-85.

Figure 8-85

Basic dimension

Feature tolerance

Ø30±.05

⊕ | Ø0.02 Ⓜ | A

50

45

Positional tolerance

Basic dimensions are required when using positional tolerances.

0.05 tolerance zone from feature tolerance

0.02 tolerance zone from positional tolerance

Figure 8-86 shows an object containing two holes that are dimensioned and toleranced using positional tolerances. There are two consecutive horizontal basic dimensions. Because basic dimensions are exact, they do not have tolerances that accumulate; that is, there is no tolerance buildup.

Figure 8-86

8-41 Creating Positional Tolerances

Figure 8-87 shows an orthographic view that has been dimensioned. Note that the hole has a dimension and tolerance of Ø1.000±.001. This is the hole's feature tolerance. It deals only with the hole's diameter variation. It does not tolerance the hole's location.

Creating the Positional Tolerance

1 Click the **Annotation** tab and click the **Geometric Tolerance** tool.

2 Locate the Geometric Tolerance.

3 Click the **No Leader** option.

4 Select the **Position** symbol from the popup box, define the tolerance as **.001**, and select the **Diameter** symbol in the next popup box.

5 Select **Material Condition** and select the **Maximum Material Condition** symbol.

6 Click **Done**.

The collective symbol would read "Apply a .001 positional tolerance about the hole's centerpoint at the maximum material condition."

7 Click the green **OK** check mark.

8 Locate the symbol on the drawing under the feature tolerance as shown.

Figure 8-87

Figure 8-87
(*Continued*)

Create basic dimensions to accompany the geometric positional tolerance. See Figure 8-88.

Figure 8-88

9 Click the **2.00** dimension.

The **Dimension PropertyManager** will appear.

10 Click the **Basic** option in the **Tolerance/Precision** box.

11 Click the **1.13** dimension and make it a **Basic** dimension.

12 Click the **1.00** dimension and make it a **Basic** dimension.

13 Click the green **OK** check mark.

14 Save the drawing.

> **TIP**
>
> Geometric positional tolerances must include basic dimensions. Basic dimensions are assumed to be perfect. The locational tolerance associated with locating dimensions has been moved to the geometric positional tolerance.

8-42 Virtual Condition

Virtual condition is a combination of a feature's MMC and its geometric tolerance. For external features (shafts) it is the MMC plus the geometric tolerance; for internal features (holes) it is the MMC minus the geometric tolerance.

The following calculations are based on the dimensions shown in Figure 8-89.

Figure 8-89

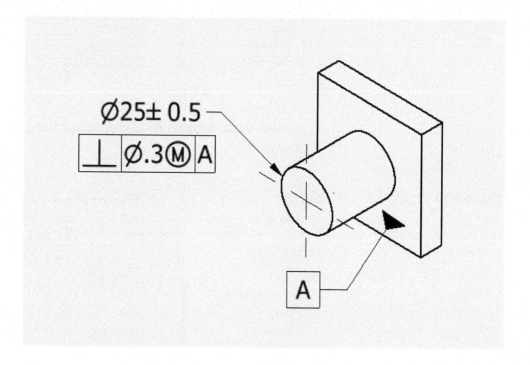

Figure 8-89
(*Continued*)

Chapter 8

$\phi25\pm0.5$

$\boxed{\oplus \; \phi.3\text{\small{Ⓜ}} \; A}$

Bottom Surface

$\boxed{A}$

Calculating the Virtual Condition for a Shaft

25.5	MMC for shaft—maximum diameter
+0.3	Geometric tolerance
25.8	Virtual condition

Calculating the Virtual Condition for a Hole

24.5	MMC for hole—minimum diameter
–0.3	Geometric tolerance
24.2	Virtual condition

8-43 Floating Fasteners

Positional tolerances are particularly helpful when dimensioning mating parts. Because basic locating dimensions are considered exact, the sizing of mating parts is dependent only on the hole and shaft's MMC and the geometric tolerance between them.

The relationship for floating fasteners and holes in objects may be expressed as a formula:

$$H - T = F$$

where

H = hole at MMC
T = geometric tolerance
F = shaft at MMC

A *floating fastener* is one that passes through two or more objects, and all parts have clearance holes for the tolerance. It is not attached to either object and it does not screw into either object. Figure 8-90 shows two objects that are to be joined by a common floating shaft, such as a bolt or screw. The feature size and tolerance and the positional geometric tolerance are both given. The minimum size hole that will always just fit is determined using the preceding formula:

$$H - T = F$$

$$11.97 - .02 = 11.95$$

Therefore, the shaft's diameter at MMC, the shaft's maximum diameter, equals 11.95. Any required tolerance would have to be subtracted from this shaft size.

Figure 8-90

SIZE	TOLERANCE ZONE
11.97 MMC	.02
11.98	.03
11.99	.04
12.00	.05
12.01	.06
12.02	.07
12.03 LMC	.08

11.97 MMC
−0.02
11.95 virtual condition

Maximum possible
fastener diameter = 11.95

The .02 geometric tolerance is applied at the hole's MMC, so as the hole's size expands within its feature tolerance, the tolerance zone for the acceptable matching parts also expands.

8-44 Sample Problem SP8-3

The situation presented in Figure 8-90 can be worked in reverse; that is, hole sizes can be derived from given shaft sizes.

The two objects shown in Figure 8-91 are to be joined by a .250in. bolt. The parts are floating; they are both free to move, and the fastener is not joined to either object. What is the MMC of the holes if the positional tolerance is to be .030?

A manufacturer's catalog specifies that the tolerance for .250 bolts is .2500 to .2600.

Rewriting the formula

$$H - T = F$$

to isolate the H yields

$$H = F + T$$

$$= .260 + .030$$

$$= .290$$

The .290 value represents the minimum hole diameter, MMC, for all four holes that will always accept the .250 bolt. Figure 8-92 shows the resulting drawing callout.

Figure 8-91

Floating fasteners

Ø.2500
.2600

Ø ?
Size and
tolerance

Object 1

Object 2

Figure 8-92

Ø .290 - tolerance and clearance

Any clearance requirements or tolerances for the hole would have to be added to the .290 value.

8-45 Sample Problem SP8-4

Repeat the problem presented in SP8-3 but be sure that there is always a minimum clearance of .002 between the hole and the shaft, and assign a hole tolerance of .008.

Sample problem SP8-3 determined that the maximum hole diameter that will always accept the .250 bolt is .290 based on the .030 positioning tolerance. If the minimum clearance is to be .002, the maximum hole diameter is found as follows:

.290	Minimum hole diameter that will always accept the bolt (0 clearance at MMC)
+.002	Minimum clearance
.292	Minimum hole diameter including clearance

Now, assign the tolerance to the hole:

.292	Minimum hole diameter
+.001	Tolerance
.293	Maximum hole diameter

See Figure 8-93 for the appropriate drawing callout. The choice of clearance size and hole tolerance varies with the design requirements for the objects.

Figure 8-93

8-46 Fixed Fasteners

A *fixed fastener* is a fastener that is restrained in one of the parts. For example, one end of the fastener is screwed into one of the parts using threads. See Figure 8-94. Because the fastener is fixed to one of the objects, the geometric tolerance zone must be smaller than that used for floating fasteners. The fixed fastener cannot move without moving the object it is attached to. The relationship between fixed fasteners and holes in mating objects is defined by the formula

$$H - 2T = F$$

The tolerance zone is cut in half for each part. This can be demonstrated by the objects shown in Figure 8-95. The same feature sizes that were used in Figure 8-91 are assigned, but in this example the fasteners are fixed. Solving for the geometric tolerance yields a value as follows:

$$H - F = 2T$$

$$11.97 - 11.95 = 2T$$

$$.02 = 2T$$

$$.01 = T$$

The resulting positional tolerance is half that obtained for floating fasteners.

Figure 8-94

Fixed fasteners

Fasteners are fixed into the object

Figure 8-95

Fixed condition

Diameter that will always fit at MMC

A

Ø.2600
.2500

$\oplus$ | Ø .030 ⓜ | A

8-47 Sample Problem SP8-5

This problem is similar to sample problem SP8-3, but the given conditions are applied to fixed fasteners rather than floating fasteners. Compare the resulting shaft diameters for the two problems. See Figure 8-96.

Figure 8-96

Base with fasteners fixed into the holes

Ø .290 - tolerance and clearance

$\oplus$ | Ø.030ⓜ | A

.50

.40

1.25

1.00

A. What is the minimum diameter hole that will always accept the fixed fasteners?

B. If the minimum clearance is .005 and the hole is to have a tolerance of .002, what are the maximum and minimum diameters of the hole?

$$H - 2T = F$$

$$H = F + 2T$$

$$= .260 + 2(0.030)$$

$$= .260 + 0.060$$

$$= .320 \text{ Minimum diameter that will always accept the fastener}$$

If the minimum clearance is .005 and the hole tolerance is .002,

$$
\begin{array}{ll}
.320 & \text{Virtual condition} \\
\underline{+.005} & \text{Clearance} \\
.325 & \text{Minimum hole diameter} \\[4pt]
.325 & \text{Minimum hole diameter} \\
\underline{+.002} & \text{Tolerance} \\
.327 & \text{Maximum hole diameter}
\end{array}
$$

The maximum and minimum values for the hole's diameter can then be added to the drawing of the object that fits over the fixed fasteners. See Figure 8-97.

Figure 8-97

8-48 Design Problems

This problem was originally done in section "8-40, Positional Tolerances" using rectangular tolerances. It is done in this section using positional geometric tolerances so that the two systems can be compared. It is suggested that the previous problem be reviewed before reading this section.

Figure 8-98 shows top and bottom parts that are to be joined in the floating condition. A nominal distance of 50 between hole centers and Ø20 for the holes has been assigned. In the previous solution a rectangular tolerance of ±.01 was selected, and there was a minimum hole diameter of 20.00. Figure 8-99 shows the resulting tolerance zones.

Figure 8-98

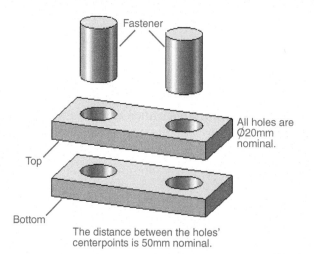

Figure 8-99

Linear tolerance zones based on ± tolerances.

NOT TO SCALE

Rectangular range: 49.98 to 50.02

Tolerance zones based on positional (⊕) tolerances.

NOT TO SCALE

Circular range: 49.97 to 50.03

Crescent-shaped areas account for the increased tolerance range of circular (positional) tolerances.

This increased area of acceptability is the result of assigning the positional tolerance at MMC.

The diagonal distance across the rectangular tolerance zone is .028 and was rounded off to .03 to yield a maximum possible fastener diameter of 19.97. If the same .03 value is used to calculate the fastener diameter using positional tolerance, the results are as follows:

$$H - T = F$$

$$20.00 - .03 = 19.97$$

The results seem to be the same, but because of the circular shape of the positional tolerance zone, the manufactured results are not the same. The minimum distance between the inside edges of the rectangular zones is 49.98, or .01 from the centerpoint of each hole. The minimum distance from the innermost points of the circular tolerance zones is 49.97, or .015 (half the rounded-off .03 value) from the centerpoint of each hole.

The same value difference also occurs for the maximum distance between centerpoints, where 50.02 is the maximum distance for the rectangular tolerances, and 50.03 is the maximum distance for the circular tolerances. The size of the circular tolerance zone is larger because the hole tolerances are assigned at MMC. In this example the MMC for the hole is 20.00; that is, when the hole is at its smallest. As the hole's feature tolerance increases from 20.00 to 20.02, the size of the tolerance zone increases.

The basic dimensions of 20 and 50 are assumed to be perfect. The original ±.01 positional tolerances assigned are still present; they are now presented as geometric positional tolerances. The hole tolerance, 20 +.02/–0, is the feature tolerance, and the geometric tolerance of .03 is the positional tolerance.

Figure 8-99 shows a comparison between the tolerance zones, and Figure 8-100 shows how the positional tolerances would be presented on a drawing of either the top or bottom part.

Figure 8-100

Figure 8-101 shows the same top and bottom parts joined together in the fixed condition. The initial nominal values are the same. If the same .03 diagonal value is assigned as a positional tolerance, the results are as follows:

$$H - 2T = F$$

$$20.00 - .06 = 19.94$$

These results appear to be the same as those generated by the rectangular tolerance zone, but the circular tolerance zone allows a greater variance in acceptable manufactured parts.

Figure 8-101

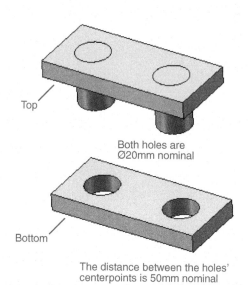

Figure 8-102 shows the parts dimensioned using baseline dimensions.

Figure 8-102

H − 2T = F
20.00 − .06 = 19.94

Subtracting .01 for
clearance results in
a maximum shaft
diameter of 19.93.

⌀ 19.93
19.91
2 HOLES

|← 20 →|← 50±0.01 →|

┤32

20±0.01

40

|← 90 →|

Assigning a shaft tolerance of .02 results
in a maximum shaft diameter of 19.91.

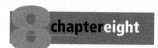
Chapter Projects

Project 8-1:

Draw a model of the objects shown in Figure P8-1A through P8-1D using the given dimensions and tolerances. Create a drawing layout with a view of the model as shown. Add the specified dimensions and tolerances.

Figure P8-1A
MILLIMETERS

1.	38±0.05
2.	10±0.1
3.	5±0.05
4.	45.50° 44.50°
5.	40±0.1
6.	22±0.1
7.	12 $^{+0}_{-.1}$
8.	25 $^{+.05}_{-0}$
9.	51.50 50.75
10.	76±0.1

MATL = 20 THK

Figure P8-1B
MILLIMETERS

1. 34±0.25
2. 17±0.25
3. 25±0.05
4. 15.00
   14.80
5. 50±0.05
6. 80±0.1
7. R5±0.1-8 PLACES
8. 45±0.25
9. 60±0.1
10. Ø14 - 3 HOLES
11. 15.00
    14.80
12. 30.00
    29.80

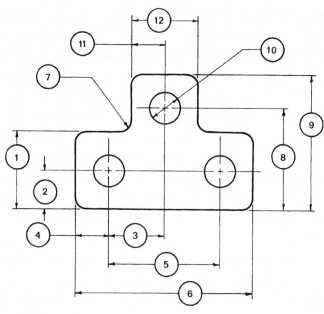

MATL = 30 THK

Figure P8-1C
INCHES

1. 3.00±.01
2. 1.56±.01
3. 46.50°
   45.50°
4. .750±.005
5. 2.75
   2.70
6. 3.625±.010
7. 45°±.5°
8. 2.250±.005

MATL = .75 THK

Figure P8-1D
MILLIMETERS

1. 50 $^{+.2}_{\ 0}$
2. R45±.1 – 2 PLACES
3. 63.5 $^{\ 0}_{-.2}$
4. 76±.1
5. 38±.1
6. Ø12.00 $^{+.05}_{\ 0}$ – 3 HOLES
7. 30±.03
8. 30±.03
9. 100 $^{+.4}_{\ 0}$

MATL = 10 THK

Project 8-2:

Redraw the object shown in Figure P8-2, including the given dimensions and tolerances. Calculate and list the maximum and minimum distances for surface A.

MATL = 25 THK

MATL = 1.25 THK

Project 8-3:

A. Redraw the object shown in Figure P8-3, including the dimensions and tolerances. Calculate and list the maximum and minimum distances for surface A.

B. Redraw the given object and dimension it using baseline dimensions. Calculate and list the maximum and minimum distances for surface A.

Project 8-4:

Redraw the object shown in Figure P8-4, including the dimensions and tolerances. Calculate and list the maximum and minimum distances for surfaces D and E.

Project 8-5:

Dimension the object shown in Figure P8-5 twice, once using chain dimensions and once using baseline dimensions. Calculate and list the maximum and minimum distances for surface D for both chain and baseline dimensions. Compare the results.

Figure P8-4
MILLIMETERS

Figure P8-5
MILLIMETERS

MATL = 20 THK

Project 8-6:

Redraw the following shapes, as shown in Figure P8-6, including the dimensions and tolerances. Also list the required minimum and maximum values for the specified distances.

Figure P8-6
INCHES

B_{min} = _____
B_{max} = _____

MATL = 1.125 THK

MATL = 45 THK

C_{min} = _____
C_{max} = _____

C_{min} = _____
C_{max} = _____

C_{min} = _____
C_{max} = _____

MATL = .625 THK

Figure P8-7
MILLIMETERS

INSPECTION REPORT

PART NAME AND NO: *10755002*

INSPECTOR:

DATE:

1.00 3 PLACES

BASE DIMENSION	TOLERANCES		AS MEASURED	RESULTS
	MAX	MIN		
① 100 ± 0.5			99.8	
② $\phi \, ^{57}_{56}$			57.01	
③ 22 ± 0.3			21.72	
④ $^{40.05}_{39.95}$			39.98	
⑤ 22 ± 0.3			21.68	
⑥ $R52 ^{+0}_{-0.2}$			51.99	
⑦ $35 ^{+0.2}_{-0.3}$			35.20	
⑧ $30 ^{+0.4}_{0}$			30.27	
⑨ $6.0 ^{+.1}_{-.2}$			5.85	
⑩ 12.0 ± 0.2			11.90	

.50 −10 PLACES

Project 8-7:

Redraw and complete the inspection report shown in Figure P8-7. Under the RESULTS column classify each "AS MEASURED" value as OK if the value is within the stated tolerances, REWORK if the value indicates that the measured value is beyond the stated tolerance but can be reworked to bring it into the acceptable range, or SCRAP if the value is not within the tolerance range and cannot be reworked to make it acceptable.

Project 8-8:

Redraw the charts shown in Figure P8-8 and complete them based on the following information. All values are in millimeters.

A.   Nominal = 16, Fit = H8/d8
B.   Nominal = 30, Fit = H11/c11
C.   Nominal = 22, Fit = H7/g6
D.   Nominal = 10, Fit = C11/h11
E.   Nominal = 25, Fit = F8/h7

F. Nominal = 12, Fit = H7/k6
G. Nominal = 3, Fit = H7/p6
H. Nominal = 18, Fit = H7/s6
I. Nominal = 27, Fit = H7/u6
J. Nominal = 30, Fit = N7/h6

Figure P8-8
MILLIMETERS

NOMINAL	HOLE		SHAFT		CLEARANCE	
	MAX	MIN	MAX	MIN	MAX	MIN
A						
B						
C						
D						
E						

NOMINAL	HOLE		SHAFT		INTERFERENCE	
	MAX	MIN	MAX	MIN	MAX	MIN
F						
G						
H						
I						
J						

Use the same dimensions given above

Project 8-9:

Redraw the charts shown in Figure P8-9 and complete them based on the following information. All values are in inches.

A. Nominal = 0.25, Fit = Class LC5, H7/g6
B. Nominal = 1.00, Fit = Class LC7, H10/e9
C. Nominal = 1.50, Fit = Class LC9, F11/h11
D. Nominal = 0.75, Fit = Class RC3, H7/f6
E. Nominal = 1.75, Fit = Class RC6, H9/e8
F. Nominal = .500, Fit = Class LT2, H8/js7
G. Nominal = 1.25, Fit = Class LT5, H7/n6
H. Nominal = 1.38, Fit = Class LN3, J7/h6
I. Nominal = 1.625, Fit = Class FN2, H7/s6
J. Nominal = 2.00, Fit = Class FN4, H7/u6

Figure P8-9
INCHES

3.75
6 equal
spaces

NOMINAL	HOLE		SHAFT		CLEARANCE	
	MAX	MIN	MAX	MIN	MAX	MIN
A						
B						
C						
D						
E						

half space

1.5 — 6.0 − 6 equal spaces

NOMINAL	HOLE		SHAFT		INTERFERENCE	
	MAX	MIN	MAX	MIN	MAX	MIN
F						
G						
H						
I						
J						

Use the same dimensions given above

Project 8-10:

Draw the chart shown and add the appropriate values based on the dimensions and tolerances given in Figures P8-10A through P8-10D.

Figure P8-10A
MILLIMETERS

MAXIMUM SHAFT DIAMETER
THAT WILL ALWAYS FIT
= ____ ?

PART NO:										10
A		B		C		D		E		10
MAX	MIN	MAX	MIN	MAX	MIN	MAX	MIN	MAX	MIN	10
										20

→| |← 20 - 10 PLACES

```
PART NO: 9-M53A

  A.  20±0.1

  B.  30±0.2

  C.  Ø20±0.05

  D.  40

  E.  60
```

Figure P8-10B
MILLIMETERS

```
PART NO: 9-M53B

  A.  32.02
      31.97

  B.  47.52
      47.50

  C.  Ø18 +0.05
           0

  D.  64±0.05

  E.  100±0.05
```

Figure P8-10C
MILLIMETERS

```
PART NO: 9-E47A

  A.  2.00±.02

  B.  1.75±.03

  C.  Ø.750±.005

  D.  4.00±.05

  E.  3.50±.05
```

Figure P8-10D
MILLIMETERS

```
PART NO: 9-E47B

  A.  18 +0
        -0.02

  B.  26 +0
        -0.04

  C.  Ø  24.03
         23.99

  D.  52±0.04

  E.  36±0.02
```

Project 8-11:

Prepare front and top views of parts 4A and 4B in Figure P8-11 based on the given dimensions.

Add tolerances to produce the stated clearances.

Project 8-12:

Redraw the Box, Top and Box, Bottom in Figure P8-12 and include dimensions and tolerances to meet the "UPON ASSEMBLY" requirements.

Figure P8-11
MILLIMETERS

Figure P8-12
INCHES

Project 8-13:

Draw a front and top view of both given objects in Figure P8-13. Add dimensions and tolerances to meet the "FINAL CONDITION" requirements.

Project 8-14:

Given the following nominal sizes, dimension and tolerance parts AM311 and AM312 in Figure P8-14 so that they always fit together regardless of orientation. Further, dimension the overall lengths of each part so that in the assembled condition they will always pass through a clearance gauge with an opening of 80.00±0.02.

Figure P8-13
MILLIMETERS

Figure P8-14
MILLIMETERS

In the assembled condition, both parts must always pass through the clearance gauge.

FINAL CONDITION

All given dimensions, except for the the clearance gauge, are nominal.

Project 8-15:

Given the following rail assembly, as shown in Figure P8-15, add dimensions and tolerances so that the parts always fit together as shown in the assembled position.

Figure P8-15
MILLIMETERS

All dimensions are nominal.

Project 8-16:

Given the following peg assembly, shown in Figure P8-16, add dimensions and tolerances so that the parts always fit together as shown in the assembled position.

Figure P8-16
INCHES

All dimensions are nominal.

Project 8-17:

Given the following collar assembly shown in Figure P8-17, add dimensions and tolerances so that the parts always fit together as shown in the assembled position.

Figure P8-17
MILLIMETERS

Collar Support

Collar

Project 8-18:

Given the following vee-block assembly shown in Figure P8-18, add dimensions and tolerances so that the parts always fit together as shown in the assembled position. The total height of the assembled blocks must be between 4.45 and 4.55in.

Figure P8-18
INCHES

Block, Vee

Vee, Top

All dimensions are nominal.

Project 8-19:

Design a bracket that will support the three Ø100 wheels shown in Figure P8-19A. The wheels will utilize three Ø5.00±0.01 shafts attached to the bracket. The bottom of the bracket must be a minimum of 10mm from the ground. The wall thickness of the bracket must always be at least 5mm, and the minimum bracket opening must be at least 15mm.

1. Prepare a front and a side view of the bracket.

2. Draw the wheels in their relative positions using phantom lines.

3. Add all appropriate dimensions and tolerances.

Given a top and a bottom part in the floating condition as shown in Figure P8-19B, satisfy the requirements given in projects P8-20 through P8-23 so that the parts always fit together regardless of orientation. Prepare drawings of each part including dimensions and tolerances.

A. Use linear tolerances.

B. Use positional tolerances.

Figure P8-19A
MILLIMETERS

All sizes are nominal, unless otherwise stated.

Ø100– 3 WHEELS

105 NOMINAL

105 NOMINAL

THICKNESS=10
3 WHEELS

Ø5–3 WHEELS

Shaft Ø = 5.00±.00
3 required

AS NEEDED

AS NEEDED

5–WALL THICKNESS
MINIMUM ALL AROUND

ROUND CORNERS

15 MINIMUM

THIS SURFACE MUST ALWAYS
BE AT LEAST 10 FROM THE GROUND.

Roller blade assembly
Part number BU 110-44

Figure P8-19B

Floating condition

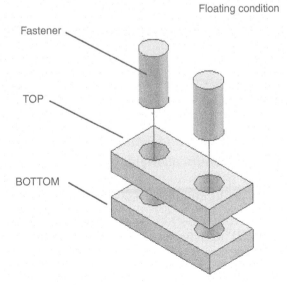

Fastener

TOP

BOTTOM

Project 8-20: Inches

A. The distance between the holes' centerpoints is 2.00 nominal.
B. The holes are Ø.375 nominal.
C. The fasteners have a tolerance of .001.
D. The holes have a tolerance of .002.
E. The minimum allowable clearance between the fasteners and the holes is .003.
F. The positional tolerance is .001.

Project 8-21: Millimeters

A. The distance between the holes' centerpoints is 80 nominal.
B. The holes are Ø12 nominal.
C. The fasteners have a tolerance of 0.05.
D. The holes have a tolerance of 0.03.
E. The minimum allowable clearance between the fasteners and the holes is 0.02.
F. The positional tolerance is .01.

Project 8-22: Inches

A. The distance between the holes' centerpoints is 3.50 nominal.
B. The holes are Ø.625 nominal.
C. The fasteners have a tolerance of .005.
D. The holes have a tolerance of .003.
E. The minimum allowable clearance between the fasteners and the holes is .002.
F. The positional tolerance is .002.

Project 8-23: Millimeters

A. The distance between the holes' centerpoints is 65 nominal.
B. The holes are Ø16 nominal.
C. The fasteners have a tolerance of 0.03.
D. The holes have a tolerance of 0.04.
E. The minimum allowable clearance between the fasteners and the holes is 0.03.
F. The positional tolerance is .02.

Given a top and a bottom part in the fixed condition as shown in Figure Figure P8-20, satisfy the requirements given in projects P8-24 through P8-27 so that the parts fit together regardless of orientation. Prepare drawings of each part including dimensions and tolerances.

A. Use linear tolerances.

B. Use positional tolerances.

Figure P8-20

Fasteners are fixed to the top part.

TOP

Fastener

BOTTOM

Fixed condition

Project 8-24: Millimeters

A. The distance between the holes' centerpoints is 60 nominal.

B. The holes are Ø10 nominal.

C. The fasteners have a tolerance of 0.04.

D. The holes have a tolerance of 0.02.

E. The minimum allowable clearance between the fasteners and the holes is 0.02.

F. The positional tolerance is 0.01.

Project 8-25: Inches

A. The distance between the holes' centerpoints is 3.50 nominal.

B. The holes are Ø.563 nominal.

C. The fasteners have a tolerance of .005.

D. The holes have a tolerance of .003.

E. The minimum allowable clearance between the fasteners and the holes is .002.

F. The positional tolerance is .001.

Project 8-26: Millimeters

A. The distance between the holes' centerpoints is 100 nominal.

B. The holes are Ø18 nominal.

C. The fasteners have a tolerance of 0.02.

D. The holes have a tolerance of 0.01.

E. The minimum allowable clearance between the fasteners and the holes is 0.03.

F. The positional tolerance is 0.02.

Project 8-27: Inches

A. The distance between the holes' centerpoints is 1.75 nominal.

B. The holes are Ø.250 nominal.

C. The fasteners have a tolerance of .002.

D. The holes have a tolerance of .003.

E. The minimum allowable clearance between the fasteners and the holes is .001.

F. The positional tolerance is .002.

Project 8-28: Millimeters

Dimension and tolerance the rotator assembly shown in Figure P8-21. Use the given dimensions as nominal and add sleeve bearings between the LINKs and both the CROSS-LINK and the PLATE. Create drawings of each part. Modify the dimensions as needed and add the appropriate tolerances. Specify the selected sleeve bearing.

Project 8-29: Millimeters

Dimension and tolerance the rocker assembly shown in Figure P8-22. Use the given dimensions as nominal, and add sleeve bearings between all moving parts. Create drawings of each part. Modify the dimensions as needed and add the appropriate tolerances. Specify the selected sleeve bearing.

Project 8-30: Millimeters

Draw the model shown in Figure P8-23, create a drawing layout with the appropriate views, and add the specified dimensions and tolerances.

Project 8-31: Millimeters

Redraw the shaft shown in Figure P8-24, create a drawing layout with the appropriate views, and add a feature dimension and tolerance of 36±0.1 and a straightness tolerance of 0.07 about the centerline at MMC.

Figure P8-21

ROTATOR ASSEMBLY

LINK
P/N AM311-1
SAE 1020

CROSS-LINK
P/N AM311-2
SAE 1020

R10 BOTH ENDS

Ø10-2 HOLES

80

10

PLATE
P/N AM311-3
SAE 1020

Ø10-2 HOLES

40

20

20   80

120

15

ROCKER ASSEMBLY

DRIVE LINK

Ø10 x 15 PEG

CENTER LINK

Ø10 x 10 PEG

PLATE, WEB

ROCKER LINK

Ø10 x 15 PEG

DRIVE LINK
P/N AM312-2
SAE 1040
5mm THK

30

R10 BOTH ENDS

Ø10-2 HOLES

PLATE, WEB
AM312-1
SAE 1040
10mm THK

ALL FILLETS AND ROUNDS = R3

ROCKER LINK
P/N AM312-4
SAE 1040
5mm THK

Ø10 BOTH HOLES

R10 BOTH ENDS

Ø10

R15

40

Ø5-7 HOLES

30

26

6 TYP

12 TYP

40

R15

80

4

R15

Ø10

R10

20

26

30

80

10

100

70

15

CENTER LINK
AM312-3
SAE 1040
5mm THK

Ø10 x 10 PEG
P/N AM 312-5
SAE 1020

Ø10

10

90

20

50

R10

Ø10

R10

Ø10

R5

R5

Ø10 x 15 PEG
P/N AM 312-6
SAE 1020

Ø10

15

Figure P8-23

Figure P8-24

Project 8-32:

A. Given the shaft shown in Figure P8-25, what is the minimum hole diameter that will always accept the shaft?

B. If the minimum clearance between the shaft and a hole is equal to 0.02, and the tolerance on the hole is to be 0.6, what are the maximum and minimum diameters for the hole?

Project 8-33:

A. Given the shaft shown in Figure P8-26, what is the minimum hole diameter that will always accept the shaft?

B. If the minimum clearance between the shaft and a hole is equal to .005, and the tolerance on the hole is to be .007, what are the maximum and minimum diameters for the hole?

Project 8-34:

Draw a front and a right-side view of the object shown in Figure P8-27 and add the appropriate dimensions and tolerances based on the following information. Numbers located next to an edge line indicate the length of the edge.

Figure P8-25

Figure P8-26

Figure P8-27

Figure P8-28

A. Define surfaces A, B, and C as primary, secondary, and tertiary datums, respectively.

B. Assign a tolerance of ±0.5 to all linear dimensions.

C. Assign a feature tolerance of 12.07 – 12.00 to the protruding shaft.

D. Assign a flatness tolerance of 0.01 to surface A.

E. Assign a straightness tolerance of 0.03 to the protruding shaft.

F. Assign a perpendicularity tolerance to the centerline of the protruding shaft of 0.02 at MMC relative to datum A.

Project 8-35:

Draw a front and a right-side view of the object shown in Figure P8-28 and add the following dimensions and tolerances.

A. Define the bottom surface as datum A.

B. Assign a perpendicularity tolerance of 0.4 to both sides of the slot relative to datum A.

C. Assign a perpendicularity tolerance of 0.2 to the centerline of the 30 diameter hole at MMC relative to datum A.

D. Assign a feature tolerance of ±0.8 to all three holes.

E. Assign a parallelism tolerance of 0.2 to the common centerline between the two 20 diameter holes relative to datum A.

F. Assign a tolerance of ±0.5 to all linear dimensions.

Project 8-36:

Draw a circular front and the appropriate right-side view of the object shown in Figure P8-29 and add the following dimensions and tolerances.

Figure P8-29

Figure P8-30

A. Assign datum A as indicated.

B. Assign the object's longitudinal axis as datum B.

C. Assign the object's centerline through the slot as datum C.

D. Assign a tolerance of ±0.5 to all linear tolerances.

E. Assign a tolerance of ±0.5 to all circular features.

F. Assign a parallelism tolerance of 0.01 to both edges of the slot.

G. Assign a perpendicularity tolerance of 0.01 to the outside edge of the protruding shaft.

Project 8-37:

Given the two objects shown in Figure P8-30, draw a front and a side view of each. Assign a tolerance of ±0.5 to all linear dimensions. Assign a feature tolerance of ±0.4 to the shaft, and also assign a straightness tolerance of 0.2 to the shaft's centerline at MMC.

Tolerance the hole so that it will always accept the shaft with a minimum clearance of 0.1 and a feature tolerance of 0.2. Assign a perpendicularity tolerance of 0.05 to the centerline of the hole at MMC.

Project 8-38:

Given the two objects shown in Figure P8-31, draw a front and a side view of each. Assign a tolerance of ±.005 to all linear dimensions. Assign a feature tolerance of ±.004 to the shaft, and also assign a straightness tolerance of .002 to the shaft's centerline at MMC.

Tolerance the hole so that it will always accept the shaft with a minimum clearance of .001 and a feature tolerance of .002.

Project 8-39:

Draw a model of the object shown in Figure P8-32, then create a drawing layout including the specified dimensions. Add the following tolerances and specifications to the drawing.

Figure P8-33

Figure P8-32

Figure P8-31

Figure P8-31 labels: 2.00, 2.00, .75, OBJECT A, 1.50, .125 × 45°, Ø1.50 NOMINAL, 1.50, OBJECT B, 2.00, 2.00

Figure P8-32 labels: 50, 20, 30, FRONT, 3, 2, 1

Figure P8-33 labels: 3, 1.005 Ø1.000, 2.00, 2, 1

A. Surface 1 is datum A.

B. Surface 2 is datum B and is perpendicular to datum A within 0.1mm.

C. Surface 3 is datum C and is parallel to datum A within 0.3mm.

D. Locate a 16mm diameter hole in the center of the front surface that goes completely through the object. Use positional tolerances to locate the hole. Assign a positional tolerance of 0.02 at MMC perpendicular to datum A.

Project 8-40:

Draw a model of the object shown in Figure P8-33, then create a drawing layout including the specified dimensions. Add the following tolerances and specifications to the drawing.

A. Surface 1 is datum A.

B. Surface 2 is datum B and is perpendicular to datum A within .003in.

C. Surface 3 is parallel to datum A within .005in.

D. The cylinder's longitudinal centerline is to be straight within .001in. at MMC.

E. Surface 2 is to have circular accuracy within .002in.

Project 8-41:

Draw a model of the object shown in Figure P8-34, then create a drawing layout including the specified dimensions. Add the following tolerances and specifications to the drawing.

A. Surface 1 is datum A.

B. Surface 4 is datum B and is perpendicular to datum A within 0.08mm.

C. Surface 3 is flat within 0.03mm.

D. Surface 5 is parallel to datum A within 0.01mm.

E. Surface 2 has a runout tolerance of 0.2mm relative to surface 4.

F. Surface 1 is flat within 0.02mm.

G. The longitudinal centerline is to be straight within 0.02 at MMC and perpendicular to datum A.

Project 8-42:

Draw a model of the object shown in Figure P8-35, then create a drawing layout including the specified dimensions. Add the following tolerances and specifications to the drawing.

A. Surface 2 is datum A.

B. Surface 6 is perpendicular to datum A with .000 allowable variance at MMC but with a .002in. MAX variance limit beyond MMC.

C. Surface 1 is parallel to datum A within .005in.

D. Surface 4 is perpendicular to datum A within .004in.

Project 8-43:

Draw a model of the object shown in Figure P8-36, then create a drawing layout including the specified dimensions. Add the following tolerances and specifications to the drawing.

A. Surface 1 is datum A.

B. Surface 2 is datum B.

C. The hole is located using a true position tolerance value of 0.13mm at MMC. The true position tolerance is referenced to datums A and B.

D. Surface 1 is to be straight within 0.02mm.

E. The bottom surface is to be parallel to datum A within 0.03mm.

Project 8-44:

Draw a model of the object shown in Figure P8-37, then create a drawing layout including the specified dimensions. Add the following tolerances and specifications to the drawing.

A. Surface 1 is datum A.

B. Surface 2 is datum B.

C. Surface 3 is perpendicular to surface 2 within 0.02mm.

D. The four holes are to be located using a positional tolerance of 0.07mm at MMC referenced to datums A and B.

E. The centerlines of the holes are to be straight within 0.01mm at MMC.

Figure P8-37

Figure P8-36

Project 8-45:

Draw a model of the object shown in Figure P8-38, then create a drawing layout including the specified dimensions. Add the following tolerances and specifications to the drawing.

A. Surface 1 has a dimension of .378–.375in. and is datum A. The surface has a dual primary runout with datum B to within .005in. The runout is total.

B. Surface 2 has a dimension of 1.505–1.495in. Its runout relative to the dual primary datums A and B is .008in. The runout is total.

C. Surface 3 has a dimension of 1.000±.005 and has no geometric tolerance.

D. Surface 4 has no circular dimension but has a total runout tolerance of .006in. relative to the dual datums A and B.

E. Surface 5 has a dimension of .500–.495in. and is datum B. It has a dual primary runout with datum A within .005in. The runout is total.

Project 8-46:

Draw a model of the object shown in Figure P8-39, then create a drawing layout including the specified dimensions. Add the following tolerances and specifications to the drawing.

A. Hole 1 is datum A.

B. Hole 2 is to have its circular centerline parallel to datum A within 0.2mm at MMC when datum A is at MMC.

C. Assign a positional tolerance of 0.01 to each hole's centerline at MMC.

Figure P8-38

Figure P8-39

Project 8-47:

Draw a model of the object shown in Figure P8-40, then create a drawing layout including the specified dimensions. Add the following tolerances and specifications to the drawing.

A. Surface 1 is datum A.

B. Surface 2 is datum B.

C. The six holes have a diameter range of .502–.499in. and are to be located using positional tolerances so that their centerlines are within .005in. at MMC relative to datums A and B.

D. The back surface is to be parallel to datum A within .002in.

Project 8-48:

Draw a model of the object shown in Figure P8-41, then create a drawing layout including the specified dimensions. Add the following tolerances and specifications to the drawing.

A. Surface 1 is datum A.

B. Hole 2 is datum B.

C. The eight holes labeled 3 have diameters of 8.4–8.3mm with a positional tolerance of 0.15mm at MMC relative to datums A and B. Also, the eight holes are to be counterbored to a diameter of 14.6–14.4mm and to a depth of 5.0mm.

D. The large center hole is to have a straightness tolerance of 0.2 at MMC about its centerline.

Figure P8-41

Figure P8-40

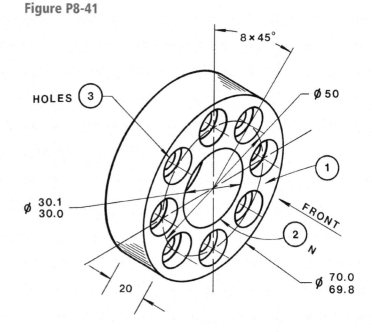

Project 8-49:

Draw a model of the object shown in Figure P8-42, then create a drawing layout including the specified dimensions. Add the following tolerances and specifications to the drawing.

A. Surface 1 is datum A.

B. Surface 2 is datum B.

C. Surface 3 is datum C.

D. The four holes labeled 4 have a dimension and tolerance of 8 +0.3/ –0mm. The holes are to be located using a positional tolerance of 0.05mm at MMC relative to datums A, B, and C.

E. The six holes labeled 5 have a dimension and tolerance of 6 +0.2/–0mm. The holes are to be located using a positional tolerance of 0.01mm at MMC relative to datums A, B, and C.

Project 8-50:

The objects in Figure P8-43B labeled A and B are to be toleranced using four different tolerances as shown. Redraw the charts shown in Figure P8-43A and list the appropriate allowable tolerance for "as measured" increments of 0.1mm or .001in. Also include the appropriate geometric tolerance drawing called out above each chart.

A. Millimeters

B. Inches

Figure P8-43A

Figure P8-42

Figure P8-43B

A

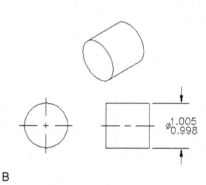

B

Project 8-51:

Assume that there are two copies of the part in Figure P8-44 and that these parts are to be joined together using four fasteners in the floating condition. Draw front and top views of the object, including dimensions and tolerances. Add the following tolerances and specifications to the drawing, then draw front and top views of a shaft that can be used to join the two objects. The shaft should be able to fit into any of the four holes.

A. Surface 1 is datum A.

B. Surface 2 is datum B.

C. Surface 3 is perpendicular to surface 2 within 0.02mm.

D. Specify the positional tolerance for the four holes applied at MMC.

E. The centerlines of the holes are to be straight within 0.01mm at MMC.

F. The clearance between the shafts and the holes is to be 0.05 minimum and 0.10 maximum.

Project 8-52:

Dimension and tolerance parts 1 and 2 of Figure P8-45 so that part 1 always fits into part 2 with a minimum clearance of .005in. The tolerance for part 1's outer matching surface is .006in.

Figure P8-44
MILLIMETERS

Figure P8-45

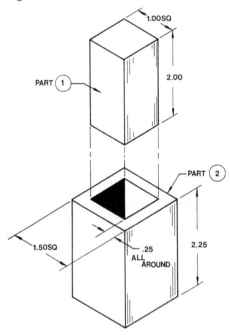

Project 8-53:

Dimension and tolerance parts 1 and 2 of Figure P8-46 so that part 1 always fits into part 2 with a minimum clearance of 0.03mm. The tolerance for part 1's diameter is 0.05mm. Take into account the fact that the interface is long relative to the diameters.

Project 8-54:

Assume that there are two copies of the part in Figure P8-47 and that these parts are to be joined together using six fasteners in the floating condition. Draw front and top views of the object, including dimensions and tolerances. Add the following tolerances and specifications to the drawing, then draw front and top views of a shaft that can be used to join the two objects. The shaft should be able to fit into any of the six holes.

A. Surface 1 is datum A.

B. Surface 2 is round within .003.

C. Specify the positional tolerance for the six holes applied at MMC.

D. The clearance between the shafts and the holes is to be .001 minimum and .003 maximum.

Figure P8-46
MILLIMETERS

Figure P8-47
INCHES

Project 8-55:

The assembly shown in Figure P8-48 is made from parts defined in Chapter 5.

A. Draw an exploded assembly drawing.

B. Draw a BOM.

C. Use the drawing layout mode and draw orthographic views of each part. Include dimensions and geometric tolerances. The pegs should have a minimum clearance of 0.02. Select appropriate tolerances.

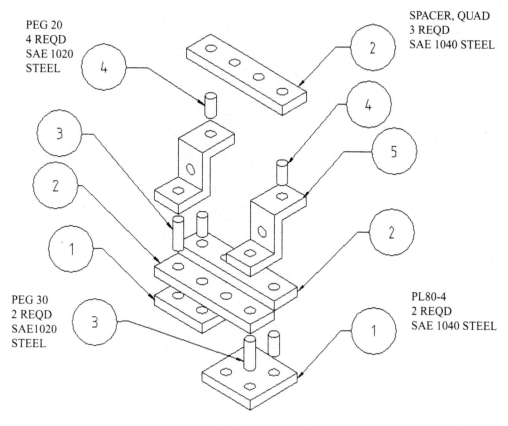

PEG 20
4 REQD
SAE 1020
STEEL

SPACER, QUAD
3 REQD
SAE 1040 STEEL

PEG 30
2 REQD
SAE1020
STEEL

PL80-4
2 REQD
SAE 1040 STEEL

CHAPTER OBJECTIVES

- Learn about sleeve and ball bearings
- Learn about fits
- Apply fits to holes and shafts
- Apply tolerances to holes and shafts

9-1 Introduction

This text deals with two types of bearings: sleeve bearings or *bushings* and ball bearings. See Figure 9-1. *Sleeve bearings*, or jig bushings, are hollow cylinders made from a low-friction material such as Teflon or impregnated bronze. Sleeve bearings may have flanges. *Ball bearings* include spherical bearings in an internal race that greatly reduce friction. In general, sleeve bearings are cheaper than ball bearings, but ball bearings can take heavier loads at faster speeds. A listing of ball bearings is included in the **Design Library**.

Figure 9-1

Sleeve bearing   Sleeve bearing with a flange   Ball bearing   Thrust roller bearing

9-2 Sleeve Bearings

Sleeve bearings are identified by the following callout format:

Inside Diameter × Outside Diameter × Thickness

For example,

.375 × .750 × .500 or 3/8 × 3/4 × 1/2

Drawing a Sleeve Bearing

Draw a .500 × 1.000 × 1.000 sleeve bearing. See Figure 9-2.

1 Start a new **Part** document.

2 Select the **Front Plane** orientation.

Figure 9-2

1. Click the **Sketch** tab, then click the **Circle** tool.

2. Draw a **Ø1.000** circle. Use the **Smart Dimension** tool to size the circle.

3. Click the **Features** tab, then click the **Extruded Boss/Base** tool.

4. Define the thickness of the extrusion as **1.00in**.

5. Click the green **OK** check mark.

6. Right-click the front surface of the cylinder and select the **Sketch** tool.

7. Use the **Circle** tool and the **Smart Dimension** tool to draw a **Ø.500** circle on the front surface of the cylinder.

8. Click the **Features** tab and select the **Extruded Cut** tool.

9. Define the Ø.500 circle to be cut through the entire cylinder and click the green **OK** check mark.

10. Save the part as **.50 BEARING**.

> **NOTE**
> No tolerances are assigned to the bushing.

Using a Sleeve Bearing in an Assembly Drawing

See Figures 9-3 and 9-4.

Figure 9-3

1. Create the support plate and Ø.500 × 2.500 shaft defined in Figure 9-3. Save the parts.

2. Create a new **Assembly**.

3. Add the support plate, shaft, and sleeve bearing (created in the last section) to the assembly.

See Figure 9-4.

4. Use the **Mate** tool and assemble the sleeve bearing into the support plate, and the shaft into the sleeve bearing. The front surface of the shaft should be offset **1.50** from the front surface of the support plate.

Figure 9-4

.50 x 1.00 x 1.00 Bearing

Ø.50 Shaft

Plate, Support

Assemble the parts

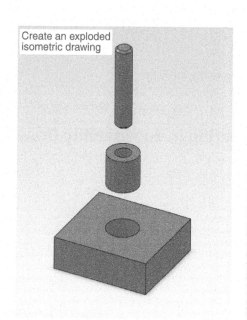

Create an exploded isometric drawing

Create a new drawing

ITEM NO.	PART NUMBER	DESCRIPTION	QTY.
1	BU-407A	PLATE, SUPPORT	1
2	BU-407B	Ø.50 SHAFT	1
3	BU-407C1	.500 ×1.000 × 1.000 BEARING	1

5 Save the assembly as **Sleeve Assembly**.

6 Use the **Exploded View** tool. Select a direction and pull the shaft out of the assembly.

See Figures 5-25 and 5-26 in Chapter 5 for instructions on how to use the **Exploded View** tool.

7 Use the **Exploded View** tool to pull the bearing away from the support plate.

8 Save the assembly with exploded view.

9 Start a new **Drawing**.

10 Click the **Annotation** tab, click the **Balloon** tool, and add the assembly numbers as shown in Figure 9-4.

11 Click the **Annotation** tab, click the **Tables** tool, click the **Bill of Materials** tool, and add a BOM to the drawing.

9-3 Bearings from the Toolbox

The SolidWorks **Toolbox** includes many different sizes and styles of bearings. In this example we will use the **PLATE**, **SUPPORT**, and **Ø.50 SHAFT** with a bearing from the **Toolbox** to create an assembly.

1 Create a new **Assembly** and add the **PLATE**, **SUPPORT**, and **Ø.50 SHAFT**.

See Figure 9-5.

2 Save the assembly as **BEARING ASSEMBLY**.

3 Click the **Toolbox**, expand **ANSI Inch**, click **Jig Bushings**, and select **All Jig Bushings**.

4 Select **Jig Bushing Type P** and drag it onto the drawing screen.

We know the shaft diameter is **.500**, so we will size the bearing's inside diameter to match the shaft diameter. Tolerances are not considered. They will be included in later examples.

5 Set the **Size** to **0.5000 (1/2)** and the **Length** to **1** and click the green **OK** check mark.

Figure 9-5

Figure 9-5
(*Continued*)

Outside
diameter

Click the Edit
Sketch tool

Edit the Ø1.00 value to Ø.75.

Figure 9-5
(*Continued*)

Chapter 9

BEARING ASSEMBLY

The completed assembly

Create an
exploded isometric
drawing

Save
the drawing

Create a
drawing and
a BOM

ITEM NO.	PART NUMBER	DESCRIPTION	QTY.
1	ME-407-1A	PLATE, SUPPORT	1
2	ME-407-2A	Ø.50-SHAFT	1
3	0.5000-P-48-16	BEARING	1

Manufacturer's part number

What is the outside diameter of the bearing? To answer this question, double-click the bearing on the screen. The dimensions used to create the bearing will become visible.

The outside diameter is defined as **.75**, so the Ø1.00 hole in the PLATE, SUPPORT is not acceptable. It must be edited.

6 Click the screen to remove the bearing's dimensions and click the arrow next to the **PLATE, SUPPORT** heading in the **FeatureManager**.

7 Click the arrow next to the **Boss-Extrude1** heading, right-click the **Sketch1** heading, and click **Edit Sketch**.

Your sketch number may be different.

8 Click the **Edit Sketch** option.

The dimension for the Ø1.00 hole will appear.

9 Double-click the **1.00** dimension and change the diameter from **1.00** to **.75**; click the green **OK** check mark.

10 Return to the assembly and assemble the components.

11 Create an exploded assembly.

12 Create a **Drawing** of the exploded assembly and add a BOM.

Note that the bearing's part number, 0.5000-P-48-16, was used as is. This is a vendor item; that is, we did not make it but purchased it from an outside source, so we used the manufacturer's part number for the bearing rather than creating a new one.

9-4 Ball Bearings

Ball bearings are identified by the following callout format:

Inside Diameter × Outside Diameter × Thickness

For example,

.375 × .750 × .500 or 3/8 × 3/4 × 1/2

A listing of standard ball bearing sizes can be found in the **Design Library**. For this example a .5000 × .8750 × .2188 instrument ball bearing will be used and will be inserted into a counterbored hole. Only nominal dimensions will be considered. Tolerances will be defined later in the chapter.

Figure 9-6 shows a ball bearing support plate.

Figure 9-6

Ball bearing support plate

1 Draw and save the ball bearing support plate.

2 Draw and save a **∅.500 × 2.50** shaft with **.03** chamfers at each end.

3 Start a new **Assembly** and insert the ball bearing support plate and ∅.500 × 2.50 shaft.

See Figure 9-7.

4 Access the **Design Library, Toolbox, ANSI Inch, Bearings, Ball Bearings**, and select **Instrument Ball Bearing – AFBMA 12.2**.

5 Click and drag the bearing into the drawing screen and set the properties as shown.

In this example a **Size** of 0.5000 – 0.8750 – 0.2188 was used. See the values in the **Instrument Ball Bearing PropertyManager**.

Figure 9-7

Ø.50 x 2.50 SHAFT
with .03 Chamfer

Block, Ball

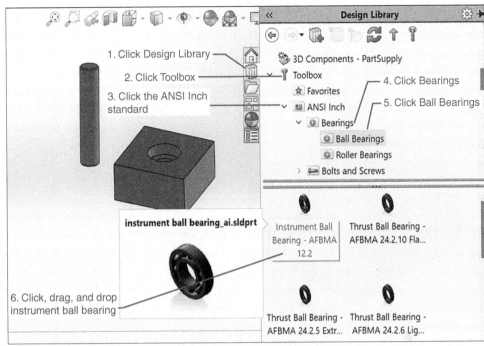

1. Click Design Library

2. Click Toolbox

3. Click the ANSI Inch standard

Design Library

3D Components - PartSupply

Toolbox

⭐ Favorites

ANSI Inch

> Bearings

4. Click Bearings

5. Click Ball Bearings

Ball Bearings

Roller Bearings

> Bolts and Screws

instrument ball bearing_ai.sldprt

Instrument Ball Bearing - AFBMA 12.2

Thrust Ball Bearing - AFBMA 24.2.10 Fla...

6. Click, drag, and drop instrument ball bearing

Thrust Ball Bearing - AFBMA 24.2.5 Extr...

Thrust Ball Bearing - AFBMA 24.2.6 Lig...

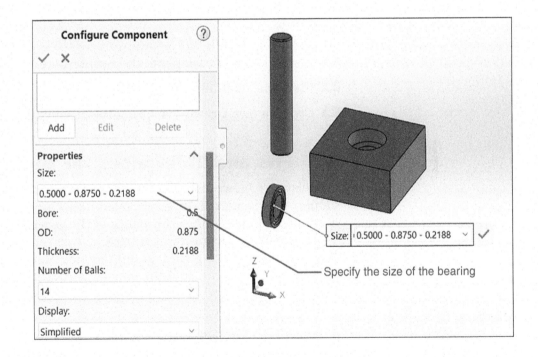

Configure Component (?)

✓ ✗

Add   Edit   Delete

Properties

Size:

0.5000 - 0.8750 - 0.2188

Bore: 0.5

OD: 0.875

Thickness: 0.2188

Number of Balls:

14

Display:

Simplified

Size: 0.5000 - 0.8750 - 0.2188 ✓

Specify the size of the bearing

Figure 9-7
(*Continued*)

Assemble the parts

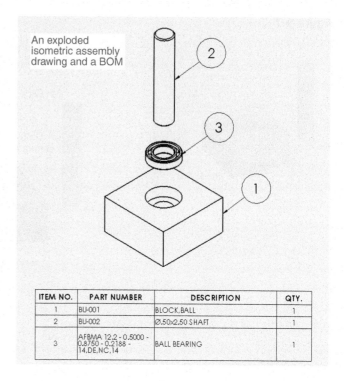

An exploded isometric assembly drawing and a BOM

ITEM NO.	PART NUMBER	DESCRIPTION	QTY.
1	BU-001	BLOCK, BALL	1
2	BU-002	Ø.50x2.50 SHAFT	1
3	AFBMA 12.2 - 0.5000 - 0.8750 - 0.2188 - 14,DE,NC,14	BALL BEARING	1

6 Insert the ball bearing into the counterbored hole.

7 Insert the shaft into the bearing.

8 Create a new **Drawing** showing the assembly and a BOM.

9-5 Fits and Tolerances for Bearings

The tolerance between a shaft and a bearing and between a bearing and a support part is critical. Incorrect tolerances can cause excessive wear or vibration and affect the performance of the assembly.

In general, a clearance fit is used between the shaft and the inside diameter of the bearing, and an interference fit is used between the outside diameter of the bearing and the support structure. A listing of standard fit tolerances is included in the appendix.

9-6 Fits—Inches

Tolerances for shafts and holes have been standardized and are called *fits*. An example of a fit callout is H7/g6. The hole tolerance is always given first using an uppercase letter, and the shaft tolerance is given second using a lowercase letter.

9-7 Clearance Fits

As an example, a Ø0.500 nominal shaft is to be inserted into a Ø0.500 nominal hole using an H7/g6 clearance fit, which is also referred to as a Class LC5 Clearance fit.

NOTE

The term *nominal* refers to a starting value for the shaft and hole. It is not the final dimension.

The following data are given in a table in the appendix. See Figure 9-8. The values are given in thousandths of an inch. The nominal value for the hole is 0.5000, so the +0.7 table value means .5007in. The –0.25 table value for the 0.5000 nominal shaft means 0.49975in. The limits of clearance values are the differences between the hole minimum value and the shaft maximum value, 0.00 and –0.25, or 0.25 absolute, and between the maximum hole value and the minimum shaft value, +0.7 and –0.65, or 1.35.

Figure 9-8

Class LC5			
Nominal Size Range	Limits of Clearance	Standard Limits	
		Hole H7	Shaft g6
0.40 – 0.71	0.25	+0.7	–0.25
	1.35	0	–0.65

Hole basis

9-8   Hole Basis

The 0 value for the hole's minimum indicates that the tolerances were derived using *hole basis* calculations; that is, the tolerances were applied starting with the minimum hole value. Tolerances applied starting with the shaft are called *shaft basis*.

9-9   Shaft Basis

The limits of clearance values would be applied starting with the minimum shaft diameter. If the H7/g6 tolerances were applied using the shaft basis, the resulting tolerance values for the shaft would be 0.50000 to 0.50040, and for the hole would be 0.50065 (.50040 + .00025) to 0.50135. These values maintain the limits of tolerance, 0.50135 to 0.00135, and the individual tolerances for the hole (0.50135 – 0.50065 = 0.0007) and the shaft (0.50040 – 0.50000 = .00040).

9-10   Sample Problem SP9-1

If a shaft with nominal values of Ø.750 × 3.00 is to be fitted into a bearing with an inside diameter bore, nominal, of 0.7500 using Class LC5 fit, hole basis, what are the final dimensions for the shaft and bearing's bore? The table values for the hole are 0/+0.5, yielding a hole tolerance of .7500 to .7505, and the shaft values for the hole are 0/–0.4, yielding a shaft tolerance of .7500 to .7496.

See Figure 9-9.

Figure 9-9

9-11   Interference Fits

When the shaft is equal to or larger in diameter than the hole, the fit is called an *interference fit.* Interference fits are sometimes used to secure a shaft into a hole rather than using a fastener or adhesive. For example, an aluminum shaft with a nominal diameter of .250in. inserted into a hole in a steel housing with a Ø.250 nominal hole using .0006in. interference would require approximately 123in.-lb of torque to turn the shaft.

In this example a sleeve bearing with a nominal outside diameter (O.D.) of .875 is to be inserted into a Ø.875 nominal hole using an LN1 Interference Locational fit. The hole and shaft (bearing O.D.) specifications are H6/n5. The following values were derived from a table in the appendix. See Figure 9-10.

Figure 9-10

Class LN1			
Nominal Size Range	Limits of Interference	Standard Limits	
		Hole	Shaft
0.71 − 1.19	0	+0.5	+1.0
	1.0	0	+0.5

Hole basis

All stated values are in thousandths of an inch. The 0 in the column for the hole indicates that it is a hole basis calculation (see the explanation in the previous section). Given the .875 nominal value for both the hole and the shaft, the hole and shaft tolerances are as follows. See Figure 9-11.

Hole: Ø.8755/.875 Shaft: Ø.8760/.8755

Figure 9-11

9-12 Manufactured Bearings

Most companies do not manufacture their own bearings but rather purchase them from a bearing manufacturer. This means that tolerances must be assigned to assemblies based on existing given tolerances for the purchased bearings.

NOTE

Companies that manufacture bearings usually also manufacture shafts that match the bearings; therefore, the tolerances for the bearings and shafts are coordinated.

Figure 9-12 shows a typical manufactured sleeve bearing. The dimensions and tolerances are included. The inside diameter (bore or I.D.) of the bearing is matched to the shaft using a clearance fit, and the O.D. is to be matched to the support using an interference fit. The procedure is to find standard fits that are closest to the bearing's manufactured dimensions and apply the limits of tolerance to create the needed tolerances.

Figure 9-12

MATERIAL:
Oil Impregnated Bronze
Self-Lubricating

Clearance for a Manufactured Bearing

Refer to the standard fit tables in the appendix and find a tolerance range for a hole that matches or comes close to the bearing's I.D. tolerance of .001 (the +.000/–.001 creates a tolerance range of .001). The given I.D. is 1.0040, so it falls within the 0.71–1.19 nominal size range. An LC2 Clearance fit (H8/h7) has a hole tolerance specification of 0.0 to 0.0008, 0.0002 smaller than the bearing's manufactured tolerance of .0010. The given tolerance is Ø1.0040/1.0030.

The limits of clearance for the LC2 standard fit are 0.0 to 0.0013. If these limits are maintained, the smallest hole diameter is equal to the largest shaft diameter (1.0030 – 0.0 = 1.0030), and the smallest shaft diameter is .0013 less than the largest hole diameter (1.0040 – .0013 = 1.0027).

Therefore, the shaft tolerances are

Shaft: Ø1.0030/1.0027

These tolerances give a tolerance range for the shaft of .0003, or .0002 less than the stated .0005 found in the table. This difference makes up for the .0002 difference between the actual hole diameter's tolerance range of 0.0010 and the standard H8 tolerance of 0.0008.

Applying a Clearance Fit Tolerance

Figure 9-13 shows a shaft with a nominal diameter of 1.0040. Enter the required 1.0030/1.0027 tolerance.

Figure 9-13

1 Click the **Limit** option in the **Tolerance/Precision** box.

2 Set the upper limit for **–0.0010mm** and the lower limit for **–0.0013mm**.

3 Click the green **OK** check mark.

Interference for a Manufactured Bearing

The O.D. for the manufactured bearing is 1.379 + .000/ –.001. Written as a limit tolerance, it is 1.3790/1.3780. The tolerance range for the O.D. is 0.001. An interference tolerance is required between the O.D. of the bearing and the hole in the support.

> **NOTE**
> An interference fit is also called a *press fit*.

A search of the Standard Fit tables in the appendix for a shaft (the O.D. of the bearing acts like a shaft in this condition) tolerance range of 0.001 finds that an LN2 (H7/p6) shaft range is .0008, or .0002 less than manufactured tolerance.

The limits of interference for the LN2 standard fit are 0.0 to 0.0013. If these limits are maintained, the smallest shaft diameter is equal to the largest hole diameter (1.3780 + 0.0 = 1.3780), and the largest shaft diameter is .0013 greater than the smallest hole diameter (1.3790 – .0013 = 1.3777).

Therefore, the shaft tolerances are

Shaft: Ø1.3780/1.3777

These tolerances give a tolerance range for the shaft of .0003, or .0002 less than the stated .0005 found in the table. This difference makes up for the .0002 difference between the actual hole diameter's tolerance range of 0.0010 and the standard H7 tolerance of 0.0008.

Applying an Interference Fit Tolerance

Figure 9-14 shows a support with a nominal diameter of 1.3780. Enter the required 1.3780/1.3777 tolerance. See Chapter 8 for further explanation on how to apply tolerances.

Figure 9-14

1 Click the **Limit** option in the **Tolerance/Precision** box.

2 Set the upper limit for **+0.0000mm** and the lower limit for **−0.0003mm**.

3 Click the green **OK** check mark.

Applying Standard Fit Tolerances to an Assembly Drawing

Figure 9-15 shows the assembly of the shaft and support toleranced in the previous section with the manufactured bearing. The standard tolerance callouts are added as follows.

Figure 9-15

1 Use the **Smart Dimension** tool and dimension the O.D. of the bearing.

2 Access the **Tolerance/Precision** box and select the **Fit** option.

3 Set the hole fit tolerance for **H8** and the shaft fit tolerance for **h7**.

4 Click the green **OK** check mark.

5 Use the **Smart Dimension** tool and dimension the I.D. of the bearing.

6 Access the **Tolerance/Precision** box and select the **Fit** option.

7 Set the hole fit tolerance for **H6** and the shaft fit tolerance for **p6**.

9-13 Fit Tolerances—Millimeters

The appendix also includes tables for preferred fits using metric values. These tables are read directly. For example, the values for a Close Running Preferred Clearance fit H8/f7 for a nominal shaft diameter of 16 are as follows:

Hole: Ø16.027/16.00   Shaft: Ø15.984/15.966

Fit (limits of fits): 0.016

The value 16.000 indicates that the hole basis condition was used to calculate the tolerances. Metric fits are applied in the same manner as English unit values.

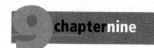
Chapter Projects

Figure P9-1 shows a support plate with three holes. A dimensioned drawing of the support plate is included. The holes are lettered. Three shafts are also shown. All shafts are 3.00 long. For Projects 9-1 to 9-8:

A. Create dimensioned and toleranced drawings for the support plate and shafts.

B. Specify tolerances for both the support plate holes and the shaft's diameters based on the given fit information.

Figure P9-1

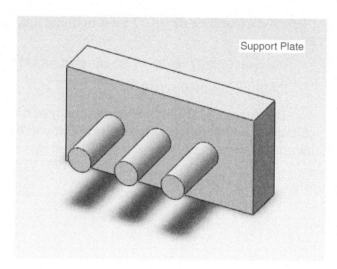

Specify limit tolerances

All shafts are 3.00 long.

Shaft D
Shaft E
Shaft F

Project 9-1: Clearance Fits—Inches

Hole A/Shaft D: H7/h6, Ø.125 nominal
Hole B/Shaft E: H6/h5, Ø.750 nominal
Hole C/Shaft F: H9/f8, Ø.250 nominal

Project 9-2: Clearance Fits—Inches

Hole A/Shaft D: H10/d9, Ø1.123 nominal
Hole B/Shaft E: H7/h6, Ø.500 nominal
Hole C/Shaft F: H5/g4, Ø.625 nominal

Project 9-3: Clearance Fits—Inches

Hole A/Shaft D: H9/f8, Ø.500 nominal
Hole B/Shaft E: H8/e7, Ø.635 nominal
Hole C/Shaft F: H7/f6, Ø1.000 nominal

Project 9-4: Clearance Fits—Millimeters

Hole A/Shaft D: D9/h9, Ø10.0 nominal
Hole B/Shaft E: H7/h6, Ø16.0 nominal
Hole C/Shaft F: C11/h11, Ø20.0 nominal

Project 9-5: Interference Fits—Inches

Hole A/Shaft D: H6/n5, Ø.250 nominal
Hole B/Shaft E: H7/p6, Ø.750 nominal
Hole C/Shaft F: H7/r6, Ø.250 nominal

Project 9-6: Interference Fits—Inches

Hole A/Shaft D: FN2, Ø.375 nominal
Hole B/Shaft E: FN3, Ø1.500 nominal
Hole C/Shaft F: FN4, Ø.250 nominal

Project 9-7: Locational Fits—Inches

Hole A/Shaft D: H8/k7, Ø.4375 nominal
Hole B/Shaft E: H7/k6, Ø.7075 nominal
Hole C/Shaft F: H8/js7, Ø1.155 nominal

Project 9-8: Interference Fits—Millimeters

Hole A/Shaft D: H7/k6, Ø12.0 nominal
Hole B/Shaft E: H7/p6, Ø25.0 nominal
Hole C/Shaft F: N7/h6, Ø8.0 nominal

Figure P9-2 shows a U-bracket, four sleeve bearings, and two shafts. A dimensioned drawing of the U-bracket is also included. For Projects 9-9 to 9-12:

Figure P9-2

A. Create dimensioned and toleranced drawings for the U-bracket, sleeve bearings, and shafts. All shafts are 5.00 long.

B. Specify tolerances for the shaft diameter and the outside diameter of the sleeve bearings based on the given interference fits.

C. Specify tolerances for the holes in the U-bracket and the outside diameter of the sleeve bearings based on the sizes given in the appendix.

D. Assign your own part numbers for the bracket and shaft. Use the manufacturer's numbers for the bearings.

Project 9-9: Inches

Clearance between shaft and bearing: H9/f8, Ø.875 nominal

Interference between the hole in the U-bracket and the bearing: H7/p6, Ø.375 nominal

Project 9-10: Inches

Clearance between the shaft and the bearing: H9/f8, Ø.875 nominal

Interference between the hole in the U-bracket and the bearing: Class FN2, Ø1.125 nominal

Project 9-11: Inches

Clearance between the shaft and the bearing: H10/h9, Ø.500 nominal

Interference between the hole in the U-bracket and the bearing: H7/r6, Ø.750 nominal

Project 9-12: Millimeters

Clearance between the shaft and the bearing: H9/d9, Ø10.0 nominal

Interference between the hole in the U-bracket and the bearing: H7/p6, Ø16.0 nominal

Project 9-13: Inches

A four-bar assembly is defined in Figure P9-3.

1. Create a three-dimensional assembly drawing of the four-bar assembly.

2. Animate the links using LINK-1 as the driver.

3. Redraw the individual parts, add the appropriate dimensions, and add the following tolerances:

   A. Assign an LN1 interference fit between the links and the needle roller bearing.

   B. Assign an LC2 clearance between the holder posts, both regular and long posts, and the inside diameter of the needle roller bearing.

   C. Assign an LC3 clearance between the holder posts, both regular and long posts, and the spacers.

Four Bar Assembly

ITEM NO.	PART NUMBER	DESCRIPTION	QTY.
1	BU09-ME1	HOLDER, BASE	1
2	BU09-ME2	HOLDER, SIDE	2
3	HBOLT 0.5000-13x1.25x1.25-N		2
4	HBOLT 0.2500-20x1x1-N		11
5	HBOLT 0.2500-20x1.25x1.25-N		1
6	BU09-P1	POST, PIVOT, SHORT	2
7	LINK-01	LINK1, ASSEMBLY	1
8	LINK-03	LINK3, ASSEMBLY	1
9	LINK-02	LINK 2, ASSEMBLY	1
10	BU09-P2	POST, PIVOT, LONG	2
11	BU09-S1	SPACER, SHORT	2
12	BU09-S2	SPACER, LONG	2

SECTION B-B

SECTION A-A

Figure P9-3
(*Continued*)

SECTION A-A
HOLE PATTERN

SECTION A-A
CONTOUR DIMENSIONS

SECTION B-B
CONTOUR DIMENSIONS

SECTION B-B
HOLE PATTERN

Holder, Side
P/N BU09-ME2

MATL THK = .50

ALL FILLETS=1.00 R

R1.00
2 PLACES

Ø.78

.50 ALL AROUND

Ø.56
2 HOLES

Ø.28
5 HOLES

1.00

5.50

14.00

15.37

9.00

5.25

1.88

8.00

.25

.375

.75

.50

5.00

5.54

13.77

LINK 1, Assembly
P/N Link-01

ITEM NO.	PART NUMBER	DESCRIPTION	QTY.
1	BU09-L1	LINK-1	1
2	AFBMA 18.2.3.1 - 12NIHI35 - 20,SI,NC,20	NEEDLE ROLLER BEARING	2

LINK - 1
P/N BU09 - L1

12.00

10×1.00 (10.00)

1.00

R.75
BOTH ENDS

Ø.375 THRU
11 HOLES

R.50 ALL
FILLETS

Ø1.00
2 HOLES

MATL = .50 THK

Figure P9-3
(Continued)

LINK 2, Assembly
P/N Link-02

ITEM NO.	PART NUMBER	DESCRIPTION	QTY.
1	BU09-L2	LINK - 2	1
2	AFBMA 18.2.3.1 - 12NIHI35 - 20,SI,NC,20	NEEDLE ROLLER BEARING	2

Link - 2
P/N BU09 - L2

LINK 3, Assembly
P/N Link - 03

ITEM NO.	PART NUMBER	DESCRIPTION	QTY.
1	BU09-L3	LINK-3	1
2	AFBMA 18.2.3.1 - 12NIHI35 - 20,SI,NC,20	NEEDLE ROLLER BEARING	2

Link - 3
P/N BU09 - L3

Short Post
Assembly

Post, Holder
P/N BU09 - 07

$\emptyset$ .14 $\underline{\nabla}$ .66
8-32 UNC $\underline{\nabla}$ .50

$\emptyset$.75

1.69

.125

.125

Disk, Top
P/N BU09 - 10

$\emptyset$1.25

$\emptyset$.19

ITEM NO.	PART NUMBER	DESCRIPTION	QTY.
1	BU09-07	POST, HOLDER	1
2	BU09--10	DISK, TOP	1
3	SBHCSCREW 0.164-32x0.4375-HX-N	SOCKET BUTTON HEAD CAP SCREW	1

Long Post Assembly

$\emptyset$1.25

$\emptyset$.75

$\emptyset$ .14 $\underline{\nabla}$ .66
8-32 UNC $\underline{\nabla}$ .50

2.38

.125

ITEM NO.	PART NUMBER	DESCRIPTION	QTY.
1	BU09-10	DISK, TOP	1
2	SBHCSCREW 0.164-32x0.4375-HX-N	SOCKET BUTTON HEAD CAP SCREW	1
3	BU09-08	POST, HOLDER, LONG	1

Spacer, Long
P/N BU09 - S2

Spacer, Short
P/N BU09 - S1

Project 9-14: Inches

Redraw the crank assembly shown in Figure P9-4. Create the following drawings.

A. An exploded isometric drawing with balloons and a BOM.

B. Dimensioned drawings of each part.

C. Animate the assembly.

D. Change the length of the links and note the differences in motion.

Figure P9-4

Crank Assembly

Parts List				
ITEM	PART NUMBER	DESCRIPTION	MATERIAL	QTY
1	EK131-1	SUPPORT	STEEL	1
2	EK131-2	LINK	STEEL	1
3	EK131-3	SHAFT, DRIVE	STEEL	1
4	EK131-4	POST, THREADED	STEEL	1
5	EK131-5	BALL	STEEL	1
6	BS 292 - BRM 3/4	Deep Groove Ball Bearings	STEEL,MILD	1
7	3/16x1/8x1/4	RECTANGULAR KEY	STEEL	1

NOTE: ALL FILLETS AND ROUNDS R=0.250
UNLESS OTHERWISE STATED.

Project 9-15: Millimeters

Redraw the Rocker Assembly shown in Figure P9-5. Create the following drawings:

A. An exploded drawing with balloons and a BOM

B. Dimensioned drawings of each part

C. Animate the assembly

Figure P9-5

ROCKER ASSEMBLY

HOUSING
P/N CH9–15A
MATL = SAE 1020

LAYOUT for the Internal Cutout

WHEEL, DRIVE
P/N CH9–15B
MATL = SAE 1020

LINK 95
P/N CH9–15C
MATL = SAE 1020

LINK 140
P/N CH9–15D
MATL = SAE 1020

PIN
P/N P10–28
MATL = SAE 3120

BEARING
P/N BG400–18
MATL = SAE 3120

PIN, LONG
P/N P10–35
MATL = SAE 3120

PIN, SHORT
P/N P10–17
MATL = SAE 3120

$\varnothing \begin{smallmatrix} 9.995 \\ 9.986 \end{smallmatrix}$ H7/G6

17

10 chapter ten

Gears

CHAPTER OBJECTIVES

- Learn the concept of power transmission
- Learn the fundamentals of gears
- Draw and animate gears

10-1 Introduction

Gears, pulleys, and chains are part of a broader category called *power transmission.* Power comes from a source such as an engine, motor, or windmill. The power is then transferred to a mechanism that performs some function. For example, an automobile engine transmits power from the engine to the wheels via a gear box. Bicyclists transmit the power of their legs to wheels via a chain and sprocket.

This section explains how gears, pulleys, and chains are drawn using SolidWorks and how the finished drawings can be animated. There is also a discussion of how speed is transferred and changed using gears, pulleys, and chains. Figure 10-1 shows a spur gear drawn using SolidWorks.

Figure 10-1

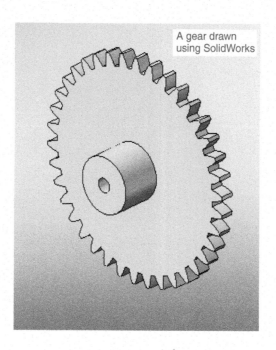

A gear drawn using SolidWorks

10-2 Gear Terminology

Gears are designed based on several factors, and proper function is dependent on these factors. The following list provides descriptions of gear terminology.

Pitch Diameter (*D*): The diameter used to define the spacing of gears. Ideally, gears are exactly tangent to each other along their pitch diameters.

Diametral Pitch (*P*): The number of teeth per inch. Meshing gears must have the same diametral pitch. Manufacturers' gear charts list gears with the same diametral pitch.

Module (*M*): The pitch diameter divided by the number of teeth. The metric equivalent of diametral pitch.

Number of Teeth (*N*): The number of teeth of a gear.

Circular Pitch (*CP*): The circular distance from a fixed point on one tooth to the same position on the next tooth as measured along the pitch circle. The circumference of the pitch circle divided by the number of teeth.

Preferred Pitches: The standard sizes available from gear manufacturers. Whenever possible, use preferred gear sizes.

Center Distance (*CD*): The distance between the centerpoints of two meshing gears.

Backlash: The difference between a tooth width and the engaging space on a meshing gear.

Addendum (*a*): The height of a tooth above the pitch diameter.

Dedendum (*d*): The depth of a tooth below the pitch diameter.

Whole Depth: The total depth of a tooth. The addendum plus the dedendum.

Working Depth: The depth of engagement of one gear into another. Equal to the sum of the two gears' addendums.

Circular Thickness: The distance across a tooth as measured along the pitch circle.

Face Width (F):   The distance from front to back along a tooth as measured perpendicular to the pitch circle.

Outside Diameter: The largest diameter of the gear. Equal to the pitch diameter plus the addendum.

Root Diameter: The diameter of the base of the teeth. The pitch diameter minus the dedendum.

Clearance: The distance between the addendum of the meshing gear and the dedendum of the mating gear.

Pressure Angle: The angle between the line of action and a line tangent to the pitch circle. Most gears have pressure angles of either 14.5° or 20°.

See Figure 10-2.

Figure 10-2

10-3   Gear Formulas

Figure 10-3 shows a chart of formulas commonly associated with gears. The formulas are for spur gears.

Figure 10-3

Diametral pitch (*P*)	$P = \dfrac{N}{D}$
Pitch diameter (*D*)	$D = \dfrac{N}{P}$
Number of teeth (*N*)	$N = DP$
Addendum (*a*)	$a = \dfrac{1}{P}$

Metric

Module (*M*)	$M = \dfrac{D}{N}$

10-4 Creating Gears

In this section we will create two gears and then create an assembly that includes a support plate and two posts to hold the gears in place. The specifications for the two gears are as follows. See Figure 10-4.

Figure 10-4

Gear 1:

      Diametral Pitch = **24**

      Number of Teeth = **30**

      Face Width = **.50**

      Nominal Shaft Diameter = **Ø1/2**

      Hub Diameter = **Ø1.00**

      Hub Height = **.50**

      Pressure Angle = **20**

Gear 2:

      Diametral Pitch = **24**

      Number of Teeth = **60**

      Face Thickness = **.50**

      Nominal Shaft Diameter = **Ø1/2**

      Hub Diameter = **Ø1.00**

      Hub Height = **.50**

      Pressure Angle = **20**

TIP

Gears must have the same diametral pitch to mesh properly.

Using the formulas presented we know that the pitch diameter is found as follows:

$$D = N/P$$

So

$$D1 = 30/24 = 1.25 \text{ in.}$$

$$D2 = 60/24 = 2.50 \text{ in.}$$

The center distance between gears is found from the relation $(D1 + D2)/2$:

$$\frac{1.25 + 2.50}{2} = 1.875 \text{ in.}$$

This center distance data was used to create the Plate, Support shown in Figure 10-4.

The bore for the gears is defined as 0.50, so shafts that hold the gears will be Ø0.50, and the holes in the Plate, Support will also be 0.50.

NOTE

Tolerances for gears, shaft, and support plates are discussed in Chapter 9.

The shafts will have a nominal diameter of Ø0.50 and a length of 1.50. The length was derived by allowing 0.50 for the gear thickness, 0.50 for the Plate, Support thickness, and 0.50 clearance between the gear and the plate. See Figure 10-4. In this example 0.06 × 45° chamfers were added to both ends of the shafts.

Creating a Gear Assembly

1 Draw the **Plate, Support** and **Shaft** shown in Figure 10-4.

2 Start a new **Assembly**.

3 Assemble the plate and shafts as shown. Be sure to align the origin of the plate with the origin of the assembly drawing.

See Figure 10-5. The top surface of the shafts is offset 1.00 from the surface of the plate.

Figure 10-5

Create the gears using the **Design Library**. See Figure 10-6.

Figure 10-6

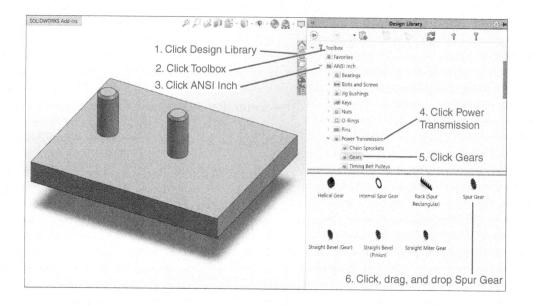

4 Click the **Design Library** tool and then click **Toolbox**, **ANSI Inch**, **Power Transmission**, and **Gears**.

5 Click the **Spur Gear** tool and drag the icon into the drawing area.

The **Spur Gear PropertyManager** will appear. See Figure 10-7.

Figure 10-7

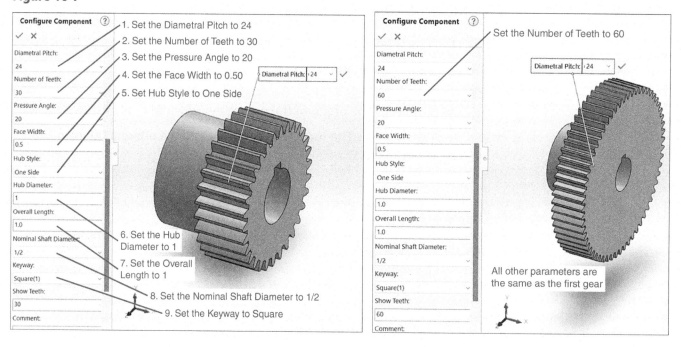

6 Enter the gear values as presented earlier for **Gear 1** and create the gear.

7 Create **Gear 2** using the presented values.

See Figure 10-8.

Figure 10-8

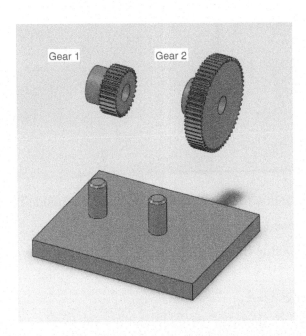

8 Use the **Mate** tool and assemble the gears onto the shafts so that they mesh. First, use the **Mate/Concentric** tool to align the gears' bores with the shafts; then use the **Mate/Parallel** tool to align the top surface of the shafts with the top surfaces of the gears.

See Figure 10-9.

Figure 10-9

9 Zoom in on the gear teeth and align them so they mesh; click the **green** check mark.

10 Click the **Mate** tool.

11 Click the **Mechanical** tab in the **PropertyManager**.

12 Select the **Gear** option.

See Figure 10-10.

Figure 10-10

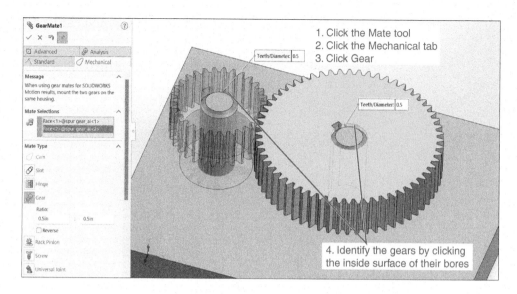

13 Define the gear mate by clicking the inside bore of the two gears.

See Figure 10-11.

14 Define the ratio between the gears.

Figure 10-11

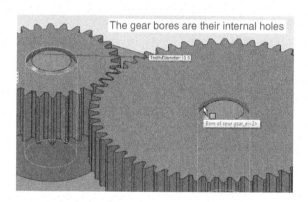

See Figure 10-12. In this example the ratio between the two gears is 2:1; that is, the smaller 30-tooth gear goes around twice for every revolution of the larger 60-tooth gear.

Figure 10-12

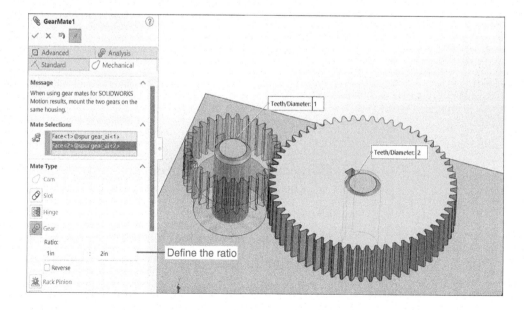

15 Click the green **OK** check mark.

16 Locate the cursor on the smaller gear and rotate the gears.

TIP

If the gears were not aligned (step 8), an error message would appear stating that the gears interfere with each other. The gears will turn relative to each other even if they interfere, but it is better to go back and align the gears.

Animating the Gears

You can see the operation of the gears in SolidWorks by animating the assembly that has appropriate gear mates in place.

1 Click the **Motion Study** tab at the bottom of the screen. If needed, click the **Expand Motion Manager** icon in the lower-right corner of the screen to expand the **Motion Manager** box.

2 Click the **Motor** tool.

See Figure 10-13.

Figure 10-13

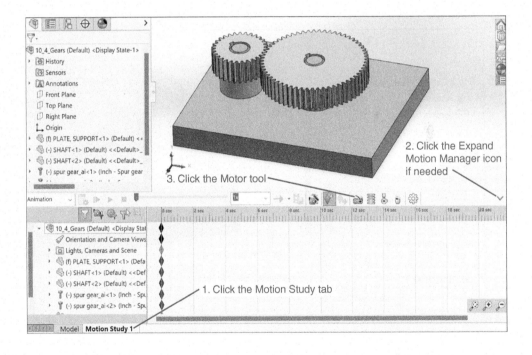

3 Click the **Rotary Motor** option in the **Motor PropertyManager**.

4 Click the smaller 30-tooth gear.

A red arrow will appear on the gear, and the gear will be identified in the **Component/Direction** box. See Figure 10-14.

Figure 10-14

5. Click the green **OK** check mark.

6. Drag the diamond-shaped **Key** on the time slider to 5s. See Figure 10-15.

7. The time for rotation of the Rotary Motor should correspondingly update to 5s.

8. Click the **Play** button.

The gears will animate.

9. Save the gear assembly.

Figure 10-15

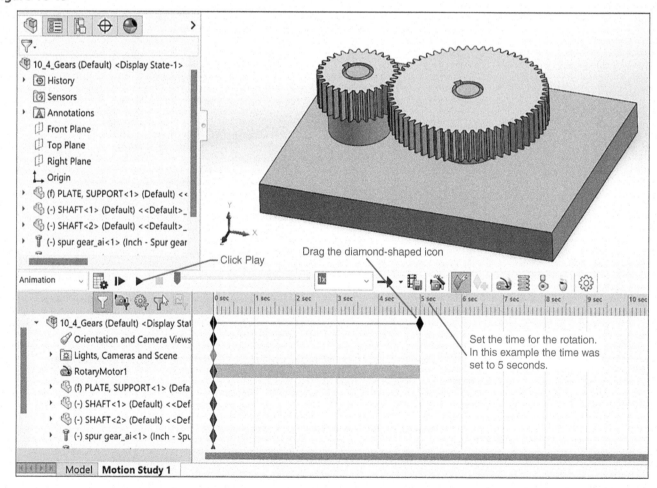

10-5   Gear Ratios

Gear ratios are determined by the number of teeth of each gear. In the previous example a gear with 30 teeth was meshed with a gear that has 60 teeth. As mentioned, their gear ratio is 2:1; that is, the smaller gear turns twice for every one revolution of the larger gear. Figure 10-16 shows a group of four gears. A grouping of gears is called a *gear train*. The gear train shown contains two gears with 30 teeth and two gears with 90 teeth. One of the 30-tooth gears is mounted on the same shaft as one of the 90-tooth gears. The gear ratio for the gear train is found as follows:

Figure 10-16

$$\left(\frac{3}{3}\right)\left(\frac{3}{1}\right) = \frac{9}{1}$$

Thus, if the leftmost 30-tooth gear turns at 1750 RPM, the rightmost 90-tooth gear turns at

$$\frac{1750}{9} = 199.4\,\text{RPM}$$

10-6   Gears and Bearings

The gear assembly created in the previous section did not include bearings. As gears rotate they rub against a stationary part, causing friction. It would be better to mount the gears' shafts into bearings mounted into the support plate. There will still be friction, but it will be absorbed by the bearings, which are designed to absorb the forces. The bearings will eventually wear, but they can be replaced more easily than the support plate.

Adding Bearings

Figure 10-17 shows the gear assembly created in the last section. The shafts are Ø.50.

1 Access the **Design Library**, click **Toolbox**, **ANSI Inch**, **Jig Bushings**, **All Jig Bushings**, and select **Jig Bushing Type P** and drag it onto the drawing.

2 Set the **Size** of the bearing to **0.5000** and the **Length** to **0.5**.

The support plate is .50 thick.

3 Add a second bearing.

Figure 10-17

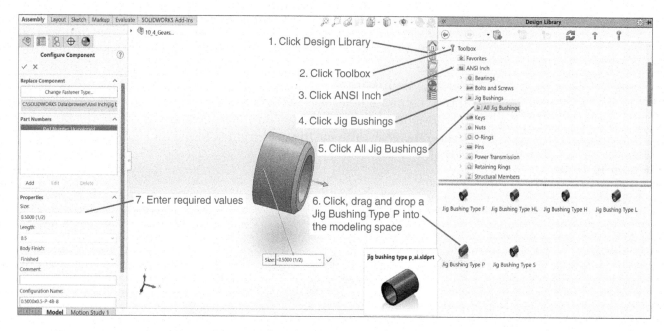

4 Double-click one of the bearings.

The dimensions used to create the bearing will appear. See Figure 10-18. The outside diameter of the bearing is .75. The holes in the support plate must be edited to Ø.75.

Figure 10-18

Figure 10-19

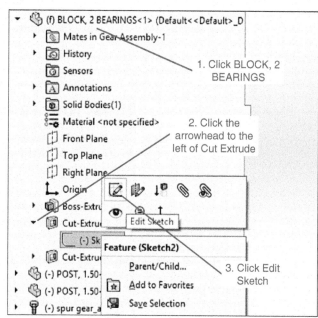

5 Click the arrowhead to the left of the **BLOCK, 2 BEARING** heading in the **FeatureManager**.

6 Click the arrowhead to the left of the **Cut-Extrude 1** heading, right-click the **Sketch 2** heading, and select the **Edit Sketch** option. Your names may differ.

See Figure 10-19.

7 Double-click the holes' **.50** diameter dimensions and change them to **.75**. See Figure 10-20.

Figure 10-20

8 Rotate the entire assembly so that the bottom surface of the support plate is visible.

9 Use the **Mate** tool to position the bearings onto the bottoms of the shafts. See Figure 10-21.

Figure 10-21

Figure 10-22 shows an exploded isometric drawing of the assembly with a BOM.

Figure 10-22

ITEM NO.	PART NUMBER	DESCRIPTION	QTY.
1	BU-2011-B	PLATE, SUPPORT	1
2	BU-2011-A	SHAFT	2
3	Inch - Spur gear 24DP 30T 20PA 0.5FW --- S30O1.0H1.0L0.5N		1
4	Inch - Spur gear 24DP 60T 20PA 0.5FW --- S60O1.0H1.0L0.5N		1
5	0.5000-P-48-B		2

10-7 Power Transmission—Shaft to Gear

When a gear is mounted on a shaft there must be a way to transfer the power from the shaft to the gear and from the gear to the shaft. Three common ways to achieve this transfer are to use set screws, keys, and splines. This section shows how to add set screws and keyways to gears. Splines will not be included.

10-8 Set Screws and Gear Hubs

This section shows how to add a hub to a gear and then how to create a threaded hole in the hub that will accept a set screw.

1 Start a new **Part** and create the **Ø0.50 × 2.25** shaft shown in Figure 10-23.

Save the part as **POST, GEAR**.

2 Start a new **Assembly** drawing.

3 Use the **Insert Components** tool and add the Ø0.50 × 2.25 shaft to the drawing.

4 Access the **Design Library** and click **Toolbox, ANSI Inch, Power Transmission**, and **Gears**.

5 Select the **Spur Gear** option and click and drag it onto the drawing screen.

See Figure 10-24.

Figure 10-23

Figure 10-24

6 Set the gear's properties as follows. See Figure 10-25.

Diametral Pitch: **24**

Number of Teeth: **36**

Pressure Angle: **14.5**

Face Width: **0.5**

Hub Style: **One Side**

Hub Diameter: **1.0**

Overall Length: **1.0**

TIP

The overall length is the face width plus the hub height. In this example the face width is .5, and the overall length is 1.00, so the hub height is .5.

---

7 Click the green **OK** check mark.

Figure 10-25

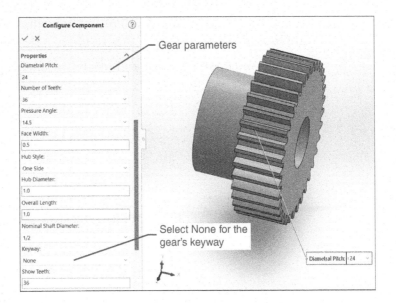

Adding a Threaded Hole to the Gear's Hub

The screen should show the shaft and gear. This is an assembly drawing.

1 Right-click the spur gear callout and click the **Open Part** option.

A warning dialog box will appear; click **OK**.

2 Rotate the gear so that the hub is clearly visible.

See Figure 10-26.

Figure 10-26

1. Right-click the gear
2. Select the Open Part option

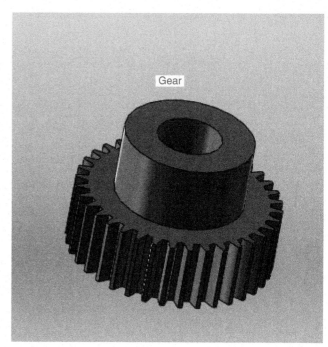

Gear

3 Click the **Hole Wizard** tool.

4 Define the **Hole Type** as a **Straight Tap** hole.

See Figure 10-27. In this example an ANSI Inch #6-32 thread was selected for the hole. The depth of the hole must exceed the wall thickness of the hub, which is 0.25. In this example a depth of 0.50 was selected.

5 Click the **Positions** tab and locate the threaded hole on the outside surface of the hub.

See Figure 10-28.

Figure 10-27

1. Click Straight Tap

2. Define the threaded hole

Figure 10-28

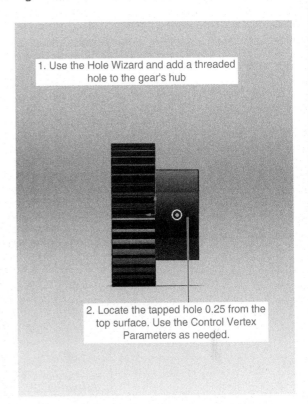

1. Use the Hole Wizard and add a threaded hole to the gear's hub

2. Locate the tapped hole 0.25 from the top surface. Use the Control Vertex Parameters as needed.

6 Click the **Smart Dimension** tool and create a **0.25** dimension between the centerpoint of the hole and the top surface of the gear teeth.

Define the dimension between the hole's centerpoint and the top surface of the gear's hub.

7 Click the green **OK** check mark.

8 Save the modified part as **GEAR, SET SCREW**.

9 Click the **Close** tool.

10 Access the **Design Library**, click **Toolbox**, **ANSI Inch**, **Bolts and Screws**, and **Set Screws (Slotted)**.

11 Select a **Slotted Set Screw Oval Point** and drag it onto the screen.

12 Define the **Properties** of the set screw as **Size #6-32** and **Length 0.263**; click the green **OK** check mark.

See Figure 10-29.

Figure 10-29

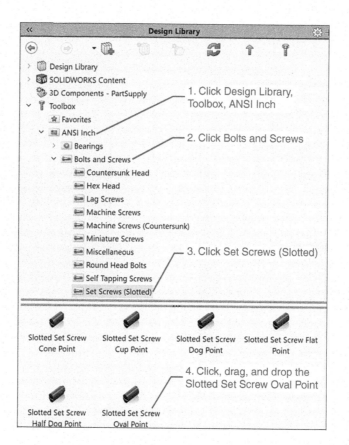

1. Click Design Library, Toolbox, ANSI Inch

2. Click Bolts and Screws

3. Click Set Screws (Slotted)

4. Click, drag, and drop the Slotted Set Screw Oval Point

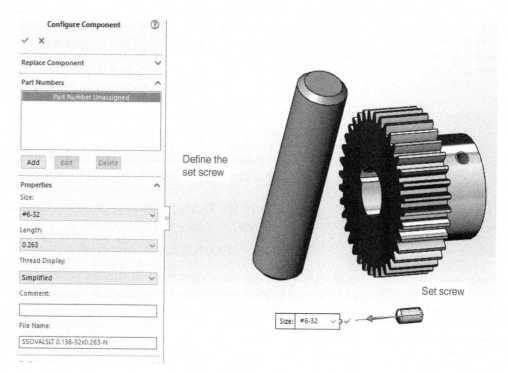

Define the set screw

Set screw

13 Use the **Mate** tool and assemble the shaft and set screw into the gear as shown.

See Figure 10-30.

Figure 10-30

The assembled gear, shaft, and set screw

10-9 Keys, Keyseats, and Gears

Keys are used to transfer power from a drive shaft to an entity such as a gear or pulley. A *keyseat* is cut into both the shaft and the gear, and the key is inserted between them. See Figure 10-31. The SolidWorks **Design Library** contains two types of keys: parallel and Woodruff.

In this section we will insert a parallel key between a Ø0.50 × 3.00 shaft and a gear. Both the shaft and gear will have keyseats.

Defining and Creating Keyseats in Gears

1 Draw a **Ø0.50 × 3.00** shaft with a .06 × 45° chamfer at both ends and save the shaft as **Ø0.50 × 3.00 SHAFT**.

2 Start a new **Assembly** and insert the shaft into the drawing.

3 Access the **Design Library** and click **Toolbox**, **ANSI Inch**, **Power Transmission**, and **Gears**.

Figure 10-31

Keyseat

Keyseat

Parallel key

A parallel key

A Woodruff key

4 Click and drag a **Spur Gear** into the modeling space.

5 Define the gear's properties as shown in Figure 10-32.

This gear will not have a hub. Define a **Square(1)** keyway.

Figure 10-32

6 Click the green **OK** check mark.

> **NOTE**
> The gear will automatically have a keyseat cut into it. The size of the keyseat is based on the gear's bore diameter.

The key will also be sized according to the gear's bore diameter, but say we wish to determine the exact keyway size. See Figure 10-33.

1 Right-click the gear and select the **Open Part** option.

A warning dialog box will appear.

2 Click **OK**.

3 Click the **File** menu at the top of the screen and click the **Make Drawing from Part** tool.

The **New SolidWorks Document** dialog box will appear.

Figure 10-33

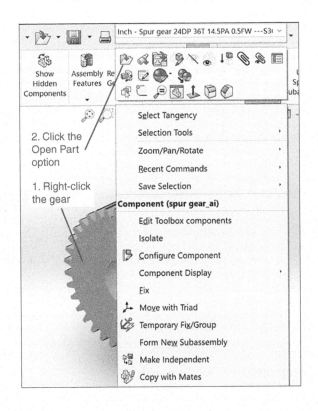

2. Click the Open Part option

1. Right-click the gear

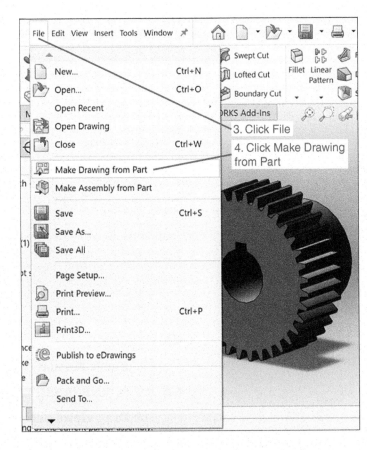

3. Click File

4. Click Make Drawing from Part

5. Click B (ANSI) Landscape

6. Click OK

7. Click, drag, and drop the Front view onto the screen

Figure 10-33
(*Continued*)

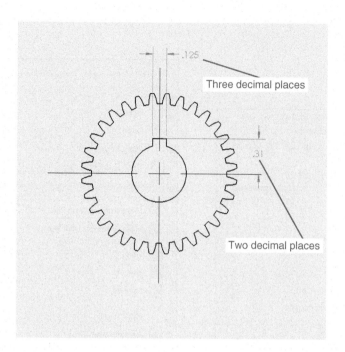

Three decimal places

Two decimal places

4 Click **OK**.

The **Sheet Format/Size** dialog box will appear.

5 Select the **B (ANSI) Landscape** sheet size; click **OK**.

The **Drag views onto drawing sheet** box will appear.

6 Click and drag a **Front** view of the gear into the drawing area.

7 Use the **Center Mark** tool to add a centerline to the gear's bore. Press **<Esc>**.

8 Use the **Smart Dimension** tool and dimension the keyseat.

Notice that the keyseat's width is .125. The height of the keyseat is measured from the bore's centerpoint. The height is defined as .31. Therefore, the height of the keyseat is .31 – .25 (the radius of the bore) = .06, or about half the width.

Returning to the Assembly Drawing

1 Click the **File** menu at the top of the screen and select the **Close** option.

Do not save the gear drawing. If changes were made to the drawing, they would have to be saved as a new drawing and the drawing closed to return to the original assembly.

2 Again, click the **File** menu and select the **Close** option.

The drawing will return to the assembly drawing. When the **Open** tool was activated, a new drawing was created, so the drawing must be closed to return to the original drawing.

See Figure 10-34.

Figure 10-34

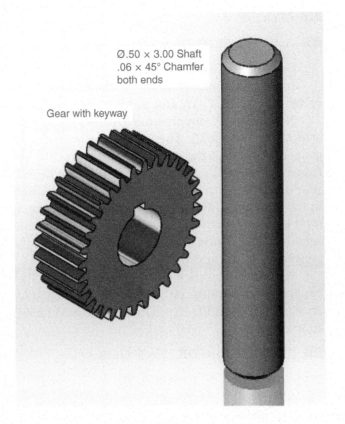

Ø.50 × 3.00 Shaft
.06 × 45° Chamfer
both ends

Gear with keyway

Defining and Creating a Parallel Key

1 Access the **Design Library** and click **Toolbox**, **ANSI Inch**, **Keys**, and **Parallel Keys**.

See Figure 10-35.

Figure 10-35

2 Click and drag the **Key (B17.1)** icon onto the drawing screen.

3 Enter the **Shaft Diameter** value and the key's **Length** value as **.5**.

See Figure 10-36.

In this example the shaft diameter is .50, or 1/2 inch (8/16). This value is between 7/16 and 9/16.

Note that key dimensions are also given as 0.125×0.125 and a Keyseat Depth of 0.0625. The key size automatically matches the keyway in the gear. The width of the gear's keyseat was .13, or .005 larger than the key. A rule of thumb is to make the height of the keyseat in both the shaft and the gear equal to a little more than the key's height. The height of the keyseat in the gear was .06, so the depth of the keyway in the shaft will be .07, for a total keyway height of .06 + .07 = .13. The calculation does not take into account the tolerances between the shaft and the gear or the tolerances between the key and the keyseat.

For exact tolerance values, refer to Erik Oberg's *Machinery's Handbook* (available from Industrial Press, Inc., at https://www.amazon.com/Machinerys-Handbook-29th-Erik-Oberg/dp/083112900X or some equivalent source).

4 Click the green **OK** check mark.

Figure 10-36

Creating a Keyseat in the Shaft

The keyway for the shaft will be $.13 \times .07$.

1 Click the top surface of the Ø.50 × 3.00 shaft.

2 Click the **Normal To** tool.

See Figure 10-37. The top surface of the shaft will become normal to the drawing screen.

Figure 10-37

2. Click Normal
To tool

1. Click the top surface
of the shaft

3 Right-click the normal surface again and select the **Sketch** option.

4 Click the **Sketch** tab, then click the **Line** tool and draw a vertical line from the centerpoint of the shaft as shown.

This vertical line is for construction purposes. It will be used to center the keyway.

See Figure 10-38.

Figure 10-38

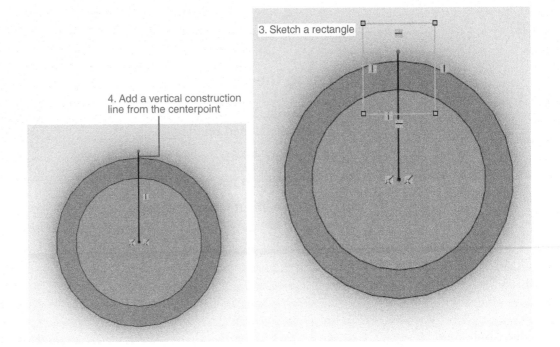

4. Add a vertical construction
line from the centerpoint

3. Sketch a rectangle

Figure 10-38
(*Continued*)

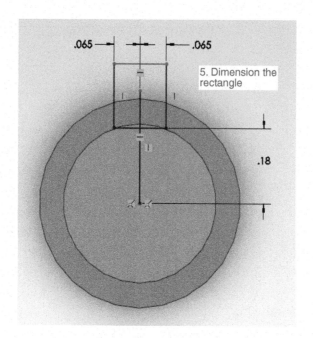

5. Dimension the rectangle

5 Click the **Sketch** tab, then the **Rectangle** tool, and draw a rectangle as shown.

Draw the rectangle so that the top horizontal line is above the edge of the shaft.

6 Use the **Smart Dimension** tool to locate the left vertical line of the rectangle .065 from the vertical construction line.

TIP

If the vertical centerline moves rather than the left vertical line, left-click the vertical construction line and select the **Fix** option.

---

7 Use the **Smart Dimension** tool and dimension the rectangle as shown.

Creating the Keyseat

1 Access the **Extruded Cut** tool located on the **Features** tab, and click the dimensioned rectangle.

See Figure 10-39.

2 Define the cut length of **0.50in**.

3 Click the green **OK** check mark.

Figure 10-39

The keyseat will end with an arc-shaped cut. The radius of the arc is equal to the depth of the keyseat. The arc shape is generated by the **Extruded Cut** tool used to create the keyseat.

Creating the Arc-Shaped End of a Keyseat

1. Right-click the inside vertical surface of the keyseat and click the **Sketch** tab.

2. Use the **Circle** tool and draw a circle centered about the end of the keyseat on the surface of the shaft, using the lower corner of the keyway to define the radius value.

See Figure 10-40.

Figure 10-40

Figure 10-40
(*Continued*)

3 Use the **Extruded Cut** tool to cut the arc-shaped end surface.

The length of the cut equals the width of the keyway, or .13.

4 Assemble the parts as shown. See Figures 10-41 and 10-42.

Figure 10-41

Assembly with
key in keyway

Figure 10-42

ITEM NO.	PART NUMBER	DESCRIPTION	QTY.
1	BU-132	Ø.50x3.00 SHAFT	1
2	Inch - 3pur gear 24DP 32T 14.5PA 0.5FW — 332N1.0H1.0L0.5S1	GEAR	1
3	Key B17.1 0.125x0.125x.5	KEY	1

10-10 Sample Problem SP10-1

This exercise explains how to determine the size of plates used to support spur gears and their shafts.

Say we wish to design a support plate that will support four spur gears. See Figure 10-43. The gear specifications are as follows.

Figure 10-43

Gear 1:

Diametral Pitch = **24**

Number of Teeth = **20**

Pressure Angle = **14.5°**

Face Width = **0.375**

Hub Style = **One Side**

Hub Diameter = **0.75**

Overall Length = **.875**

Nominal Shaft Diameter = **1/2**

Keyway = **None**

Gear 2:

Diametral Pitch = **24**

Number of Teeth = **60**

Pressure Angle = **14.5°**

Face Width = **0.375**

Hub Style = **One Side**

Hub Diameter = **0.75**

Overall Length = **.875**

Nominal Shaft Diameter = **1/2**

Keyway = **None**

Determining the Pitch Diameter

The pitch diameter of the gears is determined by

$$D = \frac{N}{P}$$

where

D = pitch diameter

N = number of teeth

P = diametral pitch

Therefore, for Gear 1

$$D = \frac{20}{24} = .83$$

For Gear 2

$$D = \frac{60}{24} = 2.50$$

The center distance (*CD*) between the gears is calculated as follows:

$$CD = \frac{.83 + 2.50}{2} = 1.67$$

The radii of the gears are .46 and 1.25, respectively.

Figure 10-44 shows a support plate for the gears. The dimensions for the support plate were derived from the gear pitch diameters and an allowance of about .50 between the gear pitch diameters and the edge of the support plate. For example, the pitch diameter of the larger gear is 2.50. Allowing .50 between the top edge and the bottom edge gives .50 + 2.50 + .50 = 3.50.

Figure 10-44

The pitch diameter for the smaller gear is .83. Adding the .50 edge distance gives a distance of 1.33 from the smaller gear's centerpoint. In this example the distance was rounded up to 1.50. The center distance between the gears is 1.67. Therefore, the total length of the support plate is 1.50 + 1.67 + 1.67 + 1.75 = 6.59, or about 6.75. The height will be 3.50.

Each of the gears has a 1/2 nominal shaft diameter. For this example a value of .50 will be assigned to both the gear bores and the holes in the support plate. Bearings are not included in this example.

Figure 10-45 shows a Ø.50 × 2.00 shaft that will be used to support the gears.

Figure 10-45

Create an **Assembly** drawing using the support plate, three Ø.50 × 2.00 shafts, and the four gears. The gears were created using the given information. Figure 10-46 shows the components in their assembled position. Save the assembly as **ASSEMBLY, THREE GEAR**. The gears are offset .60 from the support and from each other on the gear shafts.

Create an exploded drawing using the three-gear assembly in the **Isometric** orientation with no hidden lines. See Figure 10-47. Access the **Annotation** menu, add balloons, click the **Tables** tool, and select the **Bill of Materials** tool. Locate the bill of materials (BOM) as shown.

The PART NUMBER column does not show part numbers but lists the file names assigned to each part and, in the case of the gears, a listing of gear parameters.

Figure 10-46

Gear 1
Gear 2
Shaft, Gear
Support, Gear, Spur

Editing the Bill of Materials

See Figure 10-47. SolidWorks will automatically insert the part's file name as its part number.

1 Double-click the first cell under the heading **DESCRIPTION**.

A warning dialog box will appear. See Figure 10-48.

Figure 10-47

Figure 10-48

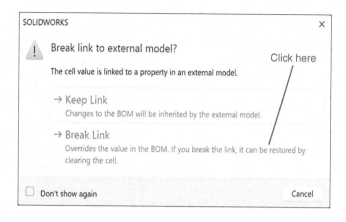

2 Click **Break Link**.

An editing text box will appear in the cell. See Figure 10-49.

3 Type in the part description.

In this example the file name **SUPPORT, GEAR, SPUR** was used, and the text was left aligned.

NOTE

The description was typed using only uppercase letters. Uppercase letters are the preferred convention.

4 Complete the editing of the **DESCRIPTION** column.

5 Click the **PART NUMBER** column and add part numbers as shown.

Figure 10-49

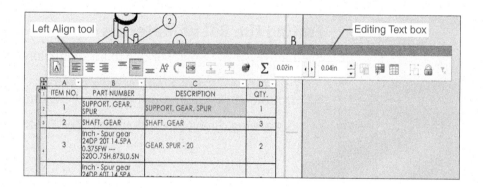

NOTE

Part numbers differ from item numbers (assembly numbers). The support plate is item number 1 and has a part number of AM311-1. If the plate were to be used in another assembly, it might have a different item number, but it will always have the same AM311-1 part number.

The gears' part numbers were accepted "as is" because they are standard numbers assigned to each gear. In general, manufacturers' part numbers are used directly. See Figure 10-50.

Figure 10-50

ITEM NO.	PART NUMBER	DESCRIPTION	QTY.
1	AM311-1	SUPPORT, GEAR, SPUR	1
2	AM311-2	SHAFT, GEAR	3
3	Inch - Spur gear 24DP 20T 14.5PA 0.375FW --- S20O.75H.875L0.5N	GEAR, SPUR - 20	2
4	Inch - Spur gear 24DP 60T 14.5PA 0.375FW --- S60O.75H.875L0.5N	GEAR, SPUR - 60	2

The three-gear assembly can be animated using the **Mechanical Mates** tool.

1 Click the **Mate** tool.

2 Click the **Mechanical** tab.

3 Click the **Gear** tool.

4 Click the edge of **Gear 1**.

The gear name should appear in the **Mate Selections** box.

5 Click **Gear 2**.

6 Set the gear ratio to **1:2**.

See Figure 10-51.

7 Create a **Gear Mate** between Gear 2 and the second Gear 1, located on the same shaft, and set the gear ratio for **1:1**.

The gears are on the same shaft, so they will rotate at the same speed.

8 Create a **Gear Mate** between the second Gear 1 and the second Gear 2 and set the gear ratio for **1:2**.

Figure 10-51

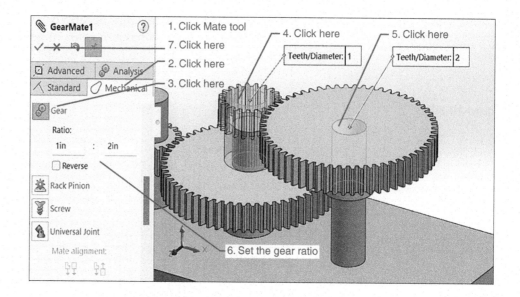

Figure 10-52 shows gear mates used to create the animated assembly.

9 Use the cursor to rotate Gear 1.

The gears should rotate.

Figure 10-52

The total gear ratio is

$$\left(\frac{3}{1}\right)\left(\frac{3}{1}\right) = \frac{9}{1}$$

Therefore, if the first Gear 1 rotates at 1750 RPM, the second Gear 2 will rotate at 194.4 RPM:

1750/9 = 194.4 RPM

10-11 Rack and Pinion Gears

Figure 10-53 shows a rack and pinion gear setup. It was created as an **Assembly** with a Ø.50 × 2.25 shaft and a rack and pinion gear from the **Design Library**.

1 Draw a **Ø.50 × 2.25** shaft with a **0.03** chamfer at each end.

2 Start a new **Assembly**.

3 Insert the Ø.50 × 2.25 shaft.

Figure 10-53

The shaft will serve as a base for the gears and a reference for animation.

4 Access the **Design Library** and click **Toolbox, ANSI Inch, Power Transmission, Gears**, and click and drag a **Rack (Spur Rectangular)** into the model space.

5 Set the rack's properties as shown in Figure 10-54.

6 Repeat step 4 but this time drag a **Spur Gear** into the model space.

The spur gear will become the pinion.

7 Set the pinion's properties as shown in Figure 10-55.

8 Reorient the components and use the **Mate** tool to insert the pinion onto the shaft.

See Figure 10-56.

Remember that the shaft was entered into the assembly first, so its position is fixed. Use the **Float** option to move the shaft.

Figure 10-54

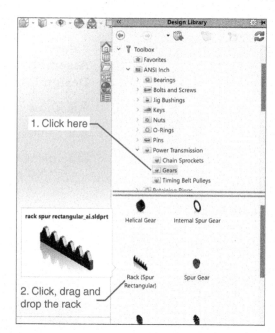

1. Click here

2. Click, drag and drop the rack

3. Define the rack's parameters

Figure 10-55

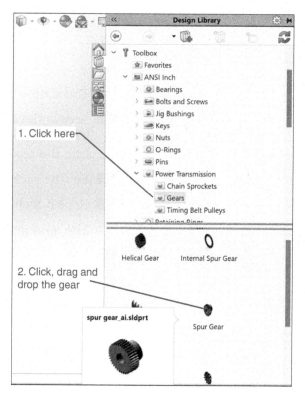

1. Click here

2. Click, drag and drop the gear

3. Define the gear's parameters

Figure 10-56

Use the Concentric option of the Mate tool and mount the pinion gear on the shaft

Figure 10-57

Mate the pinion gear to the rack teeth

9 Use the **Mate** tool to make the top surface of the pinion parallel with the front flat surface of the rack.

10 Use the **Mate** tool and align the top surface (not an edge) of one of the pinion's teeth with the bottom surface of one of the rack's teeth.

See Figure 10-57.

11 Adjust the pinion as needed to create a proper fit between the pinion and the rack by locating the cursor on the pinion and rotating the pinion.

Animating the Rack and Pinion

See Figure 10-58. This animation is based on the rack and pinion setup created in the previous section.

1 Click the **Mate** tool.

2 Click the **Mechanical** tab.

3 Click the **Rack Pinion** option.

4 Click the front edge of the rack's teeth.

5 Click the pinion gear (not an edge).

6 Fix the shaft in place.

7 Set the pinion pitch diameter.

Right-click the **Shaft** heading in the **FeatureManager Design Tree** and click the **Fix** option. An **f** should appear in the Shaft heading.

8 Click the green **OK** check mark.

9 Use the cursor to rotate the pinion.

Figure 10-58

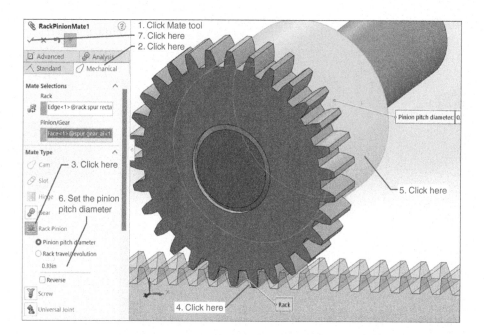

The rack will slide back and forth as the pinion is moved. Reverse the mate direction if the rack moves opposite to the pinion.

10-12 Metric Gears

Gears created using the metric system are very similar to gears created using English units with one major exception. Gears in the English system use the term *pitch* to refer to the number of teeth per inch. Gears in the metric system use the term *module* to refer to the pitch diameter divided by the number of teeth. As meshing gears in the English system must have the same pitch, so meshing gears in the metric system must have the same module.

Creating a Metric Gear

See Figure 10-59.

1 Start a new **Part** document and set the units for **MMGS**.

2 Draw a **Ø16 × 60** millimeter shaft. Save the shaft as **Ø16 × 60**.

3 Start a new **Assembly** drawing and insert the **Ø16 × 60** shaft.

4 Access the **Design Library**.

5 Click **Toolbox**, **ANSI Metric**, **Power Transmission**, and **Gears**.

6 Click and drag a **Spur Gear** into the drawing area.

7 Define the gear's properties as follows:

    a. Module = **1.5**

    b. Number of Teeth = **30**

    c. Pressure Angle = **14.5**

    d. Face Width = **10**

    e. Hub Style = **None**

    f. Nominal Shaft Diameter = **16**

    g. Keyway = **None**

Figure 10-59

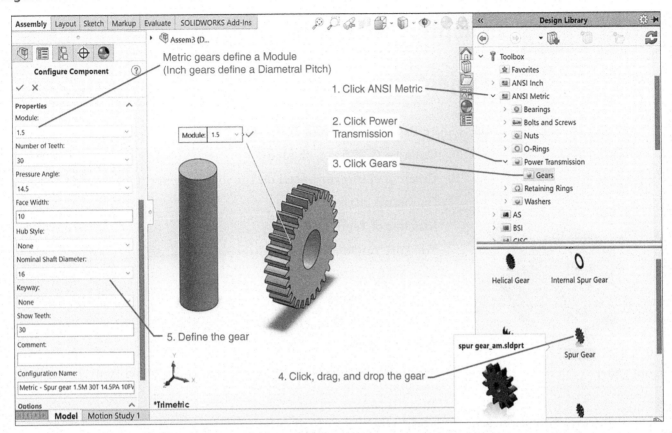

Metric gears define a Module
(Inch gears define a Diametral Pitch)

1. Click ANSI Metric

2. Click Power Transmission

3. Click Gears

5. Define the gear

4. Click, drag, and drop the gear

8 Use the **Mate** tool and assemble the gear onto the shaft.

Figure 10-60 shows the gear assembled onto the shaft.

Figure 10-60

Gear and shaft assembly

Chapter Projects

Project 10-1: Inches

Use Figure P10-1 for Projects 10-1 through 10-4.

   A. Create a Ø.375 × 1.75 shaft.

   B. Create a spur gear based on the following specifications:

      Diametral Pitch = **32**

      Number of Teeth = **36**

      Pressure Angle = **14.5**

      Face Width = **.250**

      Hub Style = **None**

      Nominal Shaft Diameter = **3/8**

      Keyway = **None**

   C. Assemble the gear onto the shaft with a .25 offset from the end of the shaft.

Ø.375 x 1.75 Shaft

.25 Offset

Spur gear

Figure P10-1

Project 10-2: Inches

   A. Create a Ø.250 × 1.50 shaft.

   B. Create a spur gear based on the following specifications:

      Diametral Pitch = **40**

      Number of Teeth = **56**

      Pressure Angle = **14.5**

      Face Width = **.125**

      Hub Style = **None**

      Nominal Shaft Diameter = **1/4**

      Keyway = **None**

   C. Assemble the gear onto the shaft with a .125 offset from the end of the shaft.

Project 10-3: Inches

   A. Create a Ø1.00 × 4.00 shaft.

   B. Create a spur gear based on the following specifications:

      Diametral Pitch = **8**

      Number of Teeth = **66**

Pressure Angle = **14.5**

Face Width = **.625**

Hub Style = **None**

Nominal Shaft Diameter = **1**

Keyway = **None**

C. Assemble the gear onto the shaft with a 0.00 offset from the end of the shaft.

Project 10-4: Millimeters

A. Create a Ø8.0 × 30 shaft.

B. Create a spur gear based on the following specifications:

Module = **2**

Number of Teeth = **40**

Pressure Angle = **14.5**

Face Width = **12**

Hub Style = **None**

Nominal Shaft Diameter = **8**

Keyway = **None**

C. Assemble the gear onto the shaft with a 5.0 offset from the end of the shaft.

Project 10-5: Inches

Use Figure P10-2 for Projects 10-5 through 10-7.

A. Create a Ø.625 × 4.00 shaft.

B. Create a spur gear based on the following specifications:

Gear 1:

Diametral Pitch = **10**

Number of Teeth = **42**

Pressure Angle = **14.5**

Face Width = **.375**

Hub Style = **None**

Nominal Shaft Diameter = **5/8**

Keyway = **None**

C. Create a second gear based on the following specifications:

Gear 2:

Diametral Pitch = **10**

Number of Teeth = **68**

Pressure Angle = **14.5**

Face Width = **.500**

Hub Style = **None**

Nominal Shaft Diameter = **5/8**

Keyway = **None**

D. Assemble the gears onto the shaft with Gear 1 offset .25 from the front end of the shaft and Gear 2 offset 3.00 from the front end of the shaft.

Project 10-6: Inches

A. Create a Ø.25 × 2.75 shaft.

B. Create a spur gear based on the following specifications:

Gear 1:

Diametral Pitch = **40**

Number of Teeth = **18**

Pressure Angle = **14.5**

Face Width = **.125**

Hub Style = **None**

Nominal Shaft Diameter = **1/4**

Keyway = **None**

C. Create a second gear based on the following specifications:

Gear 2:

Diametral Pitch = **40**

Number of Teeth = **54**

Pressure Angle = **14.5**

Face Width = **.125**

Hub Style = **None**

Nominal Shaft Diameter = **1/4**

Keyway = **None**

D. Assemble the gears onto the shaft with Gear 1 offset .125 from the front end of the shaft and Gear 2 offset 2.00 from the front end of the shaft.

Project 10-7: Millimeters

A. Create a Ø12 × 80 shaft.

B. Create a spur gear based on the following specifications:

Gear 1:

Module = **1.0**

Number of Teeth = **16**

Pressure Angle = **14.5**

Face Width = **8**

Hub Style = **None**

Nominal Shaft Diameter = **12**

Keyway = **None**

C. Create a second gear based on the following specifications:

Gear 2:

Module = **1.0**

Number of Teeth = **48**

Pressure Angle = **14.5**

Face Width = **10**

Hub Style = **None**

Nominal Shaft Diameter = **12**

Keyway = **None**

D. Assemble the gears onto the shaft with Gear 1 offset 5 from the front end of the shaft and Gear 2 offset 50 from the front end of the shaft.

Project 10-8: Inches

Use Figure P10-3 for Projects 10-8 through 10-10.

Figure P10-3

ITEM NO.	PART NUMBER	DESCRIPTION	QTY.
1	AM-311-A1	Ø.375 × 2.75 SHAFT	1
2	AM311-A2	GEAR 1 - N22	1
3	AM311-A3	GEAR 2 - N44	1
4	#6-32 UNC	SET SCREW	2

A. Create a Ø.375 × 2.75 shaft. Save the shaft.

B. Create a spur gear based on the following specifications:

Gear 1:

> Diametral Pitch = **10**
>
> Number of Teeth = **22**
>
> Pressure Angle = **14.5**
>
> Face Width = **.375**
>
> Hub Style = **One Side**
>
> Hub Diameter = **.75**
>
> Overall Length = **.75**
>
> Nominal Shaft Diameter = **3/8**
>
> Keyway = **None**

C. Create another spur gear based on the following specifications:

Gear 2:

> Diametral Pitch = **10**
>
> Number of Teeth = **44**
>
> Pressure Angle = **14.5**
>
> Face Width = **.375**
>
> Hub Style = **One Side**
>
> Hub Diameter = **.75**

Overall Length = **.75**

Nominal Shaft Diameter = **3/8**

Keyway = **None**

D. Add #6-32 threaded holes to each gear hub .19 from the top hub surface.

E. Assemble the gears onto the shaft with Gear 1 offset .25 from the front end of the shaft and Gear 2 offset 2.25 from the front end of the shaft.

F. Insert a #6-32 Slotted Set Screw with an Oval Point into each hole.

G. Create an exploded assembly drawing.

H. Create a bill of materials.

I. Animate the assembly.

Project 10-9: Inches

A. Create a Ø.375 × 3.25 shaft. Save the shaft.

B. Create a spur gear based on the following specifications:

Gear 1:

Diametral Pitch = **20**

Number of Teeth = **18**

Pressure Angle = **14.5**

Face Width = **.25**

Hub Style = **One Side**

Hub Diameter = **.50**

Overall Length = **.50**

Nominal Shaft Diameter = **3/8**

Keyway = **None**

C. Create another spur gear based on the following specifications:

Gear 2:

Diametral Pitch = **20**

Number of Teeth = **63**

Pressure Angle = **14.5**

Face Width = **.25**

Hub Style = **One Side**

Hub Diameter = **.50**

Overall Length = **.50**

Nominal Shaft Diameter = **3/8**

Keyway = **None**

D. Add #4-40 threaded holes to each gear hub .19 from the top hub surface.

E. Assemble the gears onto the shaft with Gear 1 offset .25 from the front end of the shaft and Gear 2 offset 2.63 from the front end of the shaft.

Project 10-10: Millimeters

A. Create a Ø24 × 120 shaft. Save the shaft.

B. Create a spur gear based on the following specifications:

Gear 1:

    Module = **1.5**

    Number of Teeth = **18**

    Pressure Angle = **14.5**

    Face Width = **12**

    Hub Style = **One Side**

    Hub Diameter = **32**

    Overall Length = **30**

    Nominal Shaft Diameter = **16**

    Keyway = **None**

C. Create another spur gear based on the following specifications:

Gear 2:

    Module = **1.5**

    Number of Teeth = **70**

    Pressure Angle = **14.5**

    Face Width = **12**

    Hub Style = **One Side**

    Hub Diameter = **40**

    Overall Length = **30**

    Nominal Shaft Diameter = **16**

    Keyway = **None**

D. Add M3.0 threaded holes to each gear hub 10 from the top hub surface.

E. Assemble the gears onto the shaft with Gear 1 offset 4.0 from the front end of the shaft and Gear 2 offset 80.0 from the front end of the shaft.

F. Insert an M3 Socket Set Screw with a Cup Point into each hole.

G. Create an exploded assembly drawing.

H. Create a bill of materials.

I. Animate the assembly.

Project 10-11: Inches

See Figure P10-4.

    A. Draw three Ø.375 × 3.00 shafts.

    B. Draw the support plate shown.

Figure P10-4

C. Access the **Design Library** and create two Gear 1s and two Gear 2s.

The gears are defined as follows:

Gear 1:

Diametral Pitch = **16**

Number of Teeth = **24**

Pressure Angle = **14.5**

Face Width = **.25**

Hub Style = **One Side**

Hub Diameter = **.50**

Overall Length = **.50**

Nominal Shaft Diameter = **3/8**

Keyway = **None**

Gear 2:

Diametral Pitch = **16**

Number of Teeth = **64**

Pressure Angle = **14.5**

Face Width = **.25**

Hub Style = **One Side**

Hub Diameter = **.50**

Overall Length = **.50**

Nominal Shaft Diameter = **3/8**

Keyway = **None**

D. Add #6-32 threaded holes to each gear hub .19 from the top hub surface.

E. Assemble the gears onto the shafts so that Gear 1 and Gear 2 are offset .50 from the support plate, and Gear 3 and Gear 4 are parallel to the ends of the shafts.

F. Insert a #6-32 Slotted Set Screw with an Oval Point into each hole.

G. Create an exploded assembly drawing.

H. Create a bill of materials.

I. Animate the assembly.

Project 10-12: Inches—Design Problem

Using Figure P10-4 define a support plate and shafts that support the following gears. Use two of each gear.

Parameters:

Plate: .50 thick, a distance of at least .50 beyond the other edge of the gears to the edge of the plate.

Shafts: Diameters that match the gear's bore diameter; minimum offset between the plate and the gear is .50 or greater.

Gear 1:

    Diametral Pitch = **10**

    Number of Teeth = **24**

    Pressure Angle = **14.5**

    Face Width = **.375**

    Hub Style = **One Side**

    Hub Diameter = **1.00**

    Overall Length = **.875**

    Nominal Shaft Diameter = **7/16**

    Keyway = **None**

A. Create another spur gear based on the following specifications:

Gear 2:

    Diametral Pitch = **10**

    Number of Teeth = **96**

    Pressure Angle = **14.5**

    Face Width = **.375**

    Hub Style = **One Side**

    Hub Diameter = **1.00**

    Overall Length = **.875**

    Nominal Shaft Diameter = **7/16**

    Keyway = **None**

B. Add #6-32 threaded holes to each gear hub .19 from the top hub surface.

C. Assemble the gears onto the shafts so that Gear 1 and Gear 2 are offset .50 from the support plate, and Gear 3 and Gear 4 are parallel to the ends of the shafts.

D. Insert a #6-32 Slotted Set Screw with an Oval Point into each hole.

E. Create an exploded assembly drawing.

F. Create a bill of materials.

G. Animate the assembly.

Project 10-13: Inches—Design Problem

Based on Figure P10-4 define a support plate and shafts that support the following gears. Use two of each gear.

    Parameters:

        Plate: .50 thick, a distance of at least .50 beyond the other edge of the gears to the edge of the plate.

Shafts: Diameters that match the gear's bore diameter: minimum offset between the plate and the gear is .50 or greater.

Gear 1:

Diametral Pitch = **6**

Number of Teeth = **22**

Pressure Angle = **14.5**

Face Width = **.500**

Hub Style = **One Side**

Hub Diameter = **1.50**

Overall Length = **1.25**

Nominal Shaft Diameter = **.75**

Keyway = **None**

Gear 2:

Diametral Pitch = **6**

Number of Teeth = **77**

Pressure Angle = **14.5**

Face Width = **.50**

Hub Style = **One Side**

Hub Diameter = **1.50**

Overall Length = **1.25**

Nominal Shaft Diameter = **.75**

Keyway = **None**

A. Add 1/4-20 UNC threaded holes to each gear hub 0.25 from the top hub surface.

B. Assemble the gears onto the shafts so that Gear 1 and Gear 2 are offset .50 from the support plate, and Gear 3 and Gear 4 are parallel to the ends of the shafts.

C. Insert a 1/4-20 UNC Slotted Set Screw with an Oval Point into each hole.

D. Create an exploded assembly drawing.

E. Create a bill of materials.

F. Animate the assembly.

Project 10-14: Millimeters—Design Problem

Based on Figure P10-4 define a support plate and shafts that support the following gears. Use two of each gear.

Parameters:

Plate: 20 thick, a distance of at least 25 beyond the other edge of the gears to the edge of the plate.

Shafts: Diameters that match the gear's bore diameter; minimum offset between the plate and the gear is 20 or greater.

Gear 1:

Module = **2.5**

Number of Teeth = **20**

Pressure Angle = **14.5**

Face Width = **16**

Hub Style = **One Side**

Hub Diameter = **26**

Overall Length = **30**

Nominal Shaft Diameter = **20**

Keyway = **None**

Gear 2:

Module = **2.5**

Number of Teeth = **50**

Pressure Angle = **14.5**

Face Width = **16**

Hub Style = **One Side**

Hub Diameter = **30**

Overall Length = **30**

Nominal Shaft Diameter = **20**

Keyway = **None**

A. Add M4 threaded holes to each gear hub 12 from the top hub surface.

B. Assemble the gears onto the shafts so that Gear 1 and Gear 2 are offset 10 from the support plate, and Gear 3 and Gear 4 are parallel to the ends of the shafts.

C. Insert an M4 Slotted Set Screw with an Oval Point into each hole.

D. Create an exploded assembly drawing.

E. Create a bill of materials.

F. Animate the assembly.

Project 10-15: Inches

See Figure P10-5.

A. Draw four Ø.375 × 3.00 shafts.

B. Draw the support plate shown in Figure P10-5.

C. Access the **Design Library** and create three Gear 1s and three Gear 2s.

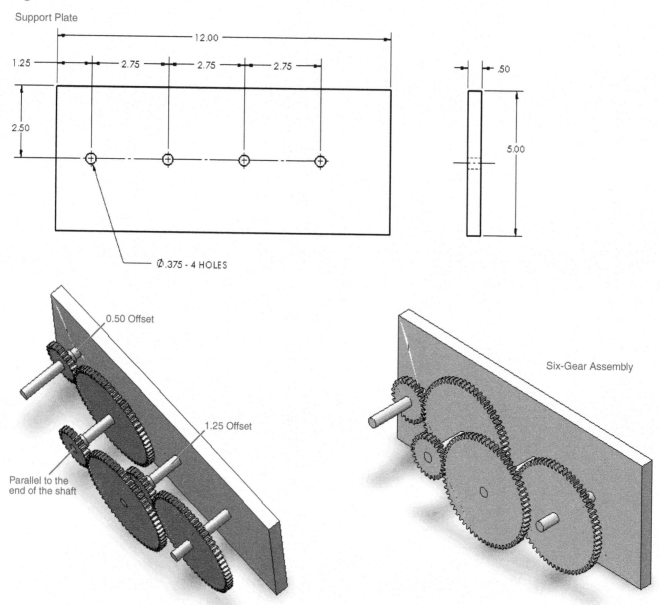

Support Plate

The gears are defined as follows:

Gear 1:

> Diametral Pitch = **16**
>
> Number of Teeth = **24**
>
> Pressure Angle = **14.5**
>
> Face Width = **.25**
>
> Hub Style = **One Side**
>
> Hub Diameter = **.50**
>
> Overall Length = **.50**
>
> Nominal Shaft Diameter = **3/8**
>
> Keyway = **None**

Gear 2:

> Diametral Pitch = **16**
>
> Number of Teeth = **64**
>
> Pressure Angle = **14.5**
>
> Face Width = **.25**
>
> Hub Style = **One Side**
>
> Hub Diameter = **.50**
>
> Overall Length = **.50**
>
> Nominal Shaft Diameter = **3/8**
>
> Keyway = **None**

D. Add #6-32 threaded holes to each gear hub 0.19 from the top hub surface.

E. Assemble the gears onto the shafts so that the offset between the support plate and the gears is as defined in Figure P10-5.

F. Insert a #6-32 Slotted Set Screw with an Oval Point into each hole.

G. Create an exploded assembly drawing.

H. Create a bill of materials.

I. Animate the assembly.

Project 10-16: Inches—Design Problem

Based on Figure P10-5 define a support plate and shafts that support the following gears. Use two of each gear.

> Parameters:
>
> > Plate: .50 thick, a distance of at least .50 beyond the other edge of the gears to the edge of the plate.
> >
> > Shafts: Diameters that match the gear's bore diameter; minimum offset between the plate and the gear is .50 or greater.
>
> Gear 1:
>
> > Diametral Pitch = **6**
> >
> > Number of Teeth = **22**
> >
> > Pressure Angle = **14.5**
> >
> > Face Width = **.500**
> >
> > Hub Style = **One Side**
> >
> > Hub Diameter = **1.50**
> >
> > Overall Length = **1.25**
> >
> > Nominal Shaft Diameter = **.75**
> >
> > Keyway = **None**

Gear 2:

Diametral Pitch = **6**

Number of Teeth = **77**

Pressure Angle = **14.5**

Face Width = **.50**

Hub Style = **One Side**

Hub Diameter = **1.50**

Overall Length = **1.25**

Nominal Shaft Diameter = **.75**

Keyway = **None**

A. Add 1/4-20 UNC threaded holes to each gear hub .25 from the top hub surface.

B. Assemble the gears onto the shafts so that Gear 1 and Gear 2 are offset .50 from the support plate, and Gear 3 and Gear 4 are parallel to the ends of the shafts.

C. Insert a 1/4-20 UNC Slotted Set Screw with an Oval Point into each hole.

D. Create an exploded assembly drawing.

E. Create a bill of materials.

F. Animate the assembly.

Project 10-17: Millimeters—Design Problem

Based on Figure P10-5 define a support plate and shafts that support the following gears. Use two of each gear.

Parameters:

Plate: 20 thick, a distance of at least 25 beyond the other edge of the gears to the edge of the plate.

Shafts: Diameters that match the gear's bore diameter; minimum offset between the plate and the gear is 20 or greater.

Gear 1:

Module = **2.5**

Number of Teeth = **20**

Pressure Angle = **14.5**

Face Width = **16**

Hub Style = **One Side**

Hub Diameter = **26**

Overall Length = **30**

Nominal Shaft Diameter = **20**

Keyway = **None**

Gear 2:

    Module = **2.5**

    Number of Teeth = **50**

    Pressure Angle = **14.5**

    Face Width = **16**

    Hub Style = **One Side**

    Hub Diameter = **30**

    Overall Length = **30**

    Nominal Shaft Diameter = **20**

    Keyway = **None**

A. Add M4 threaded holes to each gear hub 12 from the top hub surface.

B. Assemble the gears onto the shafts so that Gear 1 and Gear 2 are offset 10 from the support plate, and Gear 3 and Gear 4 are parallel to the ends of the shafts.

C. Insert an M4 Slotted Set Screw with an Oval Point into each hole.

D. Create an exploded assembly drawing.

E. Create a bill of materials.

F. Animate the assembly.

Project 10-18: Inches—Design Problem

Redraw the gear assembly shown in Figure P10-6. Create the following:

A. An assembly drawing

B. An exploded isometric drawing

C. A BOM

D. Dimensioned drawings of each part

Parts from the **Toolbox** do not need drawings but should be listed on the BOM.

Parts List				
ITEM	PART NUMBER	DESCRIPTION	MATERIAL	QTY
1	ENG-453-A	GEAR, HOUSING	CAST IRON	1
2	BU-1123	BUSHING Ø0.75	Delrin, Black	1
3	BU-1126	BUSHING Ø0.625	Delrin, Black	1
4	ASSEMBLY-6	GEAR ASSEMBLY	STEEL	1
5	AM-314	SHAFT, GEAR Ø.625	STEEL	1
6	AM-315	SHAFT, GEAR Ø.0.500	STEEL	1
7	ENG -566-B	COVER, GEAR	CAST IRON	1
8	ANSI B18.6.2 - 1/4-20 UNC - 0.75	Slotted Round Head Cap Screw	Steel, Mild	12

SECTION A-A
SCALE 3 / 4

Project 10-19: Millimeters—Design Problem

Redraw the gear assembly shown in Figure P10-7. Create the following:

- A. An assembly drawing
- B. An exploded isometric drawing
- C. A BOM
- D. Dimensioned drawings of each part

Parts from the **Toolbox** do not need drawings but should be listed on the BOM.

Figure P10-7

Figure P10-7
(*Continued*)

Parts List				
ITEM	PART NUMBER	DESCRIPTION	MATERIAL	QTY
1	ENG-311-1	4-GEAR HOUSING	CAST IRON	1
2	BS 5989: Part 1 - 0 10 - 20x32x8	Thrust Thrust Ball Bearing	Steel, Mild	4
3	SH-4002	SHAFT, NEUTRAL	STEEL	1
4	SH-4003	SHAFT, OUTPUT	STEEL	1
5	SH-4004A	SHAFT, INPUT	STEEL	1
6	4-GEAR-ASSEMBLY		STEEL	2
7	CSN 02 1181 - M6 x 16	Slotted Headless Set Screw - Flat Point	Steel, Mild	2
8	ENG-312-1	GASKET	Brass, Soft Yellow	1
9		COVER		1
10	CNS 4355 - M 6 x 35	Slotted Cheese Head Screw	Steel, Mild	14
11	CSN 02 7421 - M10 x 1 coned short	Lubricating Nipple, coned Type A	Steel, Mild	1

SECTION A-A
SCALE 1 / 2

SECTION A-A
SCALE 1 / 2

Figure P10-7
(*Continued*)

NOTE: HOLE PATTERN IS THE SAME FOR THE
GASKET, GEAR HOUSING, AND GEAR COVER.

NOTE: OBJECT IS SYMMETRICAL ABOUT
THE HORIZONTAL CENTERLINE.

220.00

74.00

74.00

R110.00

R100.00

R90.00

30.0°

45.0°

THICKNESS = 3

Ø10.00 - 14 HOLES

Ø60.00

Ø30.03
  30.01

20.00

M6x1 - 6H

M6x1 - 6H

Ø50.00

Ø25.03
  25.01

20.00

11 chaptereleven

CSWA Preparation

CHAPTER OBJECTIVES

- Prepare for the CSWA exam
- Answer types of questions likely to appear on the CSWA exam
- Practice working under time pressure

11-1 Introduction

As an undergraduate, James asked his math professor how to prepare for an upcoming exam. His response was, "Do lots and lots of problems." With that in mind, this section contains lots and lots of short problems to help you prepare for the CSWA exam.

This chapter contains a series of problems in which you will practice drawing shapes and time how long it takes you to create each shape. For example, you should spend less than 3 minutes to draw the cube in Problem 11-1. The goal is to get used to working with a time limit. Answers to multiple-choice and matching questions are provided at the end of the chapter.

11-2 Working with Cubes

Problem 11-1

Figure 11-1
MILLIMETERS

100mm x 100mm x 100mm cube

1 Draw a cube that measures $100 \times 100 \times 100$ millimeters, as shown in Figure 11-1, as a 3D model.

2 Locate and display the origin.

3 Define the material as **AISI 1020 Steel**.

4 How long did it take to draw this cube? _____

5 To determine the object's volume, after a shape has been completely drawn, click the **Evaluate** tab (see Figure 11-2).

Figure 11-2

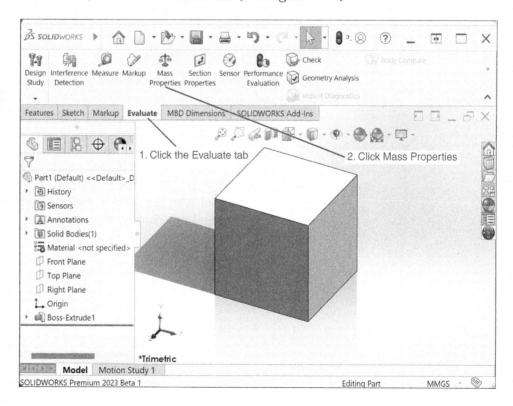

6 Click the **Mass Properties** tool.

7 Read the value listed next to **Volume** (see Figure 11-3).

8 Verify the volume by using hand calculations.

Figure 11-3

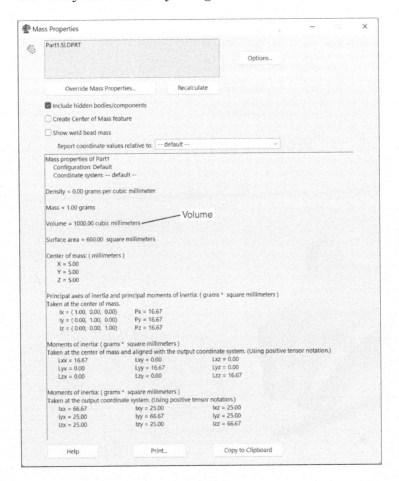

11-3 Drawing Profiles

In the following problems, you will draw a variety of *profiles*—that is, objects of uniform thickness.

Problem 11-2

Figure 11-4
MILLIMETERS

The shape is based on a right triangle with one leg 100mm long and an angle 37°.

R12   R12

40   37°   120°   120°   32   16

34

R12   R12

10

The cutout on the vertical edge is created by circumscribing a hexagon about a ⌀24mm with the centerpoint on the vertical line edge.

1 Draw the object shown in Figure 11-4 as a 3D model.

2 Define the material as **Alloy Steel**.

3 How long did it take to draw this object? _____

4 What is the object's volume, in cubic millimeters?

    A. 26,288.28

    B. 27,959.12

    C. 18,566.75

    D. 22,567.00

Problem 11-3

Figure 11-5
MILLIMETERS

1 Draw the object shown in Figure 11-5 as a 3D model.

2 Define the material as **Titanium Alloy, Commercially Pure Grade 2 textured (SS)**.

3 How long did it take to draw this object? _____

4 What is the object's volume, in cubic millimeters?

    A. 35,978.00

    B. 42,467.23

    C. 38,978.49

    D. 36,837.25

Problem 11-4

Figure 11-6
MILLIMETERS

1. Draw the object shown in Figure 11-6 as a 3D model. The circular cuts at the top of the object have a diameter of 40mm.

2. Define the material as **AISI 1020 Steel**.

3. How long did it take to draw this object? _____

4. What is the object's volume, in cubic millimeters?

    A. 75,203.69

    B. 71,663.12

    C. 75,324.89

    D. 73,779.06

Problem 11-5

Figure 11-7
INCHES

Figure 11-7
(*Continued*)

NOTE: ALL FILLETS = .19R

Dimensions for the cutout

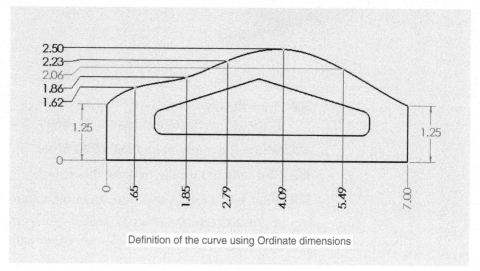

Definition of the curve using Ordinate dimensions

1 Draw the object shown in Figure 11-7 as a 3D model.

2 Define the material as **Copper**.

3 How long did it take to draw this object? _____

4 What is the object's volume, in cubic inches?

    A. 4.75

    B. 4.25

    C. 3.75

    D. 5.00

Problem 11-6

Figure 11-8
MILLIMETERS

INTERSECTION POINT IS
130MM FROM THE
CENTERPOINT

OBJECT IS SYMMETRICAL ABOUT
THE VERTICAL CENTERLINE

1 Draw the object shown in Figure 11-8 as a 3D model.

2 Define the material as **AISI 304**.

3 How long did it take to draw this object? _____

4 What is the object's volume, in cubic millimeters?

    A. 115,467.35

    B. 12,896.39

    C. 31,728.45

    D. 29,962.16

11-4   Drawing Small 3D Objects

For each of the following problems, try to draw the shape in one sitting
(that is, start the part and work straight through until it's finished). Time
yourself. It's a good idea to practice without stopping because when you
take the CSWA exam, you will have no breaks.

Problem 11-7

Figure 11-9
MILLIMETERS

1. Draw the object shown in Figure 11-9 as a 3D model.

2. Define the material as **AISI 1020**.

3. How long did it take to draw this object? _____

4. What is the object's volume, in cubic millimeters?
   - A. 154,946.33
   - B. 638,378.97
   - C. 694,556.01
   - D. 602,785.58

Problem 11-8

Figure 11-10
MILLIMETERS

1 Draw the object shown in Figure 11-10 as a 3D model.

2 Define the material as **AISI 4130 Steel**, normalized at **870C**.

3 How long did it take to draw this object? _____

4 What is the object's volume, in cubic millimeters?

    A. 1,273,282.09

    B. 1,054,492.35

    C. 990,731.79

    D. 1,805,412.78

Problem 11-9

Figure 11-11
MILLIMETERS

1 Draw the object shown in Figure 11-11 as a 3D model.

2 Define the material as **Cast Alloy Steel**.

3 How long did it take to draw this object? _____

4 What is the object's volume, in cubic millimeters?

    A. 643,535.95

    B. 58,999.10

    C. 61,598.54

    D. 62,100.46

Problem 11-10

Figure 11-12
MILLIMETERS

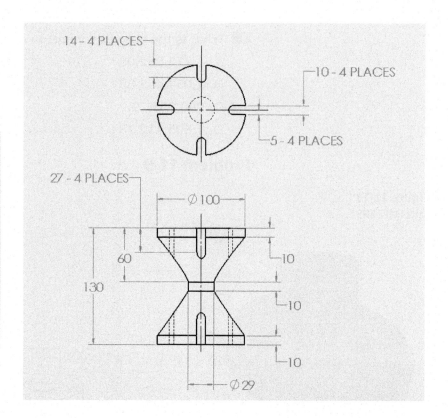

1. Draw the object shown in Figure 11-12 as a 3D model.

2. Define the material as **2024 Alloy**.

3. How long did it take to draw this object? _____

4. What is the object's volume, in cubic millimeters?

   A. 473,108.26

   B. 647,598.46

   C. 477,942.06

   D. 483,060.87

Problem 11-11

Figure 11-13
MILLIMETERS

1 Draw the object shown in Figure 11-13 as a 3D model.

2 Define the material as **Copper**.

3 How long did it take to draw this object? _____

4 What is the object's volume, in cubic millimeters?

    A. 61,766.40

    B. 647,598.46

    C. 60,713.22

    D. 59,896.01

Problem 11-12

Figure 11-14
MILLIMETERS

1 Draw the object shown in Figure 11-14 as a 3D model.

2 Define the material as **2024-T3 AL**.

3 How long did it take to draw this object? _____

4 What is the object's volume, in cubic millimeters?

    A. 999,375.24

    B. 1,744,396.50

    C. 212,050.65

    D. 1,621,578.00

11-5 Drawing Larger Objects

This section includes larger and more complex shapes.

Problem 11-13

Figure 11-15
MILLIMETERS

1 Draw the object shown in Figure 11-15 as a 3D model. The diameter of the circular cutout concentric with the Ø16 hole is Ø26mm.

2 Define the material as **Nickel**.

3 How long did it take to draw this object? _____

4 What is the object's volume, in cubic millimeters?

    A. 52,756.24

    B. 57,037.68

    C. 59,327.89

    D. 56,819.59

Problem 11-14

Figure 11-16
INCHES

1 Draw the object shown in Figure 11-16 as a 3D model.

2 Define the material as **2018 Alloy - AL**.

3 How long did it take to draw this object? _____

4 What is the object's volume, in cubic inches?

    A. 21.40

    B. 22.10

    C. 19.78

    D. 20.56

Problem 11-15

Figure 11-17
INCHES

1 Draw the object shown in Figure 11-17 as a 3D model. The center-points of the six R1.75in. arcs are located 3.88in. from the object's centerpoint.

2 Define the material as **Cast Carbon Steel**.

3 How long did it take to draw this object? _____

4 What is the object's volume, in cubic inches?

    A. 45.72

    B. 45.93

    C. 47.28

    D. 46.09

Problem 11-16

Figure 11-18
MILLIMETERS

NOTE: THE GROOVE IS CREATED FROM A 4 × 4mm SQUARE. HELIX PITCH + 20

1 Draw the object shown in Figure 11-18 as a 3D model.

2 Define the material as **Plain Carbon Steel**.

3 How long did it take to draw this object? _____

4 What is the object's volume, in cubic millimeters?

    A. 344,983.69

    B. 365,204.55

    C. 228,134.02

    D. 406,739.94

Problem 11-17

Figure 11-19
MILLIMETERS

1 Draw the object shown in Figure 11-19 as a 3D model.

2 Define the material as **Galvanized Steel**.

3 How long did it take to draw this object? _____

4 What is the object's volume, in cubic millimeters?

    A. 515,738.36

    B. 569,328.55

    C. 525,971.78

    D. 600,584.56

Problem 11-18

Figure 11-20
MILLIMETERS

1. Draw the object shown in Figure 11-20 as a 3D model.

2. Define the material as **AISI Type A2 Tool Steel**.

3. How long did it take to draw this object? _____

4. What is the object's volume, in cubic millimeters?

   A. 500,683.20

   B. 510,446.10

   C. 509,991.15

   D. 505,498.05

Problem 11-19

Figure 11-21
MILLIMETERS

1 Draw the object shown in Figure 11-21 as a 3D model.

2 Define the material as **6063-T6 AL**.

3 How long did it take to draw this object? _____

4 What is the object's volume, in cubic millimeters?

    A. 255,395.99

    B. 250,629.75

    C. 244,668.36

    D. 251,623.95

Problem 11-20

Figure 11-22
MILLIMETERS

1 Draw the object shown in Figure 11-22 as a 3D model. The overall height is 50mm.

2 Define the material as **Alloy Steel**.

3 How long did it take to draw this object? _____

4 What is the object's volume, in cubic millimeters?

    A. 88,835.33

    B. 87,934.28

    C. 89,430.75

    D. 90,385.88

11-6 Drawing Auxiliary Views

Auxiliary views are used to present true views of slanted surfaces. A slanted surface viewed in a normal orthographic view will appear foreshortened. An auxiliary view is taken at 90° to the surface and therefore shows a true view of the surface.

Problem 11-21

Figure 11-23
MILLIMETERS

1 Draw the object shown in Figure 11-23 as a 3D model and a set of dimensioned orthograph views.

2 Define the material as **Cast Carbon Steel**.

3 How long did it take to draw this object? _____

4 What is the object's volume, in cubic millimeters?

A. 147,385.58   C. 143,825.64

B. 150,553.73   D. 148,341.06

Problem 11-22

Figure 11-24
MILLIMETERS

1. Draw the object shown in Figure 11-24 as a 3D model and a set of dimensioned orthograph views.

2. Define the material as **Carbon Steel**.

3. How long did it take to draw this object? _____

4. What is the object's volume, in cubic millimeters?

    A. 92,674.96

    B. 93,319.08

    C. 89,253.60

    D. 93,548.66

Problem 11-23

This project uses three types of drawings: two orthographic views, an auxiliary view, and a detail view. Combined, these views completely define the object.

Figure 11-25
INCHES

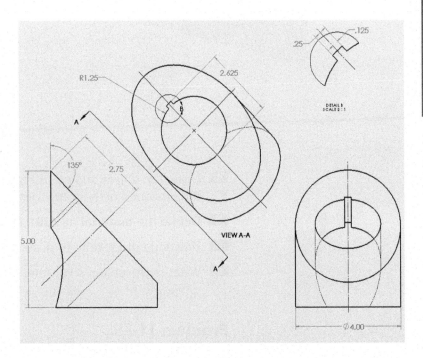

VIEW A-A

DETAIL B
SCALE 2 : 1

1 Draw the object shown in Figure 11-25 as a 3D model and a set of dimensioned orthograph views.

2 Define the material as **AISI 1020**.

3 How long did it take to draw this object? _____

4 What is the object's volume, in cubic inches?

    A. 26.05

    B. 24.71

    C. 25.07

    D. 24.96

11-7 Drawing Break Views

Break views are used to shorten long shapes so that they fit within a drawing's sheet parameters. The shapes must be of constant shape throughout their length.

Problem 11-24

Figure 11-26
INCHES

1 Draw the object shown in Figure 11-26 as a 3D model and a set of dimensioned orthograph views.

2 Define the material as **AISI 1020 Steel, Cold Rolled**.

3 How long did it take to draw this object? _____

4 What is the object's volume, in cubic inches?

    A. 35.63   B. 34.75   C. 33.85   D. 36.84

Problem 11-25

Figure 11-27
MILLIMETERS

1 Draw the object shown in Figure 11-27 as a 3D model and a set of dimensioned orthograph views.

2 Define the material as **Carbon Steel**.

3 How long did it take to draw this object? _____

4 What is the object's volume, in cubic millimeters?

    A. 62,056.35   B. 63,446.86   C. 62,831.85   D. 61,496.30

11-8 Drawing Section Views

A section view allows you to look inside an object. Often there are internal shapes in an object that are not clearly visible from the outside. Section views allow you to expose these shapes with more clarity than using just hidden lines.

Problem 11-26

Figure 11-28
MILLIMETERS

1. Draw the object shown in Figure 11-28 as a 3D model and a set of dimensioned orthograph views.

2. Define the material as **Carbon Steel**.

3. How long did it take to draw this object? _____

4. What is the object's volume, in cubic millimeters?

    A. 4,841,979.68   C. 4,293,964.08

    B. 3,495,117.34   D. 4,067,229.47

Problem 11-27

Figure 11-29
MILLIMETERS

⌀8 ⫰ 12 - 3 HOLES
FLAT BOTTOM

⌀30   30 - 3 HOLES

16

64°   100

⌀80

SECTION A-A

[1] Draw the object shown in Figure 11-29 as a 3D model and a set of dimensioned orthograph views. The 16mm deep notch has a width of 8mm.

[2] Define the material as **Carbon Steel**.

[3] How long did it take to draw this object? _____

[4] What is the object's volume, in cubic millimeters?

A. 310,663.39	C. 387,613.88
B. 335,812.94	D. 299,846.95

Problem 11-28

Cutting plane lines need not always be straight. Figure 11-30 shows an aligned cutting plane line. The resulting view is created by swinging the angle part of the line as if it were bent into the vertical position.

Figure 11-30
MILLIMETERS

SECTION A-A

1 Draw the object shown in Figure 11-30 as a 3D model and a set of dimensioned orthograph views.

2 Define the material as **AISI 1020 Steel**.

3 How long did it take to draw this object? _____

4 What is the object's volume, in cubic millimeters?

A. 46,115.01   C. 46,889.24

B. 47,335.75   D. 45,998.83

11-9   Drawing Detail Views

Detail views are used to enlarge areas of a drawing that contain small features that would be difficult to define in the drawing's initial scale.

Problem 11-29

Figure 11-31
MILLIMETERS

1. Draw the object shown in Figure 11-31 as a 3D model and a set of dimensioned orthograph views. The small holes are Ø3mm.

2. Define the material as **Brass**.

3. How long did it take to draw this object? _____

4. What is the object's volume, in cubic millimeters?

   A. 127,886.37

   B. 128,975.67

   C. 128,680.09

   D. 126,834.75

Problem 11-30

Figure 11-32
INCHES

DETAIL A
SCALE 4 : 1

1 Draw the object shown in Figure 11-32 as a 3D model and a set of dimensioned orthograph views.

2 Define the material as **Titanium Ti-5AI-2.5SM**.

3 How long did it take to draw this object? _____

4 What is the object's volume, in cubic inches?

    A. 10.47

    B. 10.05

    C. 10. 98

    D. 10.57

11-10   Drawing Lines and Views

This section tests the knowledge of the different types of lines that are used to create orthographic views.

Problem 11-31

Figure 11-33
MILLIMETERS

Technical drawings use many different types of lines. Identify the types of lines referenced in Figure 11-33 by entering the letter corresponding to the correct line type in each blank.

What type of line?	Type of lines
1 _____	a. Continuous
2 _____	b. Section
3 _____	c. Hidden
4 _____	d. Cutting Plane
5 _____	e. Extension
	f. Center
	g. Dimension
	h. Leader

Problem 11-32

Figure 11-34
MILLIMETERS

Identify the types of lines referenced and types of views in Figure 11-34 by entering the letter corresponding to the correct line type in each blank.

What type of line?	**Type of lines**
1 _____	a. Continuous
2 _____	b. Section
3 _____	c. Hidden
4 _____	d. Cutting Plane
5 _____	e. Extension
6 _____	f. Center
	g. Dimension
	h. Leader

What type of view?	**Type of views**
1 _____	i. Orthographic
2 _____	j. Auxiliary
3 _____	k. Section
4 _____	l. Detail
	m. Break

Problem 11-33

Figure 11-35
MILLIMETERS

Dimension Style 1.

Dimension Style 2.

Dimension Style 3.

Dimension Style 4.

TAG	X LOC	Y LOC	SIZE
A1	16	20	Ø10 THRU
A2	16	40	Ø10 THRU
A3	84	20	Ø10 THRU
A4	84	40	Ø10 THRU
B1	50	20	Ø16 THRU
B2	50	40	Ø16 THRU

There are different ways to dimension an object that has multiple holes. Identify the different dimension styles for the views shown in Figure 11-35 by entering the letter corresponding to the correct style type in each blank.

Style number	Name of style
1 _____	a. Ordinate
2 _____	b. Chain
3 _____	c. Hole Table
4 _____	d. Baseline

11-11 Creating Assemblies

Figures 11-36 and 11-37 are the parts and finished assembly in different configurations. In the following problems, you are asked to create and manipulate the assembly as required.

Problem 11-34

Figure 11-36
MILLIMETERS

BASE — LINK ASSEMBLY

LINK — LINK ASSEMBLY

PIN — LINK ASSEMBLY

Figure 11-36
(*Continued*)

Given the shown angular values between links, what is the value of A within one decimal place?

1 Draw the components shown in Figure 11-36 and create the link assembly.

2 Position the links as indicated by the angular dimensions.

3 What is the horizontal distance A, in millimeters?

    A. 300.0

    B. 294.7

    C. 281.0

    D. 276.4

Problem 11-35

Figure 11-37
MILLIMETERS

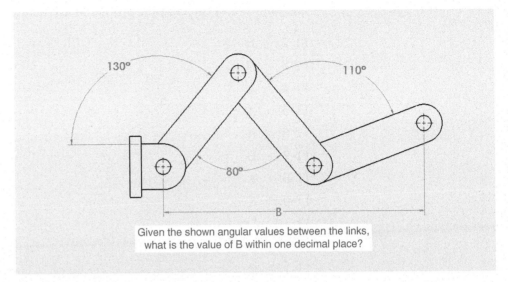

Given the shown angular values between the links, what is the value of B within one decimal place?

1 Draw the components shown in Figure 11-36 and create the link assembly shown in Figure 11-37.

2 Position the links as indicated by the angular dimensions.

3 What is the horizontal distance B, in millimeters?

    A. 353.6

    B. 356.0

    C. 354.8

    D. 357.8

NOTE

In addition to the examples presented here, students may search YouTube for more tutorials on SolidWorks.

11-12 Problem Answers

The answers to the chapter problems are below.

11-2.	B
11-3.	B
11-4.	A
11-5.	A
11-6.	A
11-7.	B
11-8.	A
11-9.	A
11-10.	D
11-11.	B
11-12.	C
11-13.	D
11-14.	B
11-15.	A
11-16.	A
11-17.	C
11-18.	C
11-19.	D
11-20.	A
11-21.	D
11-22.	D
11-23.	C
11-24.	A
11-25.	C
11-26.	A
11-27.	B
11-28.	C
11-29.	C
11-30.	A
11-31.	1. g, 2. e, 3. f, 4. h, 5. c
11-32.	Type of line: 1. d, 2. e, 3. g, 4. b, 5. h, 6. c; Type of view: 1. k, 2. l, 3. i, 4. i
11-33.	1. b, 2. d, 3. a, 4. c
11-34.	C
11-35.	B

appendix

Figure A-1

Wire and Sheet Metal Gauges

Gauge	Thickness	Gauge	Thickness
000 000	0.5800	18	0.0403
00 000	0.5165	19	0.0359
0 000	0.4600	20	0.0320
000	0.4096	21	0.0285
00	0.3648	22	0.0253
0	0.3249	23	0.0226
1	0.2893	24	0.0201
2	0.2576	25	0.0179
3	0.2294	26	0.0159
4	0.2043	27	0.0142
5	0.1819	28	0.0126
6	0.1620	29	0.0113
7	0.1443	30	0.0100
8	0.1285	31	0.0089
9	0.1144	32	0.0080
10	0.1019	33	0.0071
11	0.0907	34	0.0063
12	0.0808	35	0.0056
13	0.0720	36	0.0050
14	0.0641	37	0.0045
15	0.0571	38	0.0040
16	0.0508	39	0.0035
17	0.0453	40	0.0031

American Standard Clearance Locational Fits

Nominal Size Range Inches (Over — To)	Class LC1 Limits of Clearance	Standard Limits Hole H6	Standard Limits Shaft h5	Class LC2 Limits of Clearance	Standard Limits Hole H7	Standard Limits Shaft h6	Class LC3 Limits of Clearance	Standard Limits Hole H8	Standard Limits Shaft h7	Class LC4 Limits of Clearance	Standard Limits Hole H10	Standard Limits Shaft h9
0 — 0.12	0 / 0.45	+0.25 / 0	0 / -0.2	0 / 0.65	+0.4 / 0	0 / -0.25	0 / 1	+0.6 / 0	0 / -0.4	0 / 2.6	+1.6 / 0	0 / -1.0
0.12 — 0.24	0 / 0.5	+0.3 / 0	0 / -0.2	0 / 0.8	+0.5 / 0	0 / -0.3	0 / 1.2	+0.7 / 0	0 / -0.5	0 / 3.0	+1.8 / 0	0 / -1.2
0.24 — 0.40	0 / 0.65	+0.4 / 0	0 / -0.25	0 / 1.0	+0.6 / 0	0 / -0.4	0 / 1.5	+0.9 / 0	0 / -0.6	0 / 3.6	+2.2 / 0	0 / -1.4
0.40 — 0.71	0 / 0.7	+0.4 / 0	0 / -0.3	0 / 1.1	+0.7 / 0	0 / -0.4	0 / 1.7	+1.0 / 0	0 / -0.7	0 / 4.4	+2.8 / 0	0 / -1.6
0.71 — 1.19	0 / 0.9	+0.5 / 0	0 / -0.4	0 / 1.3	+0.8 / 0	0 / -0.5	0 / 2	+1.2 / 0	0 / -0.8	0 / 5.5	+3.5 / 0	0 / -2.0
1.19 — 1.97	0 / 1.0	+0.6 / 0	0 / -0.4	0 / 1.6	+1.0 / 0	0 / -0.6	0 / 2.6	+1.6 / 0	0 / -1.0	0 / 6.5	+4.0 / 0	0 / -2.5

Nominal Size Range Inches (Over — To)	Class LC5 Limits of Clearance	Standard Limits Hole H7	Standard Limits Shaft g6	Class LC6 Limits of Clearance	Standard Limits Hole H9	Standard Limits Shaft f8	Class LC7 Limits of Clearance	Standard Limits Hole H10	Standard Limits Shaft e9	Class LC8 Limits of Clearance	Standard Limits Hole H10	Standard Limits Shaft d9
0 — 0.12	0.1 / 0.75	+0..4 / 0	-0.1 / -0.35	0.3 / 1.9	+1.0 / 0	-0.3 / -0.9	0.6 / 3.2	+1.6 / 0	-0.6 / -1.6	1.0 / 3.6	+1.6 / 0	-1.0 / -2.0
0.12 — 0.24	0.15 / 0.95	+0.5 / 0	-0.15 / -0.45	0.4 / 2.3	+1.2 / 0	-0.4 / -1.1	0.8 / 3.8	+1.8 / 0	-0.8 / -2.0	1.2 / 4.2	+1.8 / 0	-1.2 / -2.4
0.24 — 0.40	0.2 / 1.2	+0.6 / 0	-0.2 / -0.6	0.5 / 2.8	+1.4 / 0	-0.5 / -1.4	1.0 / 4.6	+2.2 / 0	-1.0 / -2.4	1.6 / 5.2	+2.2 / 0	-1.6 / -3.0
0.40 — 0.71	0.25 / 1.35	+0.7 / 0	-0.25 / -0.65	0.6 / 3.2	+1.6 / 0	-0.6 / -1.6	1.2 / 5.6	+2.8 / 0	-1.2 / -2.8	2.0 / 6.4	+2.8 / 0	-2.0 / -3.6
0.71 — 1.19	0.3 / 1.6	+0.8 / 0	-0.3 / -0.8	0.8 / 4.0	+2.0 / 0	-0.8 / -2.0	1.6 / 7.1	+3.5 / 0	-1.6 / -3.6	2.5 / 8.0	+3.5 / 0	-2.5 / -4.5
1.19 — 1.97	0.4 / 2.0	+1.0 / 0	-0.4 / -1.0	1.0 / 5.1	+2.5 / 0	-1.0 / -2.6	2.0 / 8.5	+4.0 / 0	-2.0 / -4.5	3.0 / 9.5	+4.0 / 0	-3.0 / -5.5

Figure A-3A

American Standard Running and Sliding Fits
(Hole Basis)

Nominal Size Range Inches Over To	Limits of Clearance	Class RC1 Standard Limits		Limits of Clearance	Class RC2 Standard Limits		Limits of Clearance	Class RC3 Standard Limits		Limits of Clearance	Class RC4 Standard Limits	
		Hole H5	Shaft g4		Hole H6	Shaft g5		Hole H7	Shaft f6		Hole H8	Shaft f7
0 - 0.12	0.1 0.45	+0.2 0	-0.1 -0.25	0.1 0.55	+0.25 0	-0.1 -0.3	0.3 0.95	+0.4 0	-0.3 -0.55	0.3 1.3	+0.6 0	-0.3 -0.7
0.12 - 0.24	0.15 0.5	+0.2 0	-0.15 -0.3	0.15 0.65	+0.3 0	-0.15 -0.35	0.4 1.12	+0.5 0	-0.4 -0.7	0.4 1.5	+0.7 0	-0.4 -0.0
0.24 - 0.40	0.2 0.6	+0.25 0	-0.2 -0.35	0.2 0.85	+0.4 0	-0.2 -0.45	0.5 1.5	+0.6 0	-0.5 -0.9	0.5 2.0	+0.9 0	-0.5 -1.1
0.40 - 0.71	0.25 0.75	+0.3 0	-0.25 -0.45	0.25 0.95	+0.4 0	-0.25 -0.55	0.6 1.7	+0.7 0	-0.6 -1.0	0.6 2.3	+1.0 0	-0.6 -1.3
0.71 - 1.19	0.3 0.95	+0.4 0	-0.3 -0.55	0.3 1.2	+0.5 0	-0.3 -0.7	0.8 2.1	+0.8 0	-0.8 -1.3	0.8 2.8	+1.2 0	-0.8 -1.6
1.19 - 1.97	0.4 1.1	+0.4 0	-0.4 -0.7	0.4 1.4	+0.6 0	-0.4 -0.8	1.0 2.6	+1.0 0	-1.0 -1.6	1.0 3.6	+1.6 0	-1.0 -2.0

Figure A-3B

Nominal Size Range Inches Over To	Limits of Clearance	Class RC5 Standard Limits		Limits of Clearance	Class RC6 Standard Limits		Limits of Clearance	Class RC7 Standard Limits		Limits of Clearance	Class RC8 Standard Limits	
		Hole H8	Shaft e7		Hole H9	Shaft e8		Hole H9	Shaft d8		Hole H10	Shaft c9
0 - 0.12	0.6 1.6	+0.6 0	-0.6 -1.0	0.6 2.2	+1.0 0	-0.6 -1.2	1.0 2.6	+1.0 0	-1.0 -1.6	2.5 5.1	+1.6 0	-2.5 -3.5
0.12 - 0.24	0.8 2.0	+0.7 0	-0.8 -1.3	0.8 2.7	+1.2 0	-0.8 -1.5	1.2 3.1	+1.2 0	-1.2 -1.9	2.8 5.8	+1.8 0	-2.8 -4.0
0.24 - 0.40	1.0 2.5	+0.9 0	-1.0 -1.6	1.0 3.3	+1.4 0	-1.0 -1.9	1.6 3.9	+1.4 0	-1.6 -2.5	3.0 6.6	+2.2 0	-3.0 -4.4
0.40 - 0.71	1.2 2.9	+1.0 0	-1.2 -1.9	1.2 3.8	+1.6 0	-1.2 -2.2	2.0 4.6	+1.6 0	-2.0 -3.0	3.5 7.9	+2.8 0	-3.5 -5.1
0.71 - 1.19	1.6 3.6	+1.2 0	-1.6 -2.4	1.6 4.8	+2.0 0	-1.6 -2.8	2.5 5.7	+2.0 0	-2.5 -3.7	4.5 10.0	+3.5 0	-4.5 -6.5
1.19 - 1.97	2.0 4.6	+1.6 0	-2.0 -3.0	2.0 6.1	+2.5 0	-2.0 -3.6	3.0 7.1	+2.5 0	-3.0 -4.6	5.0 11.5	+4.0 0	-5.0 -7.5

Figure A-4A

American Standard Transition Locational Fits

Nominal Size Range Inches (Over – To)	Class LT1 Fit	Class LT1 Hole H7	Class LT1 Shaft js6	Class LT2 Fit	Class LT2 Hole H8	Class LT2 Shaft js7	Class LT3 Fit	Class LT3 Hole H7	Class LT3 Shaft k6
0 – 0.12	−0.10 / +0.50	+0.4 / 0	+0.10 / −0.10	−0.2 / +0.8	+0.6 / 0	+0.2 / −0.2			
0.12 – 0.24	−0.15 / −0.65	+0.5 / 0	+0.15 / −0.15	−0.25 / +0.95	+0.7 / 0	+0.25 / −0.25			
0.24 – 0.40	−0.2 / +0.5	+0.6 / 0	+0.2 / −0.2	−0.3 / +1.2	+0.9 / 0	+0.3 / −0.3	−0.5 / +0.5	+0.6 / 0	+0.5 / +0.1
0.40 – 0.71	−0.2 / +0.9	+0.7 / 0	+0.2 / −0.2	−0.35 / +1.35	+1.0 / 0	+0.35 / −0.35	−0.5 / +0.6	+0.7 / 0	+0.5 / +0.1
0.71 – 1.19	−0.25 / +1.05	+0.8 / 0	+0.25 / −0.25	−0.4 / +1.6	+1.2 / 0	+0.4 / −0.4	−0.6 / +0.7	+0.8 / 0	+0.6 / +0.1
1.19 – 1.97	−0.3 / +1.3	+1.0 / 0	+0.3 / −0.3	−0.5 / +2.1	+1.6 / 0	+0.5 / −0.5	+0.7 / +0.1	+1.0 / 0	+0.7 / +0.1

Figure A-4B

Nominal Size Range Inches (Over – To)	Class LT4 Fit	Class LT4 Hole H8	Class LT4 Shaft k7	Class LT5 Fit	Class LT5 Hole H7	Class LT5 Shaft n6	Class LT6 Fit	Class LT6 Hole H7	Class LT6 Shaft n7
0 – 0.12				−0.5 / +0.15	+0.4 / 0	+0.5 / +0.25	−0.65 / +0.15	+0.4 / 0	+0.65 / +0.25
0.12 – 0.24				−0.6 / +0.2	+0.5 / 0	+0.6 / +0.3	−0.8 / +0.2	+0.5 / 0	+0.8 / +0.3
0.24 – 0.40	−0.7 / +0.8	+0.9 / 0	+0.7 / +0.1	−0.8 / +0.2	+0.6 / 0	+0.8 / +0.4	−1.0 / +0.2	+0.6 / 0	+1.0 / +0.4
0.40 – 0.71	−0.8 / +0.9	+1.0 / 0	+0.8 / +0.1	−0.9 / +0.2	+0.7 / 0	+0.9 / +0.5	−1.2 / +0.2	+0.7 / 0	+1.2 / +0.5
0.71 – 1.19	−0.9 / +1.1	+1.2 / 0	+0.9 / +0.1	−1.1 / +0.2	+0.8 / 0	+1.1 / +0.6	−1.4 / +0.2	+0.8 / 0	+1.4 / +0.6
1.19 – 1.97	−1.1 / +1.5	+1.6 / 0	+1.1 / +0.1	−1.3 / +0.3	+1.0 / 0	+1.3 / +0.7	−1.7 / +0.3	+1.0 / 0	+1.7 / +0.7

Figure A-5 — American Standard Interference Locational Fits

Nominal Size Range Inches Over — To	Limits of Interference	Class LN1 Standard Limits Hole H6	Shaft n5	Limits of Interference	Class LN2 Standard Limits Hole H7	Shaft p6	Limits of Interference	Class LN3 Standard Limits Hole H7	Shaft r6
0 — 0.12	0 / 0.45	+0.25 / 0	+0.45 / +0.25	0 / 0.65	+0.4 / 0	+0.63 / +0.4	0.1 / 0.75	+0.4 / 0	+0.75 / +0.5
0.12 — 0.24	0 / 0.5	+0.3 / 0	+0.5 / +0.3	0 / 0.8	+0.5 / 0	+0.8 / +0.5	0.1 / 0.9	+0.5 / 0	+0.9 / +0.6
0.24 — 0.40	0 / 0.65	+0.4 / 0	+0.65 / +0.4	0 / 1.0	+0.6 / 0	+1.0 / +0.6	0.2 / 1.2	+0.6 / 0	+1.2 / +0.8
0.40 — 0.71	0 / 0.8	+0.4 / 0	+0.8 / +0.4	0 / 1.1	+0.7 / 0	+1.1 / +0.7	0.3 / 1.4	+0.7 / 0	+1.4 / +1.0
0.71 — 1.19	0 / 1.0	+0.5 / 0	+1.0 / +0.5	0 / 1.3	+0.8 / 0	+1.3 / +0.8	0.4 / 1.7	+0.8 / 0	+1.7 / +1.2
1.19 — 1.97	0 / 1.1	+0.6 / 0	+1.1 / +0.6	0 / 1.6	+1.0 / 0	+1.6 / +1.0	0.4 / 2.0	+1.0 / 0	+2.0 / +1.4

Figure A-6 — American Standard Force and Shrink Fits

Nominal Size Range Inches Over — To	Limits of Interference	Class FN 1 Standard Limits Hole	Shaft	Limits of Interference	Class FN 2 Standard Limits Hole	Shaft	Limits of Interference	Class FN 3 Standard Limits Hole	Shaft	Limits of Interference	Class FN 4 Standard Limits Hole	Shaft
0 — 0.12	0.05 / 0.5	+0.25 / 0	+0.5 / +0.3	0.2 / 0.85	+0.4 / 0	+0.85 / +0.6				0.3 / 0.95	+0.4 / 0	+0.95 / +0.7
0.12 — 0.24	0.1 / 0.6	+0.3 / 0	+0.6 / +0.4	0.2 / 1.0	+0.5 / 0	+1.0 / +0.7				0.4 / 1.2	+0.5 / 0	+1.2 / +0.9
0.24 — 0.40	0.1 / 0.75	+0.4 / 0	+0.75 / +0.5	0.4 / 1.4	+0.6 / 0	+1.4 / +1.0				0.6 / 1.6	+0.6 / 0	+1.6 / +1.2
0.40 — 0.56	0.1 / 0.8	+0.4 / 0	+0.8 / +0.5	0.5 / 1.6	+0.7 / 0	+1.6 / +1.2				0.7 / 1.8	+0.7 / 0	+1.8 / +1.4
0.56 — 0.71	0.2 / 0.9	+0.4 / 0	+0.9 / +0.6	0.5 / 1.6	+0.7 / 0	+1.6 / +1.2				0.7 / 1.8	+0.7 / 0	+1.8 / +1.4
0.71 — 0.95	0.2 / 1.1	+0.5 / 0	+1.1 / +0.7	0.6 / 1.9	+0.8 / 0	+1.9 / +1.4				0.8 / 2.1	+0.8 / 0	+2.1 / +1.6
0.95 — 1.19	0.3 / 1.2	+0.5 / 0	+1.2 / +0.8	0.6 / 1.9	+0.8 / 0	+1.9 / +1.4	0.8 / 2.1	+0.8 / 0	+2.1 / +1.6	1.0 / 2.3	+0.8 / 0	+2.1 / +1.8
1.19 — 1.58	0.3 / 1.3	+0.6 / 0	+1.3 / +0.9	0.8 / 2.4	+1.0 / 0	+2.4 / +1.8	1.0 / 2.6	+1.0 / 0	+2.6 / +2.0	1.5 / 3.1	+1.0 / 0	+3.1 / +2.5
1.58 — 1.97	0.4 / 1.4	+0.6 / 0	+1.4 / +1.0	0.8 / 2.4	+1.0 / 0	+2.4 / +1.8	1.2 / 2.8	+1.0 / 0	+2.8 / +2.2	1.8 / 3.4	+1.0 / 0	+3.4 / +2.8

Figure A-7

Preferred Clearance Fits — Cylindrical Fits
(Hole Basis; ANSI B4.2)

Basic Size		Loose Running			Free Running			Close Running			Sliding			Locational Clear.		
		Hole H11	Shaft c11	Fit	Hole H9	Shaft d9	Fit	Hole H8	Shaft f7	Fit	Hole H7	Shaft g6	Fit	Hole H7	Shaft h6	Fit
4	Max	4.075	3.930	0.220	4.030	3.970	0.090	4.018	3.990	0.040	4.012	3.996	0.024	4.012	4.000	0.020
	Min	4.000	3.855	0.070	4.000	3.940	0.030	4.000	3.978	0.010	4.000	3.988	0.004	4.000	3.992	0.000
5	Max	5.075	4.930	0.220	5.030	4.970	0.090	5.018	4.990	0.040	5.012	4.996	0.024	5.012	5.000	0.020
	Min	5.000	4.855	0.070	5.000	4.940	0.030	5.000	4.978	0.010	5.000	4.988	0.004	5.000	4.992	0.000
6	Max	6.075	5.930	0.220	6.030	5.970	0.090	6.018	5.990	0.040	6.012	5.996	0.024	6.012	6.000	0.020
	Min	6.000	5.885	0.070	6.000	5.940	0.030	6.000	5.978	0.010	6.000	5.988	0.004	6.000	5.992	0.000
8	Max	8.090	7.920	0.260	8.036	7.960	0.112	8.022	7.987	0.050	8.015	7.995	0.029	8.015	8.000	0.024
	Min	8.000	7.830	0.080	8.000	7.924	0.040	8.000	7.972	0.013	8.000	7.986	0.005	8.000	7.991	0.000
10	Max	10.090	9.920	0.260	10.036	9.960	0.112	10.022	9.987	0.050	10.015	9.995	0.029	10.015	10.000	0.024
	Min	10.000	9.830	0.080	10.000	9.924	0.040	10.000	9.972	0.013	10.000	9.986	0.005	10.000	9.991	0.000
12	Max	12.110	11.905	0.315	12.043	11.950	0.136	12.027	11.984	0.061	12.018	11.994	0.035	12.018	12.000	0.029
	Min	12.000	11.795	0.095	12.000	11.907	0.050	12.000	11.966	0.016	12.000	11.983	0.006	12.000	11.989	0.000
16	Max	16.110	15.905	0.315	16.043	15.950	0.136	16.027	15.984	0.061	16.018	15.994	0.035	16.018	16.000	0.029
	Min	16.000	15.795	0.095	16.000	15.907	0.050	16.000	15.966	0.016	16.000	15.983	0.006	16.000	15.989	0.000
20	Max	20.130	19.890	0.370	20.052	19.935	0.169	20.033	19.980	0.074	20.021	19.993	0.041	20.021	20.000	0.034
	Min	20.000	19.760	0.110	20.000	19.883	0.065	20.000	19.959	0.020	20.000	19.980	0.007	20.000	19.987	0.000
25	Max	25.130	24.890	0.370	25.052	24.935	0.169	25.033	24.980	0.074	25.021	24.993	0.041	25.021	25.000	0.034
	Min	25.000	24.760	0.110	25.000	24.883	0.065	25.000	24.959	0.020	25.000	24.980	0.007	25.000	24.987	0.000
30	Max	30.130	29.890	0.370	30.052	29.935	0.169	30.033	29.980	0.074	30.021	29.993	0.041	30.021	30.000	0.034
	Min	30.000	29.760	0.110	30.000	29.883	0.065	30.000	29.959	0.020	30.000	29.980	0.007	30.000	29.987	0.000

Figure A-8

Preferred Transition and Interference Fits — Cylindrical Fits

(Hole Basis; ANSI B4.2)

Basic Size		Locational Trans.			Locational Trans.			Locational Inter.			Medium Drive			Force		
		Hole H7	Shaft k6	Fit	Hole H7	Shaft n6	Fit	Hole H7	Shaft p6	Fit	Hole H7	Shaft s6	Fit	Hole H7	Shaft u6	Fit
4	Max	4.012	4.009	0.011	4.012	4.016	0.004	4.012	4.020	0.000	4.012	4.027	-0.007	4.012	4.031	-0.011
	Min	4.000	4.001	-0.009	4.000	4.008	-0.016	4.000	4.012	-0.020	4.000	4.019	-0.027	4.000	4.023	-0.031
5	Max	5.012	5.009	0.011	5.012	5.016	0.004	5.012	5.020	0.000	5.012	5.027	-0.007	5.012	5.031	-0.011
	Min	5.000	5.001	-0.009	5.000	5.008	-0.016	5.000	5.012	-0.020	5.000	5.019	-0.027	5.000	5.023	-0.031
6	Max	6.012	6.009	0.011	6.012	6.016	0.004	6.012	6.020	0.000	6.012	6.027	-0.007	6.012	6.031	-0.011
	Min	6.000	6.001	-0.009	6.000	6.008	-0.016	6.000	6.012	-0.020	6.000	6.019	-0.027	6.000	6.023	-0.031
8	Max	8.015	8.010	0.014	8.015	8.019	0.005	8.015	8.024	0.000	8.015	8.032	-0.008	8.015	8.037	-0.013
	Min	8.000	8.001	-0.010	8.000	8.010	-0.019	8.000	8.015	-0.024	8.000	8.023	-0.032	8.000	8.028	-0.037
10	Max	10.015	10.010	0.014	10.015	10.019	0.005	10.015	10.024	0.000	10.015	10.032	-0.008	10.015	10.037	-0.013
	Min	10.000	10.001	-0.010	10.000	10.010	-0.019	10.000	10.015	-0.024	10.000	10.023	-0.032	10.000	10.028	-0.037
12	Max	12.018	12.012	0.017	12.018	12.023	0.006	12.018	12.029	0.000	12.018	12.039	-0.010	12.018	12.044	-0.015
	Min	12.000	12.001	-0.012	12.000	12.012	-0.023	12.000	12.018	-0.029	12.000	12.028	-0.039	12.000	12.033	-0.044
16	Max	16.018	16.012	0.017	16.018	16.023	0.006	16.018	16.029	0.000	16.018	16.039	-0.010	16.018	16.044	-0.015
	Min	16.000	16.001	-0.012	16.000	16.012	-0.023	16.000	16.018	-0.029	16.000	16.028	-0.039	16.000	16.033	-0.044
20	Max	20.021	20.015	0.019	20.021	20.028	0.006	20.021	20.035	-0.001	20.021	20.048	-0.014	20.021	20.054	-0.020
	Min	20.000	20.002	-0.015	20.000	20.015	-0.028	20.000	20.022	-0.035	20.000	20.035	-0.048	20.000	20.041	-0.054
25	Max	25.021	25.015	0.019	25.021	25.028	0.006	25.021	25.035	-0.001	25.021	25.048	-0.014	25.021	25.061	-0.027
	Min	25.000	25.002	-0.015	25.000	25.015	-0.028	25.000	25.022	-0.035	25.000	25.035	-0.048	25.000	25.048	-0.061
30	Max	30.021	30.015	0.019	30.021	30.028	0.006	30.021	30.035	-0.001	30.021	30.048	-0.014	30.021	30.061	-0.027
	Min	30.000	30.002	-0.015	30.000	30.015	-0.028	30.000	30.022	-0.035	30.000	30.035	-0.048	30.000	30.048	-0.061

Figure A-9

Preferred Clearance Fits — Cylindrical Fits
(Shaft Basis; ANSI B4.2)

Basic Size		Loose Running			Free Running			Close Running			Sliding			Locational Clear.		
		Hole C11	Shaft h11	Fit	Hole D9	Shaft h9	Fit	Hole F8	Shaft h7	Fit	Hole G7	Shaft h6	Fit	Hole H7	Shaft h6	Fit
4	Max	4.145	4.000	0.220	4.060	4.000	0.090	4.028	4.000	0.040	4.016	4.000	0.024	4.012	4.000	0.020
	Min	4.070	3.925	0.070	4.030	3.970	0.030	4.010	3.988	0.010	4.004	3.992	0.004	4.000	3.992	0.000
5	Max	5.145	5.000	0.220	5.060	5.000	0.090	5.028	5.000	0.040	5.016	5.000	0.024	5.012	5.000	0.020
	Min	5.070	4.925	0.070	5.030	4.970	0.030	5.010	4.988	0.010	5.004	4.992	0.004	5.000	4.992	0.000
6	Max	6.145	6.000	0.220	6.060	6.000	0.090	6.028	6.000	0.040	6.016	6.000	0.024	6.012	6.000	0.020
	Min	6.070	5.925	0.070	6.030	5.970	0.030	6.010	5.988	0.010	6.004	5.992	0.004	6.000	5.992	0.000
8	Max	8.170	8.000	0.260	8.076	8.000	0.112	8.035	8.000	0.050	8.020	8.000	0.029	8.015	8.000	0.024
	Min	8.080	7.910	0.080	8.040	7.964	0.040	8.013	7.985	0.013	8.005	7.991	0.005	8.000	7.991	0.000
10	Max	10.170	10.000	0.260	10.076	10.000	0.112	10.035	10.000	0.050	10.020	10.000	0.029	10.015	10.000	0.024
	Min	10.080	9.910	0.080	10.040	9.964	0.040	10.013	9.985	0.013	10.005	9.991	0.005	10.000	9.991	0.000
12	Max	12.205	12.000	0.315	12.093	12.000	0.136	12.043	12.000	0.061	12.024	12.000	0.035	12.018	12.000	0.029
	Min	12.095	11.890	0.095	12.050	11.957	0.050	12.016	11.982	0.016	12.006	11.989	0.006	12.000	11.989	0.000
16	Max	16.205	16.000	0.315	16.093	16.000	0.136	16.043	16.000	0.061	16.024	16.000	0.035	16.018	16.000	0.029
	Min	16.095	15.890	0.095	16.050	15.957	0.050	16.016	15.982	0.016	06.006	15.989	0.006	16.000	15.989	0.000
20	Max	20.240	20.000	0.370	20.117	20.000	0.169	20.053	20.000	0.074	20.028	20.000	0.041	20.021	20.000	0.034
	Min	20.110	19.870	0.110	20.065	19.948	0.065	20.020	19.979	0.020	20.007	19.987	0.007	20.000	19.987	0.000
25	Max	25.240	25.000	0.370	25.117	25.000	0.169	25.053	25.000	0.074	25.028	25.000	0.041	25.021	25.000	0.034
	Min	25.110	24.870	0.110	25.065	24.948	0.065	25.020	24.979	0.020	25.007	24.987	0.007	25.000	24.987	0.000
30	Max	30.240	30.000	0.370	30.117	30.000	0.169	30.053	30.000	0.074	30.028	30.000	0.041	30.021	30.000	0.034
	Min	30.110	29.870	0.110	30.065	29.948	0.065	29.979	29.979	0.020	30.007	29.987	0.007	30.000	29.987	0.000

Figure A-10

Preferred Transition and Interference Fits — Cylindrical Fits
(Shaft Basis; ANSI B4.2)

Basic Size		Locational Trans.			Locational Trans.			Locational Inter.			Medium Drive			Force		
		Hole K7	Shaft h6	Fit	Hole N7	Shaft h6	Fit	Hole P7	Shaft h6	Fit	Hole S7	Shaft h6	Fit	Hole U7	Shaft h6	Fit
4	Max	4.003	4.000	0.011	3.996	4.000	0.004	3.992	4.000	0.000	3.985	4.000	-0.007	3.981	4.000	-0.011
	Min	3.991	3.992	-0.009	3.984	3.992	-0.016	3.980	3.992	-0.020	3.973	3.992	-0.027	3.969	3.992	-0.031
5	Max	5.003	5.000	0.011	4.996	5.000	0.004	4.992	5.000	0.000	4.985	5.000	-0.007	4.981	5.000	-0.011
	Min	4.991	4.992	-0.009	4.984	4.992	-0.016	4.980	4.992	-0.020	4.973	4.992	-0.027	4.969	4.992	-0.031
6	Max	6.003	6.000	0.011	5.996	6.000	0.004	5.992	6.000	0.000	5.985	6.000	-0.007	5.981	6.000	-0.011
	Min	5.991	5.992	-0.009	5.984	5.992	-0.016	5.980	5.992	-0.020	5.973	5.992	-0.027	5.969	5.992	-0.031
8	Max	8.005	8.000	0.014	7.996	8.000	0.005	7.991	8.000	0.000	7.983	8.000	-0.008	7.978	8.000	-0.013
	Min	7.990	7.991	-0.010	7.981	7.991	-0.019	7.976	7.991	-0.024	7.968	7.991	-0.032	7.963	7.991	-0.037
10	Max	10.005	10.000	0.014	9.996	10.000	0.005	9.991	10.000	0.000	9.983	10.000	-0.008	9.978	10.000	-0.013
	Min	9.990	9.991	-0.010	9.981	9.991	-0.019	9.976	9.991	-0.024	9.968	9.991	-0.032	9.963	9.991	-0.037
12	Max	12.006	12.000	0.017	11.995	12.000	0.006	11.989	12.000	0.000	11.979	12.000	-0.010	11.974	12.000	-0.015
	Min	11.988	11.989	-0.012	11.977	11.989	-0.023	11.971	11.989	-0.029	11.961	11.989	-0.039	11.956	11.989	-0.044
16	Max	16.006	16.000	0.017	15.995	16.000	0.006	15.989	16.000	0.000	15.979	16.000	-0.010	15.974	16.000	-0.015
	Min	15.988	15.989	-0.012	15.977	15.989	-0.023	15.971	15.989	-0.029	15.961	15.989	-0.039	15.956	15.989	-0.044
20	Max	20.006	20.000	0.019	19.993	20.000	0.006	19.986	20.000	-0.001	19.973	20.000	-0.014	19.967	20.000	-0.020
	Min	19.985	19.987	-0.015	19.972	19.987	-0.028	19.965	19.987	-0.035	19.952	19.987	-0.048	19.946	19.987	-0.054
25	Max	25.006	25.000	0.019	24.993	25.000	0.006	24.986	25.000	-0.001	24.973	25.000	-0.014	24.960	25.000	-0.027
	Min	24.985	24.987	-0.015	24.972	24.987	-0.028	24.965	24.987	-0.035	24.952	24.987	-0.048	24.939	24.987	-0.061
30	Max	30.006	30.000	0.019	29.993	30.000	0.006	29.986	30.000	-0.001	29.973	30.000	-0.014	29.960	30.000	-0.027
	Min	29.985	29.987	-0.015	29.972	29.987	-0.028	29.965	29.987	-0.035	29.952	29.987	-0.048	29.939	29.987	-0.061

Figure A-11

Metric Threads—Preferred Sizes			
First Choice	Second Choice	First Choice	Second Choice
1	1.1	12	14
1.2	1.4	16	18
1.6	1.8	20	22
2	2.2	25	28
2.5	2.8	30	35
3	3.5	40	45
4	4.5	50	55
5	5.5	60	70
6	7	80	90
8	9	100	110
10	11	120	140

Figure A-12

	3/16	1/4	3/8	1/2	5/8	3/4	7/8	1	1 1/4	1 1/2	1 3/4	2	2 1/2	3
Standard Thread Lengths—Inches														
#2 – 5	√	√	√	√	√	√	√	√						
#4 – 40		√	√	√	√	√	√	√	√	√				
#6 – 32		√	√	√	√	√			√	√	√	√	√	√
#8 – 32		√	√	√	√	√			√	√	√	√	√	√
#10 – 24		√	√	√	√	√			√	√	√	√	√	√
#10 – 32		√	√	√		√			√	√	√	√	√	√
#12 – 24			√	√	√	√			√	√	√	√	√	√
1/4 20				√	√	√	√	√	√	√	√	√	√	√
5/16 18				√	√	√	√	√	√	√	√	√	√	√
3/8 16				√	√	√	√	√	√	√	√	√	√	√
1/2 13						√	√	√	√	√	√	√	√	√
5/8 11							√	√	√	√	√	√	√	√
3/4 10										√		√		√

Figure A-13A

American National Standard Plain Washers					
Nominal Washer Size		Series	Inside Diameter	Outside Diameter	Thickness
No. 0	0.060	N	0.068	0.125	0.025
		R	0.068	0.188	0.025
		W	0.068	0.250	0.025
No. 1	0.073	N	0.084	0.156	0.025
		R	0.084	0.219	0.025
		W	0.084	0.281	0.032
No. 2	0.086	N	0.094	0.188	0.025
		R	0.094	0.250	0.032
		W	0.094	0.344	0.032
No. 3	0.099	N	0.109	0.219	0.025
		R	0.109	0.312	0.032
		W	0.109	0.406	0.040
No. 4	0.112	N	0.125	0.250	0.032
		R	0.125	0.375	0.040
		W	0.125	0.438	0.040
No. 5	0.125	N	0.141	0.281	0.032
		R	0.141	0.406	0.040
		W	0.141	0.500	0.040
No. 6	1.380	N	0.156	0.312	0.032
		R	0.156	0.438	0.040
		W	0.156	0.562	0.040
No. 8	0.164	N	0.188	0.375	0.040
		R	0.188	0.500	0.040
		W	0.188	0.633	0.063
No. 10	0.190	N	0.203	0.406	0.040
		R	0.203	0.562	0.040
		W	0.203	0.734	0.063
No. 12	0.216	N	0.234	0.438	0.040
		R	0.234	0.625	0.063
		W	0.234	0.875	0.063
1/4	0.250	N	0.281	0.500	0.063
		R	0.281	0.734	0.063
		W	0.281	1.000	0.063
5/16	0.312	N	0.344	0.625	0.063
		R	0.344	0.875	0.063
		W	0.344	1.125	0.063
3/8	0.375	N	0.406	0.734	0.063
		R	0.406	1.000	0.063
		W	0.406	1.250	0.100
7/16	0.438	N	0.469	0.875	0.063
		R	0.469	1.125	0.063
		W	0.469	1.469	0.100
1/2	0.500	N	0.531	1.000	0.063
		R	0.531	1.2.5	0.100
		W	0.531	1.125	0.100

Figure A-13B

American National Standard Plain Washers					
Nominal Washer Size		Series	Inside Diameter	Outside Diameter	Thickness
9/16	0.562	N R W	0.594 0.594 0.594	1.125 1.469 2.000	0.063 0.100 0.100
5/8	0.625	N R W	0.656 0.656 0.656	1.250 1.750 2.250	0.100 0.100 0.160
3/4	0.750	N R W	0.812 0.812 0.812	1.375 2.000 2.500	0.100 0.100 0.160
7/8	0.875	N R W	0.938 0.938 0.938	1.469 2.250 2.750	0.100 0.160 0.160
1	1.000	N R W	1.062 1.062 1.062	1.750 2.500 3.000	0.100 0.160 0.160

Index